THE SPECTER OF NEUTRALISM

THE SPECTER
OF NEUTRALISM

THE UNITED STATES AND
THE EMERGENCE OF
THE THIRD WORLD, 1947–1960

H. W. Brands

Columbia University Press
New York

Columbia University Press
New York   Oxford
Copyright © 1989 Columbia University Press
All rights reserved

Library of Congress Cataloging-in-Publication Data

Brands, H. W.
   The specter of neutralism : the United States and the emergence of
   the Third World, 1947–1960 / H. W. Brands.
      p.   cm.—(Columbia studies in contemporary American history)
   Includes bibliographical references.
   ISBN 0-231-07168-X (alk. paper)
1. Developing countries—Foreign relations—United States.
2. United States—Foreign relations—Developing countries.
3. Developing countries—Nonalignment.
I. Title.
II. Series.
D888.U6B73   1989
327.730172'4—dc20   89-24002
                                    CIP

Casebound editions of Columbia University Press books are Smyth-sewn and printed
on permanent and durable acid-free paper

Printed in the United States of America

c 10 9 8 7 6 5 4 3 2 1

CONTENTS

ACKNOWLEDGMENTS

For their generosity in reading and commenting on the manuscript, I thank Robert Divine, William Leuchtenburg, Robert McMahon, and Robert Stookey. I hope the exercise provided them at least a small part of what it gave me.

THE SPECTER OF NEUTRALISM

Yalta and Bandung

It STRAINS the truth only a little to describe the postwar era in international affairs as the age of the third world. Not in the sense that the nonaligned and less developed nations have dominated the arena of global politics—far from it, because almost by definition and certainly by circumstance they have played marginal parts on the global stage. But that is precisely the point, for the most important developments of the last four decades have taken place on the margins of the superpower systems. Cosmologists sometimes say that everything interesting in the history of the universe occurred in the first moments after the big bang, that the subsequent course of physical events has involved merely a working out of the consequences of that seminal burst. Something similar applies to the universe of postwar superpower relations. In this case the big bang happened on the New Mexico desert on July 16, 1945, even as the leaders of the United States, Britain, and the Soviet Union gathered to ratify the de facto division of Europe they had sketched out at Yalta five months before. Facing each other along the Elbe during that summer when the center of the continent disappeared, the armies of East and West have been frozen in position ever since.

On the other hand, beyond the occupation zones, a seething brew of nationalism and revolution prevented any such status quo from congealing. There the war's two winners (Britain soon felt the pyrrhic effects of the conflict) began contesting for preference, venting the energies Europe's stalemate stifled. It was not coincidence that the first confrontation of the cold war turned on events in the outback of Iran, nor that the American commitment to the containment of the Soviets was triggered by crises in Greece and Turkey. The Truman Doctrine was, more than anything else, a declaration of intent regarding the unclaimed regions of the earth. (It was significant that no one seriously thought of applying the doctrine to Czechoslovakia when communists staged a coup there in 1948.) For the next two generations, on battlefields from Indochina to the Caribbean and the Congo, from Angola to Afghanistan and Nicaragua, Americans and Russians fought for the hearts, minds, and resources of that large mass of humanity that eschewed alliances. Because a third world war threatened such dire consequences, the superpowers contented themselves with third-world wars.

As a result, the sternest test of American foreign policy during this period was the management of relations with the nonaligned countries. Once the Marshall Plan stabilized the economy of Western Europe and the Atlantic pact promised that the United States would, if pushed, invest blood to match its treasure, dealing with the Soviets in the European theater of the cold war rarely taxed the insight or ingenuity of American leaders. With an occasional reminder of resolve, often regarding Berlin, policy nearly ran itself. Conducting diplomacy toward the third world, by contrast, pushed Washington to the limits of insight, ingenuity, and whatever other talents Americans could muster.

At the root of the difficulty lay the fact that fighting the cold war and handling relations with the third world demanded different mindsets. For the cold war, Yalta—representing the division of Europe into democratic and communist zones—provided a convenient conceptual construct. Americans never liked the spheres-of-influence arrangement Yalta implied, since it involved accommodation of a country they feared and an ideology they despised. They never considered legitimate Russia's control of Eastern Europe. But they got used to the Yalta idea, principally because the alternatives appeared either a showdown with the Kremlin or a further loss of territory; and by 1947, when the Truman administration announced the adoption of containment, American policy rested on an acceptance, however tacit and grudging, of Yalta. Despite its drawbacks, the worst being the air of permanence it conferred on Soviet hegemony in the satellite belt, Yalta as a framework for international relations had one signal advantage: it made the world easy to understand. In a polity in which most voters do not educate themselves to the nuances of foreign affairs, this counts for a lot. Yalta provided ready categories of East versus West, "iron curtain" versus "free world," dictatorship versus representative government, atheism versus religion, evil versus good. That the Yalta arrangement survived on the ground in Europe for forty years followed principally from the existence of nuclear weapons; that it persisted in the American mind owed much to its powers of simplification.

The emergence of a third world between the blocs challenged the neatness of this arrangement. If the Yalta Conference marked the origin of the bipolar superpower order, another meeting, held ten years later at Bandung in Indonesia, symbolized the rejection of that order by countries having no part in its creation and no interest in its continuance. The Bandung Conference included more than just the nonaligned nations—Pakistan, for example, was allied with the United States, and China with the Soviet Union—and since only Asian and African countries received invitations, important neutralists like Yugoslavia were left out. But at Bandung the nonaligned movement gained self-confidence, momentum —and a name, as French journalists began speaking of "le tiers monde."

Bandung as a metaphor lacks precision; debates have never ceased regarding criteria for membership in the third world, and even whether such a beast exists. But to those in attendance and those watching, Bandung signaled a refusal to accept the bipolar scheme, to join the superpower competition, or to subscribe to either of the mutually exclusive ideologies on which that competition rested. In the decade between Yalta and Bandung, the struggle between the United States and the Soviet Union had begun to spill beyond Europe into Asia and the Middle East. Bandung symbolized resistance to this trend, a denial that the cold war applied to the world at large. In short, Bandung represented a rejection of Yalta as a model for international relations.

American leaders, intent on a global role for themselves and their country, had to deal with both the Yalta and Bandung concepts; not suprisingly their attempts to integrate the two tended to produce a certain—sometimes severe—case of cognitive and political dissonance. Yalta brought out the manicheanism Americans seem prone to; it required a focusing of attention and a narrowing of mind. It generated a siege mentality. Strapping on the ideological armor against the commu-

3

nists, Americans prepared to treat skeptics as dupes or subversives. Handling Bandung, by contrast, demanded a willingness to question premises and set ideology aside. Agnostics themselves, the neutralists looked askance at the born-again, indelicately reminding America of its long history as a conscientious objector to international combinations and of its recent alliance with the Soviet Union. Reconciling the two approaches—true belief with tolerance—proved difficult at best, occasionally impossible.

To complicate the matter further, policy toward the nonaligned countries precipitated political debates in America other parts of the world were often spared. For all the partisan harping over who did what at Yalta, for all the Republican denunciations of containment as cowardly and defeatist, for all the demands to "roll back the red tide" and "liberate the captive peoples," Yalta in practice commanded a consensus unequaled in postwar American history; and regardless of what they said in opposition, neither Republicans nor Democrats, once in power, took any concrete actions to overturn the bipolar division of Europe. Bandung, on the other hand, lay outside the Yalta framework, beyond the American cold war consensus. For politicians, pundits, and other interested observers, Yalta's convenient dichotomies provided ready guidance regarding the affairs of Europe; but they furnished few clues for negotiating the ambiguities of Bandung. Lacking a prepackaged paradigm, America's elected officials often freelanced, with unpredictable results.

Moreover, such influence as the United States wielded in the third world rested in large part on American foreign aid, the dispensation of which the executive branch shared with the legislature. To a limited degree, presidents could manage an updated dollar diplomacy with discretionary funds, but for anything major they had to go to Congress, which demanded hearings and public debate. Bandung claimed no natural constituency in America, and at a time when money for pledged allies came hard enough, requests for support of nonaligned governments faced even closer scrutiny. Further, the reasoning behind assistance to neutralists was subtle, at least by Yalta standards. In the days of McCarthyism, subtlety was not the legislature's forte.

Nor, if public statements be credited, was subtlety a strong point with policymakers. The most egregious expression on the subject of the third

4

world came from Eisenhower's secretary of state, John Foster Dulles, who declared in 1956 that neutralism was an "immoral and short-sighted conception." Spoken just before a meeting at Brioni, Yugoslavia, of the era's three most prominent neutralists—India's Prime Minister Jawaharlal Nehru, Yugoslavia's Marshal Josip Broz-Tito, and Egypt's President Gamal Abdel Nasser—Dulles' pronouncement appeared to typify the official American attitude on nonalignment.

Appearances, however, deceived—not only Dulles' contemporaries but most writers on the subject since. Historians and other commentators have tended to take the secretary of state at his word. "Dulles's hatred of 'neutrals' was the counterpart of his defiance of Communism," Herman Finer wrote while the Dullesian rhetoric still resounded. " 'Who is not with me, is against me!' " A decade's distance afforded Townsend Hoopes little added perspective; Hoopes' Dulles believed "neutrality could only be a transitional state of existence on the way to Communist control." Donald Neff in 1981 asserted that "Dulles was revolted by the concept of a Third World of nations steering an independent course between East and West." [1]

In fact, public remarks by administration officials told only part of the story, and the less revealing part at that. American policy toward the third world during the first decade and a half of the cold war demonstrated considerable insight and flexibility. If the American people and many legislators had a difficult time balancing the demands of Yalta and Bandung, the persons who handled day-to-day decisions were surprisingly adept in the exercise. Those at the policy controls scarcely lacked confidence in America's moral and ideological superiority over their country's rivals, but they were realistic enough to recognize that morality often had little to do with international politics, and that ideology often got in the way of results.

What follows is an account of American relations with the third world during the period from 1947 to 1960. The beginning date marks both the entrenchment of Yalta—evidenced by the Truman Doctrine, the Marshall Plan, and the publication of George Kennan's "X" article on containment—and the independence of India, which arguably was the single most important event in the early history of the third world. The ending date, 1960, comes just before the penultimate wave of decolonization in Africa, a development that changed the face of the third world and called for a new set of American responses; in 1960 as well, the Eisenhower administration prepared to leave office, bringing to a close the most formative period of postwar American foreign policy.

Even before widespread devolution in Africa the third world included a large number of disparate members. For manageability, and so something more useful than bland generalizations can be offered, American relations with three countries—India, Yugoslavia, and Egypt—have been chosen for close study. Several considerations prompted the selection of these three. First, Nehru, Tito, and Nasser were commonly judged the principal practitioners of neutralism during this era—the neutralist "triumvirate," in the phrase of a contemporary; the "three pioneers of the nonaligned movement," the "founding trio," and "the Brioni statesmen who made nonalignment an international movement," according to later observers.[2] Second, the geographic, cultural, and political diversity of the three countries—one Asian and democratic, another European and communist, the third African-Middle Eastern and autocratic—provides a perspective a narrower source base would not. Third, the three demonstrate some of the various ways nations have arrived at nonalignment: India by the transfer of power from Britain in 1947, Yugoslavia as a result of its 1948 break with the Cominform, Egypt following a 1952 military revolt against King Farouk. Fourth, the three charted three approaches to neutralism. Within the broad framework of nonalignment, Tito steered toward the West, Nasser edged East, and Nehru hewed more or less to the middle of the road. Fifth, these different approaches elicited divergent reactions from American leaders: Tito they embraced (gingerly), Nasser they opposed (for awhile), Nehru they tolerated (eventually). Finally, an investigation of American relations with the three countries elucidates other important aspects of postwar foreign policy. The response to India set a pattern for dealing with successor states in the former colonial world. In deciding how to handle Tito, American officials were forced to consider what the cold war was all about. Did they oppose communism, or the Soviet Union? Yugoslavia also serves as a reminder that politics, rather than economics, initially defined the third world; that nonalignment, rather than poverty, provided the unifying concept; and therefore, that the third world could, and did, include Europeans as well as Asians and Africans, and later Latin Americans. Relations with Egypt brought together the strands of political radicalism, Arab nationalism, Islamic fundamentalism, and Zionism that have tied the Middle East in knots until today.

Two themes unite the case studies. The first involves the interaction of politics and policy in America's dealings with the third world. Politics has never stopped at the water's edge, although the chilly currents of the cold war in Europe kept most swimmers ashore; but in treating the nonaligned nations American politicians positively hit the surf running. The lasting effect of such rambunctiousness is not always easy to measure. Congress rarely initiated policy toward the third world; only slightly more often did it succeed in blocking measures presidents made priorities. Much of the entertaining commentary in congressional hearings and debate amounted to posturing by legislative lightweights looking to the next campaign. Yet the fact that these individuals thought neutralist-baiting would sell on the stump indicated the presence of a sentiment the executive could not lightly dismiss; and the outsized shadow of the junior senator from Wisconsin demonstrated the dangers of underestimating the hinterland's discontent. When major party figures like Tom Connally and William Knowland registered reservations about Nehru, Tito, and Nasser, administrations thought several times before risking new departures. More than once they shelved plans they deemed otherwise desirable.

The second and more important theme reflects the interplay between ideology and geopolitics in American foreign relations. The tension between the two influences—sometimes described in terms of idealism and realism, sometimes as humanitarianism and national interest, sometimes by other language—is as old as the republic. Nor is it unique to America: every country with aspirations to shape the world at all in its image experiences the conflict in some measure. But during the early years of the cold war, when anticommunist revivalism in the United States coincided with an enormous expansion of America's global role, the contest grew sharper; and it was particularly acute—according to most accounts—in relations with the third world. Received wisdom has it that the ideologists won: that American officials, obsessed with their struggle against communism, blinded themselves to the non-ideological realities of nonalignment. The results, we read, ranged from minor damage to disaster. Thus Melvin Gurtov, in a general study explaining America's penchant for intervening in the affairs of nonaligned nations, describes a sweeping anti-leftist "ideological consensus among postwar high-level policy-makers" and declares that intervention "should be understood as resulting from the ideology's distorting effect on American officials' perception of Third World conditions." Richard Barnet, elaborating similarly on the mindset of American policymakers confronted with forces demanding radical change, asserts that such forces were "simply assumed to be the products of conspiracy by the 'forces of international communism.' " Barnet goes on to say:

> The word "communist" has been applied so liberally and so loosely to revolutionary or radical regimes that any government risks being so characterized if it adopts one or more of the following policies which the State Department finds distasteful: nationalization of foreign industry . . . radical land reform . . . insistence upon following an anti-American or nonaligned foreign policy.

Gabriel Kolko, focusing on the American response to nonalignment in the 1950s, writes, "The Manichean ideological premises of antineutralism were more all-encompassing than anything the United States was to undertake in this decade."[3]

Authors treating American relations with particular countries or regions have arrived at similar conclusions. Stanley Wolpert, examining American policy toward South Asia, contends that Dulles' "Hell and brimstone" concern with the "Red Russian Menace" led the United States into its alliance with Pakistan, a move Wolpert characterizes as "surely the worst single blunder" in a history of policy characterized by "singular incompetence." Robert Stookey describes a "rigid American posture" in the Middle East, marked especially by the lack of "a sufficient appreciation of the difference (in fact, the incompatibility) of communism with Arab nationalism and neutralism." Regarding Egypt in particular, Stookey says, the United States acted "on the assumption that Nasser's Egypt was 'controlled by international communism' and embarked on a sterile attempt to isolate her from her sister Arab states." Thomas Paterson, examining the same events, accounts American policy nearly a dead loss because American leaders failed to deal "with Middle Eastern realities rather than with Communist ghosts." Policymakers, Paterson continues, could not understand the complexities of the Middle East "because they had become Cold Warriors, hyperbolic in their depiction of the Communist threat."[4]

Thomas Noer, surveying American policy toward Africa during the

1950s, writes that Dulles' "periodic denunciations of neutralism and revolution," his "contempt for the idea of nonalignment," his tendency "to identify reform with revolution and revolution with communism," and his penchant for portraying "the Cold War as an apocalyptic struggle between freedom and slavery" alienated black Africans and helped convince them that American policy was "merely a disguise for supporting white supremacy." Regarding Central America, Walter LaFeber asserts that despite later cosmetic efforts at regional development, the Eisenhower administration's "sense of the past seemed to have stopped with the 1954 invasion of Guatemala," when the CIA helped oust the left-leaning Arbenz government. Richard Immerman states that Dulles' "extreme anti-Communism" and Eisenhower's "espousal of the cold war ideology" helped usher in "a new era in inter-American relations, an era marked by a protracted struggle between the United States and an assumed international Communist conspiracy."[5]

The most important conclusion of the present study is that this conventional wisdom, as it applies to the third world, is essentially wrong. American officials in the Truman and Eisenhower administrations often *spoke* in ideological terms. At a certain level of abstraction they *thought* ideologically. With some exceptions, however, they tended to *act* in a remarkably non-ideological fashion. Understanding what the political market in the United States would bear, they commonly packaged their policies in the wrappings of ideology; but the product they sold reflected primarily a geopolitical interpretation of American strategic, military, diplomatic, and economic interests, and it demonstrated a shrewd weighing of the effects on the international balance of power of the particular activities of specific nonaligned countries. One might say that in an era of anticommunist prohibition, they bootlegged Bandung in Yalta bottles.

To avoid confusion, a word about the objectives of this book—an extended essay, really—is in order. I make no attempt to provide a comprehensive account of American relations with India, Yugoslavia, and Egypt during the period under discussion. Other historians, political scientists, and area specialists have been and are at work describing and analyzing each bilateral relationship, with expertise and language skills I do not pretend to possess. Matters important in a different context—American efforts to mediate the India–Pakistan dispute over Kashmir, the Yugoslav role in the Greek civil war, the Suez crisis as a watershed in Anglo–American affairs, to name three—get short shrift here, partly because they deserve more attention than I can give them, partly because they are tangential to my principal concern. While I appreciate the insights of those who examine foreign relations as an aspect of societies and cultures in collision, I focus on decision-making elites. And I concentrate on Washington—rather than on New Delhi, Belgrade, or Cairo—since the essence of my story is the formulation of American policy.

My objective is to illuminate the manner in which American leaders, in a period of unrelenting cold war, perceived and addressed the potentially unsettling phenomen of neutralism—how, in short, they balanced the competing demands of Yalta and Bandung. The specter of a third world challenged their diplomatic and political skills. To a surprising and generally unappreciated degree, they successfully met the challenge.

A final prefatory note, regarding terminology: as the group of countries abjuring alliance with either superpower expanded and evolved, the labels they applied to themselves, and which outsiders applied to them, varied. During the late 1940s and early 1950s the terms "neutral" and "neutralist" enjoyed greatest currency. "Non-aligned" appears to have originated with V. K. Krishna Menon at the United Nations about 1953 or 1954. Until the 1960s—and in some circles considerably past then—the three terms were used interchangeably. When distinctions were drawn, the distinguishers often disagreed, with some seeing neutral and neutralist as more confined and more passive than nonaligned, some just the reverse. Principally because of the negative connotations neutralism carried in a West preoccupied with the cold war, the neutralist/nonaligned nations gravitated toward the latter tag. (Nasser attempted a solution by referring to "positive neutralism.") By the Belgrade conference of 1961, nonaligned was winning out. Yet the Belgrade meeting itself was initially dubbed "the Conference of the Heads of State and Government of the Uncommitted Countries," and for many years afterward confusion reigned on the subject of third-world nomenclature. For simplicity here, neutralism and nonalignment will be used synonymously.[6]

I

INDIA, NEHRU, AND THE FOUNDATIONS OF NEUTRALISM

I

Laissez Faire: 1947–1950

FROM INDEPENDENCE in 1947 India seemed to Americans the quintessential nonaligned state and Nehru the chief spokesman for neutralism. For this reason relations with India throughout the period until 1960 served as a touchstone for America's ability to deal with the third world. Coming to terms with India and Nehru took time and entailed no little misunderstanding; but American policymakers, if not always the American people and their legislative representatives, managed the feat. Precisely because of lingering prejudices in Congress and among the public at large, policymakers sometimes felt constrained to mask their acceptance of Indian neutralism. Ultimately, however, even an administration as ideologically conservative as Eisenhower's recognized that a nonaligned India might serve American purposes better than an India tied to the West.

American policy toward India between 1947 and 1960 breaks logically into three phases. During the initial phase, which lasted from 1947 until the end of 1950, American officials contented themselves with leaving India more or less alone. Pressing problems in Europe and the Far East had first call on American resources, and the modest nature of American interests in South Asia did not warrant a change in priorities. Economically the subcontinent rated below almost every other region Americans did business with: Western Europe, Canada, Latin America, the Middle East, East and Southeast Asia. Politically India counted for somewhat more, and the idea of "the world's largest democracy" never ceased to fascinate American observers; but as long as the Nationalists held out in China, the civil war there monopolized the attention of those wondering whether Asia would follow the democratic or the communist path. Strategically India stood well back from the front lines of the cold war, and what needed defending appeared adequately secured by the British, who retained considerable influence even after the transfer of power. Reflexively to begin, later more deliberately, the Truman administration encouraged Britain to maintain a sphere of influence in South Asia.

The triple shocks of 1949–50—the collapse of the Chinese Nationalists, the outbreak of the war in Korea, and China's intervention in that conflict—brought the period of secondhand American interest in India to an abrupt halt. China's leap to the Soviet alliance system constituted a major shift in the power balance in Asia, and in its aftermath American strategists scrambled to establish a fallback position. Suddenly the Indian subcontinent, the remaining great center of population on the Asian mainland, gained new geopolitical value. Likewise India acquired heightened political significance as the democratic counterweight to communist China. The war for the allegiance of Asians now seemed—and not only to Americans—to turn on the implicit contest between India and China. Was communism the wave of the future, or democracy? Moreover, as India's importance grew, so also did the danger it apparently faced. Americans, locked in bloody combat with the Chinese, were convinced as never before of the inherent aggressiveness of communism. Meanwhile Britain's ability to hold India for the West became increasingly implausible as continuing stagnation at home and multiplying troubles in the empire forced the British to retrench. With China on the march and Britain on the ropes, the United States began actively to hunt for allies, signed, sealed, paid, and delivered.

Considered narrowly, American policy toward India itself did not change greatly during this period. After some halfhearted attempts to bring Nehru aboard, the Truman administration recognized the hopelessness of the task and wrote him off as an ally. But policy toward India's neighbors shifted markedly, with inevitable repercussions on relations between Washington and New Delhi. Nehru's general aversion to alliances—as subversive of peace and distracting from the demands of development—became noisily specific when Pakistan joined up with the Americans. Not only did this arrangement bring the great-power struggle to the subcontinent, but the American weapons that sweetened the pact threatened India's security and prestige.

The third phase of American policy toward India began in the wake of the U.S.–Pakistan arms agreement of February 1954. From this low point relations between Washington and New Delhi gradually improved, although the trend line dipped back down on more than one occasion. Convinced India was not going to change its neutralist ways, American leaders learned to make the best of the situation. By the end of his summit conference with Nehru in December 1956, Eisenhower had come to a remarkably benign view of the prime minister's position. Dulles' public shots at neutralism were largely posturing; a clearer indication of the administration's intentions was its decision to fund India's economic development. In the belief that a prosperous and stable India would serve as both beacon and anchor for democracy in Asia, Eisenhower chose to underwrite the enterprise.

Throughout the three phases the fundamental American objective—an India denied to the Soviet Union, achieved at minimum cost to the United States—remained unchanged. In 1947, even after the British surrender of direct control, the balance of power in the subcontinent favored the West. American leaders sought to ensure that it would continue to do so. In the most compliant of worlds they might have asked for more, including greater cooperation from New Delhi in the United Nations and elsewhere, a pat on the ideological back, perhaps even an alliance. But wishes aren't policy, and officials in two administrations came to realize that a nonaligned India could serve American purposes satisfactorily. They sometimes bridled at Nehru's root-and-branch rejection of the Yalta model—sometimes emphasizing their annoyance for public effect. But they understood his embrace of Bandung as a logical strategy for increasing India's influence in a world of greater powers; and while their goals and his occasionally clashed, they experienced no insurmountable difficulties accepting his style of neutralism.

II

BEFORE THE Second World War American interest in India was largely confined to missionaries and their stay-at-home supporters, to business types with dealings there, and to readers of Kipling and other writers on the exotic East. In the two decades after World War I the fading afterglow of Wilsonian internationalism revealed support for Indian independence among reliable liberals like the editors of the *Nation* and the *New Republic,* but as a general matter India remained far down the list of American priorities.[1]

Following the Japanese attack on Pearl Harbor and especially after the fall of the Philippines and Singapore, the situation changed dramatically. With most of the western Pacific, the Far East, and Southeast Asia in hostile hands, India's importance, both as a geographic barrier to further Japanese expansion and as a reservoir of military manpower, became readily apparent. But the reluctance of many Indians to join the battle against Japan complicated the picture. Britain was in trouble around the globe and Indian nationalists decided the time had come for independence. Their "Quit India" campaign of 1942 declared British withdrawal a higher priority than the defeat of the Japanese. While American sympathies lay with the nationalists, American security demanded cooperation with the British, whose prime minister, Winston Churchill, displayed no intention of acceding to the nationalists' demands.[2]

In the hope of breaking the deadlock between the Indians and the British, and in the belief that American aid to Britain justified intervention in imperial affairs, Franklin Roosevelt sent two special envoys to India: Louis Johnson in the spring of 1942 and William Phillips later in the year. In the meantime the president appealed directly to Churchill to negotiate a compromise with the nationalists. American efforts proved vain, however, as Churchill stood firm. The prime minister refused to have anything to do with what he considered the Americans' ill-advised and illegitimate meddling. He rebuffed Roosevelt's emissaries and rejected the president's advice.

Roosevelt chose not to press the issue, believing Anglo-American amity took precedence over a literal reading of the Atlantic charter. While commiserating with the Indians, Roosevelt decided that winning the war came first. A letter of March 1942 to Churchill summarized the president's attitude regarding the Indian situation: "It is, strictly speaking, none of my business, except insofar as it is a part and parcel of the successful fight that you and I are making."[3]

After Churchill demonstrated that he would handle unrest in India his own way—by jailing 100,000 of the nationalists, many for the war's duration—American attention eventually faded. Roosevelt continued to raise the Indian question with Churchill though the end of 1942 and American op-ed writers denounced Britain's heavy-handed imperialism for a longer time. Roosevelt's political rivals accused the president of irresolution. Republican Wendell Willkie, recently returned from a tour of Asia, blasted Roosevelt for undermining American credibility:

> People of the East who would like to count on us are doubtful. They cannot ascertain from our government's wishy-washy attitude toward the problem of India what we are likely to feel at the end of the war about all the other hundreds of millions of Eastern peoples. They cannot tell from our vague and vacillating talk whether we really do stand for freedom, or what we mean by freedom.

But Willkie's worries about the end of the war carried little weight while the outcome of the battle remained in doubt. British repression brought relative quiet to India, and Americans turned to the more immediate business of defeating Hitler and the Japanese.[4]

III

AFTER THE war ended and Churchill fell from power, Americans watched with approval as Britain's Labor government moved toward independence for the Indians. Americans applauded the fact that India would soon command its own destiny and they could not help noting parallels between India's trials in throwing off the British yoke and their own a century and a half before. Still, most Americans saw themselves as detached well-wishers. In the aftermath of the war they wanted mostly to mind their own affairs. To the degree they cared about Asia, China commanded their attention.

Those who closely followed the negotiations leading to Britain's transfer of power realized the operation would involve great difficulties at best and mass fratricide at worst, whether the country entered independence in one piece or partitioned into two or more parts. During the several months preceding the British pullout, the Truman administration initially hoped the negotiations would yield a united India. In February 1947 Washington announced its support for Britain's efforts to create a single, federal government. The British plan for union, the administration said, offered "a just basis for cooperation." In private correspondence as well, American officials expressed their preference for an undivided India. Acting Secretary of State Dean Acheson wrote to the American embassy in London in April 1947: "We have been fully aware of the serious obstacles in the path of Indian unity but . . . have inclined to the view that our political and economic interest in that part of the world would best be served by the continued integrity of India."[5]

As the prospects for a united country diminished in the late spring of 1947 the administration retreated from its pro-federation stance to a position of neutrality regarding the outcome of the negotiations. Citing the "unique difficulties" attending the transfer of power, the State Department declared in June that "the future constitutional pattern is a matter to be determined by the Indian people themselves and whatever that pattern may be the United States Government looks forward to the continuance of the friendliest relations with Indians of all communities and creeds."[6]

The Truman administration's hands-off policy continued through the summer of 1947 as partition became inevitable. The heavy fighting and wholesale slaughter accompanying the birth of independent India and Pakistan confirmed the wisdom of this approach, for it appeared that any third party involved in the internecine strife would certainly alienate at least one side and that anything approximating evenhandedness would probably antagonize both. In October 1947 the Indian government requested the loan of ten American transport planes to evacuate 50,000 non-Moslem refugees, recently the objects of violent attack, from Pakistan to India. The American ambassador in New Delhi, Henry Grady, strongly recommended approval of the request. Humanitarianism alone argued for American assistance in the evacuation; diplomatic and geopolitical considerations strengthened the case. "I am convinced," Grady wrote, "that it is fundamental for the U.S. Government to support Nehru in every way possible. If he should fall, disintegration in India could easily follow. We do not want, I am sure, India to become another Greece. Russia would in my opinion rather control India than several Greeces."[7]

Despite Grady's urging, Truman and Secretary of State George Marshall put off the Indians, insisting on receiving Pakistan's approval for the airlift. Grady thought this response an "excellent idea but unrealistic"; the ambassador believed the deep enmity between India and Pakistan would kill any chance of cooperation. His dismal prediction proved accurate. When the Pakistanis refused to go along with the Indian plan the proposed rescue mission literally never got off the ground.[8]

Fear of making enemies in India or Pakistan or both constituted one source of the administration's reluctance to get involved in the affairs of the subcontinent; the continuing relationship of Britain with the two dominions acted as a further deterrent. As members of the Commonwealth, India and Pakistan remained, to some degree at least, within Britain's sphere of influence. Exactly what this meant and how long it would continue were open questions, since although the British intended, as their top official for Indian defense said in the summer of 1947, to "come to the rescue" in case of aggression, developments in Greece and Turkey indicated that Britain's rescuing days might be numbered. Besides, India was talking on bolting the Commonwealth, which would complicate matters considerably. Nonetheless, the Truman administration was quite happy to leave the security of South Asia to the British for the time being, and Washington carefully avoided stepping on British toes in that part of the world.[9]

This respect for British sensibilities extended even to strictly U.S.–Indian matters. After receiving the above-mentioned Indian request for air transport, the State Department checked with the British before replying. Officials at the Foreign Office, on learning that the Americans proposed to insist on the approval of both India and Pakistan, responded that they would have answered the request "in exactly the same sense." After receiving London's seal of approval the administration went ahead as planned.[10]

Henry Grady in New Delhi thought this solicitude for British opinion essentially wrongheaded. Grady, who had been closely involved with Britain's withdrawals from other parts of its dwindling empire, distrusted British motives and considered the caution British leaders urged on the United States principally a device to guarantee American inaction. "The fact is," Grady wrote, "that His Majesty's Government feels competitive toward the USA in India and does not look with favor on American cooperation with the Government of India and the Government of Pakistan in solving their very critical problems of migration." Later, at a meeting in the State Department, Grady remarked that the British had been denigrating American motives to Indian leaders. According to Grady, Lord Mountbatten, the last viceroy and at that time governor-general of India, habitually whispered evil thoughts in Nehru's ear, warning the prime minister to beware of "dollar imperialism."[11]

Grady's complaints made little impression on Washington. In 1947 the administration had its hands full elsewhere, and neither Truman nor other policymakers possessed any desire to enmesh the United States in the vexed affairs of the subcontinent. Further, even had they entertained such a notion, they could readily see that domestic American politics ruled out any South Asian initiatives. Convincing Congress and the American people to support the Truman Doctrine and the Marshall Plan had eaten into the administration's political capital; the president had no intention of squandering what remained on a dubious commitment to a region of secondary importance. If, in addition, involvement in Indian affairs threatened to irritate the British, then the administration must shun it all the more.

IV

BUT ALOOFNESS exacted a price, for the Indians were counting on American aid in making the transition to self-government. The dislocations attending partition seriously disrupted India's food production and distribution system; consequently at the beginning of September 1947 Nehru's spokesmen approached the American embassy in New Delhi with emergency requests for grain. A short time later the Indian secretary-general for external affairs, G. S. Bajpai, asked Grady about the possibility of American loans.[12]

Despite India's obvious distress the Truman administration replied noncommittally. Grady empathized, but he lacked instructions, and in any event he did not want the administration to appear overeager with aid. The ambassador therefore confined himself to telling Bajpai that once things settled down India might apply for financial assistance to the World Bank or the American Export-Import Bank, or to private American banks. Regarding shipments of food, the State Department said grain had fallen short all over the world; American pledges to Europe precluded increasing supplies for India.[13]

The administration maintained a low profile in South Asia through 1947. At year's end American diplomats stationed in the region gathered to compare notes with desk officers in Washington. At this meeting Grady described his strategy for dealing with Indian requests for financial help. "I have followed a policy of appearing indifferent as to whether or not they take our capital. This has had a good effect." The ambassador added that excessive American interest would awaken suspicions in India, and he recommended a continuation of the administration's cautious policy.[14]

Actually, Grady had more actively promoted American aid than he indicated in this meeting. A former business executive and an economist, Grady firmly believed in the need for countries like India to industrialize, but he considered private investment a more suitable agent for development than government assistance. In the autumn of 1947, after receiving requests from Indian officials for American help in flood-control, irrigation, and hydropower projects, Grady wrote to Stephen Bechtel of the Bechtel engineering and construction firm, describing the Indian proposal and urging Bechtel to set up negotiations with the Indian government at once. "I think the time is ripe for these talks and I hope you can come soon because I would like to strike while the iron is hot."[15]

Grady's recommendation to Bechtel followed not only from his faith in capitalism but also from a conviction that American assistance, private or public, held the key to winning India's cooperation in the future. "American influence should increase greatly through economic help," Grady told his colleagues at the December 1947 conference in Washington, "It is the most effective channel for keeping India on our side and under our influence."

The significance of this conference lay in the fact that it marked the first time since Indian independence that the Truman administration seriously discussed America's long-term policy toward India. Officers from the State Department and from embassies in countries near India pumped Grady for information and opinions about India and Nehru. Ray Thurston of the department's South Asian division wondered whether the administration might realistically hope to bring India into line with American policy. "We have conceived of India as a possible stabilizing influence in Asia, taking the place of the Western powers," Thurston said. "Is this overly optimistic?"

Grady thought not. He described the Indian government's diplomatic goals and its prospects of achieving them. Immediately after independence, Grady said, Indian officials had intended to assert Indian leadership in South and Southeast Asia. The communal conflict with Pakistan had frustrated this ambition somewhat but Nehru continued to work toward an Asian bloc independent of the two superpowers. Grady said Nehru and other Indians considered their country the most advanced in the area and the region's natural leader. Grady added that such a role for India did not necessarily conflict with American purposes, so long as the Indians did not get carried away.

The American ambassador to Burma, Jerome Huddle, worried that a regional grouping under Indian leadership would make American diplomacy more difficult, in that India might form "a power bloc against us." Grady disagreed. He said he saw no reason why a South-Southeast Asian alliance system would threaten American interests, especially if the United States took measures to ensure the friendliness of such a bloc.

Paul Alling, the American ambassador to Pakistan, suggested that India was more likely to cooperate with the Soviet Union than were the Moslem countries of South Asia and the Middle East, which opposed communism on religious grounds. Grady admitted that Alling had a point. "There is a strong trend in India towards socialism," he said. "India is more likely to go in the Russian direction ideologically than are the Muslims." This might present a problem, he added, especially since the Soviets had their eyes on India. "I believe Russian thinking discounts the value of India in a war with the United States, but from the standpoint of Russian expansion, India is most attractive for her material and human resources, and as a stepping stone to China and the rest of Asia."

Ray Thurston seconded Grady's opinion by mentioning a report from the Moscow embassy indicating that the Kremlin, evidently frustrated in its designs for Western Europe by the Marshall Plan, was looking to Asia. Grady amplified his remarks: "If Russia is blocked in Europe, she will certainly turn elsewhere—probably south." Grady said the Indians did not fear a Russian attack. Neither did he. Rather his concern lay in the area of "ideological penetration." The United States needed to act quickly lest the Soviets gain an edge in this field. "India is worth a lot to us. We must realize its importance ideologically."

Raymond Hare of the State Department's division for South Asia asked Grady for suggestions on how to prevent India's sliding to the left. "What can we do about it, particularly as we square off against the U.S.S.R.?" Grady replied that the administration might start with an intensified propaganda campaign. He said he himself had taken the first steps in this direction. Describing meetings he had held with Indian publishers and editors, he asserted that his efforts to gain better press coverage of the United States had been "very effective." Indians were "moving in the right direction." More work remained. "They should be quietly encouraged, but not pushed too far." At times, however, forcefulness would be appropriate. "I have told Nehru that this is a question that cannot be straddled and that India should get on the democratic side immediately."[16]

V

EXCEPT FOR his comment about getting India "on the democratic side"—since India's commitment to democracy was unshakable—Grady's assessment of Nehru's objectives hit close to the mark. The prime minister regularly denied that India intended to create an Asian bloc: nonalignment, he argued, applied to all combinations, whether of left, right, or middle. In practice, however, his "third area" or "area of peace," to the degree it assumed coherence, would function as a bloc vis-à-vis the great powers. Even before independence Nehru had written that India "cannot play a secondary part in the world." The prime minister was ambitious, for himself and for his country, and nonalignment was his device for promoting both. Should India sign on with one of the superpowers, "then we lose that tremendous vantage ground that we have of using such influence as we possess (and that influence is going to grow from year to year) in the cause of world peace." Obviously peace was one goal of nonalignment, if for no other reason than that the Indian economy could not stand the strain of war or preparation for war, but another was the achievement of a position as the balance-tipper between the blocs. And the larger the number of votes India could deliver, the greater weight it would carry.[17]

Grady was also correct in predicting that India would more readily warm to the Soviets than would Pakistan, although the secular nature of the Indian state, as opposed to the Islamic basis of Pakistan's polity, was only part of the explanation. In 1947 India was still in the process of self-definition, and like the people of many new nations, especially heterogeneous ones, Indians sometimes had an easier time defining themselves in opposition to a common enemy than in affirmation of common goals. For generations the oppressor of India had been colonialism. Although the British had formally left India, colonialism still stalked

Asia and Africa—and India, in the form of continuing economic and military dependence on Britain. Communism held no terror for Indians, who had never felt its burden, and the communists could be counted on to denounce colonialism at every opportunity. A turn toward Moscow was the most natural thing in the world.[18]

At the beginning of 1948, however, both the "third area" and the turning toward the Soviet Union remained largely in the future; India currently had all it could do with Pakistan in Kashmir. As the new year began the two countries teetered on the brink of a full-scale war over the disputed province. Notwithstanding the ad hoc character of the fighting, some 25,000 had died and many more on both sides seemed destined to join the ranks of fallen heroes.[19]

Progress toward a closer American relationship with India probably would have required involvement in the Kashmir question, but the Truman administration wanted nothing to do with it. On the contrary, Washington sought to limit its liability. Partly as a contribution to peace, equally to avoid the stigma of having Indians and Pakistanis killed with American bullets, the administration cut off the small shipments of American arms it had been allowing each side.[20]

Embargoing weapons proved easier than staying out of the affair diplomatically. Almost from the beginning of the Kashmir troubles Britain urged American leaders to offer their services in mediation of the dispute. Grady spoke accurately in claiming that Britain did not want to have to compete with the United States for India's favor, but at the same time the British recognized that the conflict between India and Pakistan might wreck their plans for safeguarding such influence as they retained in the subcontinent. A British cabinet paper pointed out that "even if India and Pakistan are both friendly to us, we cannot hope to make full use of [their resources] unless they are prepared to afford each other mutual support." Consequently London eagerly sought American intervention.[21]

At the beginning of 1948 British Commonwealth Relations Secretary Philip Noel-Baker warned American officials of an impending "holocaust" on the subcontinent. Britain, Noel-Baker said, would gladly take the lead in the search for a settlement of the Kashmir dispute, but a British initiative might boomerang in that it would look like "a reimposition of the British Raj" just six months after the transfer of power. The prestige of the United States was "extremely high" in both India and

Pakistan; as a result the United States enjoyed an opportunity to play "a decisive role" in arranging a settlement in Kashmir.[22]

Noel-Baker's American listeners at this Washington meeting drew unsettling conclusions from his description of the dire fate in store for India and Pakistan. American leaders had watched with disappointment as British India had split, their discouragement following principally from their belief that in unity lay resistance to subversion. Two states on the subcontinent possessed less stability than one, as the Kashmir quarrel demonstrated. But if India and Pakistan could solve their problems peacefully, security might yet follow. An all-out war over Kashmir, on the other hand, besides undermining the present moderate governments of India and Pakistan, threatened to splinter the subcontinent, leading to what American officials unoriginally called the "balkanization" of South Asia.[23]

Nonetheless the administration refused to get involved. At some point events might force American intervention to head off an outright war, but for now American leaders preferred to leave the matter to the British. Undersecretary of State Robert Lovett told Noel-Baker American mediation would raise problems on two fronts. First, it would distract the American Congress from the more important task of defending and rebuilding Europe. Second, it might draw "undesirable Russian attention," confounding the difficulties of the subcontinent with the competition of the cold war.[24]

Lovett's reasons did not lack validity, but they disguised the administration's chief concern regarding intervention in Kashmir: that the conflict was insoluble and would only bring trouble for the United States. Besides, as a Commonwealth matter, Kashmir fell clearly into the British bailiwick. Britain knew the territory and the idiosyncrasies of the contenders. If anyone could find an agreement, the British could.

Loy Henderson, then in the State Department but soon to replace Grady in New Delhi, stressed these points in a note to Lovett the day before the undersecretary's meeting with Noel-Baker. Referring to discussions of Kashmir at the United Nations, Henderson wrote,

> The problem is one in which British initiative is clearly indicated not only in view of the strength of the British Delegation and the familiarity which the British have with the problems of the area but also because in essence the present situation is a further development in the evolution of the political problems connected with the British withdrawal from India.

Having explained why Britain should stay in, Henderson went on to say why America should stay out.

> A pronounced American initiative, on the other hand, would not only carry with it the danger of extending our already heavy commitments in various parts of the world but might also involve an American formula which would require making a choice between giving support to the interests of India or of Pakistan, a course which we have thus far assiduously avoided.[25]

Administration officials continued to dodge British attempts to draw the United States into the Kashmir question through the beginning of 1949, when the problem became less acute as India and Pakistan agreed to a ceasefire. But even while events in South Asia provided what the CIA described as "an unexpected breathing space," simultaneous developments in the Far East created new problems for American strategists, raising the stakes throughout Asia.[26]

In the early months of 1949 the Chinese Communists tightened the noose about Chiang Kai-shek and the Nationalists; it seemed only a matter of time before China fell entirely under the socialist spell—and perhaps into the Soviet sphere, although the strength of the Moscow-Beijing axis remained unclear. As American planners considered a line of Western retreat from China they took a fresh look at India. In March 1949 the State and Defense departments produced a joint paper analyzing the import of recent events and proposing appropriate American responses.

The paper, a straightforward exercise in geopolitics, declared that the fact of overriding importance in South Asia was the withdrawal of direct British control during the previous eighteen months. Consequently the West confronted the task of filling the resulting void before the Russians or their allies moved in. Fortunately, the memo continued, the British retained a large measure of informal influence, through the membership of India and Pakistan in the Commonwealth and through the "manifold economic and cultural contacts" the British had established over many years. The United States might turn this influence to American purposes, the most important of which was the retention of India and Pakistan as "a Western salient on the Asian continent." The authors of the State-Defense report, noting the vital role of economic development in strengthening resistance to Soviet influence, advocated a coordinated Anglo-American economic policy for India and Pakistan. Development aid, however, would yield results primarily in the long term. More to the immediate purpose, the paper drew attention to the significant role British military advisers played in the armed forces of the region. Bearing this in mind, the authors stated that it would serve American interests to explore with the British the extent to which they could "continue to assume responsibility for meeting the military requirements of the South Asian area," and to encourage the British "to bear as great a share of this burden as they possibly can."[27]

The matter of urging the British to carry on in the defense of India received added emphasis in a memorandum from the joint chiefs of staff. The chiefs' paper asserted that while India possessed only modest positive strategic value for the United States, the loss of India to the Russians would be a considerable blow. Aside from its impact on the safety of the sea lanes of the Indian Ocean, a communist takeover of India would allow the Soviets to outflank Pakistan, jeopardizing American plans to build up Karachi and Lahore as bases for air operations against the central Soviet Union and in defense of the oil fields of the Persian Gulf. Further, those parts of Pakistan closest to the Soviet Union offered possibilities for "intelligence penetration."

The joint chiefs believed the greatest communist threat to the subcontinent involved not external assault but internal subversion. Forbidding geography between India and Pakistan, on one hand, and the Soviet Union and China, on the other, made a communist invasion in the near future unlikely; so also did the presence in Europe, in the Middle East, and in the Far East of targets more tempting to the Russians and their allies. The possibility of political disintegration in India and Pakistan posed a much greater danger. Therefore American policy ought to concentrate on bolstering the internal security of the two countries. In this matter the British, with their long experience in the affairs of the subcontinent and their sensitivity to the region's problems, could prove most helpful. The joint chiefs called for "collaboration and consultation" with Britain to determine the needs of the area, and they recommended strong efforts by the Truman administration to determine "the extent to which the British can meet such requirements."[28]

The idea of relying as far as possible on the British to defend India also appealed to the CIA. Like the Pentagon and the State Department, the intelligence agency considered Britain the preferred primary guarantor of Indian security. In its strategic planning the CIA assumed that an overt communist attack on India would prompt the British immediately to send military forces to repulse the challenge. To a greater degree than did their counterparts at State and the Pentagon, however, the CIA analysts questioned how long Britain could maintain such a policy. Taking into account the increasingly evident overcommitment of British resources, the CIA predicted that at some point in the not distant future Britain would try to persuade the United States to pick up the burden of Indian defense.[29]

VII

DURING THE course of 1949 the Truman administration began to hedge its bets on the British. Not ready at this stage to assume direct responsibility for the security of South Asia, the administration nonetheless shifted slightly in that direction. A logical first step involved cultivating Nehru; consequently the White House invited the prime minister to America in the autumn of 1949.

Nehru's visit, coming at what seemed a turning point in Asian history, aroused tremendous interest in the United States. Arriving just days after the formal establishment of the People's Republic of China, Nehru embodied American hopes for democracy in Asia and personified a country until now little more than an abstraction in the broad American consciousness. Commentary on the significance of the prime minister's visit poured from the press. The *New Republic*, remarking "the gathering twilight" in the East, declared that recent events had brought Nehru to the "eve of fulfillment" of his destiny as a world leader. India, according to this journal, was the "heartland" of Asia; extending the metaphor, the *New Republic* asserted, "Its future involves the future of the whole body." *Newsweek* nodded approvingly toward "the great Indian experiment in democracy," asserting that "if the Indian experiment fails . . . all Asia will fall to Communism or into chaos." *Time*, noted for its consuming interest in China, conferred on Nehru, after Chiang's defeat, the title of "Asia's key man." *Time* went on to express the hope that India would act as "a new anchor in Asia" and to describe Nehru's journey to America as "one of the century's most important visits of state." The *Nation*, leaning as usual against the wind of current enthusiasm, stood apart from much of the excitement but provided the clearest view of what India suddenly meant to "the official mind of

America": "India offers the best hope of holding back the tide of communism now flowing south through Asia."[30]

Nehru captured the imagination of the daily press no less than that of the weeklies. The editor of the *New York Times* hailed the "welcome visitor" and described the importance of Nehru's "moral personality as something of an unofficial leader of modern-minded Asiatics." A few days later the *Times* added, "India is potentially a great counterweight to China." The *Washington Post* enthused,

> He wears a halo in his own lifetime. . . . Few men in charge of great affairs are more gifted than Nehru. . . . He knows the art of being a king. At the same time he has a common touch which excites the sympathy of all kinds and conditions of India's population. He can stir millions with pen or tongue.

A writer in the *New York Post* judged Nehru "a moral figure" of "extraordinarily luminous intellect." This author declared that Nehru stood in India

> where Washington stood in the United States. . . . His visit to this country offers more than a chance to cheer a great man. It presents an opportunity to undergird democracy in Asia and to lay the foundations of an understanding that will endure in mutual dignity, a partnership of equals from East and West.[31]

Congress asked Nehru to address the Senate and House. Not all the legislators thrilled at the idea of Nehru's grand tour; some bitter-enders of the China bloc objected to Nehru's apparent displacement of Chiang in the affections of the American people. Republican Walter Judd of Minnesota signaled his disapproval of Nehru's neutralism by inserting into the *Congressional Record* an article entitled "Sleeping India Unconscious of Stealthy Tread of Russian Bear." But Judd could muster only a small following at this time. A House colleague, Democrat Emanuel Celler of New York, more nearly approximated the sense of Congress when he declared after meeting Nehru for the first time, "There is a transcendental quality about this great man; an aura of the spiritual seems to hover over him. Yet his words are those of a man who understands the meaning and significance of the practical needs of day to day living." Democrat John Kee, chairman of the House Foreign Affairs Committee, spoke to India and Nehru in the words: "This American

Republic is marching forward upon the same road with you and toward the same goal. . . . We do not expect nor ask your country to fall in behind us. No, we are inviting you to take your place at our side and keep step with us as we march into the dawn of a new day." Democratic Senator Frank Graham, whose interest in India would lead to his appointment as a mediator in the Kashmir dispute, described Nehru as "a great leader of a great people who are one of the hopes of freedom in a world threatened by another monstrous totalitarian dictatorship."[32]

Of all the legislators, none could match the effusions of Hubert Humphrey. Upon entering the Senate the Minnesota Democrat had told Assistant Secretary of State George McGhee he wanted to "specialize on India," saying he intended "to be for India what Walter Judd is for China." Throughout his long career Humphrey attempted to make good this pledge; in doing so he embodied an important strain of American liberalism that found Bandung a more congenial concept than Yalta, that would agitate for warmer relations with New Delhi, and that eventually would mobilize behind an American commitment to India's economic development. Humphrey rarely missed an opportunity to spread the word that the future of Asia lay with the 400 million Indians. In April 1949 he contrasted the sad and declining situation in China with the hopeful and improving, though economically straitened, state of affairs in India. "China is an enigma," Humphrey declared. "No one is sure what is happening—what we ought to do about it or what will happen if we do nothing. There is no question in India. She is a great and rich country, worthy of our help and needing it sorely." But American aid to India would hardly be an exercise in philanthropy. "Frankly," Humphrey said, "we need friends in Asia. We need to bolster up those forces that are aspiring to democratic goals." In October Nehru's visit launched Humphrey into further flights.

> There already exist many bonds which bind us in friendship with India. The traditional love of freedom and democracy held by the Indian people strikes a similar chord in us. We likewise believe that this democratic freedom can only flourish in a world at peace. . . . India is a member in good standing of the United Nations. She has played a consistent and devoted role to the principles of the United Nations Charter. . . . She has a deep friendship for the United States.[33]

VIII

SOMEWHAT EMBARRASSED, albeit privately, by all the excitement, officials in the Truman administration took a more skeptical view of the Indian prime minister. Assessments of Nehru had of course constituted a staple of American diplomatic reportage from India since before independence. In August 1947 Henry Grady, saying it was "hard to be optimistic" about India's future, remarked, "My disappointment is principally with respect to Nehru." The ambassador conceded that Nehru was "a man of high ideals," but he worried that the Indian leader was too much "the dreamer type." "I get the impression that he is rather letting administrative matters drift. He does not seem to have much direction. I am not sure he knows where he is going." Part of the problem, in Grady's view, lay in the fact that Nehru made a better agitator than administrator.

> His leadership in the fight for independence was based on qualities which are not particularly adaptive to the responsibilities of Government. He seems to have little interest in the vast economic problems facing the Dominion or those involved particularly with the division of the country.

Nehru's inability to prevent partition had left the Indian leader disappointed and frustrated; yet, Grady said, "Even if there had not been division, his deficiencies in administration would still be there." Grady's attempts to get Nehru to discuss pressing matters had failed. "I have tried to talk with him several times on some of the economic problems facing the country and have become quickly aware that his mind was somewhere else."[34]

Grady's remarks reflected the expectations of a businessman; those of his successor displayed the views of a career diplomat. Loy Henderson was in a sour mood on taking up the New Delhi post, having been run out of the State Department's Near Eastern division for opposing the Zionists in the White House on the Palestine question. Dealing with the Indian prime minister did not improve Henderson's disposition. "Nehru," he declared, "is a vain, sensitive, emotional and complicated person. Mixed with his vanity appear to be certain furtive doubts regarding his own ability to carry on constructive work. He is at his best when playing the role of a critic." Henderson thought Nehru found comfort only in relations with those he considered his intellectual and social inferiors, an attitude the ambassador attributed to the prime minister's educational background. "It seems that during his schooldays in England he consorted with and cultivated a group of rather supercilious upper middle-class young men who fancied themselves rather precious, and that he acquired some of their manners and ways of thinking."

The English effect, Henderson believed, extended to Nehru's perceptions of America. The prime minister's impressions of the United States reflected the opinions of British acquaintances who had "gone out of their way to prejudice him against things American." The Mountbattens especially had succeeded in convincing Nehru that Americans were "a vulgar, pushy lot, lacking in fine feeling" and that American culture, "dominated by the dollar," was "a serious threat to the development of a higher type of world civilization." Albion's pernicious influence persisted. "When Nehru visits the U.K., he is worked on by a varied collection of notables ranging from Churchill to Laski and from Bernard Shaw to Ernie Bevin."

Yet Henderson conceded Nehru's better qualities. "It would be unfair," he commented, "if I did not add that in spite of his vanity and of his petty snobberies, he is a man of warm heart, of genuine idealism, of shrewd discernment, and of considerable intellectual capacity. He is also an expert politician and a natural leader." Henderson wrote this letter while the Truman administration pondered the advisability of inviting Nehru to America; the ambassador thought such an invitation a good idea. "If the United States could capture his imagination instead of getting on his English-strung nerves or of stirring his jealousy, his visit would be more than worthwhile."[35]

Motivating all this character analysis, of course, was a desire to discover the wellsprings of Indian foreign policy. A week before Nehru arrived in New York the State Department tackled the issue more directly. In a lengthy report entitled "India's Orientation in World Affairs," the department's Office of Intelligence Research asserted that Nehru's neutralism had about it more of appearance than reality and more of philosophical posturing than diplomatic substance. In the first place, various Indian officials, including the prime minister's sister and ambassador to the United States, Vijaya Lakshmi Pandit, had "privately, but with every appearance of sincerity," assured American leaders that India's "real sympathies" lay with the West, although Nehru preferred the freedom of maneuver a neutralist approach allowed. Second, India depended economically on Britain and other countries of the West for markets, technical advice, and investment capital. Third, despite the frustrations of the independence struggle, there remained in India a widespread affinity for Britain.

> Indian hatred of the British, even in pre-independence days when it was at its height, was generally coupled with a jealous admiration of British character, culture, and ability; the repeated emphasis by the British on the superiority of things British was not without its effect on the Indian consciousness. However much Indians resented British claims they nevertheless tended to accept them.

Finally, Indian leaders recognized their country's need for protection. "The Government of India is fully conscious of the country's military and, above all, naval weakness and its consequent inability to defend itself against foreign aggression or to keep open the sea lanes upon which its commercial life depends." This fact played a crucial role in India's patently unneutral decision to remain in the Commonwealth, and it helped guarantee that for the near term at least the balance of power in the subcontinent would continue to favor the West.

The OIR paper went on to explain that Nehru's promotion of a neutral Asian community, even while India leaned heavily on the West, reflected mixed motives. No doubt the prime minister sincerely believed neutralism would increase the likelihood of peace.

> But the concept primarily expresses India's conviction of her "manifest destiny" as the leader of Asia. . . . An Asian bloc with India at its head obviously would vastly strengthen India's position as a world power and provide a basis for greater independence in world affairs.

As to Nehru's prospects for success in creating a third bloc, the chances seemed no better than "slight." Pakistan of course rejected Indian leadership entirely. The predominantly Moslem countries farther west would probably do the same. Ceylon and Nepal looked askance at anything that increased the power of their large neighbor. If the Afghans joined India they would be responding primarily to fear of Pakistan. Only Southeast Asia appeared at all receptive to the "area of peace" idea; there India might expect "qualified support" from Burma, the Philippines, and Indonesia.[36]

IX

AFTER ALL the fanfare, preparation, and analysis, the prime minister's American tour proved a fiasco. In Henderson's words, Nehru attracted "pacifists, friends of Asia and well-meaning cranks," but to those possessing what the ambassador regarded as sounder judgment the prime minister seemed "wooly and evasive." Assistant Secretary George McGhee later remembered that

> Nehru came to America with an apparent chip on his shoulder toward American high officials, who he appeared to believe could not possibly understand someone with his background. He appeared determined to appeal to the American people over the heads of the government. Needless to say, he did not accomplish this, but only succeeded in making himself so unpopular with Americans generally that it would later prove difficult to muster support for helping to meet India's urgent need for wheat.
>
> Nehru and Truman didn't hit it off at all. Rumor has it that, in his first informal meeting with the President, he was offended by Truman's extended discussion of the merits of bourbon whiskey with Vice President Alben Barkley.[37]

Acheson and Nehru got on no better. The secretary of state tried to enliven the formal dinner given for the prime minister by depicting imagined conversations between Nehru and distinguished Americans of the past whose careers paralleled the prime minister's: Washington as father of his country, Jefferson as theorist of democracy, Jackson as political organizer and strategist, Lincoln as spiritual guide amid fratricidal strife. Nehru apparently did not know what to make of Acheson's attempt at levity. "The result," Acheson recalled, "was very definitely a change from the routine and caught our distinguished Visitor unprepared, like a student who had not done his homework for what should have been a 'gut course.' He was not pleased."

Acheson invited Nehru to his home, where he thought the prime minister might unwind. This effort also failed. "I had hoped that, uninhibited by a cloud of witnesses, we might establish a personal relationship. But he would not relax. He talked to me, as Queen Victoria said of Mr. Gladstone, as though I were a public meeting." By the time the uncomfortable session ended Acheson had despaired of establishing any rapport. "I was convinced that Nehru and I were not destined to have a pleasant personal relationship." Acheson granted that Nehru played a key part on the world stage. "He was so important to India and India's survival so important to all of us, that if he did not exist—as Voltaire said of God—he would have to be invented." Nevertheless, to Acheson Nehru remained "one of the most difficult men with whom I have ever had to deal." [38]

Nehru reciprocated the ill feelings. He considered himself insulted when asked at a New York banquet what he thought of dining "with at least $20,000,000." At the National Press Club he conceded America's technological proficiency but asserted that material advancement meant little "without progress along cultural, philosophical or social lines." A CIA source, evidently close to Nehru, summarized the prime minister's reactions. Truman was "a mediocre man who, as a result of unexpected circumstances, had been placed in a role far superior to his capacities." Acheson was "equally mediocre." The State Department was "uncertain, confused, superficial, too much inclined to improvisations and at the same time pretentious and arrogant." Americans as a race were "elementary and material," possessing "no cultural drives" and wanting only "to eat and drink and to live comfortably." American designs regarding India were "fundamentally those of taking over the position which Great Britain had held in the 19th Century." Both the policy and the people were "full of arrogance." [39]

X

AT ONE level Nehru's visit did prove worthwhile. For the first time American leaders had the opportunity to discuss world events with the prime minister personally. To Acheson Nehru gave a long lecture on Asia. He accused the Dutch of dragging their feet in decolonizing Indonesia, contending that delay only put off the day of reckoning. On Indochina he spoke "with considerable force and feeling," as Acheson described Nehru's tone. France's experiment with Bao Dai in Vietnam was "hopeless and doomed to failure." While French forces controlled the cities and major lines of communication, Ho Chi Minh's nationalists held the rest of the country. The prime minister conceded that Ho was a communist as well as a nationalist, prompting Acheson to suggest the possibility that Ho's communism might overwhelm his nationalism. Nehru granted the danger and acknowledged that something similar had taken place in China, but on the whole he considered such concern "a misapplication to the East of the European experience." In India, Indonesia, and Burma communists had attempted to subvert nationalist movements and had failed. He anticipated a similar outcome in Indochina.

Expanding on the situation in China, the prime minister expressed no enthusiasm for the new regime in Beijing but hinted that India would recognize the communist government before long. When Acheson made the American case against early recognition, arguing that the international community ought to take care to determine that the communists indeed controlled all of China, that the Chinese people at least acquiesced in communist rule, and that the new government intended to meet its legitimate obligations, Nehru brushed aside these objections. He said recognition was inevitable and therefore hesitation served little purpose.

Acheson asked the prime minister to speak "fully and frankly" on Kashmir. Nehru complied, giving an exhaustive discourse on the history of the dispute. He told how Pakistani-supported tribesmen, and later regular Pakistani troops, had invaded Kashmir. He said India, at the request of the Kashmir government, had intervened to prevent a complete takeover by Pakistan. Subsequent Indian military operations had succeeded in pushing back the invaders, though the Pakistanis still controlled part of the region. In Nehru's view the Kashmir issue transcended territorial questions; rather it provided the clearest expression of an abiding ideological clash between India and Pakistan. The Pakistanis, he said, wished to create a religious state in South Asia and claimed sovereignty over Kashmir on the basis of the Moslem faith of most of the inhabitants of the province. Such a theocratic principle completely contradicted India's political philosophy, which asserted a secular state and the separation of religious from political questions. Confessional politics would generate a "profoundly unsettling effect" in the subcontinent, threatening both Moslems in India and Hindus in Pakistan. The prime minister said a plebiscite, proposed as a means of resolving the Kashmir dispute, would be "inflammatory and disastrous" for all concerned.

Nehru then backtracked a bit, remarking that he did not entirely rule out a plebiscite. But he asserted that India could not agree to a vote until the United Nations issued a statement declaring Pakistan the aggressor and until Pakistan withdrew its troops from the region. He admitted that a Pakistani withdrawal would create pressure for a similar Indian pullout, but he said the analogy did not hold. Having readier access to

Kashmir, Pakistan could "at any moment return and upset the situation." Thus some Indian troops would have to remain. He fudged further on the plebiscite issue by citing logistical difficulties in conducting a fair vote. A better solutiòn than a plebiscite would be a constituent assembly of "the natural leaders" of Kashmir, who would decide among union with India, adherence to Pakistan, and partition.[40]

Nehru's discussions with Truman were thoroughly predictable; the only other noteworthy meeting took place at the United Nations just before the prime minister left America. Perhaps Nehru felt more at ease in his own hotel suite than he had as a guest of the Truman administration; perhaps he considered formality unnecessary in conversation with mid-level officials. Whatever the reasons, he talked more freely on the topic that most interested the administration: India's views on communism and its principal practitioners. As the American memorandum describing the session commented, "He did so in a tone and attitude of equality and partnership of understanding and purpose between India and the United States."

Communism, Nehru said, possessed a natural appeal in countries like India, poor and backward and in which radical change seemed necessary. The communist model appeared to be working in Russia; the Soviets had made great strides in solving their economic problems. For a time, especially during the independence struggle, the Indian Communist party had claimed many followers and wielded considerable influence. But after 1947 things had changed. On orders from Moscow the communists had launched a campaign of violence designed to undermine the government. By this means the communists had "alienated the people" and drained the "reservoir of good will" they had created. Nehru asserted that at present the communists posed no serious threat, although the communist victory in China might spur Indian leftists to renewed troublemaking.

Nehru went on to describe what he considered the best approach for dealing with communism. He criticized the Truman administration for falling into the Russian habit of rhetorical aggression. It made no sense for the United States to take on the Soviets with "their chosen weapons of name-calling, deprecation, and verbal belligerency." The Russians excelled in this form of diplomacy and the United States should avoid it. Nehru suggested instead an indirect approach, what he called "mental jiujitsu." American leaders ought to make every gesture of "apparent cooperation" with the Soviet Union and must never openly admit a lack of faith in the possibility of compromise. Should the Soviets launch a military attack on the West, of course the United States must respond with forceful countermeasures. But Russian troops posed a lesser threat than communist propaganda; therefore the United States should work harder in the ideological realm.

Turning to China, Nehru described "a very real split" between the supporters of Mao Zedong, who held narrowly to Moscow's line, and the followers of Zhou Enlai, who sought to broaden and diversify China's international contacts. Western diplomacy, he said, ought to aim at encouraging the latter group. The attraction of communism for most Chinese lay in the fact that for decades the communists were the only ones willing to take on the overriding issue of agrarian reform. Russia had helped the communists achieve power, but China lay too far from Moscow and the Chinese people remained too stubbornly Chinese for the Soviet Union to dominate them. The prime minister predicted that something "stronger than Titoism" would soon develop in China, and he said the Western powers should do all they could to encourage it. In this light, nonrecognition of the Beijing government and continued support of the Nationalists would backfire. While the communists faced hostility from the West they could blame their failure to live up to the promises of the revolution on "foreign devils." Should they lack enemies abroad "their problems would be increased and fissiparous tendencies among them would grow."

At this point Philip Jessup of the American UN delegation asked Nehru whether it would not be a mistake to recognize the communists as long as resistance continued in part of China. Premature recognition would surely send the wrong signals to communists and anticommunists elsewhere, heartening the former and discouraging the latter. Nehru replied that the communists already enjoyed "considerable" success in imposing their will on the country. The West might delay recognition for a few months, but to avoid it indefinitely "would not be possible."

The American ambassador to the United Nations, Warren Austin, argued that any Chinese government would require foreign aid to survive. Formerly this aid had come from the West. Austin suggested that now the UN might provide it, implying that it would serve as a lever to influence the situation in China. Nehru disagreed. He declared that the Chinese could get along without external assistance for "at least a few years." The prime minister added that he believed the UN would have no alternative to recognizing China once a large number of its members had done so.[41]

XI

THE COMMUNIST victory in China prompted a searching review of American policy toward Asia. The resulting report pointed out that the only major power centers in Asia now lying beyond the communist orbit were Japan and the Indian subcontinent. Japan, still under American occupation, was secure for the time being. India occasioned more worries and, considering its importance, deservedly so. "Should India and Pakistan fall to communism, the United States and its allies might find themselves denied any foothold on the Asian mainland." Fortunately for American interests, the nationalist revolution in South Asia had not taken the communist turn it had in China, largely because of "the advanced policies" the British had followed in handing over power in India. In addition, India and Pakistan had inherited from Britain a political, military, and to some degree economic infrastructure that contributed to their stability and predisposed them favorably toward the West. Their continuing membership in the British Commonwealth also served to pull them in a Western direction.

Consequently, although India remained wedded to its policy of non-alignment, this need cause no alarm since even a neutral India constituted a "bulwark against communist expansion." Without abandoning hope of drawing India closer to the United States, American leaders should concentrate on maintaining the status quo. In this regard the Commonwealth would play a vital role. The most obvious advantage of relying on the Commonwealth was that Britain and other members would bear the weight of defending India and solving problems like Kashmir. But the Commonwealth strategy promised a bonus. At a time when American domestic racial policies were an embarassment in America's dealings with the nonwhite world, the Commonwealth, now a multiracial organization, provided more-acceptable agents of Western influence. "The cooperation of the white nations of the Commonwealth will arrest any potential dangers of the growth of a white-colored polarization."[42]

Truman, whose limited personal interest in India had diminished further after his disastrous encounter with Nehru, and who generally left India policy to the departments to thrash out, approved this paper in slightly revised form at the end of December 1949. The original version indicated the administration's desire to limit American exposure in South Asia through continued reliance on Britain and the Commonwealth; the revision put the point even more strongly. Its principal recommendations included a statement that the United States ought to examine the means by which "all members of the British Commonwealth may be induced to play a more active role in collaboration with the United States" in assuring the security of South Asia.[43]

As an initial step in the pursuit of the Commonwealth strategy the administration redoubled its efforts to get the British to find a solution to the Kashmir problem. Though war between India and Pakistan did not appear imminent, Kashmir's continued festering blocked constructive efforts for regional defense. By the beginning of 1950 India and Pakistan still had not gone beyond agreement on the principle of a plebiscite; on the practical details of a referendum they remained as far apart as ever.

In January 1950, at the urging of George McGhee, Acheson wrote to British Foreign Secretary Ernest Bevin, declaring it "unthinkable" that the two members of the Commonwealth should remain stalemated on procedural matters when they had agreed to the basic idea of a plebiscite. A Commonwealth conference then under way in Ceylon seemed to Acheson a perfect opportunity for mediation. The secretary of state said, "I would strongly urge therefore that you take the opportunity provided by the Colombo Conference to have a thorough discussion of the problem with both sides." A month later, the Colombo meeting having failed to produce a breakthrough, Acheson again urged Bevin to leave no stone unturned in the search for a settlement. Acheson asserted that Britain, as the senior member of the Commonwealth, was in "the best position to take the necessary leadership" on the Kashmir question.[44]

During the late winter and spring of 1950 Kashmir continued to worry American officials; but still they insisted that the problem belonged primarily to the Commonwealth, even as London, tiring of what the British high commisioner in Pakistan called America's "timidity" on the issue, stepped up efforts to bring the Americans in. In March the British ambassador in Washington relayed a suggestion from the Foreign Office that a distinguished American like General Marshall would make an ideal choice to head a mediation effort on Kashmir. Acheson replied dryly that the United States had only one General Marshall and could not spare him. The secretary countered by telling the British ambassador that a respected Australian or Canadian would serve quite adequately.[45]

XII

IN JUNE a new shock from the Far East interrupted this Anglo-American pas de deux over Kashmir. The North Korean invasion of South Korea put substance into what had been largely a philosophical debate between Washington and New Delhi on the relative merits of neutralism and alignment. As one Indian historian puts it, the Korean conflict was "the proving ground for Indian non-alignment." Ambassador Pandit, viewing events from the inside, characterized it as "one of the worst phases in Indo-American relations." Both comments are apt. To the Americans the North Korean attack was a clear case of communist aggression; by the light of the experience of the 1930s it required an immediate and vigorous response. Nehru, on the other hand, considered the fighting in Korea essentially a civil war; his primary concern consisted in making sure this local affair did not spread. Because both sides were right to some degree, and because the stakes—global peace—were so high, this divergence created serious friction.[46]

In the first days of the North Korean invasion, as the Truman administration attempted to gain UN approval of a resolution authorizing action to repulse the invaders, G. S. Bajpai told Loy Henderson the Indian government considered the American proposal "somewhat drastic," in that it "might well lead to a new world war." Bajpai reported that Nehru was "very troubled" over the Korean situation. The prime minister wanted to throw India's "moral weight" against aggression but feared the American resolution might initiate "a chain of events which would have unfortunate consequences in Asia." The secretary-general said Indian support for the American proposal would amount to calling on countries like India's "close associate" Burma to send assistance to South Korea. Since Burma's relations with China were "most precarious," India preferred not to take this step, which might furnish the Chinese a pretext for invading Burma. Further, Bajpai said, the Americans had damaged their case by linking resistance to aggression in Korea with assistance to anticommunist forces in Taiwan and Indochina, forces that "millions of Asians, including many Indians," considered "imperialistic, colonial, or reactionary."

Henderson thought Bajpai's objections a poor substitute for principles and said so. Prefacing his remarks with a disclaimer that they represented his own feelings and not the position of the American government, Henderson made an impassioned defense of the Truman administration's actions. He declared he had never been prouder to be an American official than he was now. Only a short while after one terrible war and in spite of its "ardent desire to remain at peace," the United States had taken the "courageous step" of mobilizing, not for the purpose of defending its own territory, but with the goal of "showing aggressors and the world at large that it took its UN obligations seriously." Characterizing the issue confronting India as a matter of "moral courage," Henderson asked Bajpai if Indians in years to come would look proudly on a government that had failed to support the United Nations in resisting aggression.

The ambassador must have been pleased at the results of his performance. He reported to Washington that Bajpai appeared "shaken" by his remarks, adding that the secretary had promised to discuss the matter with Nehru.[47]

The next day when Henderson spoke with the prime minister himself he found him "exceptionally friendly and understanding." Nehru said he generally supported the American response to events in Korea, ascribing India's hesitation in the UN to the fact that his government needed more time to consider the ramifications of the American proposals. Like Bajpai, however, the prime minister criticized the administration's decision to drag Indochina and Taiwan into the Korean situation. Indians, Nehru said, had little sympathy for French policies in Indochina. As for Taiwan, India had recognized Beijing six months before and now hoped to develop friendly relations with the new government. To associate India with the American decision to defend Taiwan would seriously jeopardize relations between New Delhi and Beijing. Nehru also asserted that overly close cooperation with the United States might weaken his ruling majority in the Indian parliament. Already he faced attacks from various factions that denounced the government leaders as "tools of the Anglo-American imperialists." The prime minister did not consider this criticism at all decisive but neither could he ignore it. Finally, he said any support India would give to the UN effort could not be in troops or money; it would have to be "merely of a moral character."

Henderson replied that India's moral support would be just fine. Washington appreciated the difficulties Nehru faced, but for India to allow these special problems to stand in the way of unequivocal support for the UN would constitute "a serious setback to the UN and to the whole principle of collective security." India was the most powerful and influential noncommunist country in Asia; if it failed to approve collective action against aggression the UN would become "meaningless so far as Asia was concerned." Public opinion throughout Asia had not solidified. At this crucial moment Indian support would "immeasurably strengthen" the forces combating aggression.[48]

XIII

THE JOB of trying to bring Nehru around to the American point of view on events in the Far East fell largely to Henderson, but it was aided—or perhaps complicated—by advice from unlikely quarters. Certain representatives of Nehru's government made little effort to hide their disagreement with the prime minister. Bajpai, for example, often seemed more favorably disposed toward American arguments than Nehru, though the secretary maintained a professional discretion about his personal views. The most striking illustration of this pro-American dissent involved the Indian embassy in the Soviet Union, where the counselor, R. P. Kapur, approached the American ambassador with advice on how to handle his superiors.

Kapur urged a three-pronged offensive. While Henderson ought to lobby Nehru and Bajpai in India, the American secretary of state should work on the Indian ambassador in Washington. Kapur had little respect for Pandit, whom he described as an "imperious, vain woman"—an opinion shared by his colleague V. K. Krishna Menon, who called Pandit a "glamour puss"—but she was the prime minister's sister and had his ear. At the same time the American representative at the UN ought to take pains to persuade the Indian delegate there. In each case American officials must definitely separate the Korean issue from collateral questions like Taiwan and Indochina, and they should make clear that Indian support for the United States in Korea in no way committed Nehru to the American position elsewhere. The Americans should leave ideology out of the picture, arguing their case solely in terms of resistance to aggression. "Asia is important to the UN, and the UN to Asia," Kapur asserted, and Nehru should be reminded of this fact.[49]

Acheson found the advice "extremely interesting" and he directed the American ambassador in Moscow to cultivate Kapur. The suggestions themselves had little effect on the way American officials presented their case to Nehru; most of Kapur's recommendations amounted to mere common sense. The significance of Kapur's missive lay in the evidence it provided of dissatisfaction with Nehru's public neutralism, for it confirmed the American impression that India was more pro-Western than Nehru liked to let on.

Further evidence came in a conversation between Henderson and Deputy Prime Minister Sardar Patel. Patel, the man whose stature in India approached nearest to that of Nehru—indeed, the two shared what many called a "duumvirate"—told Henderson that despite the prime minister's "theories and deviations" the United States could count on India's lining up on "the side of the free countries" in the event the conflict in Korea developed into general war. As to what this would mean, Patel reminded Henderson of India's former importance to the defense of the British empire, pointing out that during the Second World War India had placed twenty million soldiers in uniform.[50]

Administration attempts to capitalize on this back-channel support occasionally caused embarrassment in relations with Nehru. Late in June the Indian government announced that it would approve the Security Council resolution authorizing UN assistance to South Korea. Shortly thereafter Arthur Krock of the *New York Times* suggested that pressure from the Truman administration had figured significantly in Nehru's decision. Predictably Krock's interpretation of events did not play well in New Delhi. Henderson reported that Bajpai was "deeply irritated," adding, "I am sure Nehru is furious." Henderson believed the Krock article would "seriously injure" his relations with Nehru, despite the fact that the prime minister would recognize that the administration could not control what appeared in American newspapers. Bajpai confirmed Henderson's fears when he remarked that the article opened Nehru to charges India had become an agent of the United States.[51]

Further difficulties arose as a result of Nehru's peacemaking efforts. In mid-July the prime minister sent letters to Washington and Moscow urging action by both superpowers to resolve the conflict in Korea before it broadened into a larger war. The Soviets were still boycotting the United Nations over the exclusion of China; to get Moscow into the picture Nehru recommended that the Americans drop their opposition to Chinese membership. In his letter to Acheson the prime minister explained his reasoning. By offering the hand of compromise, he said, those countries sincerely interested in a solution to the Korea problem would put the burden of proof on the communists. Should Moscow and Beijing refuse, world opinion would "hold them responsible for the consequences." In fact the communists would probably not refuse. "My honest belief is that Moscow is seeking a way out of the present entanglement without loss of prestige and that there is a real chance of solving the Korean problem peacefully."[52]

Washington considered Nehru's peacemongering mischievous, since it threatened to undermine the resolve of the UN. At the end of July Australian Prime Minister Robert Menzies asked Acheson his opinion of the "seriousness of the damage" Nehru's peace initiative had caused. The secretary replied that while the full consequences could not yet be determined, the damage was indeed "serious."[53]

Nonetheless Nehru persisted. Again he urged that the Chinese be brought into the Korean affair diplomatically lest they feel compelled to enter in force. To Acheson's claim that allowing China a seat in the Security Council under conditions of obvious duress would give the world the impression that "the United States had made a deal with the U.S.S.R. to buy off Communist aggression in Korea," the prime minister responded that recognition of China need not imply anything of the sort. India had recognized Beijing simply because the communists controlled the country, not because India approved of either communism or China's policies. Futhermore, China's admission was necessary to preserve the credibility of the United Nations; so long as Beijing remained outside, the UN could not pretend to be representative of the modern world. And the fighting in Korea would continue.[54]

XIV

DESPITE THEIR differences with Nehru, American officials appreciated India's potential as a conduit to China. From the beginning of the fighting the administration sought to assure the Chinese that American actions in Korea and the vicinity of Taiwan did not indicate designs on China's security, and it attempted to warn the Chinese to stay clear of Korea's troubles. In mid-July Acheson sent Henderson a message to hand to Nehru:

> I understand that yours is the only non-Communist government which has effective diplomatic relations with the Peiping regime. I hope you will find it possible to apprise your Ambassador in Peiping of our position with respect to Formosa and make every effort to persuade Peiping that its own interests require that it avoid intervention in the Korean situation or an attack upon Formosa.[55]

Before the Inchon landing of September, Washington tapped into the New Delhi–Beijing pipeline only intermittently, but when the war's fortunes shifted and UN troops approached the thirty-eighth parallel the line became crowded with messages. The day after the counteroffensive began Undersecretary of State James Webb instructed Henderson to point out to the Indian government that the situation in Korea had reached "a critical stage for the aggressors." He told the ambassador to add that it was of the "utmost importance" for the Chinese to understand they must stay out of the fighting. Webb directed Henderson to ask Bajpai to relay this warning to Beijing. Hoping to utilize India's good offices as well as its instinct for survival, the undersecretary commented that the message would carry more weight if presented as a statement of India's views and not merely forwarded as a threat from Washington. The hint proved superfluous: Bajpai declared that preventing a wider war was as thoroughly India's goal as that of the United States.[56]

The Indian connection with Beijing worked both ways, of course. Throughout the summer Indian contacts informed Washington of talks between Zhou Enlai and the Indian ambassador in Beijing, K. M. Panikkar. In July Panikkar passed word that Zhou had assured him China had no wish to see the hostilities in Korea expand beyond the borders of that country. After Inchon the messages from Beijing grew more serious. In the last week of September the State Department gained access, through the British embassy in Washington, to some of the cable traffic between Panikkar and Nehru. One of the cables reported a conversation between Panikkar and the chief of staff of the Chinese army, in which the latter complained about American bombing raids on positions in Manchuria and declared that "China would not take such provocations lying down." In another telegram Panikkar stated that as a result of the

American threat to North Korea and to China itself the Chinese had decided on a more assertive policy. Panikkar described Zhou as saying that since the United Nations had no obligations to China, China had no obligations to the United Nations.[57]

As UN troops approached the border of North Korea, India increasingly urged caution on the Americans. At midnight on October 2 a messenger from the Chinese foreign ministry awoke Panikkar and summoned him to a meeting with Zhou, where the prime minister told him that if the Americans crossed the thirty-eighth parallel China would be forced to intervene. Panikkar sped the message to New Delhi, where Bajpai gave it to Henderson with the warning that Chinese involvement would "almost certainly" lead to a third world war.[58]

But Washington ignored the advice, partly because it thought Zhou was bluffing and partly because it distrusted Panikkar. Truman later commented that Panikkar had "played the game of Chinese Communists fairly regularly." Undersecretary Webb described the Indian ambassador as "dubiously reliable" and "free-wheeling," adding that "we cannot be sure what Chou-En-lai says or hears in conversations with him." For this reason the undersecretary instructed Henderson to ask Bajpai to arrange direct contact between the American and Chinese embassies in New Delhi.[59]

Henderson doubted that the suggested initiative would appeal to the Indians. The ambassador said Nehru and Bajpai probably would not wish to risk the embarrassment of a rejection. Besides, they enjoyed their "monopoly on communications." Nonetheless he went ahead with the request. Bajpai, surprised, replied that he would think the subject over. The next day he agreed that face-to-face conversations between American and Chinese representatives might help avert a misunderstanding, and he said he was working on the matter.[60]

But the proposed meeting fell through, vetoed by the Chinese on grounds that the American refusal to recognize Beijing made even informal discussions impossible; and with its collapse the last good chance to avoid a collision between the United States and China disappeared. When the wreck occurred in late November, with 300,000 Chinese regulars joining the battle for Korea, Indian officials could not resist reminding the Truman administration of the warnings they had given. The Indian representative at the United Nations told Warren Austin that the Chinese intervention matched precisely what India had been predicting for several weeks. Austin could only reply lamely that "the practice of making threats was a weapon frequently resorted to by totalitarian regimes."[61]

China's entry into the war set India, along with many other countries, even more on edge than before. Truman compounded Indian concern by careless remarks at a press conference suggesting the United States might use the atomic bomb against the Chinese. "We are on the very verge of world war," Nehru told the Indian parliament. The prime minister declared the avoidance of nuclear escalation a matter of "absolute necessity." Not only would the introduction of nuclear weapons confirm the "widespread feeling in Asia" that the bomb was something used "only against Asiatics," it would make a broader conflict "inevitable." Nehru urged Washington to agree to a conference of the great powers, including China, with the objective of an immediate ceasefire and the creation of a demilitarized zone between the two sides.[62]

When Washington ignored this advice the prime minister tried another approach. He discreetly let out that he would appreciate an invitation to consult with the president and British Prime Minister Clement Attlee, then in Washington. Acheson, disinclined to delay Truman's discussions with Attlee to wait for Nehru's arrival and unwilling in any case to give Nehru a larger forum for his peace proposals, replied that some other time would be more convenient.[63]

XV

WHEN HUMANITY survived the Far Eastern crisis of late 1950 without a nuclear disaster, and when the fighting front stabilized in the first part of the following year, Korea subsided as an issue in U.S.– Indian relations. New Delhi and Washington continued to disagree, with India refusing to support the UN resolution of January 1951 branding China an aggressor. But as the Korean question became less world-threatening such differences diminished in intensity; eventually India would play a vital part in negotiations leading to a truce.[64]

The Chinese intervention in Korea, coming hard upon the momentous developments of the previous eighteen months, prompted another rethinking of American policy toward India. From 1947 until 1949 the Truman administration had contented itself with a minor role in South Asia. Still adjusting to new responsibilities in Europe, the administration had avoided picking up any burdens it could leave to others. Because Britain was willing and still appeared able to carry on in the defense of India, the administration encouraged the British to do so. British resources were limited but so, it seemed, was the danger to the pro-Western balance of power in South Asia. The events of 1949 and 1950 changed all that. With China now in the communist camp South Asia mattered more than ever, and with the communists prepared to take greater risks than American planners had expected, the apparent threat to the subcontinent had grown. Meanwhile the thinness of British capabilities had become increasingly obvious. A year before the Korean War began the CIA had reported that in South Asia the influence of Britain and the Commonwealth was "still paramount." At the end of 1950 Britain remained paramount among the external forces in the region, but it was clearly fading. In the midst of the September counteroffensive in Korea the Foreign Office had informed Washington that commitments elsewhere required reducing military aid to India and Pakistan. The impact of British retrenchment on what the Truman administration's planners had called the "Western salient on the Asian continent" remained unclear; but under the circumstances the administration began to consider a larger American role in the neighborhood of India.[65]

II

Write-Off: 1951–1954

THE SECOND phase of American policy toward India coincided with attempts by the Truman administration first and the Eisenhower administration later to organize Asia into anticommunist alliances—to extend the Yalta framework beyond Europe. From the beginning Nehru opposed the idea of collective security pacts and made clear India would have nothing to do with them. American officials recognized the depth of Nehru's resistance and after early and largely pro forma gestures of invitation wasted little effort trying to change his mind. At the same time American leaders refused to let Nehru's outspoken criticism prevent them from gathering allies where they could. The Americans understood the force of his objections—the prime minister did not lack advocates in the United States—but those at the top of policy hill believed the demands of Yalta took precedence and that U.S.–Indian relations could survive any storms that developed over the collective security issue. Their estimate proved correct, although Eisenhower's 1954 decision to arm Pakistan in exchange for that country's pledge of support in the Middle East pushed the prediction to the limit.

During this period of correct but cool relations between Washington and New Delhi, two new factors entered the picture on the American side. The first was the ascendancy of McCarthyism, with its reflexive opposition not only to communism but to anyone or anything not as fervently anticommunist as the McCarthyites themselves. In 1950 the CIA had asserted that one of the Soviet Union's principal objectives in Asia was "to prevent India's alignment with the West and to enlist its unwitting aid in bringing the rest of Asia under Soviet domination." The Truman administration's Republican critics did not see this report, but in the atmosphere of the time they had little difficulty arguing a case that Nehru's neutralism fell into the category of "unwitting aid." Some wondered just how unwitting the aid was—especially when representatives of the Indian government like Krishna Menon at the United Nations made a decidedly unneutral habit of defending communists at American expense.[1]

The second new factor, one that added impetus to the first, was the initiation of large-scale American assistance. Economic aid to India became a significant issue in American politics in the spring of 1951, in the wake of a series of natural calamities in the subcontinent. American aid brought Congress directly into the formulation of American policy toward India. Even those senators and representatives who declined to make political hay out of wheat for India raised a reasonable question: What will India do for us in return? One might have the warmest sympathies for the plight of hungry Indians and still ask whether Nehru could find some tangible manner of expressing appreciation. If the legislators themselves hesitated to raise the issue, they knew their opponents would when reelection time came.

II

THE EVENTS of 1949–50 marked a turning point in American policy toward Asia. The Truman administration stepped up support of the French in Indochina, taking the first serious steps on the path to involvement in the Vietnam conflict. It ended the occupation of Japan by treaties of peace and alliance, putting the American relationship with that country on a basis more suited to a long-term cold war. It reinjected the United States into the internal affairs of China by effectively guaranteeing the existence of Chiang Kai-shek's regime on Taiwan. It brought Australia and New Zealand under the American umbrella. It sought to organize the Middle East into a regional defense pact. Underlying all these initiatives was the belief not simply that the cold war had spread to Asia, but that the communists, now effectively blocked in Europe, might make Asia the primary theater in that conflict.

As to South Asia, the staff of the National Security Council in January 1951 produced a paper declaring that a communist takeover of India and Pakistan, arriving on the heels of the communist victory in China, would constitute "a catastrophe of major proportions" for the United States. With the region's increased importance came heightened danger, for British power was eroding while India and Pakistan remained far apart on Kashmir. The result was a potential "vacuum," which the United States must move to fill before the communists did. At this point administration officials were not contemplating an overt American commitment to South Asia. Contrary influences, especially the weight of prior commitments elsewhere, continued strong. For the moment the United States would emphasize diplomatic efforts to resolve the Kashmir dispute and to focus the attention of the countries of South Asia on the communist threat to their security. The NSC report noted progress in this direction, although more work remained.

> The countries of South Asia are becoming increasingly aware of the foreign inspiration of domestic communist activities and of Soviet imperialism's threat to national independence, but their attention is still diverted from the communist threat by their preoccupation with the Asian remnants of nineteenth century colonial empires, their suspicions of the Western European colonial powers, and their fear that the United States will follow a policy of discrimination to the detriment of non-white Asia.

Asian distrust particularly complicated reliance on the British. Despite the relatively good relations between London and the Asian Commonwealth members, a stigma of imperialism still attached to British actions in the developing world. To the extent the United States supported the British some of the stain rubbed off. But because Britain's grip on its South Asian sphere of influence was slipping already, for American leaders to distance themselves from the British would put the region at even greater risk. The resulting dilemma informed an ambivalent recommendation.

> We consider close and friendly ties between the South Asian countries and the United Kingdom and the Commonwealth to be in our national interest and desire the British to continue to assume as far as possible the responsibility inherent in their primary interest in the area. . . . At the same time

we should endeavor to avoid operating in too intimate association with the United Kingdom, which would offend the area governments.[2]

Not surprisingly such ambivalence provided a flimsy framework on which to erect policy. The full NSC decided the report required firming up. In spite of lobbying by the joint chiefs of staff to prevent an extension of American commitments to South Asia, summarized by the strenuously voiced recommendation of JCS chairman Omar Bradley to press Britain to continue to shoulder "prime responsibility" for the region's defense, the administration chose to move in the opposite direction. The revised and subsequently approved version of NSC 98 asserted that while the United States should continue talks with the British on "the ways and means by which U.S.–U.K. policies and actions with respect to South Asia can be better coordinated," the administration should strike out more forcefully on its own. The United States should undertake "more intimate consultation" with India and Pakistan; it should expand American anticommunist propaganda activities in the area; it should boost financial assistance, "while avoiding assumption of responsibility for economic welfare and development"; and it should explore the possibility of acquiring rights for military bases. Finally, the administration ought to prepare, "as far as practicable in the light of other demands of higher priority," to provide military assistance to India and Pakistan.[3]

The adoption of this paper marked a significant departure in American policy. For the first time the United States committed itself to bankroll and arm India and Pakistan to keep them from slipping into the Soviet sphere. This change followed from no desire to elbow the British aside; had Britain been able to guarantee the continued security of South Asia the Truman administration would have been happy to stay out. But Britain was weakening in this area, as elsewhere, and the need to secure South Asia against possible communist advances seemed to require increasing the American presence. About this time an official in London's Commonwealth Relations Office remarked that India was enjoying the privileges of membership in the Commonwealth "club" without paying "any discernible subscription." From economic necessity London was curtailing these privileges, which included defense. Consequently, despite the charges of dollar imperialism and neocolonialism the new policy inevitably would elicit, the United States chose to pick up where Britain was leaving off.[4]

III

A MONTH after Truman accepted NSC 98 George McGhee flew to Ceylon for a conference of American officials involved in diplomacy toward South Asia. McGhee's journey had two objectives: to explain the change of mind in Washington and to gather reactions from those who would have to put the new policy into effect. On addressing the assembly the assistant secretary reminded his listeners of the vast changes that had swept Asia in the previous two years. Events in Korea especially had demonstrated that the Soviets and Chinese were willing to take greater risks than American planners had estimated. At the same time, growing neutralist sentiment, especially in India, and Britain's decline laid the region more open to communist encroachment. "There is now a sense of urgency and a need for assessment of our world position that has never been present before. This is a time for a serious examination of where we stand in South Asia."

Regarding the British, McGhee attempted to explain why the Truman administration's Commonwealth strategy was not working. Economic exhaustion at home enervated Britain abroad; this much anyone could see. But equally significant was the increasingly apparent divergence of goals between London and Washington. Until recently this difference had not mattered much, but with the intensification of the cold war in Asia it assumed heightened significance.

> The primary objective of the United Kingdom, to which other objectives are subordinate, is to obtain the permanent adherence of India to the Commonwealth. United States policy, on the other hand, is concentrated upon the orientation of India, in particular, and South Asia in general, toward the United States and away from the Soviet Union.

Whether or not Britain *could* draw India to the Western side by the strength of Commonwealth ties—and this appeared unlikely—it *would* not, for fear of severing its final connection to the empire's erstwhile crown jewel.

As McGhee pointed out, India refused to reconsider its adherence to neutralism—an obstinacy he attributed to a "seeming lack of understanding and appreciation" of communism's aggressive intentions—and New Delhi's stubbornness made cooperation between America and India difficult. Indian neutralism, McGhee said, was fostering a "growing unfavorable reaction in the United States, especially in Congress." This negative response stood in the way of the assistance the administration, for all Nehru's uncooperativeness, deemed necessary. In the best of circumstances the United States could not afford much in the way of aid to South Asia. "The area rates a low priority on the scale of what we can do." But Nehru's neutralist policy made matters worse. "Even the small effort which is potentially possible is greatly endangered as far as Congressional action is concerned by the attitudes and activities of the countries involved, especially India." [5]

Loy Henderson did not like the direction McGhee's comments were heading. The ambassador to India asserted that the administration would commit "a grave blunder" if it acted as though India's cooperation were out of the question. Henderson held no brief for Nehru, as numerous earlier comments indicated, but he said he was convinced that "in India underneath the crust of criticism of the United States and of constantly expressed distrust of American policies there is a hard core of basic friendliness for the United States and confidence in the motives which animate the American people." Washington should build on this under-lying good will to move Nehru in the direction of the West.

In pursuing this goal, Henderson continued, diplomatic style would count for a great deal.

> In endeavoring to bring about a change in the attitude of the Prime Minister, we should not at any time assume a cringing or flattering attitude which would give him the impression that he has the whip hand over us. We should not, on the other hand, take an attitude of truculence or hostility towards him or India which would strengthen the hands of those in India who are opposed to us.

Americans sometimes forgot, Henderson pointed out, that as an elected leader Nehru had to respond to popular moods in India. "We should always bear in mind that Nehru is not India; even now he cannot entirely ignore Indian public opinion. Events beyond his control may force him to decide to change his present tactics and methods."

Henderson advocated a steady policy toward India, based on an assumption of a fundamental community of interest. "In dealing with India we should act as though we take it for granted that India's sense of international morality is similar to that of the United States and that India is basically on the side of those forces opposing aggression."

American officials should not apologize when American views differed from India's. Citing the example of the Korean War, Henderson admitted that Nehru had engaged in harsh criticism of American policies, but he contended that the Indians "would have had less respect for us if we had faltered in carrying out these policies." Should New Delhi continue such attacks the United States must take "energetic measures" to "expose the fallacies" of the Indian approach. Yet in defending American positions the United States ought to maintain a high standard of decorum. "We should not aim our statements at Nehru or at India, but rather at the policies which India is propagating."[6]

Henderson's arguments influenced the recommendations of the conference, although not as much as he would have liked. After nearly a week of discussions the conferees drafted a list of significant conclusions, of which two stood out. The first called for "vigorous" efforts to promote the idea of collective security and for "most active opposition to Nehru's efforts to create a neutral bloc among the Asian and Arab states." The second involved military aid to Pakistan. While the NSC paper that provided the focus of discussion at the Ceylon conference displayed a bureaucratically cautious opaqueness about the relative probabilities of enlisting India and Pakistan on the side of the United States, the diplomat-conferees did not hesitate to predict that Nehru would reject immediately any American plan for a South Asian anticommunist treaty. Consequently they urged the administration to concentrate on Pakistan, which occupied a vital position geographically and appeared willing to cooperate. At an appropriate moment the United States should break the news to India gently, but under no circumstances should it allow Nehru to veto American efforts to take "every feasible military and political step" to increase Pakistan's strength.[7]

This final recommendation marked the beginning of an American tilt to Pakistan. The inclination toward Karachi had nothing to do with a preference for the Pakistanis in their country's conflict with India, although, as American officials recognized, Indian leaders would interpret it thus when such an interpretation suited their purposes. And while Americans found Nehru trying at times, the new policy had little to do with pique toward the prime minister personally. Rather the decision to pursue an agreement with Pakistan represented the considered belief that one ally on the subcontinent was better than none. Later, when American plans for a Middle East pact centering on Egypt fell through, the United States would look to Pakistan to hold down the eastern end of the "northern tier." For the time being American officials viewed Pakistan in the context of South Asia. The region needed defending, and if the Indians would not help, the United States would make common cause with those who would.

IV

AS THE conference in Ceylon broke up McGhee packed his bags for India. The assistant secretary did not expect to persuade the prime minister to join forces with the United States; rather the meeting with Nehru had the principal objective of balancing McGhee's stop in Karachi, where he *did* hope to do business. But it also gave the administration an opportunity to state its case for collective security and cover itself against claims it was offering something to Pakistan it denied India.

McGhee found Nehru evasive. Assuring the prime minister the American government did not wish differences of opinion between Washington and New Delhi to damage the two countries' "basic understanding," McGhee described administration thinking on the nature of the communist threat, especially that part posed by the Chinese. "I made it clear," McGhee reported to Acheson afterward, "that it was their apparent aggressive intent rather than their Communist ideology which gave us concern." Nehru responded with what the assistant secretary characterized as "a rather involved, and to me irrelevant, discourse." After McGhee tried to bring him back to the topic at hand, Nehru started on "an historical proof that wars do not accomplish their objectives, but merely lead to new wars." The prime minister went on to say that "Russia is what she is today largely because of the way the nations of the world isolated her when she was young." The same mistake was being made with China. To shun China risked war, and any anticommunist war would ultimately fail, for even in apparent victory the West would find itself in a world of "social and economic chaos," in which the surviving nations would be "easy prey to Communism." Besides, the democratic states could never achieve "victory" over countries as large as China and the Soviet Union; the occupation required to impose Western will dwarfed politically available resources.

McGhee, following Henderson's advice, candidly told Nehru where he thought Indian policy mistaken. The American people were making great sacrifices to defend democracy against communist aggression, he said.

> We have begun to build up our military forces, which means that normal citizens, many of whom fought in the last war, are going into uniform. . . . We have, in pursuance to the call of the UN, suffered 50,000 casualties in Korea. We have made great efforts to help arm and train other nations threatened by aggression.

Consequently it was a disappointment and a source of popular antipathy toward India to see Nehru's representative on the Security Council not only voting against the resolution condemning China as an aggressor but "actively seeking to influence other states toward a neutral position in the cold war." This "trend toward neutralism" constituted "a great danger." It diminished the strength of the "free world" and afforded encouragement to aggressors.

Nehru did not entirely disagree with McGhee's analysis. He conceded that the Russians possessed "aggressive and expansionist designs." But the Chinese were different, if only because they had too many domestic problems to engage in foreign adventures. The prime minister denied that Indochina and Korea demonstrated China's aggressive intentions. Regarding Indochina he asserted that Beijing's support of Ho Chi Minh did not yet involve anything substantial; as to Korea he argued that the United Nations had brought much of its troubles upon itself by treating China as an outcast. Declared beyond the pale, the Chinese had decided they had little further to lose. In any event, military preparations might well produce the very conflict they aimed to prevent. It was "inevitable" that in a world armed to the teeth some incident would set the juggernaut in motion.

The prime minister ended the discussion with perfunctory remarks that the United States and India ought to consult each other on matters of mutual interest. He did add in parting that it would serve both sides to discuss controversial issues through diplomatic channels rather than through the press.[8]

V

NEHRU'S LATTER suggestion made especially good sense in the context of concurrent developments in Washington. A month before McGhee went to India the Truman administration had cautiously broached to Congress the question of economic aid for India. The previous growing season had witnessed a coincidence of natural disasters in South Asia; these combined with the partition-induced dislocation in the subcontinent's food-supply system to raise a serious possibility of famine. In December 1950 Indian Ambassador Pandit told the State Department her government's experts predicted a shortfall of two million tons in India's grain crop, and she asked the administration to consider emergency assistance to relieve the deficit.[9]

From the first, administration officials looked favorably on the Indian request. Humanitarian considerations played an important role, of course; estimates of excess deaths in the absence of American aid ranged beyond ten million. But geopolitics clinched the case. Assistance to India would serve much the same purpose as Marshall Plan relief for Europe: to prevent the social disintegration on which communism thrived. Already the Indian Communist party was making inroads in the hardest hit regions. A State Department analysis of January 1951, describing the food situation in India as a "crisis of alarming proportions," assessed the challenge it posed to Nehru's government. "The political opposition, particularly the Communists, are exploiting the situation, charging the Government with indifference to the peasant's lot. The Communists have had considerable success in organizing the rural areas into autonomous districts from which Government officials have been excluded by force."[10]

George McGhee amplified the argument to the secretary of state, asserting that the impending famine in India threatened to create conditions "ideally suited" to the spread of communist influence, which already was eroding Nehru's political base. American aid would help reverse the trend. "A quick response to the Indian Government's request for food grains is the most effective means, immediately available to our Government, of counteracting Communist subversion in India." McGhee outlined the alternatives facing the United States. If the administration and Congress approved an assistance package, this action would shore up Nehru, who for all his faults held the country together and thereby served American interests. Further, McGhee asserted, with apparently unintended irony:

> The Indian people and the world at large will be impressed by our humanitarian impulses: charges that we are willing to relieve suffering only when we stand to gain politically will be counteracted; and the American taxpayer will have the satisfaction of participating in a generous project to prevent starvation in a country plagued by natural disasters.

On the other hand, if the United States rejected aid for India, assorted evils would follow.

> The present government will be weakened and India may be threatened with anarchy, a dictatorship of the extreme left, or a dictatorship of the extreme right. The possibility of Communist subversion of the country, and utilization of Indian manpower and other resources against us will be increased.

In addition, denial of aid would confirm Indians and other Asians in their belief "that we are interested in relieving human suffering only for political reasons."[11]

Acheson needed little convincing that help for India made sense, and he backed the idea immediately; but the American Congress seemed likely to prove less agreeable. Administration officials recognized that India no longer held the attraction for many Americans it had claimed only one year earlier. When Pandit first mentioned the subject of assistance, American forces were reeling from the blow of Chinese intervention in Korea. Meanwhile Nehru spoke in terms that smacked of appeasement to millions in the United States. At the same time the prime minister appeared to be putting his own cold war with Pakistan ahead of the welfare of the Indian masses; by refusing to compromise on Kashmir he exacerbated the difficulties arising from the fact that much of British India's most productive farmland now belonged to Pakistan, and he diverted resources that might combat the approaching famine.

When Congress convened in January the administration decided to take soundings on Capitol Hill. Perceiving the antagonism to Nehru that existed in the legislature, the administration wanted to find out whether an aid package for India had a reasonable chance of approval before submitting a formal resolution. This caution had two sources, one political and the other diplomatic. Politically, of course, Truman sought to avoid any more problems with Congress than he already faced. China remained a political disaster for the administration. Korea was becoming another. To add India to the list would serve only the interests of the administration's enemies. Diplomatically, a defeat for an aid bill would constitute an insult to Nehru and doubtless would intensify anti-American sentiment in India. If there appeared little chance of getting Congress to approve assistance, discretion dictated burying the proposal bureaucratically. Perhaps the administration could persuade India to withdraw the request; if not, some other excuse for sidetracking it would have to suffice. In any event, the less said publicly the better.

VI

ON JANUARY 26 McGhee met with the Senate Subcommittee on Near Eastern and African Affairs, whose portfolio included India. The tentative proposal he laid before the members called for a grant of approximately $200 million to cover the purchase of two million tons of wheat. The Indian government had initially requested a concessionary loan rather than a grant, but the administration did not consider India a good credit risk and preferred to avoid the irritations likely to follow problems in repayment.[12]

The first comments by the committee members indicated that approval of the administration's proposal would not come easily. Responding to McGhee's statement that the Indian government estimated thirteen million persons would starve in the absence of American aid, Foreign Relations Chairman Tom Connally questioned the accuracy of such predictions. "Of course they are going to say there are a lot of people that are going to starve if you don't hurry up and give them some wheat." The Texas Democrat added, "If you are going to sit down and accept what they say and what they ask, we won't have anything to eat ourselves in a little while." McGhee's assurance that the Indian estimate matched the administration's own figures did not satisfy Connally. Referring to India's large sterling account with Britain, Connally asked why the Indian government could not buy wheat as other countries did. "They are sitting there with over $1 billion owing to them by the British Government, and yet they are so poor that we have to give them $200 million worth of wheat."[13]

McGhee admitted the existence of India's sterling surplus but said it did not apply to the present case because the sterling area lacked the grain India needed. J. William Fulbright of Arkansas spotted the weakness of this argument. Fulbright would become a strong supporter of economic and technical aid to third-world countries, but he refused to accept careless reasoning. He pointed out that India could pay for American wheat with pounds, which would simply shift to the American column of Britain's ledgers. McGhee conceded the theoretical possibility of such a transaction; even so, he declared it inadvisable politically since it would frustrate American attempts to remedy Britain's balance-of-payments problems.[14]

The assistant secretary tried to turn the discussion in a positive direction by explaining how congressional support for the aid request might tip the scales in American relations with India; but Connally would not let him proceed. The Texas senator burst in, "Our relations with India now are not very good, are they? Nehru is out giving us hell all the time, working against us and voting against us. Is this a proposition to buy him? He won't stay bought, if you buy him." McGhee attempted to distance the administration from Indian diplomacy, saying, "I do not in any way want to appear in behalf of Mr. Nehru's present political policy." Again Connally interrupted: "You are appearing in behalf of Mr. Nehru now."[15]

H. Alexander Smith of New Jersey displayed greater sympathy. Smith, a Republican internationalist, had suggested to the State Department that a visit by McGhee to Capitol Hill might prove wise while the aid proposal remained in a formative stage. Now he raised the humanitarian issue, declaring that the subcommittee ought to consider India's request from the fundamental perspective of people facing death, without "balling it up" in a debate over Nehru's foreign policy. "I, as you know, am violently opposed to Nehru's whole attitude in the United Nations and so on, but I want to divorce that from the idea of starving millions that we might help." Politics inevitably crept in, however. "If they should die in great quantities, as I am told they will next summer if something is not done, and we have a surplus here . . . it seems to me we might be in a very difficult spot in our relations with the Far East as a whole."[16]

Wisconsin's Alexander Wiley, who would chair the Foreign Relations Committee when the Republicans gained control of the upper house in 1953, wondered whether the State Department had thought of asking India for a "quid pro quo, a little collaboration on the world stage." Suggesting "something in the nature of defense," Wiley said such a request would set a good precedent for other potential aid cases. He advocated announcing a general policy: "Hereafter we are going to be practical realists. We are going to do charity where charity is done, but when there is no need for charity, when our own people have to pay the bill, we owe our own people some responsibility."

McGhee responded that the State Department did not operate on a quid pro quo basis. Further, he asserted that such an approach would certainly fail with Nehru, who had repeatedly insisted that he would accept no aid with strings. To this, Democrat Guy Gillette of Iowa replied that if Nehru held such an attitude—"if thirteen million people are dying and he is willing to let them die"—then the United States ought to let him take the blame for whatever befell his country.

McGhee tried to explain the complications of the matter.

> Six months from now, if in fact these people are dying . . . they will know we had the grain, they will know they made the request, and they will know at that time that Mr. Nehru and we were on the outs over the question of Communist China. And an inference will be very strong to them that we denied this request because we did not like the political attitude Mr. Nehru expressed.

Such being the case, the United States could not avoid implication in any famine that followed congressional disapproval of aid.

Returning to the question of exacting a price for American assistance, McGhee reminded the subcommittee that Nehru, like elected officials in America, had political fences to tend. For the prime minister to accept conditions on aid would hurt his position in India, with possible consequences that might seriously damage American interests. As he had argued earlier to Acheson, McGhee pointed out that despite the annoyances Nehru caused, he provided the glue holding India together. His fall might lead to chaos, from which nothing good and much bad would follow. Moreover, for the prime minister to bow to American pressure would diminish his stature among other Asians. The Truman administration did not agree with many of the things Nehru said and did, but of the likely candidates for leadership in Asia he was the only one with a "basic orientation to the West." [17]

Connally remained unconvinced of Nehru's good intentions. Declining to identify his sources, the committee chairman said, "I understand he hates every white man and every foreigner, and he does not want any

Western people coming into Asia or doing anything about Asia. That is what I have been informed. We are told that that is his attitude."[18]

Fulbright spoke less bluntly but just as skeptically. Regardless of whether Nehru's demise would bring to power someone openly hostile to the United States, Fulbright was uneasy with the appearance of the situation. "It looks to me a great deal like blackmail, to say, 'Give it to us or we will go Communist.' " The Arkansas senator acknowledged that there would be the devil to pay in the event of widespread famine but he suggested shifting the blame to the Russians. With the international situation as dangerous as it was, the United States had to look out for itself first. "We may be confronted with a war in three months," he asserted. "There are a lot of people who think so. We may need this wheat very badly." The administration should tell India that if not for the communist threat the United States would be glad to help, but under the circumstances it was not safe to do so. "Russia is the reason why we feel squeamish about depleting our reserves. Pound that into them."[19]

Gillette challenged McGhee's statement about the desirability of supporting Nehru. "If it is a question of stabilizing Nehru's position," the Iowa Democrat said, "I am the last one who would contribute anything to stabilize his position with the attitude he has taken."

McGhee reiterated that any alternative to Nehru would prove "much worse" from the standpoint of the United States, and he said Nehru's fall would entail "a very great risk of losing India completely to the Western world." Communists had seized China little more than a year before. "If you add these 330 million in India to the masses of people who have already joined with the other Communist countries, the balance would be turned very greatly in their favor."

The committee members remained apparently unmoved. Fulbright summarized much of the opposition when he cited the extent of American commitments to regions more vital to American security and declared, "We just can't take everything under our wing. . . . If we are going to start supporting India from here on, I don't see how we can do it."

McGhee had gone to the Hill to gauge the reaction of Congress to an aid request. Gillette put it politely when he said there existed among the legislators "a notable lack of zeal" for the administration's proposal. Connally, as usual, spoke more directly: "I want to tell you right now you are going to have one hell of a time getting this thing through the Congress."[20]

VII

SPURRED BY Connally's warning and by the cool response of the other committee members, the administration stepped up its efforts on behalf of aid for India. At the beginning of February Truman met with Connally and other members of the Democratic leadership to stress the need for swift and favorable action. The president touched base with the Republicans by enlisting the support of the grand old man of American relief, Herbert Hoover, who declared, "This doesn't fall into the category of politics; it falls into the category of Christianity." On February 12 Truman took his case directly to Congress. Casting his message in the same terms of humanitarianism and self-interest that had sold the Marshall Plan, Truman emphasized the need to support democracy in India. "It is important to the free world that the democratic institutions which are emerging in India be maintained and strengthened." India's continued stability was "essential" to the future of Asia. Conceding "important political differences" between American foreign policy and that of India, Truman asserted that these differences should not stand in the way of the needs of the Indian people.[21]

Meanwhile the Indian government made matters simpler for the administration—not to mention the Indian masses—by agreeing to a ceasefire in its trade war with Pakistan long enough to strike a deal bringing to India 300,000 tons of Pakistani grain. Nehru got into the act on a personal level as well. Without making any substantive concessions to the Americans, he did his best to please, impressing even the wary Henderson. In February the American ambassador reported a conversation with Nehru.

> I found the Prime Minister in an excellent humor. In none of my previous conversations had he ever been so friendly or talked with such apparent frankness. He made use of his great personal charm and was evidently anxious to persuade. It is easy to understand how, when the Prime Minister is in such a mood, he is so frequently able to win over so many persons. . . . In fact, as I listened to him I found myself rather regretful that I could not agree with him and say with all honesty that he was quite right and was, in my opinion, pursuing the policy most likely to preserve the peace of the world.[22]

When Congress began formal hearings on the administration's aid proposal, Acheson did most of the testifying. At an open meeting of the House Foreign Affairs Committee he made the case for aid in guardedly bland terms; later, during three days of executive sessions of the Senate Foreign Relations Committee the secretary of state spoke more freely. In the latter forum Republican Henry Cabot Lodge set the tone of the discussion with his initial question: "What are the Indians going to do for us?" At first Acheson sought to evade the issue, but when Lodge persisted the secretary replied, "There is nothing they can do economically. They do not offer to do anything politically."[23]

Lodge would become a great supporter of India following his 1953 appointment as ambassador to the United Nations; now, in loyal opposition, he expressed reservations regarding aid without rejecting it outright. The Massachusetts senator reflected what turned out to be the predominant mood in Congress when he said,

> I can perfectly well see that if we don't do this we incur a lot of ill will. I am not so sure that if we do do this we get a lot of good will. Having observed Mr. Nehru and the Ambassador here, I just haven't got any faith at all that there is going to be any gratitude or appreciation or anything else.

Acheson admitted Lodge was probably right, though the secretary chose not to put the matter in quite such negative terms. If the United States failed to provide the aid, Acheson said, it stood to lose ground in the region. If it delivered the wheat, it would gain, but not much and mostly in the realm of intangibles.[24]

As during McGhee's earlier testimony, discussion centered on Nehru's approach to world affairs. As before, the administration sought to strike a balance between criticism of Nehru's foreign policy and support for the prime minister's continuation in office. In doing so administration spokesmen trod the slippery track of distinguishing between Nehru and the rest of India. The prime minister, they contended, might appear antagonistic at times, but most other Indian officials, and the majority of the Indian people, were solidly pro-American. Speaking of the Indians, Acheson's special assistant, William Pauley, declared, "I believe they are unfortunately controlled at the moment by a man whose ideologies are cooped up by too many years in prisons under the British regime." However, Pauley continued, Nehru's opinions did not mirror those of his colleagues. "I believe that the bulk of the people of the Indian Government are not sympathetic with his views." In a nice twist on the tactics of the McCarthyites, Pauley even talked numbers. "In the Cabinet, there are forty-three men who are very friendly to the United States —I mean really friendly, as much so as if they were Americans."[25]

Stanley Andrews of the Office of Foreign Agricultural Relations pursued this line of argument. He quoted an Indian minister involved in food distribution as saying, "Mr. Nehru is a great man, and I love him and all of that. It is all right for him to stay up here in the sky on these international problems. But I have got to feed the people of India . . . and we have got to have American help." This official, according to Andrews, and "hundreds of others"—like McCarthy's, the administration's list grew fast—were America's "great friends." Andrews concluded, "I was really embarrassed with the pro-American attitude of all those people right within that government."

Whether the administration was stretching things, or the Indians, with or without Nehru's knowledge, were putting on a good show to get the wheat—probably both—the latent pro-Americanism theme worked. Lodge recognized the irrefutability, given the limited exposure to India of the members of the committee, of this appeal to faith in India's silent majority, and he conceded the point. "I think there are a lot of very fine men in India who like the United States." These exemplars of perspicacity might be sympathetic to American goals. "But the head man," Lodge reminded, "is not."[26]

Senator Fulbright thought the administration erred in resting much of its case for assistance to India on humanitarian considerations. After all, if humanitarianism were the issue China could easily match India's hungry millions. Fulbright believed the Senate, if not the administration, ought to look at the question of aid to India in terms of the cold war.

> If it is not justifiable on the ground of our policy with regard to the whole situation with Russia, I think it is hard to justify. I say that it is important, but we are so constituted that we like to kid ourselves that everything is done for humanitarian reasons. . . . The real reason is because we don't want the government to collapse over there and the Communists to make headway.

Regarding the Indian government, Fulbright commented:

> These people, while they are not our friends, do not seem to be friendly to the Communists. Everybody says they shoot Communists when they find

them. That it is all to the good. Even though they do not like us, it is still better to have it that way than to let the Communists run it.

Conservative Republican Bourke Hickenlooper of Iowa objected. Hickenlooper thought Indians and Americans alike might benefit if Nehru fell. "Nehru is the fellow that is flirting with the Communists all the time." But Hickenlooper agreed with Fulbright's point regarding the limits of humanitarianism. "They have starved for years over there," he said.

Fulbright declared that to treat the Indian request as a humanitarian matter would open the United States to endless demands from the poor of the world. "I think there is no limit to it and no stopping place. . . . From a humanitarian standpoint, what is the difference between 100,000 dying and a million dying?"[27]

As with most such hearings these sessions ended inconclusively. On the whole they went better than McGhee's earlier appearance, and the tone of the questions suggested that the majority of the committee members accepted, albeit grudgingly, the idea that American interests in Asia required helping India, even if Nehru rejected conditions on assistance, which he emphatically did. From the legislators' perspective, Truman's decision to make a special request for aid for India limited their political exposure by placing most of the burden of Nehru's unpopularity on the administration. The major worry of the committee, and among legislators generally, was that assistance to India might set an example for other nations of the third world. Republican Alexander Wiley warned the administration against encouraging the notion "that Uncle Sam is going to be Santa Claus all the rest of the years." As a concession to this concern, the administration accepted an amendment making the aid a loan, as India had initially requested. With this change the bill cleared the Senate by a 52–32 margin and the House by 293–94.[28]

VIII

ALMOST INEVITABLY the debate over the aid bill and the criticism of Nehru it entailed diminished the good will the measure was designed to create. This problem would vex American relations with India throughout the period under study—as similar problems have troubled dealings with nearly every nation to which the United States has sent assistance for four decades. The administration was caught in a bind: by humanitarian arguments alone it could not summon the votes for aid, but appeals to geopolitical self-interest killed any halo effect. Nehru assuredly did not expect the United States to act other than in its own interest—the prime minister himself declared that "in the final analysis, all foreign policy concerns itself chiefly with the national interest of the country concerned"—but appearances counted for something. An Indian diplomat who worked with Nehru during the 1950s described the prime minister as miffed at the manner of dispensation of American aid. "Not that Nehru was unappreciative of the economic assistance given to India by the U.S. He was, however, irritated by frank references in the American press and in official statements to the motives for such aid." This individual, Subimal Dutt, contrasted the Americans' clumsy openness with the "more astute" approach of Soviet leaders. "They made it appear that their aid was entirely selfless, designed to help India stand on its own feet without having to depend on any foreign country."[29]

The Truman administration did not quite expect gratitude from Nehru, but neither was it ready for what it got. Even while the first wheat shipments were en route from Philadelphia to Bombay, the Indian government announced that it would not sign the recently completed Japanese peace treaty, thereby joining Beijing and Moscow in opposition. Nehru contended that the continued American presence in Japan, the American trusteeship over the Ryukyu and Bonin islands, and the failure to return Taiwan to China and the Kuriles and South Sakhalin to the Soviet Union rendered the treaty unacceptable.[30]

Had Nehru deliberately tried he could hardly have picked a worse time for such a decision. Even persons otherwise favorably disposed toward India judged this blow, as the grain ships neared their destination, too much to bear. The *New York Times* editorialized,

> Nehru is fast becoming one of the great disappointments of the post-war era. . . . Instead of seizing the leadership of Asia for its good, Nehru turned aside from the responsibilities, proclaimed India's disinterestedness, and tried to set up an "independent," third-force India, suspended in midair between the two decisive movements of our day—the communism that Russia leads and the democracy of which the United States is the chief champion.

History, the *Times* said, was not likely to forgive Nehru's "abnegation of greatness." "His statesmanship is not inspiring people and nations to do things but only to leave them undone. How the mighty have fallen!"[31]

To Henderson in New Delhi, Nehru's rejection of the Japanese treaty seemed part of a grand design to increase India's influence in world affairs. As early as a year before, Bajpai had told Henderson the Indian government would not look favorably on continued American occupation of Japan. At that time, however, Bajpai had said India would not object to America's negotiating for base rights with the Japanese government after Japan regained control of its affairs. But now Nehru appeared intent on removing American influence from Japan entirely. The refusal to sign the treaty, Henderson wrote, was a means to this end.

> We believe it represents a logical step on the part of Nehru in his efforts to attain one of his primary foreign policy objectives, that is, the eventual exclusion from the mainland and waters of Asia of all Western military power and what he would consider as Western political and economic pressures.[32]

Henderson thought Nehru hoped to gain the support of "the nationalistic and anti-white elements in Japan" by his opposition to the treaty.

> He believes that these three elements, if discreetly encouraged by such experienced Asian nationalist leaders as himself, will eventually take over power in Japan, denounce the Japanese alliance with the United States, and insist on the evacuation of all American armed forces from Japan and the return to Japanese control of such islands as the United States might be occupying.

Nor did Nehru's objectives stop there. Though the prime minister had made little progress in drawing China away from the Soviet Union, Henderson thought Nehru retained hope of doing so, apparently envisioning an Asian bloc consisting of India, Japan, and China, with himself in a central position.

Henderson gave Nehru credit for subtlety and predicted the prime minister would pursue his goals by dissimulation.

> In carrying on his campaign to attain his objectives in Asia, Nehru is not likely to move too openly or rapidly. He will not wish to arouse too much hostility or indignation in the United States. He realizes that, for some time to come, India will sorely need certain capital and consumption goods which only the United States can furnish. He is not likely to disclose his real objectives. He will probably try to appear as a democratic idealist primarily interested in the welfare of the downtrodden masses of Asia; of David who regretfully faces the materialistic and clumsy Goliath of militarism and imperialism. . . . He will continue to make minor concessions

and friendly gestures from time to time to the United States in order to keep down the tide of resentment and make U.S. officials think, "He will come to our side eventually if we are patient and handle him properly."

Admitting Nehru might not consciously have thought his plan through as far as this, Henderson nonetheless argued that these consequences inhered in the prime minister's philosophy and recent actions.[33]

At one level, Henderson's deconstruction was about right, including, probably, his comment that Nehru had not thought the design to the end. But the tone of this cable made India's aims seem part of a dark conspiracy. (Having learned his trade in Stalin's Moscow during the great purges, Henderson sometimes saw conspiracies where none existed.) In fact the rejection of the peace treaty and the other moves Henderson described followed logically from India's publicly held positions. An American protectorate over the Ryukyus amounted to a form of colonialism, which India consistently opposed. A mutual security pact between Japan and the United States contradicted the objectives of nonalignment. Indian approval of the withholding of territory from China and the Soviet Union would needlessly complicate New Delhi's relations with those countries. As for efforts to draw Japan away from the United States, Nehru did not conceal his preference for an Asia controlled by Asians. He had told the Americans directly he sought to pull China out of Moscow's orbit; Washington would have been obtuse not to suspect he intended to do the same for Japan vis-à-vis the United States. Whether the independent Asia that resulted from success in these efforts would constitute a "bloc" was a question of semantics. And if Nehru wished to see himself preeminent among Asian leaders, what world figure was not ambitious?[34]

At the same time, Henderson underestimated an important aspect of the prime minister's diplomacy: the depth of Nehru's desire for peace. Pragmatic to the point of cynicism, and representing the strongest military power in the world, Henderson believed struggle—in particular, the cold war—was an abiding feature of international relations. Nehru hoped otherwise; and his efforts to remove Western influence from Asia represented an attempt to bring this hope closer to reality. Nehru was not so naive as to think strife would cease with the removal of outside influences; his "area of peace" speeches contained a considerable dose of propagandic oversell. But he was convinced, with good reason, that local and regional quarrels would prove less damaging and easier to end if they did not get tangled in the cold war. The Korean conflict never would have begun had not Americans and Russians insisted on imposing their troubles upon the Koreans; once started it would not have escalated to world-threatening size had the United States not intervened. Now, even as the fighting in Korea continued, a similar situation was developing in Indochina.

Nehru's aim to keep the superpower contest out of Asia—to prevent the extension of the Yalta framework to India's environs—was, of course, precisely what Indian nonalignment was all about. And peace, as much as any inclination to India's aggrandizement or his own, was the objective of nonalignment. Peace was its own reward; it was also, as Nehru never forgot, the prerequisite to India's economic development. Not half a decade into independence, India still faced nearly overwhelming problems, almost none of which could be solved without raising India's standard of living. To enmesh India in war or to force India to prepare for war would slow development, perhaps halt it altogether. What would become of the country then, none could say.[35]

Eventually American leaders would gain a greater appreciation of India's desire for peace. Nehru would make a particular impression on Dwight Eisenhower, whose devotion to peace matched the prime minister's. Eisenhower would also enjoy the advantage of holding office during a respite in the cold war. In 1951, however, with Americans dying in Korea, and with Republicans blaming the Democrats, the Truman administration and its representatives were not in a mood to appreciate the nobler aspects of Indian nonalignment.

At the time Henderson delivered his analysis, Washington took the position that although America could live with a nonaligned India—it had no choice—it did not have to stand by while Nehru spread the neutralist gospel. State Department strategists argued for what amounted to a policy of containment of Indian neutralism. At one level, they contended, American officials should challenge the premises of nonalignment in all available forums, emphasizing that the key to Asian and world peace lay in collective security, not nonalignment. At another level the United States should offer moral and material support to those countries willing to buck the neutralist trend and side with the West. To the degree American policy succeeded in demonstrating the rewards of alignment it would achieve "a commensurate limitation on the ability of Mr. Nehru to maintain India as the pivotal Asian state between what he regards as the 'two power blocs.' "[36]

While these recommendations were circulating through the administration, the CIA issued a report indicating containment was the best the United States could hope for, since India's neutralism was not about to go away. Nehru, the intelligence memo said, was as determined as ever to hold the middle ground between East and West. This statement lifted few eyebrows. What *was* significant about the report was the assertion that neutralism was not simply Nehru's policy but India's. The intelligence agency did not buy the argument—however useful it might be in congressional hearings—that the Indian government sheltered scores of crypto-allies and that India's masses silently sided with the United States. On the contrary, the CIA analysts asserted that the roots of nonalignment lay deep in Indian politics and culture. No foreseeable government could easily abandon it.[37]

This paper did not overturn the predominant American belief that if Indian policy favored one side in the cold war, it favored the West; but the report fairly killed hopes that such affinity would ever become explicit, even after Nehru passed from the scene. The importance of the CIA memo lay in its implication that the United States should forget about trying to win India's open cooperation. The possibility had always seemed slim; now it was recognized to be nonexistent. American leaders had yet to arrive at a belief in the beneficence of Indian neutralism, but in conceding so clearly that the phenomenon would not disappear they faced the necessity that would form the raw material for virtue.

IX

IN THE autumn of 1951 Acheson and Truman decided to change ambassadors in New Delhi. Henderson carried out his duties capably and professionally, but his personality and Nehru's grated too much and the two shared too little in outlook on the world to make for good relations. At one point an unnamed source in Washington floated the idea of a back-channel link to New Delhi, circumventing Henderson, but Bajpai rejected the scheme. As time passed Henderson experienced ever greater difficulty concealing his dislike for the prime minister. Journalist C. L. Sulzberger, who knew both men, summarized the problem:

"Henderson detested Nehru and Nehru knew it." Besides, career diplomats usually rotated every three or four years, and the administration had other work for Henderson. The Bombay *Current,* describing the American ambassador's new posting, commented that he was heading to Iran "to pour water on troubled oil."[38]

Acheson and Truman could not have chosen a replacement more different from Henderson than Chester Bowles. A liberal Democrat, charter member of the Americans for Democratic Action, former advertising executive and recently governor of Connecticut, Bowles exhibited an outgoing style that contrasted sharply with Henderson's correct approach. And even more than did Hubert Humphrey and most other American liberals, Bowles *loved* India and everything about it, including its prime minister.

Bowles' enthusiasm, not to mention his liberalism, provoked questions at his confirmation hearings before the Senate Foreign Relations Committee. On the whole the nominee handled himself with aplomb, but he evidenced too much optimism regarding the potential benefits of American economic aid to suit Republican tastes. Alexander Smith complained of what he called Bowles' "save the world" philosophy. Owen Brewster, a McCarthyite and Taftite, conceded a role for hopefulness in diplomacy but feared Bowles would raise expectations in India that "manna is going to fall from heaven"; the inevitable disappointment would cause trouble. Brewster added that before he could support the nomination he needed assurance that the State Department was putting "brakes" on Bowles, to "restrain him from too exuberant a presentation" of American plans for aid to India.[39]

Other objections to Bowles centered on the fact that he lacked the training and experience of a career envoy Republicans contended the job in New Delhi required someone more qualified than a political creditor to the president. Smith initially thought he would be unable to accept Bowles' diplomatic opinions, but the ambassador-designate's testimony on Asian and world affairs changed his mind. "I will say that in talking to him and getting his views on China and so forth I was very well impressed with the answers he gave." Still, Smith had reservations. "I cannot help but feel that this is a political appointment and not an appointment where the President really sought throughout the country to find the one man we might need for this thing." Maine's Brewster took the same tack. "If there is any point in the world where there should be a career man, I think it should be India because of its extreme delicacy."

Democrat John Sparkman of Alabama came to Bowles' and his party's defense by describing to the committee a conversation he had recently had with newsman Marquis Childs, just returned from India. According to Childs, Sparkman said, Nehru had "a complete antipathy" to career men, apparently growing out of his unpleasant experiences with British civil servants.[40]

The Republicans on the committee continued to fight what they admitted was a losing battle. They asked whether Bowles' obvious concern for India's tremendous problems might color his reporting to the State Department. "I think it would be particularly dangerous," Brewster declared, "to have a man there who was too sympathetic with the Nehru approach." Smith granted Bowles' native ability but complained of the nominee's lack of personal experience in India. "He may be the best man on earth," Smith said. "If you asked me to vote to send him to Belgium, I would probably have no hesitation. But I would not send him to India." Smith also expressed disappointment that the Truman administration had not seen fit to consult the Senate or even the Foreign Relations Committee before nominating Bowles.

This final criticism, the last refuge of Senate obstructionists, indicated the weakness of the Republican case against Bowles. But Smith's colleagues in the party refused to yield without getting their licks. Bourke Hickenlooper did not quite declare Bowles a socialist, but the Iowa Republican came close. Hickenlooper characterized Bowles' political and economic views as expressing "the Government management theory, the Government manipulation theory." With conspicuous broadmindedness Hickenlooper did not deny Bowles' right to hold such opinions—just not in India. That country, he said, was in "very much of a state of flux"; consequently the post in New Delhi called for someone of safely orthodox tendencies.

In reality the hearings and subsequent debate on the Senate floor had less to do with Bowles personally than with the Truman administration's approach to India and the third world; in attacking Bowles the Republicans vented their displeasure at the administration's general policies. Hickenlooper charged the Democrats with overburdening American taxpayers in a vain quest to buy cooperation overseas.

We have neglected fearfully the basic and sound interests of the United States to the point where there are countries in the world that laugh at our stupidity diplomatically and take advantage of us and our bounty. . . . Behind their hands they laugh at the stupid Americans.

In a sneering reference to Bowles' marketing background Hickenlooper asked why, if India needed help as badly as Bowles indicated, the administration could not come up with someone more qualified. "If one has a very sick child or a very sick relative, he sends for a trained, experienced physician to treat the sick child or relative; he does not send for the Fuller-brush man." Describing Bowles as one of a group of persons who had been "preaching to other nations of the world the idea that we are gradually collectivizing our business, our opportunities, and our whole enterprise system," Hickenlooper denounced such individuals as "ambassadors of disservice to our country and to the freedom-loving nations of the world."

Owen Brewster decried the "economic ideology and theories" Bowles advocated, as representing not the majority of either party but only the nominee's "missionary" notions. Bowles' hopes for reforming India through foreign aid were doubly misplaced, Brewster said.

Whether it be Mr. Bowles in the guise of instructor of economics, telling them how to govern their country, or whether it be Mr. Bowles in the guise of Santa Claus, giving them hundreds of millions of dollars—the figure he mentioned was $250,000,000 a year as a starter, which we should give them—in whichever function he appears, I greatly fear that the results will be most unfortunate in our relations with India.

The big guns of the party put their views more succinctly. To William Knowland, Bowles' selection demonstrated the "bankrupt state" of American foreign policy under the Democrats. Robert Taft simply declared Bowles to be "without any qualifications" for the ambassadorship.[41]

X

AS EXPECTED, the Senate eventually sent Bowles on his way to New Delhi; but the debate over his nomination, combined with the battle for the wheat loan, so politicized India as an issue in American politics as to preclude any efforts by the Truman administration markedly to improve relations with Nehru. Crippled already with regard to China, the administration now found itself hamstrung on India.

Bowles nonetheless managed an improvement in the tone of U.S.–Indian relations. Immediately on arrival the Bowles family enthusiastically embraced Indian life. Bowles' wife adopted Indian dress; his children attended Indian schools. The ambassador patronized Indian arts and invited Indian musicians to perform at his home. The Indians found the attention flattering and a tremendous improvement from Henderson. At times, however, even they thought Bowles was getting carried away. (A British observer offered a simple explanation: Bowles was trying to corner the "coloured vote" for a future political campaign in America.) Pandit later described a dinner at the American embassy. The Indian ambassador said she had looked forward to the occasion, hoping to enjoy a taste of American cuisine, perhaps Virginia ham. To her disappointment, the Bowleses served curry and rice.[42]

Acheson once warned Bowles against "MacArthur's failing of regarding your 'theater' as the whole show"; the new ambassador's dispatches demonstrated that the warning was warranted. From the first, Bowles engaged in a concerted attempt to sell India to Washington. He described a growing Indian disenchantment with communism, especially the Russian brand. "The position of the USSR," he said, "has slipped rather substantially. ... Every top Indian official with whom I talked has gone out of his way to condemn the Soviet Union and the Communist approach to economic, social and political problems." Nehru himself had been "most emphatic" in his criticism of the communists. On the other hand the United States was gaining ground.

> I have talked to scores of peasants and working people, and I have yet to see anyone whose face did not light up when he heard I was from America. I have drunk many cups of tea in the homes of peasants who have been eager for every snatch of information about our country.

Admittedly India and the United States differed on important matters of international relations. India's geographic isolation caused Indian leaders to "rationalize away the danger of a Russian attack," and their desire for good relations with China contributed to a certain gullibility toward Beijing. Bowles likened Indian neutralism to American isolationism in the 1930s, but he added, "The Indians are one up on us! We turned down the League of Nations while they are active in the U.N."

Bowles' rosy perceptions informed his policy recommendations. The administration ought to work on building trust. "We should do everything possible to win their confidence in us, and to demonstrate our respect and admiration for the many good things which they are doing." Washington should not press New Delhi on Kashmir. "If Nehru is pushed too hard on this, he will react in about the same manner that either one of our political candidates next fall would react if he were accused of having made a secret agreement to turn Greece over to the Soviet Union." The United States ought to make the most of Indian neutralism. Rather than begrudge close ties between India and China the administration should encourage India "to remain in a position which will enable her to exert an effective modifying influence upon Communist China, with the chance that she may eventually act as an intermediary in a great effort to wean China away from the USSR." To be sure, such a split would not occur soon. But the possibility existed over the longer term and "the stakes are no less than the opening up of Russia's vulnerable rear door."[43]

Acheson refrained from comment on Bowles' suggestions, saying he would discuss them personally when the ambassador visited the United States.[44]

XI

THE SECRETARY was not the only one who wanted to talk to Bowles, and when the latter arrived in Washington in January 1952 the Senate Foreign Relations Committee invited him for a chat. During his confirmation hearings Bowles had encountered hostility primarily from the Republicans; Democrats who doubted the administration's wisdom on India and on Bowles had kept quiet out of party loyalty. This time, however, the barbs flew from both sides of the aisle.

Tom Connally did not let Bowles get through his opening statement before he began to object. The Texas Democrat disliked nearly everything about Bowles, from his Madison Avenue background and liberal political philosophy to his press-the-Indian-flesh diplomatic style. As the ambassador described his travels around India and his attempts to sample public opinion outside New Delhi, Connally cut in to ask Bowles what he thought his job was: to represent the views of the American government to the Indian government, and vice versa, or to meddle in

Indian politics. When Bowles replied that being an ambassador required him to get to know the Indian people, Connally asked sarcastically if his job also required him to "electioneer."[45]

Undeterred, Bowles continued his presentation. He explained how the situation in India afforded greater opportunities for the United States than most Americans realized. He stated that the danger to India from Soviet communism had diminished, although he admitted the Chinese version remained troublesome. When Connally demanded, "They are identical, are they not?," Bowles held his ground, saying, "One is Chinese and one is Russian, but they are sharply distinguished." The ambassador described measures Nehru had taken to combat the internal communist threat; India he said, had "more Communists in jail than any other democratic country in the world."[46]

Most of all Bowles insisted on the importance of making India "a going concern." American help in strengthening the Indian economy and raising the standard of living would "go a long way toward buttressing South Asia and the Middle East." "If we fail," he added, "we have another China on our hands, only this time it could be even worse because many other countries might fall, too." The future of India and of Asia depended on the success of India's five-year plan. "I want to be very frank; some of you gentlemen will not like it," he said, as he proceeded to recommend one billion dollars in aid to India.[47]

Since this amounted to five times what Congress had reluctantly approved the year before, on the understanding that the 1951 package represented a response to extraordinary conditions, Bowles' listeners found the notion astonishing. After catching his breath, Democrat Theodore Green of Rhode Island stated that India would become a foreign-aid sinkhole, as China had been. "Why do you think that aid given Nehru now will be more effective than the aid given Chiang in China was?" Connally considered Bowles' plan another bleeding-heart scheme to underwrite the human race. "We cannot finance the whole world, and we cannot finance India. You know good and well that the more money we give them the more they want." When Bowles responded that he was merely describing what India needed "to beat Communism so you people in Texas can live decently," Connally snapped, "We live decently enough." Unwilling to be lectured by a Connecticut Yankee, Connally added, "You are spreading your jurisdiction a little far, are you not?"[48]

Although Bowles failed utterly to sell his assistance plan to Congress, he had more luck within the administration. In part Bowles' success in the State Department reflected a sincere belief there that India's prosperity and security required the kind of help the ambassador advocated. At the same time it reflected how thoroughly the bureaucrats had learned the lesson of China. In February 1952 Burton Berry of the division for South Asia described the danger confronting India if sufficient aid did not materialize. "There is no time to lose. Communist gains in the recent elections show clearly that the conditions our program is designed to combat are being successfully exploited by Communist agents." Berry admitted Congress would never approve a large assistance plan for India, but he pointed out that if India went the way of China the State Department would have some serious explaining to do. Advocating aid was an insurance policy against that day.[49]

Acheson concurred with Bowles on the need for increasing assistance to India, but the secretary declined to mount a crusade for Nehru. By 1952 Acheson was tired of trudging up Capitol Hill to face hostile committees; he had no desire to risk the scant good will he still commanded on behalf of India. Besides, the case was hopeless. Bowles himself estimated the chances of passing an India aid bill at no better than one in ten. Acheson predicted that a request for money for India would provoke a "massacre" in Congress. The secretary preferred to put off the matter until 1953, when there would be "new faces in the Congress and in the Administration."[50]

XII

THE NEW faces, of course, belonged to Republicans. The 1952 elections delivered GOP majorities to both houses of Congress and a Republican to the presidency; they also brought increased attention to Asia. Eisenhower did not share the anti-European bias of the Asia-firsters in his party; in fact he had chosen to run in no small part to reaffirm the Republican commitment to Europe. But considering the uproar Republicans had made about China and in light of his own winning pledge to go to Korea, the new president could not have avoided paying considerable heed to the affairs of Asia.

John Foster Dulles also believed American interests required an increased emphasis on Asia. To some extent Dulles' attitude followed from a political desire to please the Knowlands and the Judds; to some degree he shared their convictions. Had nothing else accomplished the feat, Dulles' work on the Japanese peace treaty would have driven home the lesson of Asia's importance. In addition, a week after the election Dulles received a request from Ambassador Pandit for a high-level mission to India. A few days later Dulles wrote to Eisenhower that the Democrats' neglect of Asia must be "promptly corrected."[51]

As it involved India the Eisenhower administration's Asian emphasis took the form of advocating increased economic aid. On the stump the Republicans had called for "trade not aid," but in office they discovered trade would not produce the development capital India required to make even minimal economic progress. Dulles arrived early at the conclusion that a stable, non-communist India—the basic objective of American policy in the area—demanded financial support. Persuading Eisenhower took more time; bringing around others in the administration longer still.

Bowles was at least partly responsible for Dulles' precocity on the aid issue. As early as March 1952 Bowles had been selling his billion-dollar scheme to the man he suspected would become secretary of state; a year later he made the same argument in more dramatic terms. The United States, Bowles declared, had reached a crossroads with India and with Asia generally. One route led to peace, stability, and prosperity. If the world avoided a third general conflict, if Nehru remained in power, and if India's economic development progressed at a reasonable pace, there existed "a better than even chance" that India would become "the Free World's most solid bulwark between Japan and Turkey." The other road ran through economic stagnation to political dissolution and communism. If India fell, the rest of Asia likely would follow. The primary goal of American policy, Bowles argued, should be to keep India and Asia on the path of progress. At one billion dollars a stable, free continent would come cheap.[52]

Perhaps to Bowles' surprise, Dulles bought the idea, if not the price tag. The secretary of state carried the argument to an early session of Eisenhower's National Security Council, where he contended that America needed to improve its position in "the vital outpost positions" on the periphery of the Soviet bloc, especially in India. The State Department at this time was proposing a significant increase in aid for India, although, out of deference to campaign pledges, not as large an increase as department planners thought necessary. When spokesmen for the Treasury objected that the United States could not afford to shore up the entire non-Soviet world and that the administration ought to focus American resources on countries with "concrete defense implications," Dulles responded that the State Department's budget for India had been cut to the bone. He was asking $100 million for fiscal 1954; his advisers, he said, had requested $140 million and even at that level they felt "much anxiety" as to whether the request would meet the need. Dulles added that a policy of trade rather than aid sounded fine in principle, but before the administration vetoed aid it had better find the trade.[53]

XIII

A FEW weeks later Dulles left Washington for a tour of Asia. The trip was partly promotional: to demonstrate that the new administration took Asia as seriously as it had said it would; but the journey also allowed Dulles to assess the lay of the land in the East. The secretary went to India with the blessing of the Republican foreign-policy leadership in Congress; after seeing Dulles' itinerary, Senate Foreign Relations Chairman Alexander Wiley urged him to extend his time with Nehru.[54]

Literate Indians knew John Foster Dulles; many already despised him. In January 1947, while a member of the American UN delegation, Dulles had delivered himself of the opinion that "in India Soviet communism exercises a strong influence through the interim government." At a moment when India was bracing for independence and needed all the international good will it could muster, such an opinion alienated Indians by the millions, demonstrating the insensitivity and ignorance that would become Dulles' trademark in India. As secretary, Dulles got over most of his ignorance regarding India; the policies he advocated demonstrated a reasonably shrewd understanding of what that country was about. But insensitivity remained a problem. Dulles had only the faintest notion of how comments unexceptional in an American context would sound in India. In 1955 he committed what two historians of Indian foreign relations, otherwise well-disposed toward the Republican secretary, describe as "one of the most egregious blunders of his illustrious career" by referring to the Portuguese enclave of Goa as a Portuguese "province" rather than a colony. The fact that Dulles admitted using the term advisedly merely put the error in the category of what American journalist James Reston called "the planned mistake." (As wags of the time had it, Dulles was in hot water in India "from the word Goa.") The secretary's 1956 Ames, Iowa, speech describing neutrality in the cold war as "immoral"—the one time, it appears, he uttered this sentiment —reverberates in India still. Little wonder the Indian diplomat K. P. S. Menon characterized Dulles as

> The wind that sends your ship in circles,
> The wind that neither drives out Death
> Nor brings in summer.[55]

For all this, Dulles' conversations with Nehru went smoothly. "The atmosphere was intimate and we talked with great frankness," the secretary told Eisenhower afterward. Dulles explained American policy toward various of the world's trouble spots. Regarding Egypt, then locked in a dispute with Britain regarding the latter's base at Suez, he described American efforts to get the British to settle. Nehru responded that the Egyptian problem constituted a particular danger because continued tension might provoke Britain to reoccupy the country. "Of course the British can do this, but what will they do next? Bayonets are no good to sit on."

Nehru brought up the issue of Korea, questioning a recent statement by Dulles hinting at escalation if current truce talks failed. The prime minister wondered aloud where such a course of action might lead. Suggesting a way of avoiding an impasse on the principal sticking point of the negotiations, he said he hoped the United States would support India's proposal for referring the prisoner of war issue to the United Nations. Dulles responded that the communists, especially the Chinese, would probably not accept UN jurisdiction over such a sensitive matter. Nehru agreed that this might prove true. Even so he thought the proposal worth a try.[56]

One purpose of Dulles' trip, which also took the secretary to Egypt and other parts of the Middle East, was to test the reaction of regional leaders to the idea of collective security. The United States had hoped to bring Egypt into an anticommunist pact but Dulles discovered Nasser wanted nothing to do with it. Consequently American plans shifted toward the countries of the northern tier, including Pakistan.[57]

When politics or diplomacy required, Dulles could split hairs with the best of the legal and diplomatic professions. In his conversation with

Nehru he referred to concern in India that the United States was seeking an alliance with Pakistan, and he assured the prime minister that India had no cause for worry. Accurately, but narrowly so, the secretary declared it "unlikely" that the Middle East Defense Organization, or MEDO, would materialize "as originally projected." Moreover, he said the administration had "no present plans" for any military alliance with Pakistan "which could responsibly be looked upon as unneutral" with respect to India. Nehru probably had doubts about this disclaimer but he responded matter-of-factly, expressing what Dulles described as "satisfaction" at the secretary's statement.[58]

To Western observers in India Dulles' trip seemed a success. Fraser Wilkins, counselor of the American embassy in New Delhi, assessed the reaction of members of the Indian government. The Indians, Wilkins said, had initially registered disappointment at the outcome of the elections of 1952. Having taken readily to Chester Bowles, they had believed a Democratic victory would bring better relations between India and the United States than a Republican win. Further, the campaign rhetoric of Eisenhower and Dulles had sounded ominous. Dulles' visit dispelled some of the worries of Indians that the new leaders in Washington would prove as bellicose in practice as they had sounded in opposition. British diplomats agreed that the secretary had made a good showing. Dulles, in the words of the British high commissioner in India, "gave the impression of being a kindly, frank and friendly man who had come here in all sincerity to find out things for himself."[59]

To some Indians, however, including the one who counted most, Dulles, and Americans generally, remained a source of concern. An early biographer of Nehru, who conducted lengthy interviews with the prime minister during the Dulles period, describes a "lack of personal affection, understanding or trust between Nehru and Dulles." A more recent and more nearly definitive life, based on privileged access to Nehru's papers, characterizes Dulles at this time as "so obsessed with anti-communism that he was in no mood to listen to India." The author of the latter book, Sarvepalli Gopal, quotes Nehru writing to associates during this period, regarding a cultural program:

> I dislike more and more this business of exchange of persons between America and India. The fewer persons that go from India to America or that come from the United States to India, the better. . . . We have had quite enough of American superiority.[60]

85

XIV

WHATEVER ITS effect on Nehru, Dulles' 1953 tour produced a basic shift in America's Asia policy. On his return to Washington the secretary described Nehru to the National Security Council as "utterly impractical" regarding global politics, although he conceded the prime minister's realism on matters touching India directly. In contrast, Dulles had been "immensely impressed" by the Pakistanis, by their "martial" character and their willingness to join a regional defense arrangement. As a result, and despite his disclaimer to Nehru, Dulles advocated proceeding forthwith toward a northern-tier pact.[61]

Obviously an alliance with Pakistan, and the American arms it would require, would provoke a reaction from New Delhi. But Dulles judged such a reaction manageable, and his prediction received support from a joint estimate by the CIA and the State and Defense departments. According to this report, weapons for Pakistan would generate "strong Indian resentment" for two reasons: they would strengthen Pakistan's position in Kashmir and they would increase Soviet interest in the subcontinent. On the former point, assurances from the United States that Pakistan would not use its weapons against India would not significantly calm Indian fears, nor would a balancing offer of arms for India, since Nehru would reject them. Still, despite the ill feeling an American alliance with Pakistan would generate, nothing close to a rupture in U.S.–Indian relations would result, if only because Nehru valued American economic aid and considered it essential to the success of his plans for India's development.[62]

Fortified by this evaluation, the administration moved toward bringing Pakistan into a Middle Eastern alliance. Recognizing the difficulties implicit in identification of the United States as the prime mover of something that might more profitably be presented as an indigenous expression of free-world solidarity, the administration maintained a low profile. In July Eisenhower approved a proposal to "develop secretly" plans for an alliance of those states "most keenly aware of the threat of Soviet Russia" and "geographically located to stand in the way of possible Soviet aggression." Among possible candidates the NSC paper containing the proposal recommended Pakistan for "special consideration."[63]

XV

WHILE ADMINISTRATION aims for Pakistan portended future troubles with India, a relatively insignificant issue created friction at the moment. In the mid-summer of 1953 the State Department learned that an Indian firm dealing in radioactive isotopes was selling thorium nitrate to China, with the approval of the Indian government. Two years earlier the American Congress had passed a measure, commonly known as the Battle Act, mandating a cutoff of American aid to any country providing certain strategic materials to the Soviet Union or its allies. The list of proscribed commodities included thorium nitrate.

In the broad context of U.S.–Indian relations the thorium affair should have produced no more than minor problems. The sales involved small quantities, and China's purchases hardly constituted a hazard to American security. But once the Eisenhower administration learned of the sale it found itself in a delicate position. The chief difficulty arose from the fact that the Battle legislation left no room for executive discretion: a simple finding of delivery dictated an aid embargo. The administration did not want to halt aid to India. On the contrary, Dulles was trying to figure out how to get Congress to increase the support he considered necessary to ensure the stability of Nehru's government. But the legislature included many individuals who, from conviction or out of convenience, likened foreign aid to a sucker's game, especially when recipients included neutralists like Nehru. Should news of the thorium shipments leak, it would almost certainly provide the aid-busters the excuse they needed to purge India from the welfare rolls. Neither Dulles nor Eisenhower wanted to get on the wrong side of the conservatives unnecessarily; they certainly did not wish to go outside the law for Nehru's sake.

Nehru had his own problems. He desired American assistance but could hardly allow himself to be seen as knuckling under to American demands. The prime minister made this point in a conversation with the new American ambassador, George Allen. Telling Allen his government could not rescind approval of the sale, since the goods had been paid for and were now on their way to China on a Polish ship, Nehru added that even if he could physically block delivery he could not bear the political expense. The consequences, internally and in relations between India and China, would be "so serious as to render it impossible."[64]

Both Washington and New Delhi wished the issue would go away; both sides sought accommodation. Nehru told Allen "categorically and with some vehemence," as the ambassador reported to Dulles, that India "had never and would never submit to derogation of its national sovereignty in permitting United States law to determine with whom and in what commodities India could trade." But the prime minister suggested arrangements to prevent similar incidents in the future. Replying for Dulles, Undersecretary Walter Bedell Smith assured Allen, for Nehru's benefit: "We are trying in every possible way to work out a solution to the problem."[65]

From the perspective of American politics the safe answer would have been to follow the letter of the law and stop further aid; but the diplomatic repercussions of such a move might have proved disastrous, with consequences transcending relations between the United States and India. An aid embargo would undercut Nehru and cast America as an inflexible ogre. At the beginning of September Dulles explained administration thinking.

> I have been considering the possible effects of terminating aid to India because of the shipment of thorium nitrate to Communist China, and I have come to the conclusion that it would be very unfortunate to do so. Terminating aid would be interpreted as punitive not only in India but also elsewhere. We would find ourselves in the rather untenable position of believing in increased stability in India as very much to our interest but not being able to do anything about it. The boost to the communist propaganda line in India and the rest of Asia would certainly be very great.[66]

The measure of the administration's concern was the price it eventually paid to solve the thorium problem. After negotiations lasting until the middle of 1954 Washington arranged to preempt further sales to China by purchasing, at a price of two million dollars per year, the amount Beijing had been buying. At the same time Eisenhower decided to take a political chance by fudging the facts surrounding the case. The president directed his chief of the Foreign Operations Administration, Harold Stassen, to issue a secret finding that India had not "knowingly and willfully" sold the radioactive material to China and therefore that the strictures of the Battle Act did not apply.[67]

Nehru conceded nothing. Instead he got a firm contract for India's thorium at a good price. And he continued to receive American aid.

XVI

THE THORIUM episode ended happily, but the outlook for U.S.–Indian relations remained clouded as the Eisenhower administration pushed ahead with plans for arming Pakistan. In July the American ambassador in Karachi reported negotiations for a treaty going well. "A beachhead has been established," he said. A few months later Mohammed Ayub Khan, commander in chief of the Pakistani army, arrived in Washington, ostensibly for a medical checkup, in fact to discuss terms on which the United States might begin to supply weapons to his country. While in the United States Ayub whispered the purpose of his visit to reporters, intimating he and his compatriots required only American aid to take up the struggle against the godless communists. This maneuver made it easy for the administration to go forward and difficult to turn back.[68]

At the beginning of October Dulles summoned the Indian ambassador in Washington, G. L. Mehta. Expressing sympathy regarding the problems India faced, the secretary said he thought India and the United States had more in common than circumstances allowed them to demonstrate, and he added he did not believe "the thinking people of India" were really neutral in an ethical sense between communism and the West. It seemed to him "they were trying to be more neutral in deed than in spirit." Ambassador Mehta did not disagree. Dulles went on to remark that he understood how India's particular position led its leaders "to deal with the Communist issue on a different basis than that of the United States." He reminded Mehta, however, that while India's handling of communism might make sense in New Delhi, it would "not have popular appeal" in the United States.[69]

Sincerity aside, these last two points constituted a debating maneuver, for in conceding India's right to treat communism as its leaders saw fit, however unpopular their choice of strategies might be in America, Dulles implicitly claimed an analogous privilege for the United States. To the degree India honored the claim the privilege would come in useful. Eisenhower had yet to make a final decision, but all signs indicated that the American strategy for handling communism included military aid to Pakistan.

In December Eisenhower sent Vice President Richard Nixon to Karachi to discuss details of a weapons pact. On the same trip Nixon stopped in New Delhi. The vice president's talks with Nehru took place amid numerous reports that an American agreement with Pakistan was at hand, and Nehru seized the opportunity to demonstrate his displeasure at the prospect. Nixon later described the conversation: "Nehru spoke obsessively and interminably about India's relationship with Pakistan. He spent more time railing against India's neighbor than discussing either U.S.–Indian relations or other Asian problems." The vice president remained unmoved, not least because he believed Nehru's opposition to American aid for Pakistan followed less from a concern for Indian security than from worry about his individual prestige. "I was convinced that his objection owed much to his personal thirst for influence, if not control, over South Asia, the Middle East, and Africa."[70]

On returning to Washington the vice president elaborated his views for the National Security Council. Of Nehru, Nixon stated, "It is said that he has all the powers of a dictator, but doesn't use them like a dictator. I wonder." Nixon found the prime minister difficult to fathom —in contrast to the Pakistanis who had "fewer complexes than the Indians." On the substantive matter of arms for Pakistan, Nixon characterized Nehru as "very strongly opposed." Nixon did not think Nehru worried inordinately about a Pakistani attack on India; rather he ascribed the prime minister's complaints to envy. An increase in Pakistan's power, especially after India had registered strong public objections, would reflect badly on Nehru and diminish his stature internationally. Failure to preserve the principle of nonalignment in the subcontinent, of all places, would undermine Nehru's assertion that neutralism represented a viable option for Asia and Africa. Nixon granted that the administration could do a better job presenting its argument for arming Pakistan. He suggested sending another special envoy to New Delhi to reassure Nehru about America's intentions. But the vice president declared forcefully that the administration must not let Nehru prevent the United States from going ahead as planned. To balk at this late date would destroy America's credibility and risk "losing most of the Asian-Arab countries to the neutralist bloc."[71]

As the administration moved to a final decision objections arose from various quarters. Chester Bowles wrote to Dulles predicting a wave of anti-Americanism in India. Nehru, the former ambassador added, might judge it politically necessary to go along with the critics, which would produce a countercurrent of anti-Nehru feeling in the United States. The head of the American Board of Commissioners for Foreign Missions also contacted Dulles, describing his fear that arms for Pakistan would jeopardize the success and perhaps the safety of American missionaries in India. (George Allen in New Delhi suspected the Indian government of deliberately using pressure against missionaries as a device to block the weapons transfer to Pakistan.) The Indian consul-general in New York declared that the danger to U.S.–Indian relations "could not be exaggerated." In arming Pakistan, the Indian official said, the Eisenhower administration was giving Nehru's enemies "a wonderful opportunity to attack the United States." The British urged the administration to move cautiously, not wanting more trouble in the Commonwealth at a crucial moment in the Suez negotiations—and, not incidentally, not wishing to be displaced as Pakistan's chief weapons supplier. Nehru himself, perhaps concerned that he had not made his point strongly enough to Nixon, wrote to Eisenhower directly. The prime minister did not say he personally objected to the proposed deal but took the tack of suggesting he could not ignore the sentiments of his supporters who did.[72]

Eisenhower and Dulles understood what they were getting into. The secretary expected "very unfavorable reactions" in India. But he considered the deal's positive effects on regional security more important. In January 1954 Dulles summarized the argument in a memorandum to the president. During the previous few months, Dulles wrote, Karachi had expressed "its urgent desire" to receive American military aid. This desire apparently reflected "articulate public opinion" in Pakistan as well as the wishes of Prime Minister Mohammed Ali. Recently, in response to a secret approach by the administration, Pakistan and Turkey had agreed to enter into a collective security arrangement "on the understanding that the U.S. would provide military aid to Pakistan." The Defense Department considered a pact between Turkey and Pakistan a vital first step toward a larger alliance including Iran and Iraq. Closing the circle, the secretary asserted that a Turkey–Pakistan treaty "would not only be of military value but would also provide a framework of collective security which would help to justify extension of aid to Pakistan and minimize adverse repercussions in India and elsewhere."[73]

Dulles noted that although the embassy in New Delhi forecast a strong adverse response, Ambassador Allen estimated the administration could "ride out the storm without fatal effect on U.S.–Indian relations." The American ambassador in Pakistan had declared—and Dulles agreed

—that the United States would gain "a great deal" by going forward with military aid, while reneging would be "disastrous" to U.S.–Pakistani relations and to the stability of Mohammed Ali's government. Dulles added, "It would probably also be disastrous to our standing with the other countries of Asia, who would assume we had backed down in the face of Indian threats." When all the advantages and disadvantages were weighed, Dulles said, the balance came down on the side of proceeding as planned. At the same time, the secretary urged the president to announce that he would consider favorably an application by India for military aid. "India would without doubt not apply—in fact Nehru has said so—but it would help in my opinion to offset some of the distorted propaganda originating in India."[74]

After receiving this memorandum, Eisenhower met with Dulles, Defense Secretary Charles Wilson, and Foreign Operations Administration chief Stassen. Following a brief discussion the president approved the Pakistan deal. In doing so Eisenhower said the administration should take pains to describe the arrangement as not representing displeasure with India. Rather American officials should declare that aid to the Pakistanis was America's way of expressing support for Pakistan's efforts on behalf of regional security. In line with Dulles' advice, the president authorized an offer of similar aid to India.[75]

XVII

WHEN ALL the details of the Pakistan deal were in place Eisenhower officially broke the news to Nehru. In advance of the public announcement the president sent a letter to the prime minister explaining the reasons behind his decision. "I want you to know directly from me," Eisenhower wrote, "that this step does not in any way affect the friendship we feel for India." The president described the role the American government hoped Pakistan would play in the defense of the Middle East and assured Nehru American arms would not be used for any other purpose.

> What we are proposing to do, and what Pakistan is agreeing to, is in no way directed against India. And I am confirming publicly that if our aid to any country, including Pakistan, is directed against another in aggression, I will undertake immediate action both within and without the UN to thwart such aggression.

Eisenhower added that he was recommending to Congress a continuation of economic and technical aid to India and that if India asked for military assistance the administration would almost certainly approve the request. "I regret that there has been such widespread and unfounded speculation on this subject," the president concluded. "Now that the facts are known, I hope that the real import of our decision will be understood."[76]

Allen personally delivered the president's message to Nehru. The ambassador drew the prime minister's attention specifically to the passage pledging firm action in case Pakistan misused American arms. Allen appended his own comment that Nehru should not take amiss the American offer of matching weapons for India. The administration was fully aware of the prime minister's policy of not accepting arms from any foreign source. Allen said he himself had questioned the wisdom of including the offer, since it might seem to imply that the administration had not been listening or did not take the prime minister's statements seriously. Such an implication, Allen said, would be entirely erroneous. The offer was simply another way of saying that the weapons for Pakistan were not intended as a challenge to India.

After Allen's comments and after reading Eisenhower's letter, Nehru reflected briefly and then replied in what Allen described as "a pleasant and almost confidential tone." The prime minister said, "I have never at any moment, since the subject arose two or three months ago, had any thought whatsoever that the United States Government, and least of all President Eisenhower, wished to do any damage to India." Expressing his appreciation for the president's letter, Nehru told Allen that what disturbed him was not the Americans' motivation but the possible consequences of their decision. Aside from the international dangers of introducing the cold war to South Asia—dangers, he reminded Allen, he had warned of many times in public speeches—the American action might cause serious trouble between India and Pakistan. In India the vast majority of the country's forty million Moslems were fully integrated into the nation. Unfortunately there remained small groups of "extremists" among Indian Moslems who did not conceal their pleasure over the arms deal for Pakistan, hoping it might ultimately lead to a renewal of Moslem domination of India. Naturally this aroused a response among "Hindu extremists" who not only called for military preparations against Pakistan but inflamed communal tensions within

India. Turning to the situation in Pakistan, Nehru said he trusted Mohammed Ali and wished him a long term in office. But he feared that the Pakistani prime minister, by accepting American weapons, had unleashed political forces he could not control. Persons less moderate than Ali might push him aside in favor of someone who would "listen to adventurers."

Allen responded by referring again to Eisenhower's declaration that Washington would not allow the Pakistanis to use American weapons for aggressive purposes. The ambassador said the United States was supplying military hardware to some thirty or forty countries and not one of them had engaged in aggression. At this, Allen reported afterward, Nehru appeared impressed. Summarizing, Allen wrote, "The conversation was surprisingly pleasant throughout. Nehru made a conscious effort to be agreeable. He showed no adverse reaction to the President's offer to consider sympathetically any Indian request for military aid, and it is possible that he was rather pleased." Of course the prime minister would not admit any such feeling publicly. Allen had "no doubt" Nehru would issue a strong statement of criticism.[77]

III

A Virtue of Necessity: 1954–1960

THE THIRD phase of American policy toward India began with the announcement of the Pakistan weapons deal, and it involved a gradual warming of relations between Washington and New Delhi. The arrangement with Karachi marked the final admission by American leaders that efforts to bring India into an alliance with the West would fail. Had Eisenhower and Dulles retained a glimmer of hope they would not have extinguished it by shipping arms to India's foremost rival. In important respects this admission cleared the air, for it allowed American strategists to design a policy toward India unencumbered by false hopes. Nehru would not be an ally, but if handled correctly he might be a friend.

The warming did not occur overnight, nor did it preclude further difficulties between the two countries. The Geneva Conference in 1954, the Bandung Conference and the initiation of large-scale Soviet aid in 1955, and the Hungarian crisis in 1956, to cite four developments of the period, revealed continued and substantial differences between the objectives of the Eisenhower administration and those of Nehru's government. The American alliance with Pakistan rankled throughout. But despite the differences, the administration increasingly recognized the beneficial role Nehru played in India and India in the world. A signal event in this regard was Eisenhower's December 1956 meeting with the prime minister, at which Nehru gave a forceful explanation of his country's neutralist policy, convincing Eisenhower of the advantages to America's geopolitical position of a nonaligned India.

Shortly after this meeting Eisenhower approved an NSC policy paper recommending American support for India's second five-year plan. When that plan ran into trouble in late 1957 the president agreed to a major bailout scheme. This operation represented no conceptual demarche: from before the 1951 wheat loan American policy had implicitly acknowledged that India's economic stability, even under a neutralist government, was important to American interests in Asia. But the decision to close India's dollar gap made the connection between Indian development and American security explicit and actual. That Congress joined the president in committing American resources to India on a long-term basis indicated the degree to which an appreciation of India had become respectable.

II

DURING THE spring of 1954 the attention of the world focused on the final stages of the first war for Indochina. As the French struggled to retain their grip on their Southeast Asian empire, the Vietminh fought, with greater success, to dislodge them. The conflict climaxed in May in the mud of Dienbienphu. During the next two months the great powers wrote the denouement in the halls of Geneva.

Neither the United States nor India participated directly in the fighting in Indochina, although during the first third of 1954 the Americans threatened to do so; but both took important parts in the negotiations. American officials claimed places in the front row on account of America's superpower stature and deep pockets. India had to crash the gate, but once inside, Nehru's representatives became, if not quite the life of the party, in some measure the indispensables who kept the affair going when the principals threatened to leave early.

The jostling for position at Geneva began in February when the foreign ministers of the United States, the Soviet Union, Britain, and France issued a communiqué from Berlin inviting themselves, China, and "other interested states" to attend the Indochina conference. Decoding the latter part of the guest list took several weeks, as the opposing sides sought to pack the conference with cooperative partners. Any reasonable rendering should have included India, which could not be other than interested in matters concerning Southeast Asia, but the Eisenhower administration objected to an invitation for New Delhi.[1]

American opposition to India was not particularly strong, however, and it stemmed as much from fear that an Indian foot in the door would open the conference to other, less responsible, parties as from concern at problems the Indians themselves might raise. A State Department planning paper of March 1954 summarized the American view by saying that although no one could credibly deny India's stake in the negotiations at Geneva, allowing India a role might lead to "an unwieldy conference 'cluttered' with neutralists."[2]

While India's invitation remained unsent, Nehru indicated his intention to participate, by one means or another. As had been the case during the Korean conflict, Nehru's immediate objective regarding Indochina was to end the fighting before it spread. His concern increased as the French predicament worsened and Washington hinted at coming to France's rescue. The Indian ambassador in Moscow caught his chief's mood in a diary entry in April: "Dulles is at his favourite game in the Far East; and the world is on the brink of war." As Nehru explained to the Indian parliament, the crisis in Indochina "calls from us our best thoughts and efforts to avert the trends of this conflict towards its extension and intensification and to promote the trends that might lead to a settlement." To this end he offered a peace plan designed to silence the guns as quickly as possible—and therefore relatively unencumbered by political preconditions. In particular he recommended a ceasefire-in-place, complete independence for the Associated States of Indochina, and pledges of nonintervention by the major outside powers.[3]

Before American officials had a chance to analyze this plan, Nehru told, or seemed to tell, Allen that Washington should not take certain aspects of it too seriously. In his speech Nehru had stressed the nationalist character of the revolt against the French. The prime minister informed the ambassador that the Eisenhower administration must read this emphasis in the context of Indian domestic politics. Nehru knew well that the Vietminh relied heavily on China, and he assured Allen he did not wish the Chinese to dominate Indochina any more than he desired to see continued French control. But nationalism was what the Indian masses wanted to hear about, and if he did not seize the issue Indian Communists would.

Krishna Menon, who would serve as Nehru's representative at Geneva and who had helped draft the speech, spoke more directly. He reiterated the domestic purposes of the address and told Allen that India's formula did not contradict the American concept of collective security for Southeast Asia. Menon said India did not expect the great powers to leave the region entirely; his government only asked the large states other than France to pledge *military* nonintervention. India hoped to see the creation of a more or less neutralized Indochina, which would serve as a buffer against China's further expansion.[4]

A few days later Nehru took his show on the road. At a meeting in Colombo of the prime ministers of India, Pakistan, Ceylon, Burma, and Indonesia, Nehru sought cooperation in promoting his peace plan. He met mixed success. As expected, Mohammed Ali of Pakistan offered the strongest objection, declaring that if a situation reduced to a choice between colonialism and communism, as seemed to be happening in Indochina, prudence and experience dictated siding with the colonialists. The colonialists had consciences and constituents. The communists had neither.[5]

Administration officials could not have put the American case better; they must have felt they were getting their money's worth from Pakistan. But the world remained full of people less enlightened than Ali, and the administration, recognizing the attractiveness of Nehru's plan, prepared to counteract it. A few days after Nehru's appearance at Colombo the American delegation at Geneva dissected the Indian package. The first difficulty with the scheme lay in its vagueness. Nehru called for a cease-fire. No problem there. But the prime minister failed to specify accompanying political conditions, without which a halt in the fighting would mean little. A second deficiency involved Nehru's idea of limiting cease-fire negotiations to the French and their Indochinese allies, and the Vietminh. On paper India's argument looked reasonable. These parties were doing the fighting; they ought to do the talking. But aside from the fact that only the participation of the great powers had made a Geneva conference possible, exclusion of the United States, the Soviet Union, and China would work to America's disadvantage. As Charles Stelle of the State Department's policy planning staff put it,

> Given the obvious eagerness of the French to reach some sort of an agreement and the disinclination of the French to reckon the costs too

carefully, exclusion of the U.S. from negotiations for an Indochina settlement would undoubtedly tend to weaken the Western position in the
negotiations.

Further, just as an American presence at the peace talks was needed to
stiffen the Gallic spine, the Russians and the Chinese were required to
force flexibility on the Vietminh. "Since the Viet Minh are more apt
to be more interested in immediate complete victory than either the
Russians or the Chinese, exclusion of the other Communists from
the negotiations would tend to harden the Communist negotiating position."

Nehru's failure to specify terms for enforcement of a ceasefire also
threatened to work to the West's disadvantage. The French would abide
by the conditions of a truce, out of political necessity if not out of honor.
But the Vietminh knew neither politics, in the democratic sense, nor
scruples. Similar considerations applied to Nehru's call for military nonintervention by outside powers. Domestic and world opinion would
police a suspension of American arms aid; nothing comparable would
act on the communists. Besides, France depended on help from its allies
far more than the Vietminh did. Finally, the threat of more-forceful
American intervention, to the point of air strikes or even the deployment
of ground troops, remained one of the few bargaining chips left to the
Western side at Geneva.

On balance the American delegation could find little good and much
bad to say about Nehru's plan.

> The Indian proposal picks up those items of the Communist position—
> direct negotiation, cease-fire, and non-intervention—which have a danger-
> ous appeal to the French public, and which in themselves would be dam-
> aging to the Western position, and neglects any of the safeguards—politi-
> cal settlement, and controls—which might be calculated to make the non-
> Communist position in Indochina tenable.[6]

The deficiencies of Nehru's peace plan reinforced Washington's dis-
inclination to allow India a seat at the negotiations. When the conference
began in the second week of May the Americans had managed to bar
the Indians, largely because the communist side had not tried to force
passage. The possibility remained, however, that the communists might
make the attempt. If they did, the United States would continue to object
—to a point. To allow India to join the conference would increase the

impact of Nehru's proposals; but to appear stubborn on a minor issue would also cause problems.

The conference started slowly, and even after two weeks questions regarding participants remained. Walter Bedell Smith, heading the American delegation, still expected the communists to raise the India issue. Smith said that if they did, the United States would find continued resistance "very difficult." But to give in might open "a whole Pandora's box" of troubles. The undersecretary recommended to Dulles that the administration counter a communist nomination of India by proposing seats for Thailand and the Philippines, two countries that saw the threat to Southeast Asia much as the United States did.[7]

Dulles decided the costs of obstruction, should the communists make India an issue, would outweigh the expected gains. Consequently he directed Smith to make no objection or counterproposal. In fact, mulling the matter over, the secretary of state discovered traces of silver in the prospect's lining. To bring India into the proceedings at Geneva would encourage Nehru to accept responsibility for the security of Southeast Asia. The prime minister, Dulles said, might find the experience "educational."[8]

Dulles' faith in on-the-job-training had limits, and when suggestions that an Indian *chair* the conference surfaced, he and other administration officials stood firmly against the idea. Allowing an Indian to lead the negotiations would produce the problems of Indian participation in heightened form; more important, it would place the fate of Southeast Asia in the hands of the one member of Nehru's government American leaders most disliked and distrusted.

III

"NEHRU'S HARRY Hopkins" was how Indian journalist Frank Moraes characterized Krishna Menon; on another occasion Moraes said, "He is our Mr. Dulles." Both descriptions fit the man who was at once Nehru's confidant and the lightning rod of Indian diplomacy. To Canadian diplomat Escott Reid, Menon was simultaneously a "brilliant, constructive negotiator and draftsman" and possessed of a "holy obstinacy." After a Commonwealth conference Reid's boss, Prime Minister Lester Pearson, described Menon as "inclined to be both ignorant and irritable." An African delegate at the United Nations declared that "although Mr. Krishna Menon supports African causes, he treats Africans like children." One of Menon's Indian colleagues, Subimal Dutt, commented that Menon "did not always measure his words." Another, C. S. Jha, concurring with a comment that Menon was "an outstanding world statesman but the world's worst diplomat," asserted that "his lack of diplomatic finesse and the abrasive manner in which he projected and expounded India's views needlessly caused offense and did India's and Nehru's image much harm." Jha went on to say that Menon had an "acid tongue" and was often "overbearing, churlish and vindictive." The Indian ambassador to the Soviet Union, K. P. S. Menon, had a single word for him: "insufferable." [9]

Thus American leaders were not alone in finding Menon difficult. Dulles considered him "a very adroit and unscrupulous maneuverer who likes to have his finger in every pie." To the secretary of state, Menon seemed "strongly anti-American," although the Indian diplomat usually managed "to conceal this rather effectively when talking with Americans." Most of all Dulles objected to what he considered Menon's dissembling style in intergovernmental transactions. Menon was "troublesome," the secretary told Eisenhower, because of his habit of "mixing up the channels of communication." [10]

The president had even less use for Menon than Dulles did. Civil in his personal dealings with the man, Eisenhower unburdened himself in his diary.

> Krishna Menon is a menace and a boor. He is a boor because he conceives himself to be intellectually superior and rather coyly presents to cover this a cloak of excessive humility and modesty. He is a menace because he is a master at twisting words and meanings of others and is governed by an ambition to prove himself the master international manipulator and politician of the age. [11]

Menon, for his part, considered Eisenhower a cipher. Of Dulles he commented that the secretary was "a very honest man" but added: "Honesty can lead to all sorts of strange consequences. Dulles was frank; maybe that frankness came from arrogance, or from the knowledge that he was virtually the President of the United States." [12]

For reasons best known to themselves, the Russians and Chinese did not press for Indian participation and so a Menon chairmanship never became a serious issue. But even from the sidelines Menon managed to inject himself into the negotiations. As much as they wished to,

American leaders could not ignore him. India appeared likely to figure in any settlement, and Menon provided a means of communication between the Americans and the Chinese. (Asked before the conference whether he would meet with his Chinese counterpart, Dulles replied, "Not unless our automobiles collide.") Although they never knew just how much of what they said found its way to Chinese ears, or in what form, administration officials operated on the assumption Menon told all. On one occasion Dulles concluded a briefing of Eisenhower for a conversation with Menon by reminding the president that whatever he said would reach Beijing almost as soon as New Delhi.[13]

Two weeks into the conference Smith and Menon had a long conversation. Menon did most of the talking. The Indian diplomat told Smith his comments reflected only his own thoughts, not India's official position. Smith prudently disbelieved him, remarking to Dulles afterward that "he would not have spoken as he did without Nehru's authority." The negotiations had begun slowly but Menon expressed optimism that the conference would produce a settlement. He said Zhou Enlai was a man "with whom one could do business," adding that Zhou's Russian counterpart, V. M. Molotov, was growing more amenable to a solution daily. Though division of Vietnam was in the air, Menon did not think partition inevitable. He reiterated Nehru's call for a ceasefire-in-place, followed by the gradual withdrawal of the opposing forces into "pockets." When Smith asked who would oversee the withdrawals, Menon replied that any supervising authority must consist of countries acceptable to the five major powers. After ruling out most of the Western Europeans because of their formal or informal association with NATO, rejecting Latin America and Canada for overly close ties with the "American bloc," and dismissing various Asian states for similar reasons or for internal troubles, Menon suggested that India and Norway would make a good team. He added that if the five major powers concurred in requesting Indian supervision, his government would probably accept the responsibility.[14]

Some days later Smith inquired for details of Menon's proposal to supervise a settlement. Under whose jurisdiction, he asked, did India propose to act? That of the United Nations or merely the Geneva Conference? Although Smith did not say so to Menon, Washington had grave doubts about Indian supervision in any form. The communists would surely try to cheat, and it seemed unlikely New Delhi would possess the will or ability to call them to account. Politically, Geneva was already being portrayed in the United States as another Munich or Yalta, and Nehru's many American critics would see little difference between handing Indochina to the Indians and handing it straight to the communists. As to terms of reference, an Indian team answerable only to Geneva would be less susceptible to American control than one accredited to the UN, and it would derogate from the prestige of that international body, in whose name the United States had just fought a war. On the last point, Menon suggested that the conference might produce some formula by which the Geneva powers would agree on the composition of a supervisory commission and informally sound out those chosen to see if they would serve, and then turn to the UN to issue formal invitations.[15]

The plan for Indian supervision got off the ground with difficulty. Officials from the Associated States disliked it even more than the Americans did. The Cambodian delegate told Smith he found Menon completely ignorant of conditions in Cambodia; he could hardly trust an Indian supervisory team. The Laotian representative rejected Menon's idea categorically. The spokesman for the Vietnamese government remarked that the Indian formula would favor the communists, adding that the Indians had yet to prove they were neutral and not merely neutralists.[16]

Through most of June the conference made little progress, but at the end of the month a visit by Zhou to New Delhi raised India's visibility and the prospects of an Indian role in a settlement. The Chinese premier, perhaps the most brilliant diplomat of the era, was a great success in India. Nehru's official biographer concedes that the Indian prime minister was "lulled" by Zhou's soft words.

> Above all, a clever flatterer, Chou concealed his personality and sought Nehru's advice on all matters. "Your Excellency has more knowledge about the world and Asia than I have. I am not being modest. Your Excellency has participated much more in international affairs than I have. We have been shut up in our own country dealing with our own human problems."
>
> Nehru was not immune to such deference. He was aware that this could be smart tactics, but did not think it was. "He strikes one as a frank and

forthright person, which is rather unusual in the average Communist leader. He speaks with some authority and is receptive to ideas." The result was that the element of uneasiness in Nehru's attitude to China was much weakened.

Before leaving New Delhi Zhou joined Nehru in affirming India's five principles of international intercourse, or *panchasheel:* mutual respect for sovereignty and territorial integrity, nonaggression, noninterference, equality and common benefit, and peaceful coexistence. The communiqué of the meeting expressed hope that the *panchasheel* principles might lead to a solution of the Indochina problem.[17]

Also offstage but of even greater significance for Geneva was a change of government in France. Dulles immediately flew to Paris to urge steadfastness on the new prime minister, Pierre Mendès-France—a recognizably hopeless task, since Mendès-France had pledged to settle the Indochina mess within a month or resign. The acting head of the American delegation in Geneva, U. Alexis Johnson, prepared to meet Dulles. To absolutely no surprise on Johnson's part, Menon stopped in to wish bon voyage and offer some advice. By this time partition of Vietnam was inevitable; the major point of difference between the French and the communists involved the latitude of the dividing line. The Vietminh were pressing for the fourteenth parallel while the French were holding out for the eighteenth. Menon asserted that if the conference settled the other outstanding issues, a compromise on a ceasefire line would surely be possible. Although the Americans probably did not realize the fact, India had put strong pressure on the communists in the past; it might do so again. But the West would have to cooperate in finding a formula for "saving the Communists face." Such a formula offered the only hope for a settlement and provided the best way to reduce Vietminh dependence on China and Russia. Should Geneva succeed, eventually Indochina would become neutral, "more or less like India."[18]

Neither the idea of a French compromise nor the prospect of an Indochina "more or less like India" appealed to Washington, and Johnson had no intention of arguing Menon's brief in France. But by this time American leverage had largely vanished. Paris was determined to cut its losses and get out. The French agreed to division at the seventeenth parallel and to an Indian role, independent of the UN, in supervising the settlement. The Eisenhower administration distanced itself from the deal, refusing to become a party to the accord.

IV

THE FRENCH defeat in Indochina, like the collapse of Chiang Kai-shek in China and the Chinese intervention in Korea, set American planners to reassessing the position of the United States in South Asia. NSC 5409, which contained the results of their labors, was more than the usual updating of previous papers; it pointed American policy in a new direction and laid the groundwork for the decisions of the rest of the 1950s.

South Asia, the paper declared, had emerged as "a major battleground in the cold war." For the first time American strategists described the region's physical assets as vital to the West. The resources themselves had not changed, to be sure, but as the likelihood increased that the West would lose access to Southeast Asia, India acquired larger significance. Geographically India formed the center of the "great land bridge between the countries of Southeast Asia and the Middle East" and commanded the shipping lanes of the Indian Ocean. Geologically India possessed minerals potentially "most useful" to American defense, including fissionable materials of weapons grade. Demographically India constituted a human stockpile that had supported the British empire through two world wars and which retained significance even in the atomic age.

India's primary importance, however, lay in the realm of international politics. In Nehru's foreign policy one element predominated: the desire for peace. Nehru pursued peace as an end in itself, but he also considered it the key to the economic development necessary to make political independence meaningful for India's masses. The desire for peace, more than any other single factor, informed India's neutralist policy. "Nehru and other Indian leaders believe that the only way to avoid war is to avoid alignment with either the Soviet Union and its satellites or the United States and its allies." At the same time, Nehru aspired to leadership in the developing world. Already his diplomats at the United Nations had succeeded, although not single-handedly, in creating a neutralist bloc of some fifteen Asian and African states. The influence Nehru and the Indians wielded among the uncommitted nations made future cooperation with India a matter of "great importance" to the United States.

While Nehru's neutralism at times brought India into conflict with

America, it served American interests for the prime minister to continue in power. He guaranteed stability in India, to the degree anyone could, and he kept Indian Communists in check. Nehru was pivotal for the future of democracy in his country, which in turn had tremendous ramifications for Asia generally. India and China, the world's most populous states, were seeking answers to the basic question confronting all developing nations—how to provide an adequate living for the masses—by diametrically opposed routes. India had chosen a democratic, essentially Western approach; China was taking the communist road. The West could lose the developing world to communism without a shot being fired if India proved less able to deliver economic progress than China.

India's development, therefore, became a matter of great importance to the United States. India did not entirely lack resources for economic progress, but it faced serious problems. Having lost some of the region's best farmland to Pakistan in the 1947 partition, the country could expect continuing difficulty feeding its expanding population. Exports were weak and unlikely to improve soon. Industry remained in "infancy." The next few years appeared crucial to India's future. If the country managed to make a good start overcoming its development problem, it could expect a stable and reasonably prosperous future. But if it failed, economic troubles might well lead to political crisis. The development struggle would largely determine whether India would "continue to develop in the democratic framework" or "fall under communist control." [19]

NSC 5409 might almost have been written by Chester Bowles; its significance rested in the fact that for the first time American officials at the highest level directly and emphatically drew the connection between economic development in Asia and American security. Earlier papers had nodded in the direction of development, but the Truman administration before and the Eisenhower administration until this time had generally viewed foreign economic aid in narrow terms, as something to be doled out in emergencies or in thinly veiled payment for some definite strategic quid pro quo. The Marshall Plan aimed at economic development, to be sure, but it represented, first, a response to the devastation of the war in Europe, and second, a policy directed principally at countries that would become American allies. Moreover, its designers intended the Marshall Plan to render itself unnecessary within several years.

Aid for Asia was another case entirely. Asia's economic problems had developed over millennia; they would take generations to solve. Their solution might never produce the tangible payoff NATO embodied. But American interests now demanded an effort to find that solution. American assistance in economic development might not win India to the West in any overt sense, but development's failure might lose that country to the Soviet system.

V

ALTHOUGH THE authors of NSC 5409 made plain their belief that the United States should do whatever it could to promote India's development, they did not specify any particular level of economic aid. Their diffidence was well founded. Hardly one year in office, the Eisenhower administration could not conveniently drop its campaign slogan, "trade not aid," even though many administration officials recognized that the phrase made more sense as a Republican rallying cry than as a guide to policy. The skepticism in Congress of Nehru's intentions, made clear during the fight for the 1951 wheat loan and the hearings and debate on Bowles' nomination, indicated that any initiative for India would provoke a major tussle. Further, even within the administration the aiders had not yet bested the traders. Treasury Secretary George Humphrey offered the stoutest resistance; Eisenhower himself continued to have doubts, although not so many as to prevent approval of the NSC paper.[20]

Of individuals close to Eisenhower, none pressed the case for aid to countries like India more consistently and enthusiastically than C. D. Jackson. A protégé of Henry Luce of the *Time-Life-Fortune* chain, Jackson had entered the Eisenhower administration as the president's special assistant for psychological warfare. After spending most of 1953 promoting various schemes for "liberating" Eastern Europe, Jackson learned that what he had in mind was more than Eisenhower was willing to hazard, and he shifted his attention to less risky forms of confrontation. By the early part of 1954, he had become a tireless advocate of what he called a "World Economic Plan."

Jackson's proposal, which followed from work by Walt Rostow and Max Millikan at the Center for International Studies at the Massachusetts Institute of Technology, centered on a five-year, ten-billion-dollar program of loans to developing countries. Like the Marshall Plan, Jackson's scheme enlisted generosity for service in the cold war. After Stalin's death the Soviets had launched an economic offensive in the third world, aiming to gain support in India and other nonaligned countries. With the Russians, as Jackson put it, now "muscling in on Santa Claus," the United States had to respond in kind. The World Economic Plan would demonstrate to the uncommitted "that the Free West offers more than the Communist East."[21]

Dulles, considering the same problem, had reached similar conclusions. "I have become personally convinced," he told Jackson, "that it is going to be very difficult to stop Communism in much of the world if we cannot in some way duplicate the intensive Communist effort to raise productive standards." Dulles admitted the communist countries were outpacing the United States in productivity growth by a two-to-one margin. Developing nations like India fared even worse. "That is one reason why Communism has such great appeal in areas where the slogans of 'liberty,' 'freedom' and 'personal dignity' have little appeal."[22]

But Dulles also recognized the political dangers of launching a major initiative for foreign aid. An expanded aid policy could not claim unanimous support within the administration; Congress presented greater difficulties. Dulles did not intend to diminish the administration's store of support on Capitol Hill in the probably vain pursuit of Jackson's ten-billion-dollar plan. "I am 100% behind your type of investment program," he told Jackson, but he added, "As far as I personally am concerned, it is just not practical for me to be a crusader for some particular program, however good it may be."[23]

Eisenhower took longer than Jackson and Dulles to reach the conclusion that American interests in the third world demanded an active aid policy, but by the middle of his first term he was getting close. In a letter to Dulles the president reflected on "the continuing struggle between the Communistic and the free worlds." Under Stalin, Eisenhower said, the Russians had preferred military means to achieve their ends. This strategy had often proved counterproductive, actually working to the benefit of the United States. "So long as they used force and the threat of force, we had the world's natural reaction of fear to aid us in building consolidations of power and strength in order to resist Soviet advances." With Stalin's death things had changed. The Russians had dropped their threatening posture and adopted a more subtle approach, challenging the American position in Asia with "economic weapons."

At first glance, the president said, this shift seemed to play into America's hands. "We have always boasted that the productivity of free men in a free society would overwhelmingly excel the productivity of regimented labor." But certain advantages accrued to the side taking the offensive in economic warfare, just as in conflict by arms. The Soviets could choose the positions they would attack, while the United States, not knowing where the assault would come, had to defend a larger area. As an immediate objective, Eisenhower thought the United States could promote "economic associations" analogous to the military alliances the administration had been pursuing. More effective, however, would be a policy of joint economic planning with the developing countries, to set goals for "the long term."

Eisenhower believed long-range planning would allow the United States to avoid the kind of situation in which it now too often found itself: of having to react to Soviet initiatives with stopgap measures. "While we are busy rescuing Guatemala or assisting Korea and Indo-China, they make great inroads in Burma, Afghanistan and Egypt." Extended programs, of course, would require the ability to commit large sums of money over several years, which in turn necessitated congressional approval. Eisenhower recognized that this went against the grain of much of what the administration had been preaching. "As you know, I am by no means one of those people who believe that the United States can continue to pile up bonded indebtedness and fail to suffer dire consequences both economically and, eventually, in our basic institutions." But he refused to admit that in an economic contest the United States could not afford to defeat the Russians. On the contrary, America could not afford not to win. "If we, at such a time, cannot organize to protect and advance our own interests and those of our friends in the world, then I must say it becomes time to begin thinking of 'despairing of the Republic.' "[24]

Acting on these beliefs, the president sent a message to Congress in the spring of 1955, requesting approval for a $200 million Asian development fund. Describing what he called the "interwoven self-interest" of the United States and the developing nations of the noncommunist world, Eisenhower declared, "The other free nations need the United States, and we need them, if all are to be secure."[25]

The president's package represented a cautious beginning—certainly a far cry from the ten-billion-dollar program Jackson advocated—but even this seemed excessive to Congress, and by the time the development fund emerged from the appropriations process it had been sliced in half. Opposition to the aid bill came primarily from the Republican right, whose representatives objected to the neutralism of countries like India. Senator William Jenner summarized conservative opinion when he demanded, "Why should we give fifty millions to India, when India is admittedly neutral in the irrepressible conflict between human dignity and human slavery?" Criticizing the administration for "worldwide boondoggling," the Indiana Republican decried the Asian fund as indicative that the administration had fallen for "the will-o'-the-wisp nonsense that communism develops among the very poor, and that American spending in poor areas of the world will prevent Communists from getting in." This notion Jenner branded "completely fallacious," and he declared it part of a deliberate communist plot "to help us spend our way to bankruptcy."[26]

VI

WHILE CONGRESS was debating the Asia-aid bill, American policy toward India proceeded on other fronts. Nehru's official biographer describes the prime minister during this period as being at his "zenith of world influence." In the first months of 1955, when Nehru helped organize the Bandung Conference of Asian and African countries, he appeared on the verge of increasing his influence still further. To observers in the Eisenhower administration, the Bandung Conference represented an attempt by Nehru to put substance into the neutralist philosophy he had preached for most of a decade. With a few exceptions— notably China and Pakistan—the Bandung nations eschewed alignment in the cold war, and American officials expected Nehru to use the conference to denounce the evils of superpower diplomacy and promote the formation of a third force between East and West.[27]

Bandung presented the administration with two problems particularly. This first involved the possibility that Nehru's message might catch on and that Bandung would witness the founding of an India-led neutralist bloc. To the degree Nehru's proselytizing succeeded, it would undercut American collective-security efforts in Southeast Asia and the Middle East. The second difficulty arose from the participation of China, invited at Nehru's request. The administration's problem in this case was more political than diplomatic, in that the public spectacle of the Chinese rubbing elbows in all friendliness with India and other non-aligned states would set off congressional conservatives who already confused neutralists with communists. The Bandung Conference coincided not only with Eisenhower's campaign for the Asian development fund—itself something of a counter-Bandung measure—but with a confrontation between China and the United States in the Taiwan Strait, where Beijing was threatening to seize several Nationalist-held islands. While America was again on the edge of war with China, a Sino-Indian lovefest would make Nehru more unpopular than ever.

For several weeks before the conference the administration maneuvered for position. In February the members of SEATO met at Bangkok. Considering Nehru's frequently voiced opposition to the Manila pact, not least because it included Pakistan, many observers interpreted the Bangkok gathering as a preemptive American riposte to the Indonesia conclave. The SEATO session served other purposes, but it did indeed include some anti-Bandung positioning on the part of the American delegation. After considerable persuasion by Dulles the Bangkok conferees agreed to a communiqué stressing the need for cooperation in "combatting the subversive activities of international communism." In addition the Bangkok group sent its greetings to Bandung, with the hope the Indonesia conference would further the goal of ensuring that "free nations would remain free."[28]

As cold war rhetoric this was tame stuff; but that was the point. To denounce Bandung would serve no purpose: most of the attending nations distrusted the United States already. Better to speak softly and politely, and in doing so try subtly to influence the agenda and discussions at Bandung. Dulles, for one, found the work of the Bangkok meeting quite satisfactory. On his departure from Thailand the secretary cabled Eisenhower, "I believe that our message of greeting to the Afro-Asian conference is a good touch which, if properly played, can have an excellent propaganda value, and to some extent put that conference on the spot."[29]

As Bandung drew nearer the administration considered further steps in response to what obviously would be one of the year's international highlights. In the last week of March, Nelson Rockefeller, C. D. Jackson's successor at the White House, proposed a major presidential address on Asia as a means of stealing Bandung's thunder. Dulles rejected Rockefeller's proposal. As the secretary reasoned, any speech by the president treating the issues scheduled for discussion at Bandung would have to take place at least a week before the Indonesia conference "to avoid being regarded as a purely propaganda effort and having the appearance of interference from an outside party." Insufficient time remained to meet such a deadline.

While opposing a full-dress speech, Dulles suggested that a "less-formal Presidential statement on a number of more specific topics" might have "a very useful effect." As one method of packaging such a statement the secretary recommended planting questions among friendly reporters at one of Eisenhower's upcoming press conferences. As another option the president might touch on Bandung-related topics in any of the several casual talks he would be giving during the next two weeks. Undoubtedly the Bandung Conference would condemn colonialism; Dulles recommended Eisenhower reiterate America's longstanding support for self-determination. Economic development was another likely theme at Bandung; the secretary advocated making a strong pitch for the Asian development fund.[30]

Dulles' primary domestic worry regarding Bandung involved its impact on conservative opinion in Congress; but the administration had problems with liberals as well. The chief complaint from the left was that the administration was paying too little attention to the conference and to the large portion of humanity it represented. Democrat Adam Clayton Powell, Jr. charged the president with "indifference"—albeit "benevolent indifference"—toward Bandung and said the administration could ignore "a conference representing three-fifths of the earth's population" only at the peril of the American people. The New York congressman asked why the administration was not sending an observer, dismissing as sophistry the argument that the United States had not been invited. America had sent uninvited observers to conferences in the past, and other nations were not allowing non-invitation to prevent their sending unofficial representatives. To remedy the administration's neglect, Powell declared he himself would go to Bandung. "I hope that my presence there as an American and above all as a member of the colored peoples of the United States will be of some value for the peace, understanding, and brotherhood of our world."[31]

Despite suggestions from moderate Republicans that the administration might save itself considerable trouble if it upstaged Powell by dispatching a representative, Dulles held firm. Eisenhower tried to keep out of the issue entirely. Earlier the president had responded to a question whether he would appoint an observer by pleading ignorance. "I don't even know whether we have been invited to send observers. It is a question you would have to ask the State Department; I am not really up on it." As the conference opened, Eisenhower avoided direct comment, speaking instead through the secretary. Following a meeting with Eisenhower, Dulles released a statement declaring that the president had expressed the hope the Bandung Conference would heed "the universal longing of the peoples of the world" and exert "a practical influence for peace where peace is now in grave jeopardy."[32]

VII

DULLES' LAST comment referred particularly to the Taiwan Strait affair, which had reached the crisis stage by the time Nehru, Zhou, and the representatives of twenty-seven other countries headed for Bandung. Zhou almost did not make it. An Air India plane chartered to carry the Chinese delegation from Beijing to Jakarta crashed en route, and early reports, which later proved false, placed the Chinese premier on the passenger list. Less susceptible of disproof were rumors that the crash was the work of Nationalist agents, perhaps acting with the assistance of the CIA.[33]

After his death-defying entrance Zhou stole the show. Expected by many to take a hard line against the imperialists and their running dogs —including those of the latter in attendance—the Chinese premier instead proved the soul of moderation. In his opening speech he "laid the foundation," as one perceptive witness put it, "for a feeling which continued to grow among the Conference's delegation: that he was reasonable, conciliatory, and sincerely anxious to establish the genuineness of China's peaceful inclinations." Affirming the right of all nations to choose their own destinies, he surprised some delegates by asserting China's respect even for "the way of life and political and economic systems chosen by the American people." At crucial moments in debates he acted as mediator, to the point of accepting scarcely disguised criticism of the Soviet Union. And he provided the highlight of the gathering by defusing the Taiwan Strait crisis with an announcement that the Chinese government was prepared to negotiate its differences with the United States—"especially the question of relaxing tension in the Taiwan area."[34]

By contrast, Nehru made a less than favorable impression. The Indians in attendance put the best face on the affair. Krishna Menon later said, "The Bandung spirit was Nehru." C. S. Jha wrote that "Nehru's career reached its peak with the Bandung Conference." Jha conceded that Zhou "created a great impression on the conference by his courtesy, moderation and reasonableness," but the Indian diplomat claimed Zhou was "secretly resentful of Nehru's prominence in Bandung." Subimal Dutt commented that Zhou "did not seem quite sure of his position" and that "Nehru took him as a younger brother." More detached observers, however, noted that Nehru was off his form. An American scholar well-disposed toward India remarked,

> The controversies between Mohammed Ali and Nehru were more bitter than ever, and both the Indonesian and Ceylonese delegations were antagonized by what they regarded as overbearing and patronizing attitudes on the parts of Nehru and Menon.

Zhou resented the younger-brother treatment. In a later conversation with a Ceylonese diplomat the Chinese premier said, "I have met Chiang Kai-shek, I have met American generals, but I have never met a more arrogant man than Mr. Nehru." Nehru's official biographer, Gopal, granted that the Indian prime minister aroused "considerable hostility" among the delegates.[35]

Even so, the conference succeeded in achieving some of Nehru's goals. By encouraging a conciliatory attitude on Zhou's part it helped prevent another Sino-American war. By encouraging Beijing to look to Asia it facilitated a Sino-Soviet split. Most important, by demonstrating that the nations of Asia and Africa had constructive words to say to each other it laid the foundations for the nonaligned movement that would flourish in the 1960s.

VIII

FROM THE American perspective, the most significant immediate outcome of the conference was the opening it provided for a solution to the Taiwan Strait problem. Dulles declared Zhou's statement of interest in negotiations a favorable sign, although he declined to give the Chinese leader any credit. Instead the secretary congratulated the Bandung nations for making Zhou see reason. "The Bandung conference, as we had hoped, seems to have exerted a restraint on the Chinese Communists." Ignoring the fact that the administration had frowned on the idea of the conference beforehand, especially on China's participation, Dulles added, "I had always felt that it would be salutary if the Chinese Communists were confronted with the opinion of the free nations of Asia."[36]

In a broader sense as well, the administration was satisfied with the outcome. Washington had feared an outpouring of anti-Americanism; in fact restraint marked the discussions. With the exception of attacks on Israel, Dulles told Eisenhower, the United States might have felt quite comfortable in Indonesia. Indeed the final communiqué was nearly "a document which we ourselves could subscribe to." Even the expected references to colonialism were "in accord with what we feel in our hearts," though allied sensitivities prevented the administration from voicing such sentiments. Dulles considered this favorable result principally the work of "a group of friendly Asian nations" that believed in "association with the West."[37]

The administration could claim some credit for the good work of those "friendly" nations, of whom the most important were Pakistan and Ceylon. ("Pakistan made hell," Menon muttered.) A report to the National Security Council several weeks after Bandung summarized American efforts regarding the conference:

> Following a U.S. decision to attempt to influence the Bandung Conference by encouraging friendly countries to participate and supplying guidance as appropriate to those representatives, the Prime Ministers of Pakistan and Ceylon played particularly helpful roles in supporting free world positions.

C. D. Jackson as usual put the issue more colloquially when he referred to "heavy work by Allen Dulles' boys" in encouraging the conference to look as critically at the East as at the West.[38]

Regarding India in particular the administration was no less pleased.

Dulles declared Bandung "a very severe reverse" for Nehru, entailing "a great loss of prestige." Nehru had gone to Bandung hoping to gain converts to his neutralist philosophy and to stake his claim for the leadership of Asia. He had failed on both counts. Dulles explained to Eisenhower's cabinet that on the Asian leadership issue Nehru had proved unable to adapt to the pressures that developed at the conference. On the neutralist question Nehru had met no greater success. The "friendly Asian countries," Dulles said, had "put on an amazing performance at Bandung with a teamwork and coordination of strategy which was highly gratifying." As a result, Nehru's plans for a coherent third force in world affairs had foundered, while the countries leaning toward the West had gained "a new sense of self-reliance and self-confidence."[39]

Several days after Dulles' summary to the cabinet Eisenhower received another report from Bandung. The administration had not known what to make of Adam Clayton Powell's private diplomacy, beyond chalking it up to political grandstanding. Neither had the delegates to the conference, who were baffled by Powell's penchant for handing out cigars at the least provocation. The president continued to wonder whether to take Powell seriously in an interview early in May, when the New York congressman declared that the major purpose of his trip to Bandung had been to provide "living proof" of the falsity of the communist claim that Negroes in the United States were oppressed. The communists, he asserted, had intended to make American treatment of colored people a centerpiece of the meeting. As evidence, he cited plants by the Chinese and their friends of "stooges" at "all the press conferences," with instructions to ask "embarrassing questions." But his presence had given the lie to the communists' allegations. Powell did provide one significant piece of intelligence by offering an assessment of India's performance at Bandung that essentially matched Dulles'. Nehru and Menon, he declared, had been shown to be "bitter men," and the conference proved "a severe defeat" for India.[40]

IX

WHILE PLEASED that Bandung had gone as well as it had for American interests, the Eisenhower administration realized the issues Bandung raised would not go away. Already there was talk of a sequel;

Washington began to prepare its response. While the Soviets were angling for an invitation to Bandung II, Dulles plotted a different course.

In the autumn of 1955 the secretary proposed to Harold Macmillan, Britain's chancellor of the exchequer, a meeting of Britain, France, and the United States to address the question of colonialism. Dulles intended this meeting to produce a clear statement of Western aims in non-self-governing regions—a message that would "catch the imagination of the world and take the initiative away from the Soviet Communists." Macmillan, recognizing the drift of Dulles' remarks, responded, "What you are proposing is, in effect, a Bandung Conference in reverse." Dulles agreed, and the two spoke at considerable length about the project. The secretary had broached the topic previously with the French, but he only began developing his idea with Macmillan. The latter was intrigued and suggested that their two governments line up outside consultants who could provide "fertile ideas" to exploit.[41]

Actually the secretary of state had more in mind than he indicated to Macmillan. His counter-Bandung scheme was designed not only to neutralize the neutralists on the colonial question but to flush out the British and French on the same subject. A short while after his talk with Macmillan, Dulles telephoned Dean Rusk, formerly assistant secretary of state for Far Eastern affairs and now president of the Rockefeller Foundation. In asking for Rockefeller support, Dulles explained that an essential feature of a counter-Bandung would be an agreement by London and Paris to "outline plans for self-determination." Two days later Dulles further explained his reasoning to Undersecretary of State Herbert Hoover, Jr.

> As I think you know, I have over recent months, and indeed, years, taken the occasion to press the British to take a certain leadership in developing the policy of independence for the colonial peoples which would enable us to take the initiative away from the Soviets and the Communists in this matter.

On the whole, Dulles said, the United States had a good record on colonialism. But much work remained—which was the point of his counter-Bandung project. Dulles hoped to persuade the Europeans "to get together in a dramatic way to lay out an independence program." He admitted success would require great effort and some luck. "However, I think the basic idea is sound and would capture the imagination of the peoples of the world if it were handled right."[42]

Through the end of 1955 and the beginning of 1956 the conference Dulles proposed took shape. Rusk brought in the Council on Foreign Relations as well as the Rockefeller Foundation, creating what Dulles described as "an able and well-balanced group." Macmillan convinced the Royal Institute of International Affairs at Chatham House to contribute. At the end of January Macmillan described the attitudes of his colleagues Anthony Eden and Selwyn Lloyd: "The Prime Minister and Foreign Secretary know how things stand and are much interested in bringing your beneficent project to fruition."[43]

But the fruit never ripened. Perhaps sensing that Dulles wanted to push them further on the colonial question than they desired to go, the British began to lose interest. In the spring of 1956 Rusk reported that while the American study group was "quite active" and was nearing "a crystallization of ideas," he detected foot-dragging at Chatham House. He told Dulles he would be going to London soon and would attempt to find out whether the British intended to follow through on the project.[44]

Despite Rusk's attempt to pin them down, the British continued to equivocate, until Egypt's Nasser nationalized the Suez Canal Company. At that point whatever interest Eden and Lloyd may have had in discussing timetables for imperial devolution vanished; and the counter-Bandung committees adjourned sine die.

X

ZHOU'S BANDUNG offer to negotiate ended the Taiwan Strait crisis and set in motion a train of events leading to a reduction in tensions in East Asia. This loosening spilled over into U.S.–Indian relations, although the relaxation did not immediately show at the surface.

As they had for years, conservatives in the United States complained of an Indian double standard in international relations; they alleged in particular that Nehru and his associates judged the United States and its allies more harshly than they criticized the communists. In February 1955 *U.S. News and World Report* ran a feature article on Krishna Menon, describing him as Nehru's "leading troublemaker." At the UN, the article declared, Menon rarely missed an opportunity to blast American policy, while he seldom found fault with communist actions. The journal quoted an anonymous American official: "On any big problem that comes up, he is just like a mosquito that gets in everybody's way when they are trying to repair an automobile. He can't do anything to help—but he can do plenty to get everybody annoyed." Speaking in its own voice, the magazine said of Menon, "He contends he isn't a Communist, but he follows the party line."[45]

In the summer of 1955 Nehru visited the Soviet Union, marking a warming between New Delhi and Moscow that constituted one of the decade's notable diplomatic developments. Nehru's turning to the Soviets followed in no small part from a desire to offset the American alliance with Pakistan, although he took pains to distinguish between the two relationships. The prime minister told his Russian hosts: "Countries make pacts and alliances through fear of some other country or countries. Let our coming together be because we like each other and wish to cooperate and not because we dislike others and wish to do them injury."[46]

To Indian observers like K. P. S. Menon, who declared that Nehru "came, saw, and conquered," the Moscow visit signaled a triumph for nonalignment; but American commentators interpreted things differently. *Newsweek* reported the trip and toasts in detail and asserted that Nehru, to judge from appearances, was leading India straight into the Russian camp. Conceding that the Indian prime minister was probably too clever to be taken in completely, *Newsweek* predicted Nehru would "go on parroting Moscow's line without swallowing it whole."[47]

Later that year Soviet leaders Khrushchev and Bulganin reciprocated Nehru's visit, touring India in a tumultuous progress that Nehru himself described as a "feast of friendliness." Of equal significance, the Soviet politicians were accompanied by a group of industrial experts come to oversee preparations for construction of a steel plant Moscow had pledged to fund. The American press provided thorough coverage. *U.S. News* summarized the popular view in a skeptical article under the headline: "Where Reds Get Red Carpet." The *New York Times* resisted getting carried away by atmospherics, but the paper could not deny serious concern that the economic and political agreements the Khrushchev visit showcased aligned Nehru "so closely with Soviet policies as to put a large question mark behind his professed neutrality."[48]

At the level of government to government relations, however, Washington and New Delhi avoided major difficulties. Dulles' defense of Portugal in that country's dispute with India over Goa created a stir, but otherwise things went smoothly. During the several months after

Bandung the Indian foreign ministry facilitated negotiations between Washington and Beijing; one concrete result for the United States was the release of several Americans held prisoner in China since the Korean War. The summer of 1955 brought the first summit conference of the great powers since World War II, and the meeting inaugurated a minor era of good feeling in global relations. After the Geneva summit Nehru wrote Eisenhower conveying congratulations on his statesmanship. At the same time he invited the president to India.[49]

Nehru's invitation touched off some bureaucratic skirmishing within the administration. Eisenhower wanted to go; he told Dulles India was one of two countries—the other being Mexico—that "in a sense had a status of their own," and he added that he was "particularly anxious" to ensure good relations with Nehru. Dulles disliked the idea. The secretary distrusted summiteering in principle, and although he had failed to talk the president out of Geneva he was not about to let him go to New Delhi. He reminded Eisenhower of the many and burdensome duties the president already bore. To get in the habit of making goodwill trips to countries like India would "unbearably increase" his responsibilities. After the president reluctantly agreed that Dulles was probably right, the secretary concluded his argument with a suggestion that Eisenhower ask Nehru to come to America—where, Dulles no doubt calculated, he could more easily control the proceedings.[50]

While Eisenhower thought this one over, the new American ambassador to India, John Sherman Cooper, offered his opinion. Cooper was a political appointee, a former senator from Kentucky and a member of the liberal Republican faction Eisenhower constantly sought to cultivate. Cooper had made a favorable impression in India during his six months on the job; in July the editor of the *Hindu Times* told American officials at the UN that with the possible exception of Chester Bowles, no American had ever "captured the confidence and admiration" of the Indian people as thoroughly as Cooper.[51]

Bypassing Dulles, Cooper took his case directly to Eisenhower. He urged the president to come. The ambassador admitted the difficulties a presidential trip to India would entail, but such a visit, he said, would be "of incalculable value" in strengthening U.S.–Indian relations.

> It would give you the opportunity to destroy in this important part of the world the Communist slogan which has many believers, that the U.S.

wants war. It would give new strength and determination to those who are standing up against Communism. I think, from the long term point of view, its greatest effect would be a new and correct interpretation of the purposes and the actions of our country, which have been so twisted by Communists and others. These people are hungry for leadership, and your coming could conceivably set in motion events which would not only help the United States but the countries that are striving everywhere to hold freedom.[52]

Bureaucratically, of course, the contest between Dulles and Cooper was no contest at all. Whatever the merits of Cooper's arguments—not to mention the strength of his appeal to Eisenhower's vanity—Dulles held the edge in proximity and clout. In the first week of August Eisenhower sent Nehru a letter, drafted in Dulles' office, politely declining the prime minister's invitation to visit. "I can assure you that there are few things I would rather do," Eisenhower said. But the press of a president's many responsibilities did not allow him to make state visits, "however personally tempting" these might be. Noting that a prime minister had fewer constitutional duties and reminding Nehru that India had already received the vice president and the secretary of state as guests, Eisenhower asked Nehru if he might find time to come to America.[53]

Nehru refused to be put off easily. "I would like to think," he wrote, "that the reply you have sent me is not a final one and that you will give some further consideration to my request." The prime minister asserted that one of his purposes in inviting the president to India was to give the Indian people the privilege of meeting him, and vice versa. Nehru acknowledged that a prime minister's chores required less time than a president's, and he said he appreciated Eisenhower's invitation and hoped to take advantage of the courtesy at some point. Unfortunately, with India's parliament soon to convene, his calendar had no openings until the next summer.[54]

Nothing of substance came of this exchange of letters, but they were significant nonetheless. On each side the tone of the correspondence indicated friendliness and a desire to get to know the other better. It is impossible to imagine a similar exchange between Truman and Nehru after their strained meeting in 1949. From the American perspective, Eisenhower no doubt desired to use his charm, of which he was not oblivious, to improve relations between Washington and New Delhi. The president did not expect to lessen Nehru's attachment to neutralism or win India to an alliance with the United States. That issue, quite obviously, had already been settled. But within the framework of the differing American and Indian approaches to world affairs, Eisenhower sought a basis for cooperation, if only at a personal level.

Others in the administration helped shape Eisenhower's belief in the potential of personal diplomacy. Cooper contributed, of course. So did UN Ambassador Henry Cabot Lodge, who repeatedly argued that the president's popularity constituted a not-so-secret weapon for use against the communists in the struggle for the third world. In September 1955 Eisenhower suffered a heart attack—which put an end for the time being to any thoughts of an Indo–American summit. From New York Lodge wrote to Eisenhower to describe "the emotion and the outpouring of friendly feelings which the news about you caused at the United Nations." The representatives of America's allies, as anticipated, expressed their sympathy. But so also did delegates from nonaligned states, notably Krishna Menon of India. "The world, in all truth, not only admires you and regards you as essential," Lodge declared, "the world truly loves you."[55]

(Lodge's effusion was partly hype, but not entirely. In Moscow K. P. S. Menon wrote in his diary:

> Autumn has come, bringing with it the fear that the midsummer night's dream of Geneva may not last after all. The principal actor at the Geneva conference, Eisenhower, has been taken ill. The gods seem jealous of any improvement in the affairs of men, for just as Roosevelt was taken away on the eve of the San Francisco conference and Churchill had a stroke soon after his summit speech in the summer of 1953, so Eisenhower has now had a heart attack.

Menon went on to predict that with Eisenhower, the man of peace, out of action, Dulles and the militarists would recapture the initiative in America policy.[56])

Earlier Lodge had related the great impact a personal appearance by Eisenhower at the UN had had on representatives of the neutral nations. "The reaction to your visit here was tremendous." The president had impressed the delegates with what Lodge called his "encyclopedic knowledge" and his "effectiveness as a world statesman." Lodge added, "You also flattered them tremendously by making them feel they were really 'in the club.' " Throughout his term at the UN Lodge stressed the importance of personal diplomacy. He advocated goodwill trips by ranking government officials to nonaligned countries, to counter claims that America cared only for its anticommunist allies; and he advocated a higher profile for the president in relations with Asia and Africa, because Eisenhower was "the very antithesis" of the ugly-American caricature so many residents of the third world took for truth. In 1956, Lodge passed along further evidence of Eisenhower's popularity in Asia, particularly in India. At a UN reception an Indian delegate had buttonholed Lodge to say he had polled his international colleagues to determine their preference in the approaching American presidential election. Overwhelmingly, the Indian representative said, they had chosen Eisenhower. "They all feel that President Eisenhower has the touch." The delegate made a particular point of including Nehru as one of Eisenhower's admirers; he said the prime minister hoped to see the president returned to office.[57]

XI

EISENHOWER'S HEART attack precluded a trip to India during the latter part of 1955 and all of the next year. But he did want to see Nehru again—they had met on the prime minister's 1949 visit to America—so he decided to renew his invitation to Nehru to come to the United States. At the beginning of February 1956 Eisenhower told Dulles to check into the details of a tour for the prime minister. The secretary replied that although the Indian ambassador had earlier indicated a summer visit would be best, more recently he had suggested late autumn. Dulles thought the nearing elections had caused the change of mind. "Apparently they feel that Nehru is a rather controversial character in this country and that it might be a mistake for him to come here near the height of a political campaign."[58]

The Indians were right about Nehru being controversial. As noted above, the longstanding suspicion among American conservatives that "neutralist" was Hindi for "fellow-traveler" had been reinforced by the Indo-Soviet exchange of hospitality and the initiation of Russian economic aid. Even as administration officials considered how to contain the fallout from Khrushchev's Indian tour at the end of 1955, rumors surfaced of a new and potentially far more serious development. While in New Delhi Khrushchev had given Nehru a pair of Ilyushin commercial aircraft; at the same time he reportedly offered to provide bombers at half the price India was preparing to pay for British Canberras.[59]

At this time the Eisenhower administration was contending with the aftershocks of the acceptance of a similar offer of Soviet military assistance by Egypt's Nasser; for Nehru to sign a weapons pact with Moscow would throw Washington's India policy into complete disarray. Where Dulles had dispatched assistants to try to talk Nasser out of taking up the Russian offer, he made the trip to New Delhi himself.

In his meeting with Nehru, Dulles conceded India's moral and political right to purchase weapons to defend its interests; he could hardly do otherwise in the face of America's arming of Pakistan. But he wanted the prime minister to know the effect an arms pact with Moscow would have in the United States.

> You can buy planes from the British. You can buy planes from us. I cannot see why you should buy planes from the Russians knowing that it would make it almost impossible for the United States to carry on its efforts to assist you materially in your second five-year plan. That will be hard enough anyway, and this deal with Russia, I feel, would make it impossible.

Dulles added that of course Nehru recognized better than he what India's interests required, and he said he did not want the prime minister to feel the United States was trying to coerce India in any way. "I know you will not change your attitude because of foreign pressure, and I do not mention the subject in that spirit." Still, Dulles said, the prime minister must realize the probable consequences of an arms pact with Moscow.

For a combination of reasons, undoubtedly including a desire not to antagonize Washington and jeopardize American aid, Nehru opted against Soviet weapons; in this respect Dulles' trip proved a success. It was also worthwhile in providing the secretary of state greater insight into Indian thinking. "We really took our hair down," Dulles told Eisenhower. Pakistan and the American relationship with that country dominated the discussion. Until this time Dulles had believed that many of India's complaints against the United States, especially on the Pakistan question, were the expressions of extremists or the result of anti-American enthusiasm whipped up, as he put it at the time of the 1954 arms deal, "by Communist propagandists, at least one of whose number might be found in a position of importance on almost every large Indian newspaper."

Talking to Nehru, Dulles discovered the sentiment ran far deeper. In his summary of the conversation Dulles wrote,

> The one distinct impression that I gained is of their almost pathological fear of Pakistan. I, of course, knew they did not like our alliance with, and armament program for, Pakistan, but I never appreciated before the full depth of their feeling.

Dulles had assumed India's far greater size and economic strength afforded a sense of immunity from Pakistani attack. His discussions with Indian officials changed his mind.

> They feel that Pakistan, or at least West Pakistan, is essentially a military state, largely run by the Army, that they are a martial people, that they are fanatically dedicated to Islam and may develop the urge to attack India or at least to try to take Kashmir or parts of it by force.

Dulles could not help adding that he suspected at least some of India's fear of Pakistan over Kashmir resulted from a "guilty conscience," in that India itself had used force in the Kashmir dispute, flouting UN directives in the process.[60]

Dulles did not believe the United States could go so far toward soothing Indian feelings as to alter substantially the American relationship with Pakistan. That country, the hinge connecting the Baghdad pact with SEATO, mattered too much in American strategic planning. But he did think the administration might take greater pains to provide "maximum assurance" to India that American weapons for Pakistan would be used for defensive purposes only and not against India.

In the course of their talks Dulles relayed to Nehru Eisenhower's invitation to come to the United States at a time convenient for the prime minister. Nehru replied noncommittally, reminding Dulles he too had elections to worry about. The secretary sensed, however, Nehru was playing hard to get. "My strong hunch," he told Eisenhower, "is that he will accept."[61]

Dulles guessed right. Nehru scheduled a trip for the first part of December, safely after the American elections.

XII

BEFORE DECEMBER and Nehru arrived, the world had to stumble its way through two major crises, both of which created friction between the United States and India. Following Nasser's seizure of the Suez Canal in July 1956, Washington and New Delhi agreed on the necessity of preventing the diplomatic struggle over the waterway from escalating into war. But the two countries pursued their common objective by different means. At the hastily convened London conference in August, American and Indian representatives found themselves working at cross-purposes. When Dulles proposed a settlement based on the Suez treaty of 1888, Krishna Menon immediately attacked the plan as an effort "to repeal the act of nationalization," which, as Menon asserted and Dulles admitted, lay within Egypt's legal competence. Menon later declared Dulles "killed the London Conference," accusing the secretary of playing "a double game" by saying one thing to the world in public and something else to the British in private. Dulles found Menon as slippery as ever. He told Eisenhower the Indian diplomat seemed to be coordinating his activities with the Soviets, at the expense of a peaceful solution. Dulles added that India's proposals sounded "all right as generalities" but were fatally wanting in substance. On the crucial question of international supervision, Menon's resolutions offered only "pure scenery."[62]

As is well known, the diplomats failed and war came at the end of October. Almost immediately suggestions emerged at the UN for a joint effort by the United States and India to separate the warring parties and sponsor negotiations toward a settlement. In Washington Eisenhower met with Dulles and Herbert Hoover, Jr. to consider the plan. Dulles disliked the idea of American responsibility for finding a solution that might not exist, even if India accepted part of the burden. He preferred that the president serve with Nehru, if at all, on a sort of board of appeals, leaving to the disputants the first try at a compromise. Hoover shared Dulles' caution, and he urged the president to wait for the smoke to clear before making any decision, since, as he put it, there was "still bloodshed ahead." Eisenhower wondered aloud whether it might be possible to spread the diplomatic risk by inviting other world leaders to join him and Nehru, but Dulles scuttled this idea by pointing out that the Russians would be the first to accept any such offer.[63]

Although the administration decided against collaboration with the Indians, choosing unilateral pressure instead, and despite the differences at London between Dulles and Menon, by November Americans generally were finding little to fault in Nehru's handling of the Suez affair. By that time, however, they had another cause for complaint.

Substantively, the United States took no more forceful action against the Soviet invasion of Hungary than did India; but while Washington lost no time censuring the Russians in the most uncompromising terms, New Delhi waffled. At the United Nations Krishna Menon described the Hungarian crisis as a domestic affair and—acting on his own, as it turned out—abstained on a resolution condemning the Soviets. Nehru stood by Menon, declaring that his government required more information before speaking definitively; only later did he criticize the Soviet Union in tones approximating those he was using against Britain, France, and Israel for their attack on Egypt.[64]

To millions of Americans Nehru's performance seemed the most blatant indication yet of a double standard in Indian diplomacy. Conservative American critics of Nehru—and of the administration's India policy—found their opinions confirmed. More significantly, even Nehru's liberal defenders were left shaking their heads in sorrow. The *New Republic,* which at times came close to contending that Nehru could do no wrong and Dulles no right, offered the clearest postmortem: "The conjunction of the Suez and Hungarian crises caught India with its double standard exposed as it never had been before."[65]

XIII

AGAINST THIS backdrop, Nehru's visit—postponed, ironically to avoid controversy—finally took place. In advance of Nehru's arrival Eisenhower received much advice on what to expect. Paul Hoffman, millionaire automobile executive, former Marshall Plan administrator, early promoter of Eisenhower's candidacy, and a special envoy sent by the president in 1953 on an unsuccessful effort to solve the Kashmir problem, described Nehru as "supersensitive both as to himself and his country, rather ready to take offense at what he considers a slight, even though one is not intended." Yet the prime minister was nobody's fool. "Nehru's attitude toward Communism is worth knowing. He is under no illusions about it, recognizing both its limitations and the menace it carries for all free people." Another view came from Henry Wallace, the former vice president who migrated over the years from the Republicans to the Democrats to the Progressives and back to the Republicans to support Eisenhower's reelection. Wallace had known Nehru for some time but still found him puzzling. He was, Wallace said, "sufficiently oriental to go two directions at the same time very politely." Wallace also thought Nehru "somewhat cold." Norman Cousins, editor of *Saturday Review*, disagreed. "Despite all reports to the contrary," Cousins declared, "the Prime Minister is not a difficult man with whom to have rapport. He likes and responds to friendliness." Cousins described a conversation with Nehru.

> "A truly friendly man," he told me with respect to the effectiveness of emissaries, "is one of the most remarkable things in the world. You can tell a genuinely friendly man the moment he comes into the room, the moment he gets up to speak, the moment he comes toward you. No one can fail to respond to him."

Cousins suggested that "a few of the right touches" would go far toward winning Nehru's friendship. "He would rather swap stories about his grandchildren than anything else."[66]

From such intelligence Eisenhower formed some definite opinions regarding Nehru and Indians generally. The president's estimate of Krishna Menon has already been described. Though Menon seemed an extreme case, Eisenhower thought deviousness a bit of a national trait. "I don't know about these Indians," the president told his press secretary, James Hagerty. "They are funny people and I don't know how far we can actually trust them." Regarding Nehru personally, Eisenhower believed reason mattered less than emotion in the prime minister's approach to diplomacy. "I am struck," he commented to Dulles, "by the amount of evidence we have that Nehru seems to be more often swayed by personality than by logical argument. He seems to be intensely personal in his whole approach."[67]

Eisenhower's discussions with Nehru reinforced these opinions. Reflecting on the talks in his memoirs, Eisenhower wrote that he liked the prime minister and considered him deeply committed to the well-being of the Indian people. Nehru, he said, was "essential to his nation." But he was also a riddle. "Nehru was not easy to understand. Few people are, but his was a personality of unusual contradictions." Of these contradictions Eisenhower found the persistent double standard 'most striking. In part the president attributed the disparity between Nehru's reactions to the transgressions of the West and his responses to those of the communists to the prime minister's firsthand experience of British misrule. But the full explanation appeared to have deeper roots.

> As an Asian from a less-developed nation, it is possible that Mr. Nehru felt more resentment of an intangible Western condescension toward his people than he felt toward any specific act of violence that either East or West might commit. Life, after all, is cheaper in the Orient, or so it would appear; recognition as equals by the "white" race is not. Perhaps Mr. Nehru, despite his excellent Western education and flawless English, was able to identify with the Soviets at times as "fellow Asians," a point that came out continually in his hope that the West could do something to make the Soviets feel they "were not being looked down upon."[68]

For all Eisenhower's amateur psychology, the two leaders got on quite well. Their conversations were, as the president remarked afterward, "very friendly," with "no arguments or even informal debates of any kind." Nehru began with his impressions of the Suez affair. While the prime minister agreed with most conventional views regarding the causes of the conflict in the Middle East, he held a higher opinion of the Egyptian president than did many persons in the West. "Nasser is the best of the group of Egyptian Army officers and others for whom he is the spokesman," Nehru commented. "Under present conditions, if Nasser were removed there would come into power someone who would be more inimical to the West and more unreasonable in his actions." Nehru said Nasser had been "immature" at the time he had taken power but had "come quite a way" in a few years. Nehru believed the United States must not pay too much attention to the rhetoric Nasser and other Arab leaders customarily used. Arab public figures tended "to get excited" in front of crowds, and they "always talked in extravagant terms under such circumstances."

When Eisenhower described the American side of the events leading up to the nationalization of the canal company, especially the breakdown of negotiations for financing the Aswan Dam, Nehru seemed, in the president's opinion, "astonished." Eisenhower said he hoped the prime minister would use his influence with Nasser to bring peace to the Middle East and get the canal—whose closure, Nehru had pointed out, was costing India dearly—back into service. For America's part, the president stated that his administration would continue to pressure the British, French, and Israelis toward peace.

Regarding the situation in Hungary, Eisenhower discreetly alluded to American criticism of Nehru's slowness in criticizing the Russians by saying the prime minister's "stock had gone up" in the United States when he "finally" protested Soviet actions. The president added that it would serve the interests of U.S.–Indian relations if the prime minister repeated such remarks either in a public address to the American people or in a press conference. And it would be "helpful" if India offered to accept at least a token number of Hungarian refugees.

Nehru declined to commit himself on this matter, but he did offer his opinion on the importance of recent events in Hungary. The uprising in Budapest, he said, rang "the death knell of international communism." For a decade the communists had had an opportunity to convert Hungary to their way of thinking and demonstrate the claimed superiority of communism as an organizing political and economic principle. But they had failed so spectacularly that thousands of people had chosen death rather than submission to this bankrupt ideology. The prime minister believed the uprising in Hungary came as "a terrible shock" to Soviet leaders, who now had to reappraise their basic approach to foreign policy. Embarrassed by the necessity to use force, the Russians would take a less militant line in the future.

The Kremlin's intervention in Hungary, Nehru continued, was a "great blunder," and it afforded the democratic states an opening they must not pass up. Communist parties in the West and in countries like India were "badly damaged" by the Russians' heavy-handedness. The communists were losing support as they tried to justify, "with very little success," Moscow's actions. The democracies ought to seize the opportunity to strengthen the faith and hope of people who naturally preferred independence but who had been "at least partially misled by the communists' doctrine."

Turning to the other great communist power, China, Nehru again made the case for bringing the Chinese into the council of nations. Time would diminish the strength of the Nationalists, he said. Eventually, almost inevitably, Taiwan would fall to Beijing. Reality demanded that a government controlling the affairs of 600 million people not remain an outcast forever.

On the broad question of India's philosophy of foreign relations, Nehru went to considerable trouble to explain the reasons for his government's nonalignment. He told Eisenhower he used the term "neutral" in the traditional sense of maintaining aloofness from military combinations; neutrality for India did not imply indifference between forms of government based on dictatorship and those premised on the fundamental dignity of man. India might logically fear attack from only two countries: China and the Soviet Union. In each case the actual possibility of assault seemed slim. The mountains in the north provided protection and India, to be frank about the matter, offered little incentive for invasion. His country was too poor to covet and too large to occupy. It posed no threat to the Russians or the Chinese, and if a world war broke out the communists would have problems enough elsewhere without worrying about India. Finally, he remarked that India shared 1800 miles of border with China; to fortify this frontier would exhaust the country and render impossible the elevation of living standards necessary to prevent a communist takeover from within. For his country to join an alliance, Nehru concluded, would weaken not only India but the group to which India attached. Since India could not afford to defend itself, its allies would have to bear the burden.

Nehru proceeded on a tour d'horizon of international relations, from Vietnam to Germany; but Pakistan, not surprisingly, elicited his most extensive and fervent remarks. To Eisenhower Nehru still seemed "unquestionably bitter" at the British for partitioning India, and he appeared "particularly resentful" of the fact that the Pakistanis had gained independence not by their own efforts but on the coattails of Indian nationalists. India and Pakistan, Nehru said, had organized themselves on different lines. India had chosen a secular model of government; Pakistan adopted one religiously based. The difference made disputes between the two countries—over Kashmir, for example—especially vexing and contributed to popular fears in India of a Pakistani attack. This fear, moreover, inflamed by Pakistani propaganda, created the great resentment in India against the United States for supplying weapons to Pakistan.

Eisenhower reassured the prime minister that the United States had taken measures to prevent aggressive employment of American weapons. Though the Pakistanis received guns, the president said, they did not get much ammunition. Further, Pakistan's rulers knew if they misused American military aid they would receive no more. American economic assistance and the threat of its suspension provided additional arguments for good behavior.

Eisenhower came away from this meeting with "the very definite impression" that Nehru sincerely sought an improvement in U.S.–Indian relations. Eisenhower shared the goal, not least because of what he learned during the prime minister's visit. When Nehru chose to be, as he did on this occasion, he was an engaging and forceful exponent of India's foreign policy. He did not succeed in convincing Eisenhower that neutralism was appropriate for all countries of the developing world, nor did he try. But he did go far toward demonstrating that neutralism was the only course that made sense for India.[69]

XIV

AT THE end of 1956 the national-security bureaucracy in the United States included skeptics on this last point. New Delhi's opening to Moscow during the previous year had prompted the joint chiefs of staff to seek a sharp statement of opposition to Indian neutralism, since, as the joint chiefs' intelligence staff put it, "Mr. Nehru has openly followed the international Communist line in Asia (vis-a-vis the United States) under the label of Neutralism."[70]

But this turned out to be a minority viewpoint when the National Security Council updated its policy statement for South Asia in December 1956. Although the new NSC report did not differ radically from earlier papers, it provided the clearest justification yet for supporting Nehru and the most explicit directions for doing so. The report conceded that Indian neutralism continued to cause difficulties for American diplomacy and that strengthening India would tend to compound these problems.

> Nevertheless, over the longer run, the risks to U.S. security from a weak and vulnerable India would be greater than the risks of a stable and influential India. A weak India might well lead to the loss of South and Southeast Asia to Communism. A strong India would be a successful example of an alternative to Communism in an Asian context and would permit the gradual development of the means to enforce its external security interests against Communist Chinese expansion into South and Southeast Asia.

Noting the "vigorous" efforts by the Soviet Union to achieve political goals by economic means, the paper reiterated the point that "the outcome of the competition between Communist China and India as to which can best satisfy the aspirations of peoples for economic improvement will have a profound effect throughout Asia and Africa."

At present, the key determinant of the stability of Nehru's government was India's second five-year plan.

> Should India fall significantly short of the projected expansion during the crucial next five years and lose the momentum it has gained under Nehru's leadership, it is unlikely to regain this momentum during the foreseeable future. A period of economic and political decline would almost certainly set in, popular support for the Congress Party would diminish, dissension would grow both inside and outside the Congress Party, and unrest would ensue.

Consequently the report declared that "it is in our interest that India should substantially achieve the broad aims of the five-year plan." To this end the United States should provide economic and technical aid, "placing emphasis on projects and programs having the maximum potential of support for the goals and aspirations of India's second five-year plan."[71]

While the NSC drafters were putting the last touches on this paper, reports from the field indicated that American support of the five-year plan would build upon a foundation of unaccustomed good feeling. Washington's handling of the Suez affair had raised America's stature in the eyes of Indians who commonly classed the United States with the colonialists in matters relating to Asia. The embassy in New Delhi remarked that Indians credited the Eisenhower administration with having restrained Britain and France in the early stages of the confrontation with Egypt and that they appreciated the significance of the president's refusal to countenance military action when war finally came. As Frederic Bartlett, the chargé d'affaires, put the matter, prospects for improved relations were better than "at any time in the past three years."[72]

Ambassador Cooper elaborated on this theme. He admitted that a number of issues—notably Pakistan—still divided Washington from New Delhi. But the administration's stance on Suez had changed the situation immensely. Indians, Cooper said, now tended to view the president as "a man of judgment and peace." At the same time, the Russians' brutal treatment of Hungary had disillusioned many, leaving those who posited a moral equivalence between the United States and the Soviet Union with a "feeling of isolation." In sum, the climate was

"more favorable than at any time since World War II" for an improvement in relations between America and India.[73]

The pregnant moment almost passed without issue. The administration's Middle East resolution of early 1957 undid much of the good of
Suez. Nehru predictably looked askance at this new extension of the
cold war; he wrote Eisenhower to say that nationalism, not communism,
was at the heart of the turmoil in the Middle East. Eisenhower, equally
predictably, defended the new policy on grounds that a firm statement
of American resolve offered the best hope for deterring aggression in the
region.[74]

Perhaps it was the predictability of this disagreement that allowed the
good feeling between Washington and New Delhi to persist; more likely
it was India's growing economic distress. By the summer of 1957 close
observers could see that the second five-year plan was in serious trouble.
Administrative errors, bad weather, unexpected price increases, and a
variety of other ills contributed to what was shaping up as a massive
foreign-exchange shortfall. Nehru, recalling the criticism his country
had suffered at the hands of the American Congress in 1951, put off
asking for help for as long as possible; but in September he told an
American journalist his government would need some half-billion dollars to see India through the crisis.[75]

An affirmative response to Nehru's request was something of a fore-
gone conclusion; for most of a decade American policymakers had been
arguing that American interests in South Asia required keeping Nehru's
government afloat. Since 1954 the Eisenhower administration had been
committed on paper to the idea that the United States must support
India's economic development. More recently the National Security
Council and the president had explicitly affirmed the need for assuring
the success of India's five-year plan. At the beginning of 1958, therefore,
Eisenhower announced a $225 million package of loans from the
Export-Import Bank and the new Development Loan Fund. During the
following summer, the World Bank, with American support and partici-
pation, created a consortium which pledged to cover the balance of
India's needs.[76]

This period witnessed a breakthrough on the India-aid question. Not
conceptually, as noted just above; but politically. By 1958 the last of the
diehard budget-trimmers had left the administration; George
Humphrey's resignation in the autumn of 1957 marked their final re-

treat. (It was significant that Humphrey's replacement was Robert Anderson, whom Eisenhower earlier had tapped to clean up the Arab-Israeli troubles with what would have amounted to a shower of dollars.) The elections of 1958 displaced some of the most steadfast of the anti-neutralist bloc, including Knowland and Jenner, and brought to the fore a more liberal group, including Cooper, now back in the Senate, and Massachusetts Senator John Kennedy. Internationally, something of the spirit of Geneva 1955 returned. The new thaw would culminate in a visit by Khrushchev to the United States in 1959 and planning for an Eisenhower trek to Russia the following year; in the meantime, with communists being denatured, neutralists no longer provoked the reaction they once had.

The upshot of all this was the beginning of a sustained and joint commitment by the executive and legislative branches to Indian development. Until this time American aid had been a year-to-year, touch-and-go affair. Never knowing what the administration would feel brave enough to propose nor how Congress might dispose of White House requests, India found it impossible to integrate American aid into its economic planning. But during Eisenhower's last three years the two branches began working in parallel. Exclusive of the Export-Import contribution to the 1958 package, American loans and grants to India rose steadily, from $90 million in 1958 to $137 million in 1959 and $194 million in 1960. In addition to this capital funding, Washington negotiated a number of commodity agreements with New Delhi, including a four-year package in May 1960 worth one-and-a-quarter billion dollars.[77]

XV

IF AID policy brightened U.S.–Indian relations, the dark cloud of Pakistan remained. Basically the problem was intractable, for the administration was not about to cancel its commitment to Karachi to placate India, especially once U-2 spy planes began operating out of bases in Pakistan. Even had American leaders concluded that diplomatic and strategic considerations justified such a reversal, the domestic repercussions likely to result from abandonment of an ally in favor of a neutralist rendered the notion politically unappetizing. For all the recent interest in India, congressional toleration had limits.

While the problem of Pakistan refused to go away, the administration did its best to duck responsibility. At the beginning of 1958 Dulles denied an assertion by the Indian ambassador that American military aid to Pakistan destabilized the subcontinent. The secretary declared that the Pakistanis said the same thing about American economic aid to India. The Pakistanis' argument, which Dulles made his own, posited a sort of logistical equivalence between guns and butter, in that American financial assistance to India allowed the Indians to divert resources to weapons-building that nonmilitary projects otherwise would have claimed.[78]

The Indians found this combination of reason and casuistry unconvincing, and the burr continued to rub. The administration might have ignored the irritation as simply another example of Nehru's touchiness, and one about which little could be done, had this irritation threatened only relations between Washington and New Delhi. But Eisenhower, having become aware for the first time of the depth of India's suspicions of Pakistan during his talks with Nehru, feared that these suspicions might lead to a resumption of fighting between India and Pakistan, with all the ill consequences such a conflict would bring to the subcontinent.[79]

As American officials perceived the situation, renewed fighting could begin in either of two ways. The Indians might prove right: Pakistan might risk Washington's displeasure and use American weapons to settle the Kashmir question once for all. Or the Indians, anticipating such an attack, might launch a preemptive strike. Even if the two sides managed to avoid war, continued tension would divert Indian resources from economic development, canceling the beneficial effects of American aid. And New Delhi might turn to the Soviet Union for military assistance, raising another set of problems.

For these reasons, the Eisenhower administration planned a new initiative on Kashmir. In April 1958 Dulles sent Eisenhower a memorandum suggesting a high-level approach to the governments of India and Pakistan as part of an effort to break the deadlock. Dulles had not worked out any details; he wanted to get the president's reaction first. On one point, however, Dulles was specific. Considering the explosive nature of the Kashmir situation, and in light of the broader ramifications for the morale of other client states of an American effort to strong-arm Pakistan into a deal with India, the secretary insisted that any Kashmir proposal go forward only "in strict secrecy."

Eisenhower thought the plan a good one. "I'm all for this," he replied. The president said he would be willing to invite the prime ministers of India and Pakistan to Washington for negotiations. If that would not do, he himself would fly to South Asia. With Dulles, Eisenhower appreciated the need for discretion; he told the secretary to move forward, but "in the utmost secrecy."[80]

The Kashmir dispute, however, proved no more amenable to solution at this time than before. After some further preparations for a conference, Eisenhower offered his services as a mediator to Nehru. The prime minister politely declined. No third party, Nehru declared, could usefully intervene in a matter India and Pakistan would have to settle themselves. And until Pakistan modified its policy of hatred for India, nothing could be done.[81]

XVI

THE AMERICAN intervention in Lebanon in the summer of 1958, described in the section below on Egypt, provoked annoyance in New Delhi and defensiveness in Washington, with the prime minister criticizing and the president justifying the use of military force; but it had little lasting effect on U.S.–Indian relations. When the National Security Council produced a new statement of American objectives toward India, the drafters simply lifted large sections from earlier papers. During the previous year, the State Department's Office of Intelligence Research had noted a "growing weariness" in Nehru and a certain "declining vigor" in the Congress party, but the NSC did not consider these afflictions serious. Nehru remained in charge, essentially unchallenged. Communism in India constituted a worry but not a danger. Economic development held the key to India's future. American aid should increase.[82]

A visit by Eisenhower to New Delhi in 1959 constituted the highlight of Indo–American relations during the president's final two years in office, and it came at a moment of inversion in the cold war when the United States and the Soviet Union spoke of peaceful coexistence while India and China were at bayonets' points over border questions. On his arrival, large and enthusiastic rallies greeted the president. "It was an overwhelming experience," Eisenhower wrote. An especially exuberant crowd surrounded the official motorcade from the airport, forcing it to a halt and prompting Nehru to sally forth into the mass of bodies, flailing to left and right with his walking stick in an effort to clear a path for his and the president's car. A "lively non-violence," Eisenhower chuckled.[83]

During two days of discussions, Eisenhower and Nehru again reflected on the state of the world. Eisenhower assured the prime minister he did not share the opinions of those in America who criticized India's neutrality. Considering India's particular situation, he would have it no other way. He studiously refrained from comments construable as reflecting an I-told-you-so attitude regarding China's incursions into Indian territory, but he allowed himself to wonder aloud whether India might be willing to make common cause with Pakistan against the Chinese. Nehru rejected the idea. He said he did not need Pakistan's help, only assurance Pakistan would not stab him in the back while he dealt with China. Eisenhower declared that his administration would take strong action to prevent any such move.[84]

The trip was one of the personal triumphs of Eisenhower's career. Nehru likened Eisenhower to Gandhi as a person who had touched the hearts of the Indian people. Paul Hoffman, returning from India shortly after the president, declared that "never in his life" had the standing of the United States there been higher. Eisenhower himself described his trip to an associate as "infinitely rewarding"; it had demonstrated the "great friendship" the people of India felt for America.[85]

In September 1960, Eisenhower spoke with Nehru for the last time. When the prime minister came to New York for meetings at the United Nations, Eisenhower flew up from Washington. Relations between the superpowers had again chilled and the president, commenting on recent blasts by Khrushchev, told Nehru he appreciated the prime minister's presence at a moment when the world especially needed calm voices. Eisenhower congratulated Nehru on an agreement between India and Pakistan regarding division of the waters of the Indus basin, characterizing it as a step toward peace. The two men discussed troubles in the Congo, where both supported UN intervention to alleviate a post-independence crisis. They exchanged views on disarmament and friction between China and the Soviet Union; here they differed about as often as they agreed. The conversation held no surprises, and Eisenhower and Nehru parted as they had met, in a mood of personal friendship, respect, and tolerance for divergent opinions.[86]

II

YUGOSLAVIA AND THE TITO OPTION

IV

Bolt from the Blue Danube: 1948–1950

INDIA'S NEUTRALIST preferences had been evident from the beginning and Nehru's choice of a nonaligned policy surprised no one; but the same could hardly be said of Yugoslavia and Tito. Indeed, the developments that brought the Yugoslavs to the ranks of neutralism caught American officials and most Western observers off guard. Although the Truman administration reacted with relative swiftness to the 1948 split between Tito and Stalin, American suspicions of the genuineness of the rift lingered for many months—among some skeptics, for years.

Yet where the American attitude toward Indian neutralism matured from tolerance to appreciation only over the better part of a decade, Washington perceived at once the advantages of a nonaligned Yugoslavia. To the United States, Yugoslavia's significance resided in the fact that the country lay, metaphorically, at the intersection of Yalta and Bandung, where the third world collided with the bipolar superpower order. By defecting from the Soviet system to neutralism and shifting the balance of power in Central Europe in favor of the West, Tito improved America's strategic posture. As in the Indian case, geopolitics set the tone of the American reaction; ideology took a back seat. Indeed, when they considered ideology at all, American policymakers hoped Tito would remain a reliably orthodox disciple of Marx and Lenin, so he could become a guiding light to other would-be national communists in the Soviet sphere. Needless to say, those formulating policy did not trumpet this heretical view in public.

As matters turned out, Tito required no encouragement in his continued distaste for capitalism and democracy. In 1946 Yugoslav warplanes had attacked two American transports alleged to have encroached on Yugoslav airspace; during that year and the next, harassment of employees, to the point of arrest and trial for espionage, had become a fact of life at the American embassy in Belgrade. Following the break with Stalin the situation improved only marginally, and Tito and his spokesmen lost few opportunities to denounce American imperialism in the most uncompromising terms.

For all his prickliness, Tito's independence served American security interests, and the Truman and Eisenhower administrations took measures to support it—first diplomatically, then economically, and finally by military means. That the American government, at the height of the cold war, at a moment when an almost unthinking anticommunism inflamed American politics, shipped not only food but weapons to a communist regime, was in itself noteworthy. It became all the more remarkable after Stalin's death in 1953 when the Kremlin's new masters made their peace with Tito. Despite the Yugoslav–Soviet rapprochement American aid continued to flow. As with India, American leaders managed, in a time known for its pervasive ideology, to put ideology aside and confront the issue of a neutralist Yugoslavia on its geopolitical merits.

For the present purpose American policy toward Yugoslavia in the dozen years after Tito's break with Moscow divides into two unequal parts. The first comprises the period from June 1948, when American officials initially discerned the split, until the end of 1950, when the Truman administration persuaded Congress to fund economic aid for Yugoslavia. These thirty months receive what might seem disproportionate attention because that is precisely what they demanded of American officials grappling with the questions Tito's defection raised. How deep and how permanent was the schism? What would the Soviets do to bring Tito to heel? Could Yugoslavia survive on its own? Could it survive even with American help? Would American aid do more harm than good? Would Congress countenance such aid? Such issues occupied American analysts, planners, and decision-makers during the entire period from 1948 to 1960, but they drew special interest during the first, formative years. By the end of 1950 the Truman administration felt sufficient confidence in the answers it had discovered to take its case to the people and their representatives.

With congressional approval of economic aid to Yugoslavia, American policy entered the second phase, which lasted until the end of Eisenhower's tenure. In the main, American officials during this period simply extended and elaborated the earlier decision to support Tito. But various new developments repeatedly called that decision into doubt. When Truman asked for military aid to Yugoslavia many individuals who had acquiesced in economic assistance wondered whether weapons ought to follow. Greater skepticism surfaced after Stalin died, when Moscow and Belgrade gave every indication of burying the hatchet. Even proponents of aid to Tito found this detente unsettling; critics considered it a boon to their plans to force a cutoff. Although the critics won occasional battles, the proponents won the war. Through it all, until Eisenhower left office, American policy remained relatively steady, generally supportive, and, considering the mood of the period, surprisingly broad-minded.[1]

II

IF AMERICAN officials did not foresee the events of June 1948, they had sensed for some time a desire on Tito's part to reduce his dependence on the Soviet bloc. At the founding of the Cominform in 1947 the Yugoslavs had emphasized that they, in contrast to the leaders of the other "people's democracies," had acquired power by their own efforts rather than as part of an occupation by the Red Army; and they insisted on the respect due equals. The Russians had other ideas. Boris Kidrić, one of Tito's closest advisers, recalled a few years later that "Stalin treated us not as a socialist country but like any other nation which, as he and his associates felt, belonged to their sphere of influence —that is, under their hegemony." At base the contest was a political struggle, turning on the issue of who would rule Yugoslavia and other parts of the Balkans; but at the beginning of 1948 most of the skirmishing took place in the economic sphere. Preoccupied with their own reconstruction, the Soviets aimed to enlist—to enforce—Yugoslav cooperation in building up Russia's industrial plant, which implied a subordinate position for Yugoslavia. As Kidrić put it, "Their purpose was to keep Yugoslavia as an agricultural and raw-materials-producing appendage."[2]

The full import of the differences remained hidden from American view, but in January 1948, the American ambassador in Belgrade, Cavendish Cannon, caught a glimpse in a meeting with Tito. The Yugoslav leader indicated he was not receiving the economic support he had expected from Moscow, with the result that the current five-year plan was in trouble. In particular Yugoslavia needed industrial machinery, and the marshal made clear he hoped to buy such equipment from the United States.[3]

But Tito was not about to get the tools. The Truman administration had no interest at this stage in digging Tito out of his hole. Besides, the Yugoslavs possessed no ready cash. Although Belgrade had nearly fifty million dollars on account, the majority in gold, with the Federal Reserve Bank in New York, Washington had frozen these assets pending settlement of lend-lease debts and various claims by Americans.

By the end of May Tito's troubles were mounting—which appeared to Cannon all to the good. "For the first time," the ambassador wrote, "the confidence of the local regime in its ability to move forward boldly in the new Stalinist world seems to be faltering." In contrast to "the surging optimism" of several months before, despondency had overtaken Belgrade. "Today the Yugoslav Government seems groping for those new directions that will give it once again a sense of having the lead in the Balkans, of being in fact the spearhead of evangelical and expansionist communism." Tito could find "little comfort at home or abroad." Signs of domestic "economic ill-being" grew more evident as the five-year plan remained stalled. In foreign affairs Yugoslavia's backing for communist guerrillas in Greece had yielded few returns; its hopes for greater influence in Austria had been rebuffed; its designs on Trieste had run up against a revived Italy. These difficulties, Cannon argued would keep Tito out of mischief. Anticipating no basic shifts in Yugoslavia's position, the ambassador recommended holding the current course. "I find our basic lines still eminently good and have no fundamental changes to suggest."[4]

Within ten days, however, this complacent comment grew outdated. On June 18 Robert Reams, the counselor of the embassy in Belgrade, noted signs of a rift between Tito and Stalin. Ostensibly the disagreement involved a proposed conference on navigation rights on the Danube River. The meeting had been scheduled for Belgrade at the end of July, but on June 12 Moscow announced its preference for a change of venue. When Tito resisted the move the American embassy realized something unusual was afoot. Reams commented that the Yugoslav rejection marked the "first direct and irrevocable challenge by any satellite to the supreme authority of the Communist overlords in the Kremlin." Reams went on to make the assertion that Tito's decision to question Stalin's leadership might well be "the most significant political event here since U.S. recognition." He added, "For the first time in history, the Soviet Union is faced with a consolidated Communist regime in power outside its own borders willing to risk an independent or even contrary course."

Reams credited Tito's personal ambition as a factor in the dispute, although he pointed out it was "inconceivable" that the marshal would have acted without the solid support of the rest of the Yugoslav government. While such of the dispute as had surfaced in public was couched in theoretical language, Reams doubted theory played a role. Rather Tito's evident ambition to carve a sphere for Yugoslavia in southeastern Europe "must have cumulatively irritated and perhaps alarmed the Kremlin." Conversely, Tito was increasingly alienated by Moscow's apathy toward Yugoslavia's five-year plan. Whatever the precise reasons for the quarrel, Reams believed the Yugoslav leader must feel quite sure of himself. "Tito cannot be unaware of the experience of Communists who have opposed the Kremlin." On balance, the evidence appeared conclusive. "I am convinced that a definite split exists."[5]

Events of the next several days proved Reams correct. On June 28 representatives of the Cominform, meeting in Bucharest, adopted a resolution condemning the leadership of the Yugoslav Communist party for pursuing a policy unfriendly to the Soviet Union and for violating the basic tenets of Marxism. The thrust of the resolution showed clearly through its restrained language: Stalin had accepted Tito's challenge and intended to thrash the rebel, by one means or another.

Naturally this news sent a pulse of excitement from the American embassy in Belgrade to Washington. Reams described the situation as "brilliantly fluid," characterizing Tito's challenge to Stalin and his expulsion from the Cominform as "potentially the most important events since the Japanese surrender." The military attachés at the embassy cabled urgently for instructions:

> We might be asked any minute the following questions:
> 1. Will the West support Tito against Russia? If so, how?
> 2. Diplomatically through the UN, economically, or with direct military action?
> 3. How soon and to what extent in each respect?
> 4. What commitments or guarantees must Tito make in return for such support?

In requesting an immediate reply Army Colonel Richard Partridge and Navy Captain Willard Sweetser expressed their preference for the "boldest possible exploitation of this defection in the keystone of the Soviet satellite structure." Alone, Tito could not long withstand the Kremlin's fury. However, "if he really wants to try and is given full support from the West, he would have a good prospect of a success which would lead to the solution of our major problems in Europe."[6]

Not everyone in the administration was quite so breathless regarding the probable consequences of the Belgrade-Moscow split. As soon as reports of the Cominform's anti-Tito resolution reached Washington the State Department's Policy Planning Staff set to analyzing its significance. "For the first time in history," George Kennan, the PPS director, wrote, "we may now have within the international community a communist state resting on the basis of Soviet organizational principles and for the most part on Soviet ideology, and yet independent of Moscow." But Kennan advocated caution in reacting to the schism, since any response would set a precedent for policy toward similar defections in the future, and because the right approach might encourage such defections.

Other considerations entered into the planning staff's recommendation for "extreme circumspection." For one thing, all the evidence indicated Tito remained as thoroughly devoted to communism and as belligerent toward the United States as ever. Though he might feel forced to make common cause with the West, Tito's cooperation would come at his convenience only. "It would therefore be a frivolous and undignified error on our part to assume that because Tito has fallen out with Stalin he could now be considered our 'friend.'" Moreover, the crack in the Cominform had probably unsettled the Yugoslavs as much as it had the Russians. "These events must be profoundly humiliating and disagreeable to all the parties concerned." As a consequence the United States ought to expect efforts on one side or both to patch over the dispute, if only for the sake of appearance. Finally, the Soviets would certainly take advantage of any false steps by the West in responding to the Yugoslav break, in order to use such errors to bring Tito down and discourage would-be imitators. On balance the situation called for careful realpolitik. The United States should prepare to collaborate with Yugoslavia, but only where such collaboration clearly served American interests. The principal objective ought to be a Yugoslavia independent of Moscow. American–Yugoslav cooperation toward this goal should not depend on any domestic reforms by Tito, which were unlikely in any event. On the latter point Kennan spoke explicitly: "If Yugoslavia is not to be subservient to an outside power its internal regime is basically its own business."[7]

The CIA's assessment of the situation did not differ markedly from that of the State Department, although the intelligence agency took longer to sort rumors from facts. CIA Director Roscoe Hillenkoetter suggested to Truman that the denunciation by the Cominform might be a device to cover up a coup in Belgrade. According to this scenario Tito had already been arrested; news of his fall would trickle out at a time and in a fashion convenient to Moscow. Hillenkoetter did not put much faith in this argument, but it seemed plausible enough to deserve forwarding to the White House. By the next day, however, the agency's suspicions of a Russian ruse had evaporated. In a second memo to Truman, Hillenkoetter remarked that if Tito survived, his defection might have important repercussions in other parts of the Soviet bloc. Especially in Bulgaria and Hungary, the Yugoslav challenge would give heart to "nationalists" among local cadres and diminish the prestige of "internationalists."[8]

Other interpretations arrived in Washington from the various embassies in Europe. London reported that the British advocated utmost caution. Not entirely convinced of the genuineness of the split and suspecting that even an independent Yugoslavia would pursue unacceptable objectives in such sensitive areas as Greece, the Foreign Office recommended that the West make "no gesture" toward Tito until the situation grew clearer. Paris described similar suspicions. "The Quai d'Orsay is very 'reserved' in expressing an opinion on the Yugoslav situation. They do not believe it involves a break between Moscow and Tito."[9]

Yugoslavia and the Tito Option

In the Soviet Union, Ambassador Walter Bedell Smith remarked the tight-lipped reaction of the Kremlin and the confusion of the Yugoslav mission in the Russian capital. "Very little Soviet comment thus far," Smith wrote, adding that Tito's representatives were "apparently completely disconcerted and groping for an explanation." As usual in such circumstances, Smith had compared notes with his counterparts in the embasssies of friendly countries; he considered their doubts unfounded. Responding to a British suggestion that the whole affair had been staged as a means of relieving Moscow of the burden of supporting Yugoslavia economically—an impression seconded, interestingly enough, by cynics in Yugoslavia—Smith said,

> The Kremlin must realize that it would take a long time to establish Tito in a position where he could persuade the U.S. to give economic aid to the creaking Yugoslav five-year plan, while the great concern shown by the Russian people and adverse effect elsewhere are indicative of the high price which would have to be paid for such a remote prospect.

Smith based his argument partly on his personal knowledge of Tito, whom he had encountered during World War II and on several occasions in Moscow. Smith had noted an "arrogance, truculence and independent attitude" in Tito and his advisers, which contrasted sharply with the subservience characterizing the leaders of other Soviet-bloc states. As much as anything, this convinced Smith of the reality of the rift. And there would be no turning back. "Tito must realize that recantation would be the prelude to his own official and probably personal demise, and that of his main supporters."[10]

Smith had arrived at his Moscow post after a career in the army; his assessment of events added a soldier's perspective to that of the diplomat. Another evaluation from the military side came from the commander of American forces in Austria, Lieutenant General Geoffrey Keys. Keys agreed that the current uproar probably represented "a real and serious breach" between Belgrade and Moscow. Consequently he considered it wise to anticipate "drastic steps" by the Kremlin to bring Tito back into line. "If strenuous diplomatic and psychological efforts fail, the possibility of prompt and forceful military measures should not be overlooked." The United States ought to do what it could to frustrate Soviet plans and guarantee that the split between Yugoslavia and Russia reached "full maturity." Keyes specifically recommended a direct approach to Tito's government to determine whether the Yugoslavs desired American assistance, and to indicate willingness to provide that help. Keyes cautioned, however, that any such initiative should be "as secret and discreet as possible," for a number of reasons:

(A) To avoid embarrassing Tito by public evidence of western "interference";

(B) To leave a way open to denial of an official approach if Tito's reaction is hostile or generally unfavorable; and

(C) To avoid adverse reaction upon the Greeks, Italians and other western European nations which might object to unilateral United States approach and action.

If the first contact elicited a suitable response an openly acknowledged mission to Belgrade should follow. Such a public display of support would have "an electrifying effect not only in Yugoslavia, but in other satellite nations which are thought to be restive and perhaps are seeking relief from the oppression inherent in satellites' position within the Soviet orbit."[11]

III

BETWEEN THE promise of promoting unrest in the Russian bloc and the demands of discretion, the Truman administration opted for the latter. Early in July Tito sent an emissary to the embassy in Belgrade to test the American reaction to a request for aid. Reams replied noncommittally, preferring to draw out his visitor. But he did remark offhandedly that of course Yugoslavia would not wish to participate in the Marshall Plan—to which the Yugoslav official immediately responded, Why not? The State Department found this conversation interesting but insufficiently unambiguous to warrant a direct answer. "While we should not repulse any advances by Tito toward closer association with the West," Secretary Marshall said, "we should await Tito's approaches."[12]

Few in the administration questioned the general wisdom of such a stance, but differences emerged regarding just how forward the United States ought to expect the Yugoslavs to be. W. Averell Harriman, formerly ambassador to the Soviet Union and currently supervising distribution of American aid in Europe, believed the contact Reams described deserved a friendly response. Harriman suggested the administration let

Tito know through informal channels it would be happy to discuss improvements in trade relations. Worried coolness would prove counterproductive, Harriman wrote that "this seeming lack of interest on our part may adversely affect Tito's current actions."[13]

Smith in Moscow agreed Reams might have reacted "a little more warmly" to the Yugoslavs' feeler. Smith conceded the wisdom of caution, out of concern not only for American prestige but for Tito's survival. "We might easily do him a great deal of harm by alienating sections of Communist support in Yugoslavia proper as well as such covert Communist support as he may have elsewhere in the Balkans." But discretion had its limits. "While I still believe that any concrete approach should come from Tito, I think hints might be dropped in the proper quarters to the effect that his overtures would not be summarily rejected."[14]

In mid-July the administration found occasion to drop such hints. In fact it went further. On July 19 American officials agreed to an arrangement releasing Yugoslavia's blocked gold. At about the same time the administration joined the British in a favorable reply to an indirect Yugoslav request to purchase Western petroleum, to the amount of some 50,000 tons.[15]

Tito responded in kind, inviting the former governor of California, Culbert Olson, then traveling in Yugoslavia, for an interview. Tito stressed two points, which he encouraged Olson to pass on. First, Yugoslavia wished to negotiate commercial agreements with the United States, although such agreements must not contain political conditions. Second, Yugoslavia had no intention of altering its opposition to the Cominform. Time would demonstrate the correctness of his government's convictions; meanwhile he would stand firm.[16]

Even the cautious Marshall agreed that this statement indicated an unmistakable interest in rapprochement. Telling Truman Tito's challenge had "severely shaken" the Kremlin, the secretary advocated action to keep the crevasse from closing. He directed Reams to inform Yugoslav officials at the earliest opportunity that the American government had noted Tito's remarks to Governor Olson and would be pleased for Yugoslavia to elaborate its thinking.[17]

With Washington working unobtrusively toward an understanding, Tito publicly maintained a position of undiminished antagonism toward the West. In a widely publicized speech the deputy prime minister,

Edvard Kardelj, castigated American imperialism in unusually violent terms. At the United Nations Yugoslav representatives remained as unhelpful as ever. When the much-discussed Danube conference took place, Belgrade's delegation hewed to a completely pro-Soviet line.[18]

American officials recognized the pressures under which Tito operated, and they did not place much weight on these official expressions of commitment to communist solidarity. In Cannon's view Tito cloaked his real diplomatic objectives behind several layers of propaganda. The most superficial layer appeared at the Danube conference, where no hint of the rancor of the previous six weeks was allowed to intrude. At a slightly deeper level the Yugoslav government adopted the position that such differences as did exist between Yugoslavia and the Soviet Union merely represented debates within the communist fraternity and had nothing to do with intergovernmental relations. At a third level—"more incisive but not yet realistic"—Tito was working toward a diplomatic ceasefire with the Kremlin, claiming reconciliation would come as soon as Moscow admitted the error of its ways. Beneath all the rhetoric, which Cannon considered aimed partly at a Yugoslav audience and partly at the world beyond, the ambassador perceived Tito preparing for a protracted struggle—"a long-term affair with no possibility of compromise for the present."[19]

Reams concurred with this opinion, and at the end of August the chargé d'affaires expanded on what such considerations suggested in terms of an American response. Outlining the principles that in fact would inform Washington's reaction to the Tito–Stalin split, Reams wrote:

> Our policy toward Yugoslavia in this new situation must be conceived almost exclusively in terms of its effect on the U.S.S.R. . . . Our strategy should seek maximum exploitation of the increasing opportunities to widen the gulf between Yugoslavia and the U.S.S.R. and to extend Tito's influence among the Soviet satellites.

Reams admitted that supporting Tito entailed risks, but he deemed these minor and worth taking. "Ultimately, Tito's brand of communism may well be more alluring to non-Communist countries than Stalin's; his nationalism may well be a truer internationalism; but these possibilities are speculative and remote." Tito's rebellion represented "the outstanding political possibility in the Soviet sphere" and the United States ought to work to ensure its success. "We must be prepared to extend affirmative forms of assistance whenever the situation shall require them." [20]

The State Department agreed with Reams that policy toward Yugoslavia ought to be conditioned by the continuing competition between the Soviets and the West; but for the moment it derived a different conclusion from this premise. A few days after Reams' cable arrived in Washington, representatives of three American oil-equipment companies contacted the department about a purchase proposal they had received from the Yugoslav embassy in Washington. The department studied the proposal seriously but ultimately turned it down. Marshall explained: "After consideration we feel that, while now rendered less likely because of the Tito–Soviet rift, the possibility still remains that some of this equipment might go to the Soviets, who are desperately in need of such items." Besides, there appeared little to choose between Belgrade and Moscow regarding relations with the West. "Yugoslav actions at the Danube Conference and in the Security Council indicated that they are still faithful supporters of Soviet foreign policy." Yet, while keeping the door closed for the time being on American assistance to Yugoslavia, the secretary did not want to bar the way forever. The administration would deny Yugoslavia's request for drilling rigs, but it would claim shortness of supply as the critical factor in the decision and would hint that the situation could change in the future. Marshall added that playing hard to get might pay off. If the Yugoslavs needed the equipment badly enough, perhaps they would be willing to make "significant concessions." [21]

While Marshall worried that American technology might fall into Soviet hands through a Yugoslav–Soviet reconciliation, the CIA feared a similar outcome by different means. In mid-September the agency asserted that even though a Russian attack on Yugoslavia was not likely, the possibility could not be ruled out. As the CIA saw matters, the Yugoslav situation presented the Kremlin with two basic alternatives, both unsatisfactory. To move forcibly against Tito would invite world condemnation while involving the Red Army in a difficult and costly campaign. To suffer Tito's defiance, on the other hand, would threaten Soviet hegemony in the satellite states. Agency officials thought the latter consideration might ultimately decide the issue. For the moment Stalin stayed his hand, but if he concluded that Tito's example threatened Soviet control of Eastern Europe, war would seem the lesser evil. [22]

Reams in Belgrade concurred that the central question for the Russians was the impact of Tito's defection on the states of the Soviet bloc. The chargé contended that this constituted the crucial issue for America as well. The late summer of 1948 witnessed great tension between the United States and the Soviet Union: with the Russians blockading Berlin, a war for Germany seemed possible, even likely to some. Commenting on a suggestion from the American embassy in Moscow that open conflict would nearly compel Tito to rejoin the Russian camp, Reams disagreed. An outbreak of hostilities, he argued, would more likely enforce neutrality. "If Tito enters a war on the Soviet side, he must realize that he will be finished in the long run regardless of where victory lies." A decision by Yugoslavia to stay on the sidelines would yield significant benefits to the United States. "Yugoslav neutrality would have considerable effect upon the completeness of the support accorded by the satellites to the Soviets. It would decrease pressure on areas vital to the West, such as Trieste and Greece." Finally, taking a cold-blooded approach to the matter, Reams commented, "It would possibly lead to a Soviet attack on Yugoslavia, which could be to our interest."[23]

The State Department remained unconvinced that Tito's position possessed enough stability and that his neutrality promised sufficient rewards for the United States to provide direct assistance. Acting Secretary of State Robert Lovett questioned Reams' assertion that Tito could not fight alongside the Russians without risking his own neck. Lovett suggested that Yugoslavia might announce itself a Soviet ally but not allow Russian troops into the country. Besides, the Kremlin might moot the issue of Yugoslavia's preferred position; it seemed entirely likely that the Soviets, on the outbreak of fighting, would secure their southwestern flank by liquidating Tito.[24]

Reams stood by his argument that Tito could not side with the Russians without signing his regime's and probably his own death warrant. If the United States defeated the Soviet Union, a Yugoslavia that had joined the losers could hardly expect sympathy. If the Soviets won, they would remember Tito's earlier sins and dispose of him at their leisure. Regarding Lovett's final point, Reams agreed that the Russians would certainly *try* to liquidate Tito; but he did not think they would necessarily turn the trick. And their success or failure would depend in large part on American actions in the meantime. "They are unlikely to succeed if we give economic support to the present regime." Even Tito's assassination by Soviet agents, Reams thought, would not topple his government. If the Russians invaded Yugoslavia, the chargé hoped Washington would respond with "immediate positive action." As before, Reams pressed hard for steps to ensure the survival of the dissidents. "I feel strongly that the importance of maintaining an independent, defiant Yugoslavia cannot be overestimated. I believe that its pull on other satellites may well become irresistible if time permits Tito to fully consolidate his position." [25]

IV

WHILE THE embassy in Belgrade and the State Department argued about Tito's reaction to a war over Germany—a controversy Tito encouraged by telling an American visitor who inquired about the matter that only time would reveal Yugoslavia's plans—the terms of the larger debate began to shift. With each passing week fewer American observers questioned the reality of the Moscow–Belgrade split. (One of the more persistent holdouts was Dwight Eisenhower, who suggested to Truman's National Security Council as late as February 1949 that the apparent divergence between Tito and Stalin "might not be an honest defection by Yugoslavia but merely an extremely subtle trick.") In October 1948 Reams relayed a message from Tito's inner circle declaring that the quarrel with Moscow had become "a fight to the death." In November the CIA renounced completely its earlier doubts, asserting that Yugoslavia's defiance constituted "the first major rift in the USSR's satellite empire" and struck "at the very core of the Stalinist concept of Soviet expansionism through world Communism." Both parties, the CIA said, had backed themselves into positions that made compromise nearly impossible. The Soviets retained the capability to crush Tito, but the longer the Kremlin delayed, the more expensive such a move became. [26]

As the administration grew convinced that Tito would not return to the Cominform any time soon, the issue for American policymakers regarding help for Yugoslavia became a matter less of whether than of how. The State Department continued to counsel caution but it gradually acquiesced in a loosening of trade restrictions. During the course of the autumn the Yugoslavs had sought to purchase supplies for their truck fleet, requesting especially fuel, tires, and spare parts. In addition they had renewed their earlier request for oil-drilling equipment. While the department continued to veto the oil rigs, it indicated in November that it would expedite shipments of the other materials.[27]

The decision to increase trade reflected a growing awareness in Washington of the economic problems confronting Yugoslavia. A survey by the State Department's Office of Intelligence Research noted that while Yugoslavia remained generally self-sufficient in foodstuffs, such industry as the country possessed depended heavily on imports of fuel and machinery. Previously Yugoslavia had looked east for these essential items, but confronted by the Cominform's economic blockade, Tito was turning west. To date he had had some luck, but not enough. The CIA concurred with the OIR's analysis, declaring early in 1949 that Yugoslavia's plight was becoming more serious by the day.[28]

From Belgrade Ambassador Cannon wrote that events were moving "much faster than anticipated." Tito's need to replace embargoed goods from the Soviet bloc had forced him to improve relations with the Western Europeans, and such trade as had developed was having the fortuitous effect of easing the burden of Marshall Plan reconstruction. Cannon suggested that this fact might bear mentioning when distrustful Americans asked what Tito had done for the United States. But the Europeans could not fill all Tito's requirements and undoubtedly he would seek American assistance. Cannon warned, however, that despite Yugoslavia's obvious distress Tito would not make political concessions to receive such aid.[29]

The CIA registered a slight reservation on this last point. The intelligence agency agreed that Yugoslavia would not willingly relax its belligerent posture, but "as Tito's economic situation grows more desperate and his economic dependence on the West (particularly the United States) intensifies, he may be forced to modify his hitherto vigorous anti-Western foreign policy." Still, the agency hesitated to make predictions regarding the direction of Yugoslavia's diplomacy. Describing Tito's position as "paradoxical," the CIA characterized the factors conditioning his actions as "fundamentally contradictory." Summarizing, CIA analysts wrote:

a. A significant political deviation toward Western democracy would turn away his devoted Communist supporters.

b. The only quick solution of his economic problem lies in development of more comprehensive trade links with the West.

c. The development of trade links with the West requires a modification of his vigorous anti-Western foreign policy.

d. Effective accommodation with the USSR can only be had on the basis of absolute subservience because Soviet relations with her entire satellite bloc do not permit the toleration of nationalist policies.

e. Recantation is impossible because it would deprive Tito of the strength he presently draws from Yugoslav nationalism.

Since his break with Moscow Tito had attempted to put off choosing from among the options he faced, but time was running out. "Tito is coming steadily nearer to the point at which he must make fundamental choices." The situation was becoming "more fluid and hence more susceptible to U.S. influence and manipulation." Nonetheless the agency advocated moving slowly. "A careful loosening of export controls might now serve a useful political end if it enabled Tito to keep his head above water month after month, but did not commit the US to saving him."[30]

V

DURING THIS period the Truman administration began to feel pressure from Congress regarding Yugoslavia. For years treatment of dissent in the Soviet bloc had provided a convenient vehicle for legislators wishing to demonstrate their anticommunist convictions, but their expressions of outrage at the heavy-handed tactics of the Soviets and their allies had carried little weight with the State Department. In the absence of American leverage with the governments doing the oppressing, moral outrage placed few demands on the professional diplomats. With the Belgrade–Moscow break, however, and especially with Yugoslavia's growing interest in American aid, the situation changed markedly. In February 1949 the House of Representatives unanimously approved a resolution condemning the imprisonment of the Yugoslav Roman Catholic archbishop, Aloijž Stepinac, and calling on the administration to take appropriate action to free the prelate. Several months later the Senate approved a similar measure. In addition to these public expressions of the sense of Congress, individual legislators raised the Stepinac issue in meetings with State Department officials. A few days after the vote in the House, Democrat John McCormack, the majority leader and a key supporter of the Truman administration's cold-war initiatives, made a special point of reminding department officials of the importance of the Stepinac case and impressing on them the need to take advantage of the new opportunity to force favorable action by Tito.[31]

For the moment the administration merely noted these opinions. The congressional issue surfaced only obliquely in a State Department paper describing means to "gain maximum advantage for the United States out of Tito's deviation from Kremlin hegemony." The authors advocated supporting the "self-made Tito regime," since it offered a "potent example" of successful opposition to Moscow, useful not only in Eastern Europe but in Asia. "This fact, particularly as it applies to China's equally self-made Communist conquerors, is of great political and strategic significance to the United States." The dire condition of the Yugoslav economy demanded swift action, lest Tito fall and America lose the possibility of encouraging a "cancer in the Cominform apparatus." The authors recognized that even such a harmless measure as relaxing trade controls would encounter congressional opposition, so they recommended that such changes in policy be handled in "a quiet routine manner" to avoid attracting attention.[32]

In February the National Security Council incorporated these views into a policy paper. Reiterating the by-now generally—but not unanimously—accepted view of a "profound" rift between Belgrade and Moscow, the NSC paper asserted that the "obvious" interests of the United States required the survival of "Titoism." Tito's revolt possessed significance for Eastern Europe, to be sure, but its larger importance lay in the challenge Tito posed to Soviet influence in China.

> His revolt may very well condition or even bring about a crisis between the Chinese Communist Party and the Kremlin. Mao Tse-tung appears to be capturing power in China without dependence upon the Red Army and Mao himself might already be infected by the Tito virus.

Admitting that the anti-Western character of the Yugoslav regime had softened little, the paper nonetheless urged that Tito's position "not be made more difficult by any action on our part" and it advocated an easing of controls on trade with Yugoslavia.[33]

VI

WHEN TRUMAN approved this paper, slightly modified, he put American policy on a definitely pro-Tito path; but he did not quite quell debate within the administration. By early 1949 the State Department had come around to the view pressed from the beginning by the embassy in Belgrade, that the United States should do all it could to support Tito and demonstrate the viability of opposition to the Kremlin within the communist world. The Defense Department, on the other hand, while conceding the reality and importance of Yugoslavia's defection, remained hesitant about turning over to communists of any stripe material that might increase their military capacity. This reluctance set the stage for a classic bureaucratic battle; when Yugoslavia applied for a license to buy a steel blooming, or finishing, mill, the curtain went up.[34]

Acheson played the lead for the State Department; the new secretary of defense, Louis Johnson, spoke for the Pentagon. Johnson lacked Acheson's diplomatic background, but he possessed experience managing military affairs, having served as assistant secretary of war under Franklin Roosevelt, and he had the right political connections, having been Truman's chief fund-raiser in 1948 and a heavy contributor personally. Further, Johnson had allies: the top military brass supported his opposition to the Yugoslav steel mill. But Acheson also had friends, including Charles Sawyer, the secretary of commerce, who represented the views of exporters eager to open new doors for American trade.[35]

Legally Sawyer's approval should have ended discussion of the subject, since export licenses fell into his bailiwick. In one sense it did, for shortly after Commerce gave the nod the State Department told the Yugoslavs they would get their mill. But the Pentagon refused to give in and Johnson marshaled his troops for a counteroffensive.

In mid-July the defense secretary and Lieutenant General LeRoy Lutes, the Pentagon's expert on munitions, met with Acheson and lesser officials from the State and Commerce departments. Johnson began by challenging the basis of the decision to license the mill for Yugoslavia, asserting that the military risks involved in the transfer far outweighed the political benefits of cooperating with Tito. Johnson added that America's leading military officers were unalterably opposed to the action. For good measure he declared that he would feel obliged to advise the president that approval might "set loose such a wave of public indignation as to seriously threaten the ability of the present administration to win the 1950 elections."[36]

Johnson bolstered his position further by producing an eminently leakable staff study enumerating the dangers implicit in allowing the

Yugoslavs to acquire the steel mill. First, the technology involved was "absolutely essential" to the production of modern weapons. Second, it would multiply sevenfold Yugoslavia's steel capacity and would add significantly to that of the "Soviet sphere." Third, the proposed location of the mill rendered it susceptible to capture by the Russians, by conquest or invitation. Fourth, approval of the mill by the United States would "open the door and possibly lead the way" to the export of other "highly strategic facilities" to Yugoslavia by the countries of Western Europe. Fifth, the positive psychological effect on Tito of American approval might be outweighed by its adverse effects on public opinion in America and among the Europeans. In sum, the export of the mill was "inimical to the national security of the United States."[37]

Acheson retaliated with a counter-study and a long letter to Johnson. The secretary of state rejected the Defense Department's basic argument: that the steel mill might somehow be used against the United States. Acheson found it difficult to believe that the American military leadership still questioned the reality of the Yugoslav–Soviet split. "It is clearly impossible to predict with accuracy what a dictator will do, but nearly every week brings a new development further separating Tito and his former masters in the Kremlin." The Pentagon's suggestion that Tito might permit the Red Army to enter Yugoslavia struck Acheson as ludicrous. "Tito could never allow Soviet troops in his country without reducing his life expectancy to an extremely short period." The secretary conceded that Tito might be assassinated. But Tito's associates "are as compromised as he in the eyes of the Kremlin and are doubtless well aware of the fate that would await them should they again fall under the power of Moscow." Acheson discounted the prospect of Yugoslavia's succumbing to invasion, citing a report by the general staff of the U.S. Army indicating that nothing short of a direct commitment of Russian troops could do the job. Satellite forces alone would not suffice. As to an internal rising against the Tito regime, such seemed improbable, and in any event an overthrow was precisely what American assistance was intended to prevent. Finally, the secretary pointed out that the administration had already notified the Yugoslavs of approval of their licensing request; to reverse the decision would damage American credibility.[38]

Four days after receiving this letter Johnson met with Acheson and Sawyer. Recognizing the strength of the combined opposition, the defense secretary tactically retreated. He said he would object no further to the steel plant at this point but insisted on a review of the decision when the actual shipments commenced. Additionally he required that Acheson and Sawyer rewrite the NSC directive governing such decisions, to grant the Pentagon a louder voice. When they agreed, the battle of the blooming mill ended.[39]

VII

THROUGHOUT THIS period Tito kept up his drumbeat of criticism of American foreign policy, speaking in terms that struck Ambassador Cannon as "straight Kremlinity." To the CIA this seemed not only good Yugoslav politics but an indication that Tito remained as suspicious of Washington's intentions as of Moscow's. "His main strategy is to avoid final and irrevocable commitment to the West until the West is both able and willing to guarantee the life of his particular regime." Tito's aloofness rendered Yugoslavia more vulnerable to Soviet attack, since the Russians had little to fear in the way of a direct Western response. But the possibility of such an assault, in the CIA's opinion, was slim. A stepped-up war of nerves appeared more likely. "The USSR probably hopes to achieve a revolution by generating tension and confusion within Yugoslavia."[40]

The State Department basically agreed with this analysis, although the Policy Planning Staff thought it prudent to prepare for the worst. Kennan's group described four courses of action open to the Soviet Union and outlined an appropriate American response to each. If the Kremlin chose not to escalate its campaign of harassment, it would simply continue its present economic and psychological activities. In this case current American policies would suffice to keep Tito in power. The first rung on the ladder of escalation would involve Soviet support for raids from bases in Bulgaria and Albania. Should the Russians opt for this Tito would require military assistance within a few months. If the Soviets took a still more forceful approach—invasion by satellite troops or by Russians in allied uniforms—Tito would find himself in serious trouble unless he received Western military equipment at once. The most direct and least likely course for the Kremlin would be an outright attack by the Red Army. A Russian blitz would overrun the flat north and capture Belgrade with relative ease; the Yugoslavs would retreat to the mountains for an indefinite campaign of guerrilla resistance. In this case the United States should supplement economic and military support with diplomatic initiatives to bring this gross violation of Yugoslavia's sovereignty before the United Nations.[41]

This final recommendation—to counter a Soviet invasion with money, weapons, and an appeal to world opinion—demonstrated the limits of American interest in preserving Tito's independence. When, in the event, Belgrade complained to the UN of Soviet harassment, the American delegate voted for the resolution, but officials in the Truman administration admitted that if the Soviets wanted badly enough to force Yugoslavia back into the fold the United States could reasonably do little to stop them. An independent Tito might mean much to the West as an irritant to Moscow and a role model for restless nationalists in Eastern Europe and China, but he was not worth a war with the Soviet Union.

Still, if the administration could not countenance sending American troops to Tito's rescue, the fact that it considered supplying American weapons, with the prestige that attached to them, indicated the importance American leaders placed on Tito's survival. In November the NSC staff circulated a new draft statement of American policy; its most noteworthy recommendation called for telling Tito he could expect "at least a limited amount of support in military supplies from the West."[42]

Omar Bradley, responding for the joint chiefs of staff, expressed general concurrence with the NSC draft. Tito's defection, the joint chiefs chairman said, offered "significant security advantages" to the West, and the United States ought to underwrite its author's survival. "Because of the advantages which we may obtain through this rift, the Joint Chiefs of Staff believe that, from the military point of view, United States aid to the Tito regime, both economic aid and military aid short of participation, is sound." But Bradley added a significant reservation.

> At the present time, the Department of Defense is faced with a supply situation which does not admit foreign military aid other than to an extremely limited extent without impairing our ability to prosecute a war, if war were now forced upon us.

For this reason the government's capacity to provide weapons on a grant basis was "practically negligible." Nonetheless the joint chiefs had no objection to letting Yugoslavia purchase weapons in the United States, and they would even support legislation providing funds to finance such purchases.[43]

The version of this paper the NSC approved expanded on the question of military aid. Analyzing the probable reactions of the Tito regime to intensified Soviet pressure, NSC 18/4 asserted that the prospect of increased assistance from the West might play a crucial role in encouraging Yugoslav steadfastness.

> In particular, the expectation of receiving at least a limited amount of support in military supplies from the West would be an important factor in the calculations of the Yugoslav leaders. Assurances from the United States that military supplies would be obtainable in the event of direct or indirect Soviet aggression, even without specific commitments to provide fixed quantities of arms, would strengthen their determination to resist such aggression. Such assurances would aid the top leaders in keeping the support of their subordinates in key positions of the party and the army and in maintaining army morale.

Therefore, the NSC paper concluded, the United States ought to give the Yugoslavs "general assurances as to the availability of limited military supplies in the event of attack." Reflecting the concerns of the joint chiefs, the paper added that the provision of military equipment to Yugoslavia must not diminish American preparedness.[44]

To observers in the field, the assurances the NSC paper spoke of could not have been more timely. The CIA relayed the message that the Soviets were more "seriously troubled" at Tito's rebellion than ever, implying greater efforts to bring him down. The State Department, responding to reports of dissent in Yugoslavia, investigated the possibility of a Kremlin-inspired coup and compiled a 172-page roster of important Communist party members in Yugoslavia thought to support the Cominform. From Belgrade, Reams described a common feeling in the Yugoslav capital that Moscow had decided Tito's removal was essential and worth pursuing at any cost.[45]

Awaiting the Kremlin's next move, the administration kept secret its decision to help Yugoslavia acquire arms, but still it managed to make its support for Tito known in general terms. In December 1949 the White House named George Allen to replace Cannon. Following a meeting with Truman before leaving for Belgrade, the new ambassador described the discussion to reporters.

> The President confirmed that the United States is unalterably opposed to aggression wherever it occurs or threatens to occur. Furthermore, the United States supports the principle of the sovereignty of independent

nations. As regards Yugoslavia, we are just as opposed to aggression against that country as against any other, and just as favorable to the retention of Yugoslavia's sovereignty.

Allen later thought he might have overstated the case; he wrote to a friend that he feared observers had gotten the impression that "the U.S. had given up its support of democracy and was now willing to support Tito or any other dictator who did not like Soviet Russia." But when reporters asked Truman whether Allen had accurately portrayed the administration's attitude, the president responded, "We are opposed to aggression against any country, no matter where situated." Did this signify a change in American policy?, his questioners asked. "Not at all, not at all. That has always been our policy."[46]

VIII

AT THE beginning of 1949 Yugoslav leaders had retained a slight hope that reconciliation with Moscow was possible; by the end of the year they were committed to going it alone. During the summer and autumn the Soviets and their allies denounced their treaties of friendship and aid with Belgrade; the Red Army undertook maneuvers along Yugoslavia's frontiers with Hungary and Rumania; show trials, featuring defendants charged with and convicted of—to conspiring with Tito and the the Americans were staged in the Eastern European states. In the face of this provocation Yugoslav theorists concluded, as Milovan Djilas put it, that the dispute with the Russians was based not on "misunderstandings," but on the Soviets' sin of "revising Leninism." The Kremlin, Djilas declared, had reached "extravagant conclusions in theory and practice," with the result that the conflict would "inevitably sharpen."[47]

Under the circumstances, Tito's government greeted Allen's and Truman's supportive remarks with "great pleasure," in the words of the Yugoslav ambassador in Washington, who went on to say that the comments had had "a very heartening effect" in Yugoslavia and had given his compatriots "a feeling of safety."[48]

All the same, the administration was not particularly surprised when Tito publicly asserted that the West was doing Yugoslavia no favors in liberalizing trade and offering assistance, that America and its allies would help Yugoslavia only so long as such aid promised to further Western objectives—because such assertions were entirely correct, as

Acheson frankly admitted. The secretary told the Yugoslav ambassador that America was supporting Yugoslavia "not for sentimental reasons" but simply because it was "in the interest of the United States" for Yugoslavia to maintain its independence.[49]

In this mutual pursuit of self-interest the Truman administration sought to discover just how Tito defined his half of the bargain. Fathoming Tito's intentions was always uncertain business; in this case the Americans got help from a Yugoslav informant, considered reliable by the CIA. "Tito will make the most of his singular political position," the source said, outlining several courses of action. Yugoslavia would:

a. Develop to the maximum commercial transactions with the United States.

b. Seek to acquire loans and backing from banks and private credit firms. The loans must carry no political clauses.

c. Collaborate with Ambassador Allen in the removal of satellite countries from the Soviet orbit. [This same source declared that the Yugoslav government considered Allen "the key man of the U.S. anti-Soviet policy." The informant added that Belgrade expected Allen to attempt to "widen the Tito–Cominform breach."]

d. Accept eventual military aid from the United States but avoid military pacts and combines organized on an anti-Communist and anti-Soviet basis. Permission will not be given for a U.S. Military Commission to Yugoslavia, if requested.

e. If Ambassador Allen makes the request, the Yugoslav Intelligence Service will collaborate to the extent of Yugoslav defense against Cominform politico-military maneuvers.

f. Also upon request by the United States Government, the Yugoslav Government is ready to consider the possibility of establishing future Yugoslav-United States collaboration (nature unspecified) in Satellite capitals.

g. [Express] willingness to create schisms within Stalinist parties in the West, particularly in France and Italy, if the United States advances the proposal. However, the struggle must be under the leadership of the Anti-Cominform Commission in Belgrade, with the United States rendering support to Yugoslav agents and encouraging dissident elements to revolt.

h. Concomitantly, [the Yugoslav Government] will make the most of American–British rivalry, especially in the Balkans. The policy, however, is to be so conducted as to avoid Yugoslav isolation in the international political camp.[50]

As with most such intelligence, the accuracy of this document could only be gauged by comparing it with information from other sources; in this case the general fit was good. Although George Allen probably did not see this report, he would have found little to contest in its statement of Yugoslav aims. As the ambassador explained to Acheson, he considered Tito's position entirely understandable. Commenting particularly on Tito's refusal to accept political conditions on foreign help, Allen pointed out that however important liberalization in Yugoslavia might be to potential givers of aid, at this stage Tito was in no position to loosen up at home. Surrounded by enemies and knowing Western support would continue only while it served Western purposes, Tito preferred to keep a tight grip on the situation.

But the United States, Allen contended, might turn Tito's stubbornness to America's benefit, and Tito's refusal to compromise ideologically might prove advantageous. An unrepentantly communist Yugoslavia would most efficiently serve the American purpose of undermining the Kremlin's hegemony, while a Tito gone over to the West would lack drawing power for aspiring nationalists in the socialist movement. "Yugoslavia has the greatest immediate value to us as a Communist state independent of both East and West." Convincing Tito to liberalize domestically could wait. "Our ultimate aim of course must be democratic institutions in Yugoslavia, but for the moment a Marxist state independent of Moscow suits our purposes." Allen went even further, asserting that Tito's independence of the West as well as the East was "essential" to America's purpose of "promoting disharmony in the ranks of world Communism and thus weakening the Kremlin's aggressive power."[51]

IX

A YUGOSLAVIA poised between East and West suited American purposes, but it did not make life easy for American diplomats in Belgrade. In March 1950 Allen described the situation there. To the extent a social life existed at the embassy it comprised only Westerners; Yugoslavs remained as distant as before the break with Stalin. "The officials pride themselves on being strict communists and do not wish to be too chummy with the 'reactionary capitalists of the West.' " But Allen appreciated their problems.

The Yugoslavs, in fact, are in a tough spot. They hate the Russians and other communist countries even worse than they do us, and by comparison their relations with us seem almost friendly. At the same time, Tito and his clique, who are all old-school commies and still believe explicitly in Karl Marx and all his teachings, are deeply suspicious of us. They think we are pretending to be friendly at the moment because we want Yugoslavia to help us in our quarrel against Russia, but that as soon as Yugoslavia is no longer useful to us, we will turn against Tito and Co. and do our best to destroy them.

Allen concluded, "My principal job is to try to convince them that this is not true—that is, as long as Yugoslavia is peaceful." [52]

None could argue with a "peaceful" Yugoslavia as an American goal, but Allen's advice to avoid drawing Yugoslavia closer to the West was more problematic. Once the administration decided Tito deserved significant support, it had to sell the idea to Congress and the American people. "He is a Communist and must be expected to act like a Communist," Acheson said. But if Tito acted *too* much like a communist, why should Congress favor his shade of red? [53]

For as long as possible the administration kept decisions regarding aid to Yugoslavia within the executive branch. In the winter of 1950 Yugoslavia faced a balance-of-payments crisis induced by Tito's insistence on maintaining his industrialization schedule in the face of the Cominform boycott, which necessitated that supplies formerly obtained from the East now be purchased from the hard-currency countries of the West. George Perkins, the assistant secretary of state for European affairs, predicted that for 1950 alone the Yugoslavs would have to come up with nearly $30 million in external financing. Perkins strongly advocated American help.

> To maximize U.S. political gains from the Yugoslav secession from the Soviet bloc, it is believed that the aim should be to enable this nation to continue as an independent state, able to maintain itself and to show some improvement in economic conditions. Yugoslavia would thereby continue to establish before world opinion that the primary target of U.S. foreign policy is not any particular economic system per se but Soviet imperialism; and its continued existence as an anti-Soviet but still Communist state should create the maximum dissension within and magnetism upon the other satellites.

Perkins identified sources of American assistance: the Export-Import Bank, the Marshall Plan, and special aid legislation. He preferred the first. The Eximbank would require the fewest political concessions, thereby allowing Yugoslavia to remain an orthodox communist state capable of creating the "maximum dissension" he spoke of. In addition the Eximbank had a low profile in the United States. The Marshall Plan was Perkins' second choice. Marshall grants entailed strings that would diminish Tito's credibility; the program also drew lots of attention in America and would raise political problems for the administration. As for a special congressional appropriation, Perkins deemed this "a last and rather desperate resort." [54]

Perkins' arguments persuaded Acheson, who in turn convinced Treasury Secretary John Snyder, Eximbank director Herbert Gaston, and Truman; and in March the administration approved a $20 million Eximbank loan. [55]

This credit marked no new departure in American policy, since the bank had provided similar loans before; but this one came at a crucial moment for Yugoslavia's economy, and Allen reported that Foreign Minister Edvard Kardelj greeted news of the administration's decision with undisguised relief. Whether from gratitude (unlikely), from a desire to get more aid in the future (likely), or from a belief that increased tension with the East required relaxation toward the West (equally likely), Belgrade made a deliberate effort to spruce its image. The CIA noticed the trend; Kardelj personally provided evidence by telling Allen that Yugoslavia desired to end its quarrel with Greece. "It is encouraging," Allen remarked, "to note an apparent all-around improvement in Yugoslav relations with neighboring non-Cominform countries at this critical time." [56]

X

THE SAME events that occasioned a reconsideration of American policy toward India during the summer and fall of 1950 forced a rethinking of Washington's approach to Yugoslavia. In fact, to a degree previously unknown in postwar American planning, the outbreak of fighting in Korea brought together the Asian and European strands of American cold-war strategy. Just as the conflict in the Far East raised the stakes for American security in South Asia, so it heightened the importance of Tito's defection in Central Europe. Just as the Chinese intervention in Korea pushed the United States to increased activity in the Indian subcontinent, so it spurred the Truman administration to a more forward posture on Yugoslavia. And just as the Korean crisis led American leaders to conclude that Nehru, neutralist warts and all, deserved American support, so it prompted a greater appreciation of Tito's nonalignment.

The beginning of the fighting elicited an ambivalent response from Yugoslavia. Allen explained Tito's abstention on the initial UN vote condemning the North Korean invasion:

> Yugoslavia is trying to straddle the Korean issue, which put it in a serious dilemma in the Security Council. On one hand Yugoslavia is dependent on the UN in the event of Soviet aggression, while on the other it is anxious to show sympathy for Far Eastern Communism in order to encourage Titoism.

Allen added that even though Yugoslavia chose not to commit itself in public, Tito privately applauded the American decision to send troops. As the fighting progressed Yugoslavia took a clearer position, supporting the "Uniting for Peace" resolution, which allowed the General Assembly to bypass a Soviet veto in the Security Council; but it later hedged by backing India's efforts to end the war.[57]

Pushing Tito toward the West was an increase in Soviet-sponsored activities around Yugoslavia's borders. During the month after the commencement of fighting in Korea the CIA described a twenty-five percent buildup of military forces in Hungary, Rumania, Bulgaria, and Albania. In addition, Soviet divisions in Austria were mobilizing in a manner consistent with plans for an attack on Yugoslavia. Tito's representative at the UN told his American counterpart that he was becoming "more and more concerned" about the potential for aggression against Yugoslavia by the Russians and their allies.[58]

In response to these developments and to a general fear that Moscow would use America's preoccupation in Korea to jump Europe, the Truman administration stepped up consideration of military aid for Yugoslavia. Until now American planners had assumed that the likelihood of a direct invasion from the Soviet bloc was diminishing with time—that Stalin, having failed to move forcibly in the immediate aftermath of Tito's challenge, would find it more difficult to do so as the rift solidified. The North Korean assault on South Korea challenged this reasoning. Evidently the communists had fewer reservations about war than Americans had thought. To be sure, the Soviets had not joined the fighting in

Korea, but few administration officials doubted that the Kremlin had given Kim Il Sung the nod. Considering the war preparations under way among the Soviet allies on Yugoslavia's borders, it seemed only prudent to prepare for similar adventurism in the Balkans.

The day after Truman approved the use of American troops in Korea Acheson told the embassy in Belgrade that it would be "desirable" to establish contacts with Yugoslav military authorities. The secretary did not intend to offer any guarantees of assistance at this point, and he did not want the Yugoslavs informed of the earlier NSC decision to provide weapons in case of emergency. The initiative, he believed, should come from Tito. He added, however, that "in the event that the threat of aggression should become more imminent and the Yugoslavs should specifically request military supplies, a new situation would arise." [59]

Meanwhile the State and Defense departments worked out a detailed plan regarding what types of military assistance Yugoslavia would require and what this aid might be expected to accomplish. On the latter point the State-Defense study concluded that with the cooperation of other Western powers the United States could deliver sufficient weapons and ammunition to enable Tito to rebuff an attack by the satellite states. In other words, the war-by-proxy approach, which the Kremlin seemed to be pursuing in Korea, would fail in Yugoslavia. However, if Stalin threw Soviet troops into an all-out offensive, American and Western military aid would allow only a retreat to the mountains of southwestern Yugoslavia and a defense of that regions. [60]

Simultaneously, the joint chiefs of staff reconsidered their position on military assistance. From their earlier reluctant and qualified acquiescence, the chiefs shifted to more active support. They remained unwilling to deplete American reserves to arm Yugoslavia, but they judged the threat to the Western position around the Balkans serious enough to warrant greater efforts on Tito's behalf. Should Yugoslavia fall, the chiefs declared, the situation in the region would change substantially for the worse. Greece would face a far greater risk if confronted with Soviet-controlled troops on its border; so would Italy. Now-isolated Albania would acquire heightened significance as a threat on the Adriatic, and the security of the Western zones in Austria would be called into question. For these reasons the chiefs declared that the United States should take "all possible steps" to enable Yugoslavia to receive military aid in case of aggression. Matériel earmarked for Tito should be stockpiled in Trieste, North Africa, Western Europe, or the United States, for immediate shipment when needed. The State and Defense departments should draft legislation for submission to Congress. And the administration should inform Tito of the new policy.[61]

Truman did not choose to endorse the recommendations of the joint chiefs in detail, but at an NSC meeting two days later he agreed to a review of the administration's policy. This review required several weeks, during which the situation in Korea went from bad to good to disastrous. At the same time a new threat to the stability of Tito's regime arose.[62]

XI

A WARM, dry spring on the plains of Yugoslavia had turned into a hotter, drier summer. As the drought continued into the autumn it became evident that Yugoslavia, normally self-sufficient in basic food crops, would need help to survive the winter. In October Kardelj visited Washington to request American assistance. The foreign minister said his people were prepared to "tighten their belts," but only relief from abroad could prevent a drastic drop in living standards, which would threaten the internal security of the state and afford the Soviets an opportunity to "make trouble." Stressing the importance of refuting Russian claims that Yugoslavia could not survive economically after its break with the Cominform, Kardelj asserted that his country would require $100 million, half for food and the balance to purchase raw materials agricultural exports normally paid for. He added that his government had decided not to ask for Western military aid, since this would only fuel Soviet propaganda. Consequently Yugoslavia had to continue to use its own limited resources to provide for defense.

Acheson replied cautiously but not unsympathetically. Intent on getting the request in writing, the secretary commented that he would be happy to receive a formal application. He went on to say that while the American government "fully understood" the critical nature of Yugoslavia's problems, Yugoslavia in turn must consider the political situation in the United States. The administration did not have $100 million on hand. Congress might appropriate funds, but it had recessed. When the legislators returned they would respond to an aid request with searching questions about Yugoslavia's government and policies; in the meantime, therefore, the Yugoslavs could help their case "by putting relations with the U.S. and with Yugoslavia's Western neighbors on the best possible basis."[63]

The next day Acheson persuaded Truman to ask a forthcoming special session of Congress for assistance for Yugoslavia; in the weeks that followed the administration engaged in what John Campbell, the State Department officer in charge of Balkan affairs, later characterized as "some ingenious interpretation of existing aid legislation." Administration officials requisitioned $14 million from the Mutual Defense Assistance Program, ostensibly to pay for food for the Yugoslav army; they transferred $12 million in Marshall Plan flour from Germany and Italy to Yugoslavia; and they rechanneled part of the Eximbank loan to purchase grain.[64]

At the end of October the administration set in motion a campaign to convince Congress that aid to Yugoslavia served the American national interest. Acheson wrote to leading members of the committees responsible for foreign affairs in the Senate and House, explaining the twin premises of the administration's policy:

(1) Tito's defection from Kremlin control represents the first setback to Soviet imperialism and as such is an important political symbol; and (2) Tito controls the largest fighting forces in Europe except the Soviet Union. . . . These forces constitute an important element in the defense of Western Europe against Soviet aggression.

Invoking the prestige of General Marshall, who, Acheson said, urged aid to Tito "without delay," the secretary declared that unless Congress acted at once Tito's ability to control subversive elements in Yugoslavia would be "seriously, if not fatally, undermined," and the capacity of Yugoslavia's armed forces to beat back an attack would be "dangerously weakened."[65]

At the end of November—just two weeks, as it turned out, before the Indian ambassador laid India's request for American aid before the administration—Truman asked Congress for $38 million in assistance for Yugoslavia. As he would with the Indian appeal, the president argued the administration's case in terms of humanitarianism and self-interest, although, expecting stiffer resistance for help to Belgrade, Truman especially stressed the latter. "The continued independence of Yugoslavia," he declared, "is of great importance to the security of the

United States and its partners in the North Atlantic Treaty Organization, and to all nations associated with them in their common defense against the threat of Soviet aggression."[66]

XII

DURING CONGRESSIONAL hearings on the Yugoslavia aid bill administration witnesses took a similar line. In one respect, selling the idea of aid for Tito was more difficult than pitching help for Nehru: the Yugoslav leader did not even pretend to be a democrat. On the other hand, Yugoslavia promised a very specific quid pro quo for aid, simply by the fact of its nonalignment, which had eased military pressure on the Central European front. Naturally the administration's spokespersons emphasized the latter consideration.

On the morning of November 29 George Perkins led off before the House Foreign Affairs Committee. The assistant secretary's opening statement provided the fullest explanation to date of the administration's thinking on Yugoslavia, and committee members listened carefully. Perkins did not blink at the issue of Tito's domestic repression. "Yugoslavia is a Communist state. It is a dictatorship. No attempt is being made to disguise those facts." But at the moment this mattered little.

> The issue here is a different one. Yugoslavia is resisting Soviet imperialism. The issue is the right of that country to national independence, and the will and ability of its armed forces and of its people to defend that independence against outside pressure and aggression.

Perkins delineated what Yugoslavia meant to the United States. Tito's defection, he said, represented a rolling back of the iron curtain.

> The western limit of absolute Soviet power in that part of the world—if we exclude Albania which is now only an isolated outpost—runs through the middle of the Balkan Peninsula instead of along the shores of the Adriatic Sea.

More importantly, especially with a war on in Asia, Yugoslavia acted as a force for peace in Europe.

> Its people, in their determination to defend their independence, serve the independence and the security of other peoples. And their army is a factor in the world balance. The existence of this force, ready to defend its

homeland, is a deterrent to adventurous policies and aggression, both in the Balkans and elsewhere in Europe.[67]

Perkins and other administration officials preferred to argue the case for aid strictly at this level of continental and global strategy and solely in terms of American interests. Making a worthy recipient of American aid out of Nehru, in the hearings on India, was difficult enough; defending Tito on grounds besides shared enemies was impossible. But the committee members insisted on turning the discussion in an uncomfortable direction. Democrat Abraham Ribicoff of Connecticut asked if Tito hadn't brought on Yugoslavia's troubles by socialist mismanagement. "Don't some of Yugoslavia's problems in the matter of food stem from their program of collectivization of the peasants?" Perkins replied that he had no figures on the subject; in any event the collectivization campaign had "substantially slowed." Ribicoff suggested that an excessive eagerness to industrialize had led the Yugoslav economy into difficulty. Perkins conceded this point; here again, however, he asserted that improvements were in the works. It was "a very bitter pill" for the Yugoslavs to admit that they had overreached themselves in their drive to industrialize. "But they seem to be alert to that and are willing to talk sense in their investment program."[68]

A generally sympathetic Republican, Frances Bolton of Ohio, described correspondence she had received from constituents of Yugoslav descent complaining that Tito's commissars were using relief for political purposes, withholding help from individuals who were not "out-and-out Titoists." "The poor little people at the bottom," Bolton claimed, "are getting nothing." L. Randolph Higgs of the office of Eastern European affairs, who had accompanied Perkins to the hearing, responded that the situation was changing for the better in this area also. Higgs stated that the Yugoslav government had recently abolished preferential treatment for Communist party members.[69]

Republican Lawrence Smith of Wisconsin wanted to know if the Yugoslavs had offered any guarantees—or if the administration had asked for any. "Are we going along on faith, simply hoping and praying that they will do what is right?" Perkins replied that the administration would insist on equitable distribution of aid, fair pricing, and the right of inspection. This was not what Smith was asking. "No definite conditions as to the disposition of the vexing problem of Trieste?" he demanded. "Nothing so far as guaranteeing freedom of speech or the right to have free elections?" When Perkins admitted that the administration had not proposed such conditions, Smith asked how the administration would respond if the House added them as amendments. Perkins replied that he and his colleagues would oppose them "as strongly as we could." The Yugoslavs had broken with the Soviet Union, he said, because they were tired of being told what to do. It would be "very embarrassing and unwise" for the United States to adopt "Kremlin tactics" and try to order the Yugoslavs around. "We believe basically that our strength is getting on with free people, and not in dictating to them."

Perkins had ventured onto treacherous ground, as he soon realized. Smith queried, "Do you think the people in Yugoslavia are free today?" "Relatively free," Perkins replied. "They are freer than the rest of the people back of the iron curtain." Smith objected. "If I understand your statement, you said that it was an absolute dictatorship." Perkins waffled. "That is true, but there are degrees of dictatorship." Smith: "Define them." Perkins did the best he could under the circumstances, asserting that Yugoslavs enjoyed "a certain amount of free speech" and that Tito's group had "a more liberal attitude toward religion" than did other communist regimes.[70]

Another Republican, Chester Merrow of New Hampshire, inquired whether the administration had tried to get Yugoslavia to consider "assisting the Atlantic community in stopping the drive of communism to engulf the earth." Perkins responded that the administration had weighed the idea but set it aside as premature. Merrow complained that this was typical of mistakes the administration had made "all along the line" in the foreign-aid field. He added, "We have not attached any conditions to the aid that we have extended. . . . How can we expect cooperation and assistance if we do not lay down some conditions as we go along?" Perkins responded that the congressman was missing the point. "I think the question is, Do you expect cooperation if you lay down conditions?" The United States, he said, would have "great difficulty" eliciting Tito's cooperation if it began making demands.

Republican James Fulton of Pennsylvania wondered how the administration's aid proposal dovetailed with its overall policy for opposing communism. "This program cannot be fitted into the United States program in Greece and Turkey of containing communism, can it?" Perkins answered, "Not completely; no." Fulton: "Well, not at all, because Yugoslavia is a Communist government." Perkins: "The question is what communism we are talking about containing." Fulton thought Perkins was splitting hairs. Noting that Tito had recently characterized himself as a Leninist, the Pennsylvania congressman asked, "Would you then say that the Lenin type of communism and dictatorship is better than the Stalin type of communism and dictatorship, and therefore, because of that ideological difference, the government of Yugoslavia should be aided?"

Perkins retreated, saying he did not claim expertise on the varieties of communism and could not speak knowledgeably on the matter. But he did assert that Tito was challenging some of the worst features of Stalinism, the most important being the demand for subservience to Moscow. Fulton remained unconvinced.

> Suppose that you had two tigers in the back yard, a little one and a big one. Would you go out every morning and feed the little tiger? If he does not like you any better than does the big one, would it not be possible that in a short time you might have two big tigers instead of a big tiger and a little tiger?

Perkins declined to talk tigers, while admitting the possibility of what Fulton suggested. Many things were possible, however, and other countries for which Congress had voted aid might also turn against the United States at some time in the future. "We have to figure on the law of probabilities, I think, and there are certain calculated risks that have to be considered."

Fulton judged the administration's calculus too machiavellian. "American policy must not be just arms, bombs, and bread." There must also be "something of the spirit." In assessing degrees of despotism the administration had entered a tangled thicket. "We must make sure we are not gardening a group of pet dictators." If such occurred the United States would not have "arms and bread enough to sustain the world," since principle would not be on America's side, nor a standard to which "the wise and just" might repair.[71]

Perkins could hardly agree that American policy lacked principles or standards; he again took the tack of saying his questioner had confused the issue. "What we are concerned with is containing, or driving a wedge, if you will, into Communist totalitarianism, and in containing in particular the Stalin breed of communism." The United States should support Tito because he had challenged the Kremlin, successfully so far, and because Yugoslavia's effort might mark the beginning of a momentous trend. "If we let that effort fail, whether we like Mr. Tito or not, it will be a very devastating thing from the point of view of anybody else who is going to think about trying to break away from the Stalinist doctrine."[72]

XIII

EVEN AS the committee listened to Perkins, Chinese troops were lacerating American forces in Korea; only hours later Truman would hint at the use of nuclear weapons to stave off a rout. As in the case of American policy toward India, the Chinese intervention marked a turning point in American relations with Yugoslavia. To the uninitiated, Yugoslavia might have seemed far removed from the troubles of East Asia; in fact American strategists worried that if the Korean fighting escalated, the Soviets would attack the West in Europe. Consequently the Foreign Affairs Committee paid strict attention to the opinions of the administration's next witness, Joint Chiefs Chairman Omar Bradley.

Bradley asserted that Yugoslavia's economic distress afforded the United States an opportunity "to seek further gains in exploiting the Yugoslav-Soviet break in behalf and in the interest of the West." To make himself unmistakably clear, he continued: "We believe it is in the military interest of the United States that this break be exploited as much as possible." Citing "significant security advantages" to the United States, "especially if Tito's example gives impetus to defections by other satellite states," Bradley described the proposed food aid as a lever for exploiting the situation. "In other words, we consider this an opportunity to further this rift to the military advantage of the west."

As in the earlier questioning of Perkins, committee members wanted to know what the United States could expect in return for its aid to Yugoslavia. Bradley responded that the matter of conditions principally concerned the State Department, but he added, "It is always nice to get something for something. On the other hand, sometimes when you furnish certain aid with the idea that you gain good will now, it pays off materially later on." Chester Merrow tried to pin Bradley down. "The Yugoslav Army would be very valuable in helping in the defense of the Atlantic community if we got into difficulty, would it not?" "Yes, sir," Bradley replied. "Any force of that size on our side would be of material assistance." Merrow wanted to know if the joint chiefs had considered attaching Yugoslav forces to those of the Atlantic pact. When Bradley answered that bringing Yugoslavia into NATO was primarily a political issue, Merrow sharpened his question. "I do not know that I was thinking so much of including it, as I was thinking of some commitment in regard to helping the Atlantic community if we get into a great deal of trouble in stopping the movement of international communism."

Bradley responded that if war began in Europe, Yugoslavia's armed forces could provide assistance in a number of ways, from merely sitting out the conflict to overt collaboration.

> Whether or not they took an active part, or were committed to take an active part ahead of time, or whether or not they are of great value as a threat on the flank of any movement, is something you would have to weigh. They would be of assistance in either case. In the first place, if we could even take them out of the hostile camp and make them a neutral, that is one step. If you can get them to act as a threat, that is a second step. If you can get them actively to participate on your side, that is even a further step and then, of course, if you had a commitment, where their efforts were integrated with those of ours on the defense, that would still be a further step. . . . You can see the advantages to all of them.

James Fulton asked Bradley to indicate more specifically how many Soviet divisions the Yugoslav army could tie down in the event of war. Bradley responded that he could not answer the question with confidence, since such an estimate would depend on whether the Yugoslavs were attacking, threatening attack, or simply defending.

> I think the most you can say is that a force of this size, of some thirty or more divisions, on our side in that particular position, could not help but be very effective, whether they are used as a deterrent or as a flanking threat, or in participation. . . .
> Certainly from a military point of view we would like to have those divisions on our side.

Bradley remarked that the American strategic position had already benefited from Tito's defection, in that when Yugoslavia cut off its support of the Greek rebels it saved the United States "an awful lot" of money and effort.[73]

Republican John Davis Lodge of Connecticut thought Yugoslavia's break with Moscow might prove useful for more than just defensive purposes. Pointing to a map of the Adriatic, Lodge asked Bradley whether it would further American interests if Albania "were somehow to become part of our team rather than to be part of the Communist team." Bradley replied that the significance of such a strategic reversal was "apparent to anyone." The geography of the situation alone made Albania important. Lodge said he had expected as much and went on to recommend completing the transformation of the power balance in the area via "the liberation of Albania." Such a development might have consequences far beyond the Balkans. "I think it would have a very salutary effect on a great many other countries if, for once, the tables were turned and liberation were to come about in a real sense instead of in the usual upside-down-language sense."

Bradley replied in a professionally vague manner to this suggestion, but when another questioner, returning to the matter of conditions on American aid, asserted that without a firm commitment from Tito American planning in the region amounted to nothing more than wishful thinking, the general reacted sharply.

> I should think it is more than just wishful thinking. There has been a tendency on the part of Tito and his government to lean toward the West ever since his break with the Russians. Just how far that has gone, and how far he would go in an emergency I do not believe anybody could vouch for. This has all been an attempt to encourage him and see that he does not suffer too much for having broken with the Cominform and thereby not discourage anybody else from ever doing it. So, from a military point of view, as I say, we think we ought to do anything we can to encourage him, to help him, in his breaking away, and thereby not discourage anyone else, but rather to encourage other countries to break away, if they see fit.[74]

XIV

WHEN THE aid resolution came up for formal debate administration supporters succeeded, although not completely, in focusing the discussion on strategic themes. Tom Connally expressed a common sentiment when he said, "If any Senator two years ago had suggested that I would today be standing on the floor of the United States Senate advocating $38,000,000 for aid to Communist Yugoslavia, I should have called him to order." But the situation had changed. Reciting the list of countries that had fallen under Soviet control, Connally continued, "Yugoslavia was once a member of this extinguished list of independent states. While I have never had a good thing to say for a Communist or for Communism, Marshal Tito is one Communist who knows when he has had enough." Although Tito was a despot, that mattered little at present. "In times like these we cannot demand perfection as a price for our assistance." Connally said he believed in fighting fire with fire. "We now have a Communist backfire burning in Yugoslavia. I want to keep that fire burning."[75]

Connally's argument did not go unchallenged. Conservative Democrat John McClellan of Arkansas—who held the government-operations chairmanship McCarthy would make notorious—saw nothing to choose between Tito and Stalin. "A Communist is a Communist." Because communism opposed the principles supported by "every real red-blooded American," the Senate had the duty to deny the administration's aid request. McClellan did not buy the "hypothesis" of a serious schism between Yugoslavia and the Soviet Union. "How do we know? Who can vouch for it?" Even should the split prove genuine, quarrels among communists were no business of the United States. Neither did McClellan consider Tito in significant danger. "I can see no reason on earth why Stalin should provoke a war with Yugoslavia, with world conditions as they are today." If the Russians wanted to attack Europe, their "natural and likely" strategy would be to bypass Yugoslavia. "Then what would we have? We would have Yugoslavia sitting there as a neutral." And an unreliable neutral at that. "I dare say that if the situation ever developed to the point where Tito thought the Kremlin was going to win, he would be found hastening to join the Soviet Union for the kill."[76]

Owen Brewster of Maine lambasted the administration's policy toward Yugoslavia as being of a piece with the Democrats' inept handling of foreign affairs in other parts of the world. "After Tito's break with Moscow, some of Mr. Acheson's master minds evolved the theory of Titoism. . . . The State Department loved this theory of Titoism so much that they applied it to China." But no one had bothered to read the script to the Chinese Communists. "Today, as I speak, those Chinese Communists are butchering Americans in cold blood in the snow-bound passes of North Korea. If that is what Titoism means in China, why should we expect it to be something different in Yugoslavia?"[77]

Republican William Langer of North Dakota, one of the Senate's last isolationists, insisted that Tito had only himself to blame for Yugoslavia's problems. "The actual condition in Yugoslavia is not the result of drought. It has developed because Tito did what the Russians did when Russia killed more than 5,000,000 farmers a few years ago." Collectivization, Langer asserted, had taken a tremendous toll in lives, and the Truman administration, in proposing to bail Yugoslavia out of its self-inflicted mess, was asking Congress to vote "millions of dollars to a bloody Communist outfit which murdered hundreds of thousands of families."

William Knowland, returning to Brewster's China theme, sought to sidetrack the administration's bill by adding a rider blocking the $38 million for Yugoslavia until the administration spent an equal amount on Taiwan. In the House, Ohio Republican John Vorys attempted to amend the measure to make the money for Yugoslavia a loan rather than a grant.[78]

But the dissenters constituted a minority. In the shadow of world war, most of the lawmakers agreed with William Fulbright, who said, "General Bradley and others advised us that the mere existence of thirty divisions on the flank of Russia is worth a great deal to us, whether they ever fight anybody or not." When the aid bill came to a vote in the Senate, supporters outnumbered opponents by a 60-21 margin. Two days later the House approved the resolution by a count of 225-142. One month after presenting his request to Congress Truman signed the measure into law.[79]

V

The Devil's Due: 1951–1960

As the events of 1950 had transformed American policy toward India, by demonstrating the geopolitical significance of the subcontinent, so the same events occasioned a shift in Washington's approach to Yugoslavia, for similar reasons. Just as the Korean scare had inclined Congress to vote for aid to India, so it greased the ways for grain ships heading for Yugoslavia. Once the administration persuaded the legislators to accept economic assistance to Tito, it moved to broader and more potent forms of collaboration.

Congressional acceptance of the administration's aid bill resulted from a coincidence of needs: at the moment Yugoslavia most needed American food to stave off a famine, the United States most needed, or thought it might need, Yugoslav troops to distract the Soviet Union. Put another way: Tito looked good because everything else looked so bad. Had the situation in Korea not preoccupied Congress and the American people, and had the oft-expected third world war not filled their thoughts, they would have given closer scrutiny to the administration's decision to prop up a communist regime. Considering the anticommunist atmosphere of the time, it seems doubtful that the aid package could have survived such examination. Nor did it hurt matters, from the administration's perspective, that the crisis in Yugoslavia climaxed *after* the 1950 election. From Tito's point of view it probably helped to get in the aid line ahead of Nehru.

In any event, the aid measure did pass, and it placed American policy for Yugoslavia on a new footing. The first bite on the bullet tasted worst; once Congress conceded that even a communist state might serve American purposes, further administration requests for assistance appeared less radical. When the administration included Yugoslavia in the 1951 mutual security bill, the action provoked relatively little controversy, although some legislators detected a significant difference between feeding communists and arming them.

The great challenge to the policy of support for Tito's neutralism came during the first years of the Eisenhower administration, when Stalin's heirs dropped their predecessor's belligerent posture and repented for his sins. From 1948 the American approach to Yugoslavia had rested on an enemy-of-my-enemy theory. Yugoslav-Soviet rapprochement eroded this foundation. Yet the policy survived. Not completely and not without interruption: resistance forces in Congress won occasional rounds and usually required the Eisenhower administration to accept less than it wanted. But on the whole the pragmatists carried the day. Just as in the Indian case, they recognized the advantages to the United States of a Yugoslavia poised between the blocs; they understood how Bandung could be made to serve the interests of Yalta.

II

AS DESCRIBED in the previous chapter, the Truman administration had been considering weapons for Yugoslavia for more than a year. By his approval of NSC 18/4 in November 1949 Truman had accepted the idea that military aid to Belgrade should figure in American contingency planning. Still, the administration insisted that the initiative in the arms transfers come from the Yugoslavs.

Tito was in no hurry to make a request, although he deliberately kept the door open. At the end of December 1950 the Yugoslav leader explained his position to Allen.

> I am satisfied that my standing army is well equipped, or will be in the near future. I cannot ask for arms from the West even if I wanted to. My object is that Yugoslavia should remain neutral—until, at any rate, a third

world war breaks out. In the latter circumstance I realize I shall be drawn in. But to remain neutral I must act neutrally. I cannot have people saying, "That is an American tank. Those are British guns. Yugoslavia is an Anglo-American base." I will give no provocation to the other side.

Nonetheless, to Allen's question whether Yugoslavia could defend itself without military aid from abroad, Tito replied, "Not if Russia invades us. Then we will need help from the West."[1]

Tito made this view public several weeks later in a speech to a congress of Yugoslavia's Communist party. The marshal defended his decision to seek American economic aid and cultivate trade relations with the West, but he indicated forcefully that he would never lead Yugoslavia into the Western camp. The West, Tito declared, offered help not from altruism but from fear that the Russians would become too strong if allowed to overrun Yugoslavia. Regarding arms, he stated that Yugoslavia preferred not to seek Western assistance, instead concentrating on developing its own munitions industry. He added, however, that if a Soviet attack appeared inevitable he would not hesitate to ask for military aid. But under no circumstances would Yugoslavia become a satellite of the West. "I would prefer to fight barehanded than be anyone's satellite."[2]

Washington considered this speech partly bravado for the folks at home; American officials expected Tito to turn West for weapons before 1951 ran out. In a memo to the Pentagon, Deputy Undersecretary of State H. Freeman Matthews explained that a senior Yugoslav general had said his government intended to enlarge the armed forces by fifty percent. Matthews guessed this was an exaggeration, that the point of the message was to test American willingness to equip an expanded army. Matthews predicted an arms request "before many months."[3]

At the end of January, in a meeting with Allen, Foreign Minister Kardelj conspicuously disavowed any intention to request American weapons—so conspicuously that Allen concluded the subject must be under discussion. "It is obvious that a serious and possibly critical debate is taking place inside the politbureau on the question of seeking economic and military assistance from the West, particularly from the U.S." Kardelj seemed grim and under strain; Allen suspected that the foreign minister had been pushing for American arms but had been overruled at a top-level meeting the previous night. Allen anticipated a change of heart on high. Although certain Yugoslav officials found a request for American weapons distasteful, "stern necessity would force them to it."[4]

The administration decided to give necessity some help. When a delegation of American legislators visited Yugoslavia to review the arrival of American grain, Representative John Kennedy—most probably at the behest of the State Department—asked Tito directly whether he wanted American weapons. Tito responded that Yugoslavia had a "moral right" to seek weapons from the United States or any other country, especially since the Russians were arming Yugoslavia's neighbors. But he preferred to move cautiously because he did not wish to take steps that might provoke a Cominform attack. Even so, the marshal specified what his armed forces needed most: tanks, jets, and anti-aircraft guns. Apparently Kennedy had expected to discuss less substantial items; the Massachusetts Democrat asked Tito if he could use any bazookas. Tito said he already had bazookas, and in any event they would not do the job he required. His soldiers needed heavier equipment. But he would not ask for foreign troops. "I have plenty of men. With arms, we can do all that is necessary."[5]

Some in the State Department judged this hint close enough to a formal request to deserve a straightforward response. Robert Joyce of the Policy Planning Staff argued that the administration's reluctance to declare publicly its intention to come to Yugoslavia's aid was giving Moscow the wrong idea.

> The Kremlin may believe that it might be able to take over Yugoslavia without unleashing a general conflict, perhaps on the basis that Yugoslavia is a Slav state and that an attack against Tito by the Communists might be considered a "family quarrel" within the Soviet world, at least to the extent that there would not be a total reaction on the part of the Western alliance of which Tito is not a member.

To counter such a misconception, or at least to prevent such an attack, Joyce recommended three courses of action. First, the United States and other NATO countries should establish in Trieste an "impressive" stockpile of arms and equipment especially for Yugoslavia. Initially the United States should keep the buildup secret, to forestall a preemptive move by the Soviets. But once the weapons were in place Washington should make the fact known, along with the arms' intended use. Second, the president and other Western leaders should prepare statements for release in case an offensive against Yugoslavia appeared imminent, to the effect that any aggression in Europe would destroy the fabric of peace. A pointed reminder that Yugoslavia, like Korea, was a member of the United Nations would also be in order. Finally, if the Soviets or their allies seemed about to strike, NATO ought to stage naval and air maneuvers in the Adriatic and the eastern Mediterranean.[6]

Although others in the administration declined to buy all of Joyce's argument, his memo increased the momentum toward an arms deal. The joint chiefs of staff agreed to the stockpiling arrangement Joyce suggested; several weeks later they recommended initiating discussions between American and Yugoslav military officers "at the earliest possible date." In response to an indirect request from Tito the State Department approved the transfer of $3 million worth of rifles and light artillery.[7]

In June the Yugoslav chief of staff, Koča Popović, visited the United States. At the Pentagon Popović signed an agreement calling for the shipment of a modest amount of military equipment to Yugoslavia. Just before leaving Washington Popović met with Acheson at the State Department. The secretary asked whether he had been satisfied by the discussions. "Reasonably satisfied," Popović replied, commenting that he regarded the agreement as an initial step toward further cooperation. Acheson said the American government felt similarly.[8]

The secretary then asked, in effect: Where do we go from here? The general expressed a desire for military talks. George Perkins, also at the meeting, commented that American officers strongly recommended that such talks take place in Yugoslavia, so that the Americans could become familiar with Yugoslavia's equipment and techniques. Popović demurred, saying that for "political reasons" an American military mission to Yugoslavia would be "premature." The meetings should begin in Washington; perhaps at a later date they could move to his country. In reply to a question about his opinion of Russia's intentions, the general said the Soviets undoubtedly still intended to destroy Yugoslavia's independence. The issue was not whether they would take action, but when. Mobilization in the satellite countries, especially Bulgaria, had proceeded to a point where an attack might come at any time.[9]

III

TEN DAYS later the State Department received a formal request from the Yugoslav government for military assistance. Because the Truman administration had been planning for this eventuality for eighteen months and had been supplying weapons informally for nearly half a year, a positive response from the White House was nearly automatic. But the precise nature of the response and the manner of its presentation to the public remained to be determined.[10]

Immediately the administration prepared to expand discussions then under way with the NATO allies regarding aid to Tito. The British in particular had mixed feelings about supporting Yugoslavia. While their assessment of the desirability of keeping Belgrade independent broadly coincided with the Americans', some in the Foreign Office believed a surprise reconciliation between Tito and Stalin, on the order of the Molotov-Ribbentrop pact of 1939, could not be ruled out. Others feared Washington would strangle any aid program in red tape. The British defense ministry worried that assistance to Yugoslavia would short-circuit a strengthening of NATO.[11]

Eventually, however, London agreed to military assistance, and the Pentagon readied for shipment some of the weapons it had stockpiled. The administration demonstrated further support at the beginning of August when it accepted Tito's request for a visit by Army Chief of Staff General J. Lawton Collins to Yugoslavia. A short while later, the Defense Department received a delegation of Tito's top officers.[12]

At about the same time, Tito asked Averell Harriman, then in Tehran attempting to negotiate a settlement of the Anglo-Iranian oil dispute, to stop in Belgrade on his way back to Washington. After some discussion within the State Department Harriman accepted the invitation. The flight to Belgrade demonstrated that U.S.–Yugoslav collaboration might not be easy. Harriman flew via Athens. Leaving the Greek capital early in the morning, Harriman's plane circled while waiting for clearance to enter Yugoslav airspace. Remembering the fate of the American fliers shot down by the Yugoslavs a few years previous, Harriman's crew hesitated to cross the border without authorization. After some delay the pilot radioed Athens for an explanation of Belgrade's silence. The Greeks reported that nothing was amiss; the airport in the Yugoslav capital just did not open until nine o'clock. Harriman, confident that Tito's gunners would look more charitably on an American plane now than they had before, gave the order to proceed.[13]

In Harriman's meeting with Tito the marshal came right to the point. He said his country needed not only weapons and ammunition but the industrial plant to produce them. Tito remarked that the Kremlin probably did not want war at this time, but sometimes wars started accidentally. In any event it was best to prepare for the worst. Harriman mostly listened. Avoiding commitments, he said the American government hoped to be of assistance but that it too faced shortages. How much it could supply at the moment was difficult to determine.[14]

In the wake of this inconclusive meeting Tito took measures that improved his image in the United States. He moved—albeit slowly—toward a settlement of Yugoslavia's dispute with Italy over Trieste. He told a visiting American senator who had commented that "thirty million Catholics" in the United States could not remain indifferent to the plight of the imprisoned Archbishop Stepanic, that his government had decided to let Stepanic travel abroad. But the Vatican had refused the offer. The senator, Brien McMahon of Connecticut, suggested that the regime might at least release Stepanic from prison and allow him to live in a monastery, as it had recently done for an Orthodox bishop in similar circumstances. Tito said he would consider the idea.[15]

American officials realized that these image-enhancing measures were not entirely for the benefit of Congress. Regarding Trieste, with trouble threatening from the East, Tito logically sought calmer relations with Italy. As to Stepinac, when the marshal told another visiting legislator that the archbishop indeed would be released, Allen suggested Tito was trying to liquidate his Stepinac problem without having to liquidate the prelate. Trading Stepinac for American weapons, as it were, got Tito off the hook with old partisans who still considered the archbishop an enemy of the people.[16]

The administration interpreted other liberalizing tendencies in similar fashion. For some time the CIA had been receiving reports of low morale in the Yugoslav army. An intelligence summary of late 1950 cited an informant who stated flatly that the rank and file would desert, taking their guns, before they would fight for Tito. Yugoslav expatriates told a similar story. Tito's relaxation seemed designed to calm unrest within Yugoslavia and create a feeling among the masses that the regime was worth defending. As Allen commented, however, in describing Yugoslavia's reforms, Tito's definition of freedom remained thoroughly communist: "freedom to agree with the regime and the outlawing of dissenters."[17]

With these developments on the political front American and Yugoslav officials haggled over the size and terms of reference of the American military mission that would supervise an assistance program. Having had his fill of Soviet snooping into Yugoslav affairs, Tito objected to the presence of American watchdogs. The Truman administration agreed to a smaller mission than usual but refused to dispense with supervision entirely. As Allen explained to Tito, oversight was necessary to eliminate "suspicions" in the United States regarding the program. The Yugoslav leader still resisted, saying the sight of American officers examining barracks, depots, and military installations would undermine the spirit of the army. He added that while he greatly desired American assistance he would rather do without than run "any risk whatever" of giving his troops the impression that the United States was assuming the role recently played by the Soviet Union.[18]

Not surprisingly the supervision issue proved a troublesome point in talks between the administration and members of Congress. Because the administration folded military assistance to Yugoslavia into its omnibus mutual security proposals the arms shipments provided Tito's critics fewer clear shots than had the previous year's special economic aid bill. During debate over the mutual security package Yugoslavia came up but evoked little controversy. Owen Brewster thought the United States had already been "very generous" to Tito, adding, "I have no objection to aiding anyone who will fight communism behind the iron curtain, but I think it is possible to overdo it." At the time, however, with Korea very much a live issue and a Russian invasion of Western Europe still a sobering possibility, opponents had difficulty drumming up indignation. Nonetheless the administration deemed it prudent to stay on top of the matter, and Acheson sent the deputy director of the State Department's European division, Randolph Higgs, to apprise the House Foreign Affairs Committee of recent developments.[19]

Even while Higgs spoke, negotiations continued between General Collins and his Yugoslav counterparts regarding the American supervisory mission. As Higgs explained to the committee, the major impediment in the discussions was the Yugoslavs' unpleasant memory of their experience with Soviet advisers.

> The Russians had these people all over the country, and they were telling the Yugoslavs they had to do this and that. It got into the Yugoslavs' hair to an unbearable extent. . . . Now they were afraid we are going to send in a mission which will act just like the Russians do.

General Collins was trying to convince the Yugoslavs that the United States had no such intentions, that an American oversight group would merely ensure that the weapons provided met Yugoslavia's needs and were used properly. On this point, Higgs said, the administration would not compromise. "If they do not buy that, they will not get military assistance."[20]

Responding to committee members' questions about popular support for Tito, Higgs conceded that as few as fifteen percent of the people backed the government on domestic matters. "Almost anybody you stopped on the road and said, 'What do you think of the regime?' he would say that he thinks it stinks. Our people run into that all the time." On Tito's handling of external affairs, however, especially relations with the Soviet Union, the situation was quite different. "All of the observers that we have been able to talk to who have been in there since the break with the Cominform are agreed that the people of the country support him in his stand against the Cominform."

Higgs admitted that it was conceivable that these observers might prove mistaken. In a crisis the peasants might not fight. He described a "pretty clever" ploy by the Cominform to undermine Yugoslav morale. Soviet and allied agents had spread rumors that the United States would never let Yugoslavia fall back under Russian domination; the peasants therefore could sit out a war and let Tito fall, secure in the knowledge that the Americans would come to their rescue against Stalin. Higgs said such rumors, to the degree they gained credence, created a "dangerous situation." Fortunately they did not seem to be taking hold, and the administration thought the people would stand behind Tito. "They feel that they would be much worse off if the Russians should get back in control of the country." While this attitude obtained, Tito remained a "good bet."

As administration officials had done since the question of assistance to Yugoslavia first arose in 1948—and as they did in discussions of aid to India—Higgs took pains to point out that aid to the government did not imply endorsement of all the government's actions. With India the problem was Nehru's foreign policy; in the case of Yugoslavia it was Belgrade's handling of domestic affairs. Higgs emphasized the administration's disapproval of Tito's repression of dissent. "We do not like it. We have said so publicly and privately. He is personally aware of that." But given the absence of a plausible, more democratic force in the country, the administration was compelled to work through Tito. "If there were any such force, I think everybody would be much happier." Higgs concluded with a comment that summarized American policy: "As long as we do not have any choice except between Tito and the Russians, we will support Tito."[21]

IV

AFTER NEGOTIATIONS lasting several more weeks the Truman administration and the Yugoslav government finally came to terms on the composition and objectives of the American military advisory group. Following this agreement military aid flowed more freely. As it did, the administration's unenthusiastic support of Tito became firmly cemented into American foreign policy. Until Truman left office little happened to call this support into question. Tito began to revert to authoritarian form as the Korea-inspired war scare dissipated; when the State Department suggested that he watch his step he countered with complaints about American restrictions on the activities of Yugoslav journalists. Despite earlier hints of compromise Trieste remained a point of annoyance; Acheson told the Yugoslav ambassador that Washington was "very much disturbed" at the lack of progress with the Italians. When renewed drought conditions elicited further American economic assistance the administration sent with the money a warning that unless Yugoslavia mended its ways it should not count on help in the future.[22]

But none of this was new, and until the early part of 1953 American policy toward Yugoslavia continued on the track already laid out. Collins returned from Belgrade and declared that American interests in Europe demanded a stronger Yugoslavia; on the basis of this recommendation the administration decided to overlook Tito's failings and send more weapons. The Pentagon, encouraged by a Yugoslav–Greek–Turkish treaty of friendship, began preparations for direct U.S.–Yugoslav strategic planning. Events were moving less quickly than before, but they still had a direction favoring the United States.[23]

V

SUCH WAS the relationship Eisenhower and Dulles inherited in January 1953, and neither the new president nor his secretary of state inclined toward changing it. Eisenhower, after his early skepticism, had come to recognize the depth and significance of the split between Tito and Stalin. As commander at NATO he had appreciated the degree to which Yugoslavia's dealignment from the Soviet bloc lessened the pressure on the southern flank of the Atlantic alliance; as American commander-in-chief he continued to understand the break's importance.

For Dulles Yugoslavia possessed additional significance. Author of the "liberation" plank of the 1952 Republican platform, Dulles had committed himself and the administration to an attempt to undo the Soviet seizure of Eastern Europe. In some respects, of course, "liberation" had simply floated aloft on the hot air of the campaign, and Dulles the diplomat realized that rolling back the communist tide was not as easy Dulles the campaigner made it sound. But "peaceful liberation" was not entirely oxymoronic. A model existed: Yugoslavia. Tito had lifted the iron curtain, and so long as Yugoslavia kept its heresy alive it served as an inspiration to other countries still under Soviet control. That Tito oppressed his own people mattered, but in the global scheme of things, not much. Dulles told the Yugoslav vice-minister for foreign affairs that the United States had no use for Tito's internal policies; even so, he continued, Yugoslavia was "symbolic of the possibility of breaking up the Soviet empire without war."[24]

VI

STALIN'S DEATH, six weeks into Eisenhower's first term, threatened to change all this. Much of the impetus for the Moscow-Belgrade rift had derived from the personal rivalry between Stalin and Tito, and the former's disappearance promised to drain the dispute of much of its bitterness. In Belgrade Tito's associates toasted the dictator's passing. "Thank you for the lovely news," Vladimir Dedijer told an English correspondent who woke him with the report. Milovan Djilas suggested that Stalin's last thought must have been "Ugh, Yugoslavia is not giving in."[25]

In Moscow the contenders for power had other things than Yugoslavia to worry about—namely, each other—in the immediate aftermath of the death of "Comrade Stalin, whom we have all loved so much and who will live in our hearts forever," as Molotov lied. Historian Adam Ulam describes the post-Stalin events in the Soviet Union as "a veritable *coup d'etat."* (Djilas, commenting from Yugoslavia at the time, came to the same conclusion: "an anti-Stalinist coup.") Although the struggle for the succession took three years to produce a clear winner, within weeks a new foreign-policy line emerged. In marked contrast to the Stalinist argument on the intractability of the clash between capitalism and communism, the Kremlin's now spokesmen described the necessity to avoid the world war that would devastate both sides and advocated peaceful resolution of conflicts.[26]

A revised Soviet approach toward Yugoslavia soon surfaced. In May the Kremlin received the Yugoslav chargé d'affaires for the first time since 1948. In June Moscow proposed to exchange ambassadors. Tito, suspicious but willing to accept the surrender, agreed. In July Lavrenti Beria, on whom Khrushchev dumped the blame for the Soviet-Yugoslav misunderstanding, was denounced as a "double-dyed agent of imperialism." During the next several months the Cominform dropped its boycott of Yugoslavia. (The organization itself grew moribund, finally expiring in 1956.) In November 1954 Khruschev visited the Yugoslav embassy in Moscow and offered a toast to "Comrade Tito."[27]

Predictably, this rapid turnabout prompted a reconsideration of American policy. As officials of the Truman administration had repeatedly told congressional committees and as Yugoslavia's supporters in Congress and elsewhere had explained to critics, the United States backed Tito to preserve Yugoslavia's independence in the face of Soviet aggression or the threat thereof. With Stalin fulminating in Moscow, the danger to Yugoslavia had appeared fully evident and the need for American help nearly so. But now the bellowing had given way to cooing, and the threat, if it had not vanished, certainly had changed in form. Whether American assistance continued to serve American interests required pondering.

The new state of affairs had just begun to take shape when the CIA compiled the best estimates of the American intelligence community regarding the likely direction of relations between Belgrade and Moscow. According to this summary, Yugoslavia would probably move only very cautiously toward closer ties with the Kremlin. Soviet-Yugoslav distrust antedated the 1948 split; Allen Dulles later remarked that Moscow's suspicions of Tito had been quite evident during World War II. Tito would realize that although the personnel in the Kremlin had changed, Moscow's basic objectives remained as before. The Soviet still intended to regain control over Yugoslavia. They had simply exchanged Stalin's bullying for a Leninist zigzag, seeking, as the CIA report put it, "to undermine Tito's position and weaken his ties with the West through increasingly conciliatory gestures."[28]

This being the case, the Eisenhower administration saw no reason to alter Truman's basic policy. Yugoslavia continued independent of Moscow, and while it did collaboration with Belgrade might further American interests. Tito had his faults but naiveté was not among them. Although he would probably take advantage of the Kremlin's change of strategy, aiming to lessen his dependence on the West, he would certainly not accept any Soviet help that compromised his freedom of maneuver. In other words, instead of being almost a de facto member of NATO—the month of Stalin's death found Tito in London, where Churchill declared that "should our ally, Yugoslavia, be attacked, we would fight and die with you"—he would become a genuine neutralist.[29]

This confidence in Tito's desire and ability to remain neutral in the face of Soviet blandishments provided the basis for the Eisenhower administration's policy toward Yugoslavia—just as a similar assessment informed policy toward India. Before long the administration had occasion to put its confidence to the test. In the autumn of 1953, feeling pressure from Italy, Eisenhower and Dulles decided to lean on Tito to settle the Trieste dispute. The Yugoslavs would not like the plan; the administration recognized that. But as C. D. Jackson reasoned, it was highly unlikely that "a Trieste solution which didn't give Tito everything he asked for would drive him back into the arms of Moscow."[30]

Events proved Jackson correct, although Yugoslavia reacted sharply to an Anglo-American announcement, in the works for some time, that the allied governments would turn their zone of Trieste over to the Italians. The next day a mob attacked the headquarters of the United States Information Service in Zagreb; the American consul there described the looting as far from spontaneous. On the contrary, with police standing by while vandals sacked the USIS building, the riot gave every indication of being "thoroughly organized." Dulles admitted that this response was "much more violent" than he had expected, but the administration refused to back off. When Tito declared that Yugoslavia would consider any Italian attempt to militarily occupy its new zone an act of aggression, Eisenhower sent a detachment of the Sixth Fleet to patrol the Adriatic near the contested region.[31]

The president had no intention of actually using force; the American huffing and puffing was for the benefit of Italian voters who were tilting toward the Communist party in that country, in no small part because of the Communists' irredentist stand on Trieste. According to Ambassador Clare Booth Luce the Communists had moved to within four percentage points of a plurality at the polls and continued to gain strength. Luce contended that the surest way to undercut the Communists was to steal Trieste as a nationalist issue. Putting her argument to verse she wrote,

> For the want of Trieste, an issue was lost.
> For the want of an issue, an election was lost.

And so on, up to

> For the want of Italy, Europe was lost.
> For the want of Europe, America . . .?[32]

Posturing had its limits, however, and when Rome and Belgrade indicated a mutual desire to resolve the issue peacefully the administration readily lent its good offices. The negotiations, beginning early in 1954, went slowly. For three months American representatives, with British assistance, hammered away at the Yugoslav position. Then they set to work on the Italians. After an exhausting half-year the gap between the two sides had narrowed considerably. Convinced that Rome had moved as far as it could safely go, Eisenhower prepared a final offensive against Tito.[33]

For the last push Eisenhower turned to Robert Murphy, his wartime political attaché and now deputy undersecretary of state. Murphy was an old hand at delicate bargaining—he had engineered the Darlan deal in 1942—and he knew Tito from the war. Furthermore, he was an accomplished raconteur who broke ice and scored points at the same time. In his first meeting with the marshal, Murphy joked that the Trieste affair was a terrific fuss for a small bit of territory. He often played golf, he said, at the Chevy Chase course near Washington, where regulars had named the eighth hole "Trieste." Why? Because it encompassed about as much dirt as the Italians and Yugoslavs were quarreling over. Murphy also told of a Texas friend who found the whole dispute incomprehensible. Before Murphy left, this individual had said to tell Tito that if Yugoslavia was really so hard up for land he would buy him a whole county in Texas.[34]

After lunch over war stories Murphy handed Tito a letter from Eisenhower. The letter included the usual arguments for flexibility and compromise, but the kicker was a strong hint that a settlement would bring increased American aid. The offer held special attraction for Tito at this time, since Yugoslavia faced another acute shortfall in wheat production.[35]

Murphy's persuasiveness and Eisenhower's offer turned the trick. Tito agreed to a deal on Trieste and Murphy announced that the United States would release some 400,000 tons of grain for Yugoslavia.[36]

VI

THIS NEW aid package did nothing to diminish Tito's attachment to neutralism, as he made clear to Edwin Kretzmann, the first secretary of the embassy in Belgrade. The marshal described the easing of tensions since Stalin's death as a good thing Yugoslavia would encourage. He said he intended to pursue détente with the Kremlin. But he declared that even as the diplomatic channels widened, Yugoslavia would "man the ramparts." Further, his country would take advantage of the breathing spell afforded by the Soviets' desire for rapprochement to strengthen its ties with the West. At the same time, Yugoslavia would avoid dependence on the West and would keep its distance from the Atlantic pact. A middle course was what he planned. "The small frog does not jump into the pond but talks to the big frogs from the edge, thus having the best of both worlds."[37]

This declaration of neutrality suited the Eisenhower administration well enough. Both the president and Dulles appreciated the force of George Allen's earlier argument that a neutral Yugoslavia would have greater attractive power for Eastern Europe and China than a Yugoslavia tied to the West; and they lobbied for continued American support. Eisenhower made a special and favorable mention of Yugoslavia in his 1955 State of the Union address, patting himself on the back for the successful conclusion of the Trieste negotiations and citing with approval the Balkan pact between Yugoslavia and NATO members Greece and Turkey. In a message to Congress urging approval of the mutual security budget, he declared that Yugoslav defenses required "further strengthening." New appropriations, the president asserted, were needed to continue America's "cooperation" with Yugoslavia.[38]

When the Soviet leadership visited Yugoslavia in May Dulles treated the trip as a vindication of the policy of supporting Tito and an argument for its continuance. The secretary's office issued a press release describing Khrushchev and company's "humble pilgrimage to Belgrade" as a journey "to honor the defector, whom, until recently, the Soviet Communists had abused and reviled." Dulles told the House Foreign Affairs Committee that the lesson to be learned was that "independence is rewarded, and heresy is condoned." This, Dulles averred, was "bound to have a profound effect throughout the Soviet zone."[39]

VII

IF DULLES appeared to protest too much, he had reason. From the break in 1948 until Stalin's death in 1953, to the extent moderates and conservatives had gone along with assistance to Tito they had done so in the belief that Yugoslavia was moving toward the United States. As late as October 1953, for example, fully half a year after the changing of the guard at the Kremlin, *U.S. News and World Report* continued to describe Yugoslavia as "America's Communist ally." But as the reality of the thaw between Moscow and Belgrade sank in, and with it the fact that Tito aspired to a genuine neutralism, such appeal as he had had for many Americans evaporated. If the democratic nonalignment of Nehru —also being wooed by Moscow at this time—caused irritation, Tito's communist version threatened to provoke revolt. At the beginning of 1955 Democrat Walter George, the new chairman of the Senate Foreign Relations Committee, spoke for many in both parties when he suggested that if Tito insisted on a neutralist path he might have to forgo American support.[40]

Attacks increased as the genuineness of Tito's neutralism grew more apparent. Among the blander items appearing in *U.S. News* was a warning to the White House that Tito was playing America for a "sucker." The administration was losing its "billion dollar gamble" on a man who possessed "the profile of Goring" and "the scowl of Mussolini." One writer for the journal, under the head "How Tito Fooled the U.S.," flatly declared, "The United States has suffered humiliation at the hands of Tito." *Time* considered Tito a shrewd opportunist. The Yugoslav leader, *Time* said, was angling for the best deal he could get on weapons. In doing so he appeared all too ready "to play off onetime enemies against oldtime friends." *Newsweek,* assessing the impact of Khrushchev's visit to Belgrade, thought the Russian leader had scored a success.

> Last week it appeared that the Soviet party boss knew what he was doing when he led his kiss-and-make-up pilgrimage to Yugoslavia. Marshal Tito might not have been lured back into the Soviet camp, but he was turning an increasingly cold shoulder Westward.

Even the *New Republic,* viewing events from a more liberal perspective, admitted that Tito was cautiously but definitely moving to the left. "The Yugoslavs seem firm in their resolve that they will never again be participants in Soviet plans, although as spectators they are interested and might even be sympathetic." The *New Republic* later wondered, "Should the U.S. now treat Tito as if he had re-entered the enemy's camp and at once cut off his American supplies? It is not a simple question."[41]

Congress asked precisely this question in the spring and summer of 1955 as it debated the administration's foreign-aid request. As earlier, the matter of supervision complicated the discussion, and when the administration's bill came up for debate critics attacked both the general notion of aid to Tito and a claimed lack of adequate supervision. House Democrat Michael Feighan of Ohio opposed inclusion of Yugoslavia in the mutual security program on several grounds. First, Feighan denied the reality of Yugoslav independence. Citing "common gossip along the highways and byways of Europe that the relationship between the Russian Communists and Tito Communists has always been on a most friendly and cordial basis," Feighan declared that Tito's value as a potential ally had never been more than a figment of overwrought bureaucratic imaginations. "In the hysteria created by some of our striped-pants negotiators, we have deserted some of our best friends and strangely have now accepted as our supposed friends proven advocates of world socialism." Second, even if Tito chose to fight on the side of the West the oppressed Yugoslav people would never follow his lead. Instead they would either "take advantage of war to liquidate Tito," or be "forced to fight against the West with Russian machine guns at their backs." Third, no one could tell what Tito had in mind for the weapons and money the administration proposed to give him. Referring to problems of inspection Feighan asserted,

> The hard cold facts are that we do not know what Tito does with all the military and economic aid he has inveigled from the United States. It is quite possible that military equipment received from the United States has been filtered into Albania, or to Hungary, Rumania, or Bulgaria by Tito and his henchmen.

Denouncing the recent "love feast" between Yugoslav and Russian leaders, Feighan characterized Tito as a "main cog" in the Kremlin's "global strategy of neutralism." Should the United States continue to support Yugoslavia, such support would hasten the inevitable. "It will be only a matter of a few years before the so-called neutral belt is firmly attached to the ever-expanding Russian-Communist empire."[42]

The alleged neutralist conspiracy inspired other members of the House as well. Alvin Bentley announced that although he had supported aid to Yugoslavia in the past, he could in conscience do so no longer. The Michigan Republican said he had defended Tito—"sometimes," he bravely added, "before bitter anti-Tito groups"—because he had believed the Yugoslav leader was "genuinely opposed to the Kremlin." But times had changed.

> What are we to think when we observe the growing friendship between Belgrade and Moscow? What are we to believe when Tito announces his intention to visit Moscow as an honored guest? What are we to say when our military representatives in Yugoslavia are barred from seeing the disposition of the jet planes we have sent to strengthen the Yugoslav air force? How can we take a Communist dictator to our bosom who has received millions of dollars from us and has not paid out one cent of reparations, who has not even expressed his regrets, over shooting down American planes and killing American boys only nine years ago?

Like a number of other speakers, Bentley considered Tito's neutralism of a piece with that preached by Nehru, and he denounced Yugoslavia and India together. "I sometimes think that Tito and Nehru are engaged in a contest to see who can hew more closely to the Communist line without actually becoming a satellite of Moscow." Bentley scoffed at the argument that denying Tito aid would force him into dependence on the Soviets. "I tell you that Tito would not dare to go back to the Kremlin even if he wanted to. He is enough of a realist to know that he could never be fully absolved from the sin of Communist heresy no matter how much he recanted." Regardless of what Congress decided about aid, Tito would "never abandon his pretense of independence and so-called neutrality."[43]

Republican Paul Fino of New York also found it convenient to blast Tito and Nehru in a single breath.

> Both India and Yugoslavia have been taken in by the current Moscow tactic, "peaceful coexistence," a timeworn propaganda device and nothing more. It would be better termed "peaceful infiltration," for such is fundamentally the Communist intent. . . .
>
> Neutralism is not a doctrine calculated to strengthen our cause; nor are the gestures of conciliation, compromise, and appeasement by Yugoslavia and India to the Communist world calculated to encourage the ranks of the free world.[44]

Other critics of aid to Tito were less florid in their commentary but no less opposed to Yugoslavia's inclusion in the mutual security program. Pennsylvania Republican James Fulton read a list of newspaper headlines convicting Tito of crimes against religious freedom, civil liberties, and American sensibilities; and he offered an amendment withholding jet aircraft, which Belgrade especially desired, until Tito agreed to align with the West. Democrat Edna Kelly of New York took the simpler expedient of trying to cut Yugoslavia out of the aid bill unconditionally.[45]

VIII

HOPING TO disarm this opposition, Eisenhower twice invited Republican congressional leaders to the White House. On June 14 the president opened a meeting with the legislators by acknowledging the growing sentiment for halting all aid to Tito, but he urged them to remember the symbolic role Yugoslavia had played in the politics of Eastern Europe for more than half a decade. "Yugoslavia," he said, "is something of a showcase of the suffering experienced under Communist satellite status. . . . To throw Tito back into the arms of Moscow would be the most tragic thing the United States could do."

Responding for the conservatives, William Knowland made the same case against aid to Yugoslavia he customarily leveled at support of India:

that here was a neutralist receiving friendlier treatment than avowed allies like Taiwan. The California senator asked how the administration could back Tito when it refused to provide equivalent aid to Chiang, especially when Tito consistently took the wrong side of issues like the unification of Germany and the admission of China to the United Nations.

Though he declined to do so in public, Eisenhower defended Tito on these issues to Knowland. Regarding Germany, Eisenhower suggested that the Yugoslav position had to be understood in the light of European history: the Yugoslavs had traditionally feared Germany. Considering what had happened during the Second World War, who could blame them? Of Yugoslavia's support for UN membership for China, Eisenhower said this was "almost inevitable since Yugoslavia, too, wanted to get into the UN." (Eisenhower was confused on this point: Yugoslavia had been a member of the UN since 1945. Knowland, however, did not object to the president's reasoning, nor did anyone else at the meeting.)

Knowland then pursued the topic in terms of Yugoslavia's continuing complaints about aid supervision. Again bringing in China, Knowland commented that the United States had gotten itself into trouble by not checking how effectively American aid to the Nationalists during the civil war had been used. Knowland warned against making exceptions for Tito. America's allies submitted to thorough inspection; so must Yugoslavia.

Eisenhower replied that he would look at the inspection issue more carefully, but he asserted that in any event a cutoff of assistance was not the answer. America's relationship with Yugoslavia was "one of our greatest victories of the cold war." He characterized Yugoslavia as "a thorn in the Russian flesh," citing as evidence the eagerness of Stalin's successors to reestablish ties with Belgrade. Referring to recent intelligence reports, the president said Tito had "stood his ground well" in discussions with the Soviets. Despite what some observers might have claimed, the Russians could not regard their visit as an unqualified success.[46]

Two weeks later Eisenhower had the same group to the White House again. Dulles handled the briefing this time, explaining how Yugoslavia fitted into the administration's general approach to foreign aid. Dulles stated that since the Soviets remained in an interregnum, not yet having settled on a dictator to replace Stalin, they hoped to ease strains on their policy abroad. Consequently they sought rapprochement with Yugoslavia. Describing the mutual security program in terms of "preparedness," the secretary said the administration intended to use foreign aid to heighten the pressure on the Kremlin. The Russians could not hope to keep up with the United States indefinitely in an aid race; this was no time to let up. Assistance to Yugoslavia was "the best leverage" America possessed for encouraging independence among the satellites, which would increase Moscow's troubles all the more. Khrushchev had "eaten humble pie" at Belgrade, and the United States should do nothing "to drive the Yugoslavs back to their Russian connections."

By this time Knowland had tactically softened his opposition. The minority leader said he did not want to see Yugoslavia, or India either, dropped from the assistance program, but he deemed it vital for the administration to insist on adequate inspection. If Tito flouted American law in this matter, the United States would find itself in the untenable position of treating neutralists better than allies. Knowland took the opportunity for a similar swipe at India, declaring that aid to Nehru created the impression that the United States rewarded neutralism.

Dulles retorted that the administration did no such thing. The United States gave "much more assistance" to nations "willing to stand up and be counted." On the matter of inspection in Yugoslavia, the secretary stated that the administration was negotiating the issue with Tito. In a tactical maneuver of his own, Dulles, while not quite encouraging Knowland and the others to criticize the president in public, suggested that a certain amount of congressional pressure would make it easier for the administration to reach a satisfactory solution to the supervision problem.[47]

IX

EISENHOWER AND Dulles eventually persuaded Congress to pass their foreign aid package, somewhat reduced, but even so they deemed it necessary to step up their efforts on inspection. In September Eisenhower again pulled Robert Murphy from his desk at the State Department for a mission to Yugoslavia. The president, in telling Tito that Murphy was coming, added that the deputy undersecretary would discuss further aid. Eisenhower was not so blunt as to draw the connection directly, but he made it clear that the extra assistance would require a successful resolution of the inspection issue. As an added incentive the president had originally intended for Murphy to invite Tito to the United States. In August, in the wake of the successful Geneva summit, Dulles suggested that Eisenhower ask Tito to visit Washington; the president replied that he liked the idea. In the event, Eisenhower suffered his heart attack two days before Murphy left for Belgrade, suspending all such plans.[48]

On his arrival in Yugoslavia Murphy found Tito in good humor and a cooperative mood, and before long the two men agreed in principle to inspection measures both governments could live with. Among lower-echelon Yugoslav officials, however, Murphy encountered greater difficulties. The officers who would actually have to open doors to American inspectors exhibited what Murphy considered a combination of the prejudice of partisan guerrillas against nosy outsiders, a once-burned reluctance born of experience with pushy Russians, and "traditional Slavic suspicions." The individual who caused Murphy the most trouble was Tito's vice president, Svetozar Vukmanović, a wartime hero who had acquired the nom de guerre Tempo—translated "hurry"—for his impatience. "Tempo did not request or attempt to negotiate," Murphy wrote later. "He demanded." When Murphy offered 300,000 tons of wheat for immediate delivery as a way to resolve the inspection problem, Tempo insisted on 500,000 tons—annually.[49]

After considerable haggling, Murphy got his deal and Tempo his wheat. Despite the price Dulles characterized Murphy's trip as "most successful," telling Eisenhower that the agreement had "pretty well cleared up the points of friction" between the United States and Yugoslavia. So encouraged was Dulles that he decided to go to Yugoslavia himself.[50]

X

IN SOME respects Dulles' Yugoslavia trip represented an important concession by the secretary of state. Dulles shrank from public association with communists; the previous year he had refused to take part in the Geneva conference on Indochina, not wishing to be connected with what he feared would become "a second Yalta." At a pre-conference reception he had declined even to shake hands with Zhou Enlai. Dulles had opposed the Geneva summit of 1955, and when he could not dissuade Eisenhower from going he urged the president to maintain an "austere countenance" in photographs with Soviet leaders. In each case Dulles worried that the sight of American leaders mixing and signing agreements with communists would create an impression that the administration was lowering its guard in the cold war. Dulles was sufficiently realistic to understand that the United States might make deals with communists, but he did not wish to broadcast the fact.[51]

The visit to Brioni, however, appeared necessary. With the Soviets sending their top people to Yugoslavia the United States could do no less. And with the president out of action for an indefinite period the burden of personal diplomacy fell on the secretary of state. Still, Dulles did not intend to overdo things. His trip to Yugoslavia lasted only several hours, filling a break in a conference of Western foreign ministers in Geneva. Moreover, visiting Tito in Yugoslavia, and in an out-of-the-way location at that, meant less publicity than a meeting elsewhere would have entailed.

Dulles had been in the business of international relations long enough not to be easily impressed by atmospherics; but within a short time of his arrival Tito had stripped the secretary of most of his skepticism. All his life Dulles was an avid sailor. When he wanted to escape the pressures of work, he would repair to a log cabin on an island in Lake Ontario where he chopped wood and savored the rustic life. Tito, apparently well-briefed on Dulles' affinities, whisked the secretary away in a two-seat launch to an island not far from his seaside villa, where they enjoyed the sun and salt breeze, where Tito showed off his garden and rude construction projects, and where they spent most of the afternoon talking in a small stone hut.[52]

Dulles was thoroughly taken by it all. "The day with Tito was one of the most interesting I have ever spent," the secretary reported to Eisenhower. "He was extremely open and friendly." Tito was "a frank man" who "spoke what he believed." The discussion covered a wide range of topics, from Germany to various trouble spots in Asia and the Middle East. Regarding the latter, Tito pointed out that he would be visiting Cairo within the month to talk to Nasser. He said he had told Nasser in the past that the best route to peace lay in direct relations with Israel. The Egyptians, however, had "protested vigorously," and the Israeli raid on Gaza several months earlier had not disposed them toward cooperation. Still, Tito thought the idea of Egyptian-Israeli contacts should not be abandoned, and he told Dulles he would be "frank" with Nasser when they met.

Regarding the Balkan alliance, Tito commented on tension that had developed between the Greeks and Turks. He said he had instructed his representatives to tell the two sides to calm down. After this warning the tension had diminished considerably. While denying reports that Yugoslavia intended to terminate the military aspects of the alliance, Tito conceded that in light of the changed international situation his government preferred to emphasize the political, economic, and cultural parts of the pact.

Dulles explained the political problems the administration faced in providing aid to Yugoslavia. A major difficulty, he said, arose from the fact that large numbers of Catholics in the United States thought the Yugoslav government was persecuting their coreligionists. Willing to give Tito the benefit of the doubt, Dulles asked "whether it was not true that there was very large freedom of religion" in Yugoslavia. Tito assured the secretary that Catholics, as well as Moslems and Orthodox, had "complete freedom." The trouble, Tito said, came from people like Stepinac. Yugoslav courts had "definitely proved" that the archbishop had collaborated with Germany during the war, and they had justly sentenced him to ten years in prison. The government had been magnanimous enough to release him after four. He was now free and working in a church; if he wished to leave and go to Rome he was welcome to do so. (In his memorandum of this discussion Dulles noted parenthetically, "In connection with this matter, Tito showed the first sign of emotionalism that he had exhibited during the entire visit. He spoke with considerable heat.")

The secretary remarked that the post-Geneva thaw in the cold war had somewhat loosened ties among the noncommunist countries, and he suggested that a comparable process must be occurring in the Soviet bloc. Communist authority, Dulles said, was being "diluted and diversified." Tito agreed, and he was able, as Dulles told Eisenhower, "to document this thesis on the basis of his knowledge, more intimate than ours, as to what is going on, particularly in the satellite states." At this point Tito injected the comment that China was "in no sense" a satellite of the Kremlin.

On the whole Dulles left Brioni with a high opinion of Tito, and he came away convinced that despite Tito's growing detente with the Soviets Yugoslavia would stick to a neutralist path. He wrote to Eisenhower:

> The talk confirmed me in my opinion that while Tito undoubtedly likes to be in a position to get the best of both worlds, he has no intention whatever of falling back into the clutches of the Soviet, and he feels that while Bulganin and Khrushchev are definitely trying to substitute new and more tolerable policies than those of Stalin, there is still a very strong Stalinist element within the Soviet Union representing those who were indoctrinated with Stalinism and there is always a danger that they could take over and resume rough policies.[53]

XI

DULLES' CONVICTION that Yugoslavia would remain independent of Moscow was reinforced two months later when Tito joined Nasser in declaring the virtues of nonalignment. Although a bit unsettling regarding Nasser—the administration was still trying to get Congress to approve aid for Egypt's Aswan Dam—the joint communiqué seemed to warrant confidence that Tito was not heading for the Soviet camp. This confidence enabled the administration to weather a new storm of criticism following a much publicized visit by Tito to Russia in June 1956.[54]

Many Americans already suspicious of neutralists viewed the friendly treatment Tito received in Moscow in much the same way they interpreted Nehru's exchange of hospitality with Khrushchev—as portending a sellout to the Kremlin. In the House of Representatives, then debating the next round of mutual security legislation, Republican August Johansen of Michigan asked which of his colleagues would be willing to "pass the hat in their congressional districts" for Tito in light of the accounts of "the enthusiastic, vodka-drinking, prodigal-son welcome this Yugoslav commie received in Moscow where he swore, by whatever it is he regards as good and holy, that he and his Kremlin comrades would never again be parted." In the Senate Democrat Russell Long cited the error of previous forecasts that Tito would be forever barred from the circle of communist comity. "It was thought that if he went to Moscow he might be boiled in oil." Obviously such predictions had missed the mark, and Long believed conclusions drawn from this faulty premise ought to be junked as well.

Yugoslavia and the Tito Option

> My feeling is that if Tito can walk the streets of Moscow treading on rosebuds, enjoying the plaudits of the Communist multitude, then it is no longer necessary that we squeeze the resources out of our hard-pressed taxpayers to give him arms to protect himself from his old and new friends.

Senator Styles Bridges, ranking Republican on the crucial appropriations committee and chairman of the GOP policy board, asked, "What have we got in exchange for the billion dollars we gave to Tito?" Bridges knew the answer, of course.

> We get a Tito honeymoon staged in Moscow. We get a statement from Marshal Zhukov to Tito that in war the Kremlin and Tito will fight "shoulder to shoulder." We get an official statement that Tito and the Kremlin "will make stubborn efforts" to see that Red China is admitted to the United Nations.

Bridges considered the administration's treatment of Tito a disaster on its own merits, but he also judged it symptomatic of a deeper "moral crisis in American foreign policy," which was most clearly revealed in relations with neutralist states like Yugoslavia and India. Neutrality, Bridges said, had made sense in the era when empires clashed over territorial, economic, and dynastic objectives. But the struggle with the Soviet Union was of an entirely different nature. "There is no quarrel between America and Russia on any such traditional grounds. If those were the issues, we would have no trouble coming to terms with the vast Soviet empire, just as we did with the British and other expanding empires in the past." The conflict with the Soviets above all involved "human, moral, and spiritual questions." American leaders had forgotten this fundamental fact in designing policy toward the neutralists.

> Every time a spokesman for the free world speaks of "neutrality" in the old sense in relation to our present dilemma, he cheapens the issue and betrays the high purpose of the free world. He helps make it seem—as the Kremlin wants it to seem—simply an old-style duel for power.

Neglect of the moral element in American policy had led to support for India's Nehru, a man of "weasel words and idle pretension" who had yet to denounce "slave-labor, torture, trial without jury, political violence, and all the absolute ruthless dictatorship that goes with Soviet Russia." Tito and Yugoslavia were no different. "It was a disdain for moral values which maneuvered us into the folly of building up the dictator Tito."

Knowland of California, who joined Bridges in offering an amendment to strike military aid to Yugoslavia from the mutual security bill, admitted that a reasonable case for assistance to Yugoslavia could have been made when Tito and the Soviets were at swords' points. But the situation had changed. "When Tito goes to the Kremlin and makes his bed with the men in the Kremlin, then an entirely different situation confronts us." Such justification as formerly had existed for sending weapons to Yugoslavia had vanished. American aid now simply would entrench the despot. "It will permit Tito to continue to prevent the people of Yugoslavia from ever getting their freedom, because it will put such power into the hands of the Communist dictator that the people will never be able to throw off the yoke of the oppressor." Further, Tito's example would invite imitation by other communist countries. If the administration granted aid to Yugoslavia merely on Tito's word that he continued to be independent of Moscow, logic would demand a like response to similar statements by Hungary, Bulgaria, Poland, and so forth. Finally, aid to neutralist Yugoslavia devalued America's alliances and lent support to communist movements in Western Europe. According to Knowland, Communist party leaders in Italy and France could say, "Look, there is no danger in voting for Communists. There is no danger in establishing a Communist government, because we can show you Yugoslavia. The United States not only gives Yugoslavia economic aid, but it gives Yugoslavia replacement parts, and sends Tito new jet planes and guns and howitzers, and other equipment."[55]

Responding to this criticism, Dulles explained to reporters the administration's assessment of the evolving relationship between Yugoslavia and the Soviet Union. Speaking at the end of June, Dulles admitted that the full impact of Tito's visit to Moscow remained unknown, but he asserted, "We do not believe that anything that has happened conclusively shows that Tito has gone back to any role of subserviency to the Soviet Union." Moreover, for Tito to return to any such relationship would be "almost incredible," given that he had risked a great deal, including his own life, to establish Yugoslavia's independence. "Why, under present conditions, he should have given it up I can't see; nor do I find in what has been said any evidence that he did give it up."

Dulles described "very strenuous efforts" by the Soviets to "trap"

Tito into statements construable as indicating a willingness to follow the Kremlin's lead in international affairs. But these attempts had failed, at least according to information then available. Conceding that new evidence might force a revision of this estimate—and, by implication, perhaps a change in administration policy—Dulles contended that prudence required a steady course for the time being.

> I think it would be a very grave mistake indeed, so long as the matter is subject to reasonable doubt, if action were taken which would make it impossible for us to proceed on the assumption that he was still independent or to help him maintain his independence.

The "action" Dulles referred to was a cutoff of aid to Yugoslavia. "The verdict is not yet in, and until we have a much clearer view of the situation I would hope very much that there would be no congressional action which would foreclose the issue."[56]

The secretary's plea failed. By the time the administration's mutual security package made it through the authorization and appropriation process, new military aid for Yugoslavia had been deleted, with the exception of funds for maintenance of equipment already shipped. Further, Congress mandated a termination of all aid within ninety days unless the president issued a finding declaring that Yugoslavia remained independent of the Soviet Union, that Yugoslavia was not attempting to spread communism by aggression, and that aid to Yugoslavia would serve American national interests. Foreign aid as a whole fared badly during this session: the legislature eliminated the Asian development fund and lopped more than twenty percent from the administration's original request.[57]

XII

THE NEW stricture on economic assistance and on spare parts for military equipment already shipped required the administration to weigh its next move carefully. The clock started ticking on July 18; thus the president had until the middle of October to find for or against continued aid. In some respects the decision was preordained. From the time American assistance to Yugoslavia had begun in 1949 its essential premise had always been that such aid promoted American interests precisely because Tito was independent of Moscow. Despite the recent warming between Belgrade and Moscow, Tito appeared as independent as ever.

The condition that Yugoslavia not be engaged in aggression amounted to little; Tito was hardly in a position conducive to adventurism. In reality the congressional demand for a presidential finding amounted to an exercise in buck passing. By shifting the burden of judgment to the White House, the legislature got itself off the hook with constituents who still wondered why Tito's communism was better than the Kremlin's. In heightening the administration's exposure Congress reduced its own.

Through the end of the summer administration officials considered their response. In September the issue briefly arose at a meeting of the National Security Council. Treasury Secretary George Humphrey described a recent conversation with his Yugoslav counterpart, in which the latter expressed a desire to get an affirmative decision as soon as possible. The Yugoslav finance minister had been less concerned about an embargo on military equipment, Humphrey said, than about the possibility of a cutoff of economic aid. Yugoslavia, the minister had explained, could get hardware from other sources, including Moscow. What it really needed was cash, convertible to Western currency, which the Soviets did not supply.[58]

Two weeks later Dulles, accompanied by Undersecretary Hoover, discussed the question with the president. Dulles said the State Department had studied the issue of a presidential determination with great care. As a result of this study and of much thought on his own, the secretary recommended that the president find in favor of continued aid. Dulles admitted he did not know as much as he would like about the recent meetings between Khrushchev and Tito. But all the evidence indicated that Yugoslavia remained independent of Moscow "in the sense of not being subject to dictation by the Soviet Government or the Soviet Communist Party." Dulles told Eisenhower that Tito "jealously safeguarded" his freedom of action and could count on support in this matter from a majority of the Yugoslav Communist party. Although Congress had blocked money for new weapons, perhaps the administration could in the not distant future discover some way around the congressional ban. Tito considered acquisition of modern jet aircraft a matter of pride, and if he could not get the planes from the United States he would turn to the Russians. In the meantime American economic aid would allow the United States to keep a foot in the door. Moreover, a food shortage again threatened the country. So desperate had the situation become, in fact, that Dulles feared a cutoff of American aid might force the Yugoslavs "to go on their knees to Moscow."

Dulles went on to assert that the administration's policy of backing Tito was beginning to pay off elsewhere in Europe. There quite evidently existed "an increasing desire on the part of the satellites for independence," and despite outward appearances of amity between Moscow and Belgrade, on the subject of Eastern Europe there remained "considerable strain." Under these circumstances it would be "a great misfortune to our whole policy toward Eastern Europe" if Tito's economic predicament forced a capitulation to the Kremlin. Only a favorable presidential finding would avert the disaster.

The tenor of Dulles' argument suggests he thought Eisenhower needed convincing. With the presidential election only three weeks away, this was not an unreasonable concern. Undoubtedly a pro-Tito determination would create political problems. Further, the joint chiefs of staff were cooling on the usefulness of Tito as a distracter of Soviet attention; Chairman Arthur Radford thought American resources could be used better by the United States than by Yugoslavia. Needless to say, the chiefs' skepticism would strengthen the oppositionists' case.[59]

All the same, Eisenhower followed Dulles' advice. Speaking of military aid, the president told Dulles and Hoover that the great importance of supplying weapons to a country lay in the fact that the recipient became dependent on the supplier for ammunition and spare parts. Obviously it would benefit the United States for Tito to look to America rather than the Soviet Union for resupply. Hoover concurred, adding that American military aid to Yugoslavia afforded entry for American military advisers, who provided useful intelligence. A cutoff of military equipment would also cut off the flow of information.[60]

Despite his ready agreement, Eisenhower chose not to announce his decision before Dulles' staff provided a cautiously worded defense, one designed to deflect as much criticism as possible. A few hours later, in response to a direct question on the subject of aid to Yugoslavia, Eisenhower told reporters that on such delicate subjects "the final decision is never made and published until the last minute." Four days afterward, however, the president sent a letter to the leaders of the Senate and the House, officially finding that Yugoslavia remained "independent of control by the Soviet Union," that it was not participating in any activity "for the Communist conquest of the world," and that American assistance served the "national security of the United States." The president qualified this determination with the usual disclaimers that aid to Yugoslavia did not represent approval of Tito's regime. He said he was aware that the designs of the Soviet Union against Yugoslavia were "more subtle than heretofore," and he admitted that Tito perhaps did not adequately appreciate those designs. Most important, the president stated that his finding did not commit the United States to any particular level of aid: it merely restored discretion to the executive to provide or withhold assistance as Yugoslavia's behavior dictated. The administration would keep the issue under "constant review."[61]

XIII

JUST AS the dual crisis of the autumn of 1956 threw an unfavorable light on Indian neutralism—and by implication on the Eisenhower administration's India policy—so the Hungary-Suez affair generated increased criticism of Tito and of the administration's handling of Yugoslavia.

At first this new threat remained hidden; if anything, the events of October appeared to demonstrate the correctness of the administration's position. The restiveness among the satellites indicated that Titoism lived. George Kennan, although no longer in the government, expressed a common sentiment when he wrote that "the dream of a socialist federation in southeastern Europe, friendly to Russia in principle but not slavishly beholden to the Kremlin, seems now—after Stalin's death— well on the way to realization." On October 24 Robert Murphy spoke for the administration in explaining that current events were demonstrating "the value to the free world and to enslaved peoples" of Yugoslavia's independence. The Soviet Union's diplomatic offensive of the previous three years had required the Kremlin to make its peace with Tito. "But acknowledging the 'respectability' of Tito in turn made Titoism in some measure respectable, and this has lent encouragement to the other satellites in seeking greater independence from Moscow." The administration could claim at least partial credit. "Our aid to Yugoslavia has helped to bring about some loosening of the bonds upon the once-free nations of Eastern Europe. It has helped create problems for the Communist leaders which they have not yet been able to resolve."[62]

Within two weeks, however, the situation changed completely. At the end of October Khrushchev and Georgi Malenkov flew to Brioni to talk with Tito. Immediately the Yugoslavs suspected something was up. "They behaved in an extremely cordial manner, as never before," Veljko Mićunović, the ambassador to Moscow, noted in his diary.

> As I am writing this I still seem to feel Malenkov's fat round face, into which my nose sank as if into a half-inflated balloon as I was drawn into a cold and quite unexpected embrace. We had not exchanged kisses with the Russians at our previous meetings; we hadn't even talked to them for nearly seven years, but now they decided that we should kiss each other in the difficult circumstances which had arisen—for them, rather than for us.

What the Soviets wanted was Yugoslav support in their suppression of the Hungarian revolution. They got it, but it did not come unalloyed. Caught between a desire to preserve good relations with Moscow and an inclination to defend those who followed the path he had marked out, Tito vacillated. After having denounced the first Soviet intervention of October 24, he defended the invasion of November 4 as the "lesser evil" compared to the triumph of "reaction" in Hungary. He had applauded the formation of the Nagy government, but after its fall he quickly recognized the successor Kádár regime. He granted asylum to Nagy in the Yugoslav embassy, but upon receiving assurances of safe conduct for the fugitive he turned him over to Kádár's representatives, who gave him up to the Russians, who later shot him. Meanwhile, as time allowed, he castigated the British-French-Israeli attack on neutralist Egypt.[63]

Critics who charged Nehru with applying a "double standard" during this period zeroed in on Tito as well. The *New York Times* summarized the mainstream American view in expressing its "horrified amazement" at Yugoslavia's actions. Speaking of the pro forma regrets Belgrade issued over the loss of life in Budapest, the *Times* declared, "Yugoslavs did not use such language when Stalinist troops killed Yugoslav border guards. Why do they use it now when Khrushchev's troops murder Hungarians?" Referring to Yugoslavia's abstention on a Security Council vote condemning the Soviet invasion, the paper's editors wrote, "It seems astonishing that the Government of Yugoslavia, which itself lived so long in daily terror of Soviet attack, should condone the Soviet crime in Hungary."[64]

XIV

THE ONLY redeeming feature of the affair was that Tito's attempt to straddle the fence alienated the Soviets even more than it disturbed Americans. The aftermath revealed a new fissure between Belgrade and Moscow, neither so wide nor so deep as the 1948 rift and far less acrimonious, but sufficient to quiet some critics who blasted the administration for supporting a Kremlin front man. Meanwhile Eisenhower and Dulles considered how to take advantage of the contretemps.

By the beginning of 1957 the president and the secretary thought the dust might have settled sufficiently to allow a visit by Tito to Washington. They soon discovered their mistake. Critics in the House gunned down an administration trial balloon, circulating a petition protesting any invitation to Tito and rapidly gaining the signatures of 168 representatives from 41 states. Republican Congressman Gordon McDonough of California brought to the attention of his colleagues a poll showing that 61 percent of those questioned believed a visit by Tito would serve no useful purpose. Other opponents supported a resolution barring the use of federal funds for entertaining the Yugoslav leader. In the Senate Styles Bridges, leading the anti-Tito faction, cited heavy constituent mail in announcing his opposition to an invitation.[65]

The White House refused to oppose this adverse sentiment and dropped Tito from its guest list; but otherwise the administration moved toward reaffirming its ties to Belgrade. In May 1957 Eisenhower announced a decision to send Tito jet fighters procured under programs of previous years but not yet shipped. Explaining his decision, the president asserted that events during the six months since his earlier finding had confirmed the administration's belief that Yugoslavia remained independent of Moscow, that Yugoslav independence served the American national interest, and that American aid would materially help Yugoslavia maintain its freedom. "Soviet hostility to the cause of national independence in Eastern Europe, which has led to the renewed harassment of Yugoslavia, makes it even more imperative that the United States adhere to its established policy of lending support to those countries seeking to withstand Soviet pressures." Alluding to, but not explicitly mentioning, the role of Congress in halting weapons deliveries, Eisenhower declared that the suspension had led to "serious disadvantages" for Yugoslavia's military posture vis à vis the countries of the Warsaw Pact, which were receiving supplies of modern Soviet weapons.

> Yugoslav soldiers, sailors, and airmen trained to operate and maintain American equipment have lacked even those quantities of items needed to keep up their training and proficiency. Ground installations, and particularly jet-plane fields built by the Yugoslavs at sizable expense, are lying idle.

Therefore, the president concluded, the United States must once again deliver major arms systems, including jet aircraft, to Yugoslavia. As a minor concession to critics, he added that the administration had chosen to stretch out the delivery schedule.[66]

This announcement provoked surprisingly little criticism; but Eisenhower still considered it wise to protect his flanks. A week after the announcement the president invited Senator Bridges to the White House for a chat. Eisenhower began with a defense of foreign aid generally. Bridges interrupted, saying he was a longtime supporter of foreign aid. It was only aid to neutralists, countries that "would contribute nothing to the mutual security," that he opposed. Eisenhower continued, describing the role of aid in his administration's foreign policy. "I want to wage the cold war in a militant, but reasonable, style whereby we appeal to the people of the world as a better group to hang with than the Communists." The president denied a standard complaint by conservatives that the United States sought to buy allies. "I am not concerned with buying friends or purchasing satellites or any other thing—that is all false. As a free country, the only ally we can have is a free ally, one that wants to be with us." The Russians, of course, did not play by the same rules; Eisenhower commented that one purpose of American assistance was to keep neutral countries from falling into dependence on the Soviet Union.

Turning specifically to Yugoslavia, the president asserted, "Tito is the only man in Europe who succeeded in breaking away completely from the Soviets. I do not by any manner or means want Tito to find that he has no place to go except back to the Soviets." This especially applied to military aid, since Tito's air force included only a handful of jets— "which we now consider to be obsolete." Eisenhower rejected as ridiculous the argument of some critics that American weapons supplied to Yugoslavia might some day be turned against the United States. Under no conceivable circumstances could that country pose a threat to America. "I would say that two bombs in Yugoslavia would make the country helpless." Although the administration did not intend to interfere in Belgrade's domestic affairs, Eisenhower assured Bridges he was doing his best to get Yugoslavia "to act decently, to be a decent member of the family of nations."[67]

XV

THROUGH THE rest of 1957 Yugoslavia remained quiescent as an issue in American politics, even though Tito and Khrushchev once again found common ground. Yugoslavia's recognition of East Germany caused a minor blip of unfavorable attention but little more. In December Tito assured an even lower profile for his country by informing Washington that he required no further military aid.

Soon after this Eisenhower's National Security Council reviewed the American position with respect to Yugoslavia. Coming not quite ten years after the initial schism between Belgrade and Moscow, NSC 5805 surveyed the results of the decade's policies toward Tito. From the military standpoint the most significant consequence of the split was "the continued denial to the USSR of important strategic positions and other assets." Politically, Yugoslavia's defiance of the Kremlin had resulted in "a break in the 'monolithic' Communist bloc." American economic and military aid had been "of crucial importance" in keeping the Tito regime viable in the face of severe and sustained Soviet pressure; moreover, by demonstrating American interest in Tito such assistance had deterred Soviet attack. As to cost, the paper tallied a total of some $1.4 billion through 1957, almost equally divided between military and economic aid.

Looking to the future, the NSC paper described the primary aim of American policy as the maintenance of "an independent Yugoslavia outside the Soviet Bloc, capable of withstanding Soviet political and economic pressures, not actively engaged in furthering Soviet Communist imperialism, and with a potential for weakening the monolithic front and internal cohesiveness of the Soviet Bloc." The emphasis here quite clearly was on Yugoslavia's independence. A distinctly secondary goal, one to be pursued "without jeopardizing the above objectives," was to bring Yugoslavia closer to the West and to encourage domestic liberalization.

In pursuit of these objectives the United States should continue to provide diplomatic support to Yugoslavia. It should promote political and cultural exchanges, valuable in their own right but equally significant as counters to similar Soviet activities. More substantially, despite Tito's recent rejection of American weapons aid, the United States should let Belgrade know that arms remained available, on either a grant or purchase basis, in the amount needed by Yugoslavia "to avoid dependence on the Soviet bloc." The administration should also facilitate military training programs. In addition it ought to encourage cooperation in the field of atomic energy, including technical assistance and the transfer of fissionable material. At the economic level the American government should treat Yugoslavia on the same basis as the "free European nations" in arranging terms of trade. Export licenses should be granted to Yugoslavia so long as Tito provided guarantees against reexport to the Soviets. Desirable, but not essential, was the promotion of private enterprise within Yugoslavia. The administration should "attempt to influence Yugoslavia to give greater play to free economic forces," but again only "to the extent possible without prejudicing the above primary objectives."[68]

It was an ambitious statement of purpose, noteworthy—although at this late date not unusual—for the degree to which it considered cooperation with Yugoslavia, even atomic cooperation, in the American interest. Defense Secretary Charles Wilson overstated the case in a 1957 NSC meeting when he declared that Yugoslavia was "so to speak an ally of the United States." But there was no question that the administration still considered Tito's Yugoslavia a country with which America might usefully make common cause.[69]

This conviction gained support from a fresh outbreak of the Yugoslav-Soviet dispute in 1958, in which the Kremlin charged Tito with "revisionism" and other sins, and Belgrade denounced the execution of Nagy. Together with Tito's decision to terminate military aid and a gradual decline in American economic assistance, this development served further to reduce Yugoslavia's visibility in American politics.[70]

The last years of the Eisenhower administration witnessed nothing like the loud and bitter debates of earlier days. Diehard oppositionists continued to criticize aid to Yugoslavia; significantly, however, when critics in the House sought to amend the 1958 mutual security bill to bar technical assistance to Yugoslavia, the first speaker to rise in protest was conservative Walter Judd. The Minnesota Republican declared,

> Mr. Chairman, I have consistently opposed military aid to the Government of Yugoslavia. . . . But concrete help to improve the lives of the people of Yugoslavia is a different matter. I believe that the best hope of our country to avoid an ultimate showdown, perhaps atomic war with the Communist world, lies in the people behind the Iron Curtain. . . . It seems to me that to adopt this amendment would serve notice on the people of Yugoslavia that they are being abandoned.[71]

Judd's remarks, and the fact that a person like Judd could make them, indicated the degree to which Yugoslavia had disappeared as an issue. No significant differences ruffled relations between Washington and Belgrade; in May 1959 the American ambassador, Karl Rankin, commented that "everything was going well." Through 1960 the administration continued to chart a constant course, and no new developments on the world scene—neither the downed U-2 nor the broken summit that followed—deflected it from its path.[72]

Four months before he left the White House Eisenhower finally met Tito. Although by this time the administration could have issued a formal invitation with little risk of setting off a right-wing uproar, no such formality was required. At the same UN session at which he had his last conversation with Nehru, Eisenhower spoke with Tito.

The two old soldiers began by swapping war stories. Tito said that ever since 1945 he had looked forward to meeting the allied supreme commander. The president responded in kind and joked that while he had parachuted troops into Yugoslavia he himself had been unable to make the trip. He added that when he had been stationed at NATO in the early 1950s politics had precluded a visit. To the president's inquiry about the health of Yugoslavia's economy, Tito replied that his country was making good progress. The agricultural sector, he hoped, was on the verge of a breakthrough, due in part to assistance from the United States. Industrial production promised to be up by twelve to sixteen percent from the previous year. To Eisenhower's remark that a major problem in the United States was the disposal of excess grain stocks, Tito replied from experience that it was "better to have too much than too little."

When the conversation turned to diplomatic affairs Eisenhower mentioned recent reports that Tito, as a neutralist, intended to exercise a mediating influence in the conflict between East and West, and he wished the marshal luck. The president commented, however, that "we hope a man who is neutral is neutral on our side." The Yugoslav foreign minister, Koča Popović, interjected that his government did not want to be called neutral if the term meant passive. Eisenhower responded that there could be no neutrals on questions "of moral values, or right and wrong."

Whether it came about through the mediation of neutrals or otherwise, Eisenhower believed a relaxation of tensions would be a blessing. The arms race, he said, exacted a "tremendous" economic cost, in addition to the psychological strain involved. A reduction of forces, to a level sufficient for domestic order, would mark "a great step forward." Moreover, consequent savings in the United States would allow Americans to be "much more helpful to other nations." Tito picked up on the idea, suggesting that funds set aside for underdeveloped countries be specified in advance, so the recipients could make appropriate plans.

The marshal remarked that America was not alone in bad relations with communist countries. Though tension between the Soviet Union and Yugoslavia had diminished somewhat, Yugoslavia remained on very bad terms with China. "The Chinese hate the Yugoslavs more than they hate the United States." Nonetheless China should be admitted to the UN. "They do amount to 600 million, they are arming rapidly, and they may have atomic weapons at the present time or soon." Eisenhower responded that the question of China constituted "a difficult problem for the whole world"—and for an American president particularly. "Hatred for the Chinese Communist Government is very intense in the United States. . . . Any political leader in the United States who tried to bring the Chinese Communists into the UN would be rejected." The president cited the conventional reasons for Americans' ill will toward the Chinese, including their invasion of Korea, their mistreatment of American prisoners, and the pressure they continued to exert on Southeast Asia. "All these combine to develop in our people a deep psychological feeling." Americans were "much less hostile" toward the Soviet Union.

The conversation concluded with an exchange of good wishes. Eisenhower said that although the United States opposed "some elements of the Yugoslav system of government," Americans hoped to see Yugoslavia progress. Tito replied that his compatriots were "very friendly" toward the American people, and he said they would never forget the help America had provided. Such an attitude provided "a sound and durable basis" for continued profitable relations between the two countries.[73]

III

EGYPT AND NASSER:
THE NEUTRALIST AS RADICAL

VI

The Riddle of the Sphinx: 1952–1956

N̲EHRU AND Tito managed to chart nonaligned courses for their countries not least because India and Yugoslavia lay off the beaten track of postwar geopolitics, possessing relatively little worth fighting for and holding the shortest route to nowhere in particular. With most of a subcontinent to itself and plenty of problems of its own, India could and did remain aloof from the worst of the cold war's first decade and a half. Yugoslavia was more in the thick of things but only by a little. If Tito's defection challenged the Kremlin ideoloically it did not strike at the heart of Soviet security, as a similar revolt in the invasion alley of East Germany or Poland would have. An independent Yugoslavia annoyed Moscow, but from a strategic perspective it constituted no direct threat.

Egypt, on the other hand, had the misfortune of occupying one of the most sensitive spots on earth. For thousands of years Egypt had commanded vital transportation routes; in the postwar period the export of neighbors' oil added to Cairo's import. Whatever the preferences of the country's leaders and people, the great powers would not let Egypt sit out the cold war. Nasser eventually succeeded in carving a nonaligned niche for Egypt, but his was less the sideline neutralism of Nehru and Tito than an ongoing struggle to hold midfield between competing heavyweights.

A principal contender, of course, was the United States, and once

223

Egypt and Nasser: Neutralist as Radical

American officials recognized Nasser's neutralism as such they opposed it, at least so long as they believed opposition viable and while they discerned a pro-Western alternative. As the previous sections have shown, the Truman and Eisenhower administrations had nothing against neutralism per se. Where neutralism served American geopolitical interests, as it did from the first in Yugoslavia, and as they eventually recognized it would in India, they supported it. Put otherwise, where they could turn Bandung to Yalta's ends, they gladly did so. But a neutral—that is, independent—Egypt, in a region heretofore dominated by the West, represented a net loss to the American alliance system. By the end of World War II the United States had become the essential status quo power. In the Middle East the status quo and all it implied in terms of access to oil markedly favored the West; hence the basic American objective in the area was the preservation of as much of the status quo as possible for as long as American leaders could manage. By challenging the status quo Nasser challenged American security as Washington defined it.

Change, of course, always threatens those on top; what made Nasser appear more dangerous than the average boat-rocker was the virulence and potential contagiousness of the neutralism he preached. Nehru was often a pain in the neck but his variety of nonalignment was relatively innocuous. Tito's dealigning neutralism was beneficent but did not travel as well as Americans had hoped. Nasser's neutralism, by contrast, was both malignant, in that it undermined Western hegemony in the Middle East, and infectious. If Nasser managed to graft his philosophy of nonalignment onto radical Arab nationalism—the other principal influence in the Middle East—the West might lose all the region worth controlling.

Stated thus, American policy toward Egypt appears simple and straightforward. In practice it was anything but. For one thing, it took American leaders considerable time to fathom Nasser's plans; indeed they required many months after the coup of July 1952 simply to figure out that he was running Egypt's new show. Once they discovered that Nasser and not General Muhammad Naguib held the balance of power in Cairo, they still hoped Egypt might choose to cooperate with the United States. Nasser needed money and arms, and although he early vetoed Egyptian membership in an American-sponsored Middle East

Defense Organization, the possibility remained that he might purchase what he needed with some less formal type of collaboration.

Two other factors muddied the waters. The first was Britain, which from Washington's view appeared to be doing everything in its power to destroy the future of the West among the Arabs. American officials initially humored the British, preferring not to alienate an ally and hoping to squeeze a last bit of usefulness out of Britain in regional defense. Patience appeared to pay off in 1954 when the British agreed to terms of withdrawal from their Suez base. But Eisenhower and Dulles underestimated Britain's capacity for anachronism, and two years later, when misjudgment blossomed into madness, Washington felt compelled to put the British in their place.

The second complicating factor was Israel. On its own merits Egypt usually counted for little in American politics, and other things being equal American decision makers might have pursued their Egyptian designs unconcerned about the domestic implications. But other things were never equal in matters touching the security of Israel, and every time the Eisenhower administration pondered overtures to Cairo it had to consider the effects of its actions on the Israelis. Eisenhower was hardly a hostage to the Zionist lobby, as his conduct during the Suez affair on the eve of the 1956 elections demonstrated. But he was a president, not a czar, and he recognized the necessity of getting along with those in Congress and among the public to whom Israel meant more than it did to him.

For the present purpose American policy toward Egypt divides into two and a half phases (but only two chapters). The initial phase carries the story from the summer of 1952 until the beginning of 1956. During this period the United States sought to cultivate Egypt's new leaders— hesitantly at first, out of a desire not to upset the Suez negotiations, more forthrightly after London and Cairo cut a deal in mid-1954. Until the early spring of 1956 American officials believed Nasser might be willing to cooperate in the search for security in the Middle East. After they gave up on MEDO they still hoped he would agree to a settlement with Israel, which would do more than a dozen MEDOs to stabilize the region. These hopes vanished in the first months of 1956 when Nasser rejected the peace proposals of Eisenhower's special envoy, Robert Anderson.

Egypt and Nasser: Neutralist as Radical

The collapse of the Anderson mission marked the beginning of the second phase of American relations with Egypt. In the estimate of Eisenhower and Dulles, Nasser deserved most of the blame for Anderson's failure. The Egyptian leader appeared totally uncooperative and obstructionistic; his agenda, they now believed, had nothing to offer the United States. As a result American policy shifted from a collaborationist mode to one of opposition. The administration went about its task of depriving Nasser of influence more subtly than did the British, French, and Israelis; but Eisenhower and Dulles differed with the Suez invaders on methods only, not on objectives. In the American view the tripartite attempt to topple Nasser compounded the problem he posed by making the Egyptian leader more of a hero than ever in the eyes of the Arab masses. Better to oppose Nasser indirectly, by devices like the Middle East resolution of 1957.

But opposition had its limits, as the administration discovered in Lebanon in 1958, and even before the occupation of Beirut ended, American leaders admitted the irresistibility of the movement Nasser represented. Consequently they began to shift back toward a policy of accommodation of Nasser and the nationalists. Events of 1959 and 1960 reinforced this trend, demonstrating that Nasser in fact might not be the worst of a bad lot. After the 1958 revolution in Iraq, communists in that country gained an influence Nasser had consistently denied them in Egypt, even in the palmiest days of Egyptian-Soviet friendship. Not coincidentally that friendship was cooling rapidly as Baghdad, Cairo's traditional rival for Arab hegemony, drew closer to Moscow.

Eisenhower never quite lost his suspicions of Nasser, and the tilt back toward Egypt had only begun by the time the president left the White House; but when Nasser reciprocated an inclination toward more cordial relations, the administration decided American interests required and circumstances allowed an effort to make peace with Nasser's brand of neutralism.

II

FROM 1945 until the early 1950s American policy for the Middle East had one goal above all: keeping the Soviets out of the region. In 1946 Washington took a firm diplomatic stance against Moscow's meddling in Iranian affairs, with the result that the Russians completed the overdue withdrawal of their armed forces. The 1947 crisis in Greece and Turkey elicited the Truman Doctrine, announcing America's intention of opposing communist subversion in those countries and elsewhere. In 1948 the Truman administration supported the founding of Israel, over the opposition of State Department officials who predicted that the injection of such an unsettling element into Middle East politics would open the way to Soviet trouble-making; but in 1950 the administration attempted a remedy by joining with Britain and France in the "tripartite declaration," a statement guaranteeing the status quo and warning against efforts to overturn it.[1]

Yet despite these manifestations of concern for the region's security, Washington still hoped the Middle East could remain essentially a British bailiwick. As late as December 1951 the joint chiefs of staff declared that "the defense of the over-all area of the Middle East is a British strategic responsibility." Unfortunately, Britain's strength was failing here as everywhere else, and by May 1952 the State Department's Policy Planning Staff was judging the chiefs' position untenable. Paul Nitze, the planning director, characterized Britain's capabilities as "wholly inadequate" to defend the region against Soviet aggression. "It appears doubtful," Nitze added, "that they are adequate to provide the minimum requirements for even the shortest line of defense east of the Suez Canal." After citing examples of American success in checking Soviet advances elsewhere in the world, Nitze said that in the Middle East "the general picture appears to be one of such continuing weakness as to constitute an invitation to a shift in the theater of primary pressure if further Communist progress were to be successfully blocked in other areas."[2]

Nitze's comments indicated that if the United States hoped to deter Soviet adventurism in the Middle East, Washington had better look to its own devices. But the military logistics of the matter, at a moment of strain around the globe, were unfavorable; and the political logistics were even worse. In January 1952 Winston Churchill had visited Washington to request help. Believing, as he told a colleague before departing London, that if the West intended to hold the Middle East it was "of the utmost importance to get America in," Churchill tried his best to do just that. Labeling British forces at Suez "servants and guardians of the commerce of the world," and declaring the dangers of the region to be "not less than those which the United States have stemmed in Korea," the prime minister asked a joint session of Congress for an American military commitment to the Middle East.[3]

The lawmakers wanted nothing to do with what appeared a bald scheme to transfuse American blood and money into a dying British colonialism. Republicans especially disparaged the thought. Anticipating such a British maneuver, Senator William Langer of North Dakota requested that the pastor of Boston's Old North Church hang two lanterns in the tower. (The reverend, perhaps believing the revolutionary code inapplicable to Churchill's airborne invasion, declined.) Walter Judd expressed little surprise at the prime minister's ploy. "Naturally he wants to get his country tied as closely as possible to the United States. What other hope has it?" George Malone declared that Churchill aimed to attach American military power to a "colonial slavery system." The Nevada Republican predicted that if the United States fell into Churchill's Egyptian snare, involvement in imperialist struggles in Malaya and Indochina would soon follow. "No wonder Russia can make friends in these areas by simply announcing that they intend to free the inhabitants from the yoke of colonial slavery." When Truman and Churchill concluded their conversations with a harmless communiqué, the Republicans refused to concede that the danger had passed. Seventeen GOP senators issued a demand for full disclosure of the talks, especially of any secret agreements not covered by the communiqué.[4]

More than American congressional opinion barred the way to a commitment to Middle East defense. The people of the area itself demonstrated scant interest in any Anglo-American plan. In March the intelligence offices of the State Department, the army, the navy, the air force, the joint chiefs of staff, and the CIA worked up an estimate of the prospects for a regional anticommunist pact. In a word, these prospects were dismal, and they would remain so even in the unlikely event Britain and Egypt settled their dispute at once.

> Arab fears and suspicions and intraregional rivalries would continue to plague negotiations for the development of an effective organization. Public opinion, as well as many leaders, would continue to underestimate, ignore, or be fatalistic about the threat of Soviet aggression, which they would regard as far less tangible than the question of Western "interference" or the Arab-Israeli dispute. Arab leaders would remain suspicious

of Western motives, and would be concerned lest the defense organization be used as a means of applying collective pressure on them or re-establishing spheres of influence. Moreover, nationalist resentment against foreign interference in the Arab states might be turned against the regional defense organization, and lead to a demand for the withdrawal of foreign technicians from the Suez Canal base and other Middle East bases. In general, most states would remain motivated primarily by a desire to exploit Western fear of Soviet aggression in order to improve their military strength vis-a-vis their neighbors.[5]

Harold Hoskins, writing for the State Department's planners, expanded on the political difficulties confronting the United States in the Middle East. Hoskins warned of a "growing danger" that significant parts of the region would be lost to the West not through overt Soviet attack but "through neutralism or through communist penetration by methods short of open war." He remarked the decline of British and French prestige and asserted that this decline was beginning to affect the United States as well. Identifying the most important developments in the area as "the rising tide of nationalism and the growth of neutralism," Hoskins argued that America's problem "boils down to an attempt to reconcile what are sometimes considered as two irreconcilable objectives": namely, placating the nationalists and staying on friendly terms with the colonialists. There were no easy answers. The best the United States could do was pressure the British and French to face the fact that their days of special privilege were over and that repression had become counterproductive. "Force will not succeed and will divert already badly needed manpower from Western Europe and to that extent weaken the whole free world structure." At the same time American leaders should jawbone the Arabs to convince them that their safety lay in "effective cooperation for defense, not neutralism."[6]

Convincing the Arabs was a formidable task, however, so long as Britain and Egypt remained at loggerheads and the United States was stuck, as Acheson glumly commented, at "dead center" between the two. Egypt, the administration believed, held the key to a Middle East pact. As the State-Defense-CIA estimate of two weeks earlier put the matter, "Egypt will not join until its controversy with the U.K. is settled, and under the present circumstances no other Arab nation is likely to if Egypt does not."[7]

American planners pondered how to circumvent this difficulty, but solutions did not come easily. In a June meeting with officials from the State Department, Joint Chiefs Chairman Omar Bradley described a military defense of the Middle East as "not too realistic," in light of the opposition of the Egyptians, the weakness of the British, and American commitments elsewhere. Army Chief of Staff J. Lawton Collins expressed greater optimism but premised his hopefulness on a change in American thinking. The original Egypt-centered design for MEDO had to be scrapped, Collins said. He suggested a shift to the north. "The real hope of Middle Eastern defense is Turkey." As they demonstrated by their adherence to NATO, the Turks constituted a reliably pro-Western force, and they seemed willing and able to expand their role eastward. Collins predicted that if the United States could find a friendly government for Iran—"one which would talk turkey with the Turks"—the situation would improve further. The northern approach had the additional advantage that it would allow a forward defense of the oil fields. "If we are going to hold Middle Eastern oil, we will have to hold a line in Iran."

Henry Byroade, the assistant secretary of state for Near Eastern affairs, offered another argument for translating the focus of regional defense from Egypt to the northern tier. Having just visited the Middle East, Byroade believed British strength in the region was overrated. For all Churchill's tough rhetoric, Byroade worried that the British might pull a Palestine. "It seems to me that there is a real possibility that the British are going to get out of that area in a rather disgraceful way." The assistant secretary especially worried about Egypt. "I think we have got to watch the Egyptian thing very carefully."[8]

III

EGYPT BORE watching all right, and never more than during the next several weeks. Early in July Harold Hoskins returned from a tour of the Middle East convinced that the situation there was going from bad to worse.

> The tides of neutralism and nationalism, with which communism has successfully allied itself to an increasing degree, continue to rise. One impressive development since my trip last year is the surprising increase in the number of acknowledged communists in the Middle East and their

growing influence, despite the Moslem religion which many, including King Ibn Saud, felt would form an effective barrier.

Under the circumstances, Hoskins thought the idea of working with rather than against the neutralists bore considering. "If it were possible, could we build 'areas of neutrality' which are benevolently directed toward the free world?" The plan had attractions. Allies would not come cheap in the Middle East if they came at all, and if a pro-neutralist strategy succeeded there it might set a pattern for "a growing area of benevolent neutrality in other parts of the non-Soviet world."

But hard necessity forced Hoskins to reject his own suggestion. Depending on neutralists, he argued, at least in the Middle East, was just too risky. The location and resources of the region mattered too much in the balance of world power to entrust their care to governments the West could not control. Nonaligned regimes might *try* to hold the Russians at bay, but their success, especially at combating Soviet-inspired subversion, could hardly be guaranteed. Czechoslovakia had aimed at neutralism and been lost. Losing the Middle East would do far greater damage to the United States.[9]

Control was the crux of the issue. Neutralism in the Middle East challenged Western control. Of course neutralism in India challenged— indeed denied—Western control of that country; but Nehru appeared strong enough to resist Soviet advances, and India's adherence to the Commonwealth and its various other ties to the West ensured a continued friendly influence with his government. Yugoslavia was not under Western control; but because it had just recently seemed under Soviet control neutralism in Belgrade represented a change for the better. The Middle East, by contrast, *was,* effectively, under Western control. A shift to neutralism would signify a net loss; and since nonaligned regimes in the Middle East might not manage to keep the communists under control, neutralism might not be the last stop on the road to the left. Furthermore, neither India nor Yugoslavia was as central to Western, and therefore American, security as the Middle East. Without the region's oil Atlantic Europe would be at risk; without Atlantic Europe the United States would be in danger. At the moment—early 1952—the Middle East remained a Western sphere of influence. By one means or other American leaders intended to keep it that way.

Events in Egypt in July complicated matters, although the degree of complication only gradually became apparent. Since January, when open fighting between Egyptians and British troops had left scores dead, King Farouk had been shuffling his cabinet in an attempt to diminish dissent and hold his throne. His success diminished daily. Among those most disaffected was a conspiracy of colonels calling themselves the Free Officers, dedicated to the expulsion of the British from their country and headed by Nasser. The existence and activities of the group were not exactly secret: according to participant accounts the CIA had kept tabs on the colonels for some time, learning in March of a planned revolt. But revolution was a staple on the Cairo rumor market—"Talk of a coup d'etat is in the air," American Ambassador Jefferson Caffery had written in 1950—and until something happened one had to treat the rumors with skepticism.[10]

During the third week of July Caffery described "excited barracks room meetings of junior officers," with the dissidents lining up behind General Naguib. On the night of July 22 the officers staged a bloodless revolt against Farouk. The king appealed to the American embassy—as well as to the British—for help, declaring that his government could survive only with outside assistance. "I count on you," Farouk told Caffery, "to pass this message along to the right people." But neither Washington nor London had much interest in a countercoup and Caffery soon declared the Egyptian matter settled. The king had "completely lost control." Naguib held "undisputed command."[11]

Beyond this—even this far, as events demonstrated—Caffery had a difficult time sorting things out in Cairo. Naguib seemed to command but who followed and where they were all going remained unclear. Caffery worried that the rebels were riding a tiger they could not control. Although the leaders of the coup appeared moderate enough themselves, there seemed "a very real danger, as military influence grows and stabilizing influences decline, that extremist groups, particularly the Moslem Brothers, will play an increased role."[12]

Not surprisingly, considering the condition of the world and the frame of American minds, officials in Washington wanted to know the extent of communist influence among the new leaders of Egypt. On this count Caffery offered reassurance. He personally saw no evidence that communists wielded any significant clout, and the embassy had received unequivocal declarations from Naguib of "the complete anti-communist nature" of the revolt.[13]

The State Department tried to figure out just what had happened.

According to Alta Fowler of the department's Near East division, the uprising had been two decades coming. Since 1929 the Egyptian government had been sending promising young college graduates to England to study, on condition that they take commissions in the army on their return. As a consequence a middle echelon of well-educated and relatively idealistic officers had developed. But the monarchy had failed to make room for the advancement of this group, and they resented the fact that their careers were blocked by less educated and less capable commanders. During the Palestine war of 1948 the incompetence of the older generation had become alarmingly apparent. ("Overfed, lazy, and selfish," was how Nasser characterized his seniors, adding that they filled their time with "eating, drinking, gambling, carousing, smoking hashish, and engaging in many different forms of tyranny and corruption.") The worst of the lot had been sacked, but some, having the king's favor, eventually found their way back into positions of power, to the dismay of the colonels. Farouk's recent attempt to find a place for one of the most unsavory of the generals, Hussein Sirry Amer, had touched off the chain of events that utlimately led to the revolt.[14]

Consequently, Fowler suggested, the United States should experience little difficulty getting along with Egypt's new regime. From the beginning Naguib had assured foreigners that their persons and property would remain secure. As to potential radicalism, the Moslem Brotherhood possessed influence among the armed forces and doubtless had backed the coup, especially since the goals of the Brotherhood and of the Free Officers—"a purge of all corruption, whether in material, moral or religious matters"—coincided. Moreover, several members of the officers' group were closely identified with the Brotherhood. But Fowler did not think the religious radicals posed a serious threat. As to communism: "There is apparently little or no Communist influence in the army, and there have been no evidences of Communist elements at work in this latest upheaval."[15]

For most of a month after the coup American officials confined themselves to a posture of "stand-offishness," as Caffery put it, but by the middle of August they began to play a more forward role. After indications by Naguib's representatives of friendliness toward the United States and interest in presently receiving American aid, Caffery accepted an invitation to dine with the general and several associates. The evening went well and Caffery returned to the embassy favorably impressed. He described Naguib as "not brilliant" but possessing "good common sense and some qualities of leadership." His conversation with Naguib had convinced him that reports that the general was merely a figurehead were untrue. Of the junior officers no individual stood out.

> These young men look all to be in their thirties-forties. I believe they are well intentioned, patriotic and filled with desire to do something for Egypt. On the other hand, they are woefully ignorant of matters economic, financial, political, and international. However, they seem anxious to learn and have learned a lot in the last few weeks.

The entire group seemed eager to establish good relations with America. "They again emphasized their desire to be particularly friendly with the United States; they affirmed again that they hope in due course to receive 'help' from the United States." Caffery had assured them of America's sympathy and had congratulated them on the peaceful and orderly fashion in which they had effected the change of government, as well as on the "moderation" they continued to demonstrate.[16]

Caffery's favorable assessment largely determined the public response of the Truman administration. At the ambassador's urging Acheson applauded the "encouraging developments" in Cairo, declared relations between the United States and Egypt "most friendly and cooperative," and wished the new government "every success."[17]

IV

THE BRITISH, who had the most-direct Western stake in Egypt, were monitoring developments in Cairo even more carefully than were the Americans—and they were monitoring the Americans as closely as they were the Egyptians. Churchill and Eden wanted to get the United States into Egypt but only on Britain's terms. To the British, America was the wild card in the Middle Eastern deck, potentially trump or joker depending on when and how it was played. By dangling aid the Americans might lure Cairo to a Suez settlement. By actually delivering aid, however, they might spoil everything. Even before the July coup one Foreign Office observer noted that the Egyptians were counting on the United States to enter the picture as a "deus ex machina to persuade us to give way to Egyptian demands." The Free Officers' revolt heightened London's worries, since the colonels were shamelessly, in Britain's view, cozying up to the Americans.[18]

Acheson's sign of approval for the revolutionary regime provoked an immediate reaction from London. One British diplomat complained about the "double game" the Egyptians were now able to play between the United States and Britain. Another predicted that the American statement would convince the Egyptians that there was "no longer any need for restraint." Anthony Eden warned Acheson that "in these circumstances it is even more important than ever that British and American policy should keep in step, and anything that the Egyptians can interpret as appeasement by the United States is likely to encourage extremists at our expense." [19]

The British were especially suspicious of Caffery; the ambassador reciprocated fully. At the beginning of September the Revolutionary Command Council forced the resignation of Prime Minister Ali Maher in favor of Naguib. Maher's exit, Caffery reported, with more than a hint of satisfaction, left the British "out in the cold." "The military will not only have nothing whatever to do with them, but they are convinced that the British are attempting to sabotage their movement." The ambassador added that the regime had jailed most Egyptians who had treated the British "with any attempts at understanding." Moreover, Naguib had indicated that Egypt would "much prefer" American aid to British and that his government would like "a working alliance with the U.S. to the exclusion of the U.K." This suited Caffery. "They recognize their need for a strong friend, and we are nominated." [20]

Caffery thought the British had thoroughly mucked things up already; when he learned of Eden's warning against "appeasement" he could scarcely contain his annoyance.

> London's Foreign Office tactics have been wrong, and over and over again I have predicted the consequences. They are wrong again. . . . We trust the Department will refute Eden's innuendo that the US is "encouraging more extreme elements in Egypt." The US is encouraging a reform movement headed by an honest soldier who presides over a civilian cabinet and who is after all in control of Egypt.[21]

V

THROUGH THE late summer and autumn of 1952 Caffery continued to argue for a policy of friendliness and support for the new regime. In September one of the colonels, Abdel Amin, visited the embassy to tell Caffery that Egypt's government, after two months of concentration on domestic matters, now wished to turn to international affairs. Reaffirming that General Naguib and his colleagues were "completely on the side of the United States" and "unalterably opposed to Communism," Amin requested American military and economic assistance. He assured Caffery that Egypt did not ask something for nothing: in exchange for American aid his government would commit itself to a regional security pact or perhaps an alliance with the United States. General Naguib believed, however, that for the present such a commitment must remain confidential, lest it play into the hands of the government's enemies. After making his pitch Amin asked two questions: "(1) Would the United States be interested in such cooperation? (2) What sort of secret commitments would the United States want?"[22]

Washington moved cautiously in response to this approach. On one hand, Truman hesitated to get too closely involved with what was, despite its evident idealism, essentially a military dictatorship. On the other, the president did not wish to foreclose any options. Consequently he approved a reply by Acheson indicating close and sympathetic American consideration of the Egyptian request, but no more. The secretary directed Caffery to tell Naguib that the administration shared Egypt's desire for cooperation and would appreciate a further delineation of what the general had in mind. In addition Acheson told Caffery to drop a hint that a gesture or two of good will toward the West would make cooperation easier. The effect of such a move on public opinion, the secretary said, would be "most important in connection with efforts to help Egypt."[23]

Meanwhile American officials probed the Egyptians for a more definite declaration of what they would be willing to do in return for American aid. In particular Washington sought an explicit commitment to a regional pact. Early in November the embassy in Cairo received the clearest statement to date of Egypt's intentions toward MEDO. Naguib said that as soon as he reached an agreement with Britain regarding the final withdrawal of British troops, his government would be prepared to give assurances that its "ultimate objectives" included cooperation with the United States and other friendly powers in "planning for the common defense of the area."[24]

Acheson considered this assertion sufficiently solid to warrant a meaningful American response. After talks with Pentagon officials the secretary authorized the release of police equipment originally ordered by Farouk but withheld in the wake of the coup.[25]

At about the same time, Acheson met with Egypt's foreign minister, Ahmed Farraq Tayeh, then in the United States for a meeting of the UN General Assembly. The Egyptian diplomat said his government greatly appreciated the sympathy the United States had shown, adding that he hoped "this sympathy could be turned into material support." After describing Egypt's need for military assistance, he went on to inquire whether the United States might purchase Egyptian cotton at a price above that of the world market. Indicating that his government had taken to heart the secretary of state's earlier suggestion regarding the importance of good impressions, the foreign-minister asserted that Egypt had been endeavoring to create "a favorable atmosphere" for American help. He pointed to progress in the negotiations with Britain and to Cairo's decision to compensate families of foreigners killed during the riots the previous January.

Acheson acknowledged that these actions had been "most helpful," but he refused to commit the administration to further aid. Cotton purchases would create political and economic problems in America; as to military assistance, he would be happy to discuss the matter in greater detail at a future date.[26]

From Cairo Caffery continued to press for a more positive American policy. At the end of November the ambassador spoke with Naguib on the subject of aid. The general said he valued what the administration had done so far, in terms of releasing the police equipment, but his government needed further help. Radicals continually denounced the United States as a British lackey, claiming the Americans talked a good anticolonial game but failed to support their words with substance. Military assistance would go far toward proving these critics wrong. Naguib reiterated that his government remained staunchly opposed to communism but hinted that without external backing he might be forced to make concessions to those less adamant. Finally, he commented that American aid would ease cooperation with the West. "I may be dreaming, but if you could find a way to let us have 100 tanks, various doors would be opened, including one leading to Middle Eastern Defense."[27]

Caffery had not become an ambassador by accepting such statements at face value; still, he took Naguib seriously. As he reminded the State Department, military aid meant more to a regime like Naguib's than in some other cases. After all, Naguib's was a military government and tended to think in military terms. "The officers composing the Military High Committee are convinced that they can only maintain the support of the armed forces by a tangible show of military aid from the Western powers." Caffery added, "I believe they are right."[28]

At this time the ambassador also spoke with Nasser, who confirmed Caffery's opinion that the United States needed to move fast. Describing the colonel as "the strongest member of the Military High Committee" but also, interestingly, "probably the most moderate," Caffery found him unshakably anti-British. Nasser told Caffery that Britain had poisoned Egyptian minds against cooperation with the West and that the poison was seeping into relations with America. "The British are losing this country, and you with them, because you are tied to their policy. ... Already we are being accused of treason and selling out to the Americans." Under the circumstances, collaboration with Washington, as in a defense pact, grew increasingly difficult. (In a conversation with journalist Kennett Love, which Caffery may or may not have heard secondhand, Nasser addressed the MEDO issue more directly: "This hammering, hammering, hammering for pacts will only keep alive the old suspicions in the minds of the people—and the Communists know well how to exploit these suspicions.")[29]

To Acheson Caffery argued that continued deference to Britain, however advisable on Atlanticist grounds, threatened irreparable harm to American interests in Egypt. Unless the United States reinforced its verbal support of the Naguib regime with "tangible assistance," one of two bad results would likely follow: either the current rulers of the country would grow totally disillusioned with America or Naguib and Nasser and the others would become "more vulnerable to attacks from extreme nationalists and Communists."[30]

Although the suggestion of such "tangible assistance" provoked another sharp response from Britain, with Eden objecting on grounds of "inexpediency" with respect to the Suez negotiations and the defense ministry complaining that American arms would diminish Egypt's dependence on Britain, Acheson sided with Caffery. Without great difficulty the secretary swung the joint chiefs into line, and by the end of December the State Department and the Pentagon had agreed to a $10 million weapons package for Naguib.[31]

VI

YET THE largest hurdle, the White House, remained. Neither the State Department nor the military brass could entirely ignore the domestic political implications of a decision to arm Egypt, but the diplomats and generals tended to place other considerations foremost. (The attitude of the joint chiefs became evident a few months later when they only grudgingly agreed to include Israel in a Middle East aid request, admitting that Congress might reject the entire package if Israel were left out.) The president, on the other hand, while generally content to let the executive departments formulate policy toward India and Yugoslavia, took a personal interest in relations with Israel. In particular he paid close attention to the activities of the Zionist lobby. Knowing this, the State Department's Near Eastern division provided Acheson a briefing paper outlining arguments designed to win the president's support.[32]

State's case rested on two themes: the importance of Egypt to the West and the importance of Naguib to Egypt. Regarding the first, Egypt was "the key to the establishment of a Middle East Defense Organization and to a new relationship between the West and the Arab states." But Egypt's cooperation depended on reciprocal cooperation from the United States, which to the present regime implied military aid. As to Naguib, he had shown himself "both reasonable and skillful" in handling the myriad challenges facing an untested government vexed by internal and external problems.

> He represents our best chance to establish a relationship of confidence between his country and the West. We must support him if he is to overcome opposition which will undoubtedly increase unless he has something to show for his present reasonable and courageous attitude.[33]

On his way to the White House Acheson tested these arguments on Averell Harriman, then director of the administration's mutual security program. Acheson had hoped to bring Harriman aboard before the Israelis got wind of the plan and mobilized opposition; but Harriman informed him that the counteroffensive had already begun. Israel was placing two requirements on its acquiescence in an arms deal for Cairo: a similar package for Israel and Egypt's agreement to peace talks. As Tel Aviv no doubt knew, these conditions were impossible. "If they were put on," Acheson commented, "it would be better not to offer aid at all."[34]

Acheson decided to push forward, taking his case to Truman at the beginning of January 1953. The secretary described Naguib as "the best hope" for a pro-Western Egypt, for the establishment of MEDO, and for peace in the Middle East. Conceding the legitimacy of Israeli concerns, Acheson nonetheless asserted that Israel's future as fully as America's interests depended on Naguib's survival. Should the general's regime collapse and an "uncontrollable nationalism" seize Egypt, the entire region would be at risk. Naguib's survival demanded American arms.[35]

Harriman, who came along to the meeting to ensure that Truman not do anything rash in his last days in office, granted Acheson's arguments but contended that time would not allow the president to follow through on a favorable decision regarding military aid. Committing the incoming Republicans to a course as fraught with controversy as arming Egypt would be unfair and unwise.

Truman agreed. He admitted that the accomplishment of American objectives in the Middle East probably required weapons for Egypt; he would so advise his successor. But he did not believe he should make a promise he personally could not fulfill. Therefore he declined to grant Egypt arms. As a sop to the Egyptians he said he would let them *purchase* weapons in the United States—which meant little since Cairo lacked cash.[36]

VII

INHERITING THIS policy, the Republicans gave no serious thought to changing it during their first months in office. Eisenhower recognized the need for greater attention toward the Middle East; shortly after the 1952 election he told Dulles that mending fences with the Arabs would be a priority in his administration. But for the reasons mentioned in previous chapters—Stalin's death, Korea—he and Dulles did not get around to the Middle East until May when the secretary toured the region.[37]

By this time the State Department was coming to the realization that Naguib reigned more than ruled. "The real direction of affairs ..." Caffery asserted, "is in the hands of Nasir." Consequently, although protocol demanded that Dulles spend most of his time with the general-prime minister, he found his conversations with the colonel the most enlightening part of his visit.[38]

American policy needed enlightenment. For most of a year American leaders had been groping for a handle on the Middle East—a posture all too common during the four decades since World War II. Caught between a desire not to alienate the British, whose help was necessary to the defense of Europe, and a recognition that association with the colonialists, especially in hotbeds of nationalism like Egypt, was destroying the credibility of the United States, Washington drifted. Plenty of evidence, including Nasser's own testimony, indicated that Egypt would have nothing to do with a West-sponsored defense pact. As various American analysts had been pointing out for many months, the Egyptians, like Arabs generally, gave little thought to any Soviet threat; they worried instead about the European imperialists and the Israelis. Some Pentagon thinkers were gravitating toward the northern tier, but MEDO, sustained by the kind of life-support system bureaucracies specialize in, lingered on.

Dulles' Cairo visit pulled the plug. On the afternoon of his second day in Egypt the secretary led a group of eight Americans into a meeting with Nasser and three other members of the Revolutionary Command Council. After the usual formalities Dulles made his pitch for regional defense. Nasser responded that although collective security in the abstract might be a good idea, while the British remained in Egypt there would be a "psychological block" against cooperation with the West. The Egyptian people viewed MEDO as a "perpetuation of occupation," and they felt the Russian danger only dimly if at all.

> I must tell you in all frankness that I can't see myself waking up one morning to find that the Soviet Union is our enemy. We don't know them. They are thousands of miles away from us. We have never had any quarrel with them. I would become the laughing-stock of my people if I told them they now had an entirely new enemy, many thousands of miles away, and that they must forget about the British enemy occupying their territory. Nobody would take me seriously if I forgot about the British.

Dulles pointed out that evacuation of British troops from the Suez base was now "assured in almost all respects." Would this not make a difference in mitigating popular concerns? Nasser responded that every vestige of the British occupation must "entirely disappear." The people would settle for nothing less. Dulles countered that while he understood the importance of public attitudes, he wondered whether the government might modify the thinking of the people. Nasser replied, "We can influence the people on every point except this." [39]

Dulles could not tell how much of this opposition to all things British derived from an accurate assessment of popular sentiment and how much to Nasser's personal feelings of affront, but the colonel's increasing control made any difference academic. In a cable to Eisenhower the secretary said Egypt's "deep basic distrust" of British motives overrode any fear of the Soviets; consequently Egypt's participation in an anticommunist pact was highly unlikely. [40]

Writing to the State Department Dulles exhibited still greater pessimism. "I have found the situation in Egypt more serious than the Department generally has recognized. Observers here are convinced, and I share their view, that the possibility of open hostilities in the near future is real." Nasser had described to an American journalist what such hostilities would entail: "Not formal war. That would be suicidal. It will be a guerrilla war. Grenades will be thrown in the night. British soldiers will be stabbed stealthily. There will be such terror that, we hope, it will become far too expensive for the British to maintain their citizens in occupation of our country." Dulles thought Nasser and his associates recognized that a guerrilla campaign would bring their demise—that "chaos and the destruction of the ruling regime would inevitably be an aftermath"—but he was convinced that they preferred such an outcome to concessions to Britain. "Their emotions are so great that they would rather go down as martyrs than concede. . . . It is almost impossible to over-emphasize the intensity of this feeling. It may be pathological, but it is a fact." [41]

A few days later, following talks with other Arab leaders, the secretary of state reflected on American prospects in the region. He found little cause for encouragement. "Bitterness toward the West, including the United States, is such that while Arab goodwill may still be restored, time is short before the loss becomes irretrievable." Despite American professions of support for nationalist goals, the Arabs were fast losing faith that Washington would ever break with Britain and Israel. "The remaining hope will quickly dissolve unless our acts seem here to show the capacity to influence British and Israeli policies, which now tend to converge in what is looked upon as a new phase of aggression against the Arabs."

Dulles told Eisenhower that after his talks in Cairo he recognized Naguib was little more than a "popular figure through which the revolutionary group operates." This intelligence clarified matters but afforded scant reassurance, since the dominant figures in the government, including Nasser, had "little political experience or understanding of international problems." Consequently the administration would have to change its plans. "We had come here with the belief that Egypt afforded the best opportunity for Arab leadership toward better relations with Israel and the West." The recent discussions had destroyed that belief. Indeed, not only had the secretary concluded that MEDO was "impracticable," he feared Egyptian hostility toward Britain might result in the entire region's turning its back on the West. "The United Kingdom–Egypt problem is most dangerous, and if unsolved it will find the Arab world in open and united hostility to the West and in some cases receptive to Soviet aid." [42]

(For his part Nasser thought the talks with Dulles had gone well. Reporting to his associates, Nasser commented:

> The Americans are very energetic. I continually ask myself what they really want, and sometimes wonder whether their aim may not be exactly the same as that of the British, but to be accomplished in a different style and by different means. In any case, the British and American approaches seem to be diverging, and may actually conflict. So we should have some time in which to manoeuvre between the two. The best that could happen is that the Americans actually mean what they say; the worst is that it could turn out they mean what we suspect them of meaning.

Regardless of whether the United States desired only to prevent the Soviets from attacking the Middle East, or really aimed at replacing Britain in control of the region, Egypt might benefit from the Americans' entry into a situation heretofore dominated by the British. "If we manage to exploit the gap between the two we shall have achieved something." [43])

On his return to Washington Dulles briefed the National Security Council on his trip. He reiterated his view that Naguib was merely a front for Nasser's group and that the Revolutionary Command Council was preparing a guerrilla offensive against the British. Should Britain meet force with force the results might be "disastrous" for the West. Even if by some miracle the Egyptians and the British achieved a peaceful settlement, Egypt would prove a thin reed for regional defense. Economic distress and political instability would wrack the country for years, making it more a liability than an asset. Consequently, Dulles said, MEDO was "finished."

But some hope remained. Despite "the complete preoccupation" of most of the Arabs with local problems, certain countries of the area were thinking along American lines. Dulles had been especially impressed by Turkey and Pakistan. The former had already demonstrated its support for collective security; the latter could be made "a strong loyal point." Syria and Iraq also "realized their danger" and probably would be willing to join an alliance. Iran was a question mark, "the obvious weak spot in what could become a strong defensive arrangement of the northern tier of states." The northern approach might work, Dulles said, "if we could save Iran." The administration's immediate need, therefore, was "to concentrate on changing the situation there." As to the countries of the southern part of the region, including Egypt, they were "too lacking in realization of the international situation to offer any prospect of becoming dependable allies."[44]

VIII

DULLES' HARPING on the Arabs' "lack of understanding" of the international situation reflected a comprehension gap of his own. Nasser's assessment of the relative threats to Egypt's independence by East and West hit much closer to the mark than did Dulles', as the Suez war would prove. But more importantly, the secretary's complaints demonstrated a divergence of interests, which Dulles and other American leaders recognized all too well. Nasser demanded independence for Egypt, just as Nehru demanded independence for India and Tito for Yugoslavia. As did his neutralist confreres, Nasser understood that independence required nonalignment—which for Egypt necessitated breaking the bonds that bound the country to Britain and the West. But the United States in the mid-1950s had no use for an independent Egypt, even less than the Soviets in the late 1940s had for an independent Yugoslavia. An independent, neutralist Egypt was an Egypt out of American control, as Harold Hoskins had pointed out in rejecting a benign attitude toward Middle Eastern neutralism. In such a sensitive region independence had its limits.

But Dulles also recognized, to a far greater degree than his public pronouncements suggested, that diplomacy was the art of the possible. Nasser had killed MEDO; the United States must fall back to the next best position. In regional terms this meant the northern tier. Regarding Egypt it implied a search for influence short of alliance.

A policy paper produced for the NSC during the month after Dulles' Cairo visit summarized American objectives. The United States, the report declared, would be "critically endangered" if the Soviets gained a substantial foothold in the Middle East. Unfortunately trends in the region were working to the Russians' advantage. American support for Israel damaged relations with the Arabs; but the really grave threat arose from Britain's confrontation with Egypt, which could escalate into armed hostility at any time.

> Given the present state of tension in the Near Eastern states, such hostility could result in inflammation throughout the Arab states to the point where they would endeavor to exclude Western influence. . . . This might not only affect the availability of the resources of the area to the West and strategic operating rights and bases, but extend to expulsion of all Western influence.

With the stakes this high—"expulsion of all Western influence"—the United States could not remain aloof. Despite the risk of bruising Britain's feelings, London must be made to realize that retaining troops in Egypt had become "a political impossibility." More to the point, the American government must prepare to supplant Britain by a program of American aid, including weapons.[45]

Accordingly the Pentagon drew up a proposal for arms assistance to countries of the Middle East. The joint chiefs conceded that an alliance based on widespread Arab cooperation would not materialize in the near term. Nevertheless they believed military aid would provide a useful down payment toward future collaboration—"a priming operation designed primarily to establish a politico-military climate favorable for obtaining the participation of the individual states in planning for the defense of the Middle East." As it pertained to Egypt the chiefs' proposal specified providing equipment for two infantry divisions and one armored brigade, twenty-seven naval vessels ranging from destroyer escorts to LSTs, and one squadron of fighter planes.[46]

IX

ALTHOUGH PLANS for gaining Egypt's cooperation even short of MEDO turned out to be wishful thinking, American leaders could be partly forgiven for their error on account of the mixed signals emanating from Cairo. At the beginning of June the Egyptian ambassador told Undersecretary of State Walter Bedell Smith that his government recognized the logic behind Washington's promotion of a regional security pact. He said he understood that an attack on Egypt from the West was "inconceivable" and that "the only threat is from the East." Even so, collaboration with the Western allies was impossible, since the Egyptian people considered Britain "their number one enemy." A few weeks later, however, Nasser asked Caffery to transmit a request for military aid to Washington. In particular Nasser wanted some shiny hardware to boost army morale; he said he hoped to build pro-American sentiment in the armed forces in preparation for future cooperation.[47]

During this period Nasser was consolidating his power. On June 18 Egypt proclaimed itself a republic. Naguib assumed the office of president while continuing as prime minister; but Nasser as deputy prime minister packed the cabinet with his own supporters. To Dulles' question whether the shakeup diminished Naguib's control over policy, Caffery replied with the confidence of hindsight: "Naguib never had effective control over policy; therefore, no change. . . . Effective control has always been in the hands of Nasir and his friends."[48]

Now recognizing Nasser as the man to cultivate, Caffery continued to consider weapons the appropriate means. The Republicans had extended Truman's embargo on grant military aid pending a summit conference with Britain and France; but the fall of the Mayer government in Paris, then Churchill's illness, then Eden's, pushed the conference back through the summer and into the autumn. Caffery contended that arms for Egypt could not wait. He urged Dulles to approve Nasser's request for military aid, saying prompt approval would have

> the highly desirable effect of (a) strengthening the regime internally in the most vital area (Army), (b) encouraging the pro-American and thus prowestern orientation of Egypt and (c) avoiding disillusionment at a moment when a lingering hope of American intervention is virtually the only factor forestalling an even more adamant Egyptian stand on the issue of British evacuation.

246

Expanding on the last point, Caffery explained that to date Nasser and his friends had been patient, hoping the Americans would talk sense into the British. "An important reason why the R.C.C. have promised us to keep things quiet until our government has had time to take up the matter with the British is that they have confidence in us." Caffery argued that weapons held the key to maintaining this confidence.[49]

Dulles might have agreed, but Eisenhower refused to inject a new and unsettling element—one guaranteed to antagonize the president's old friend Churchill—into an explosive situation. So even while he warned Eden that the United States could not withhold aid indefinitely without "very grave effect" on American relations with the Arab world, the secretary put aside the issue of arms for Egypt.[50]

Having lost on the issue of guns and tanks, Nasser's backers in the State Department turned to money. The Near Eastern division worked up a proposal for some $25 million in American economic aid; in November Henry Byroade presented the plan to Dulles.[51]

Although the secretary and the president both liked the idea, they moved slowly, hoping to find a way around the inevitable British objections. The delay proved costly. On matters relating to Israel the Eisenhower administration leaked less than Truman's sieve, but reports soon surfaced that the White House was considering support to Israel's number-one enemy. Could such reports be true?, asked members of Congress when the legislature convened at the beginning of 1954. The version Thomas Pelly had heard involved weapons; the Washington Republican denounced arms for Cairo as "a terrible mistake." Citing the uncertainty surrounding events in Egypt, Pelly said, "Let us have it clearly in mind that we are dealing with a two-edge sword. A loaded gun is not the thing to hand to someone who you are not sure will use it the way you intend." Democrat Emanuel Celler of New York, an ardent Zionist, objected on grounds that Nasser unlawfully barred Israel from using the Suez Canal. "Today Egypt arbitrarily excludes Israel from access to the canal. Who knows but that the time may come when Egypt would arbitrarily proscribe any other nation, including the United States, from access?"[52]

The anti-Nasserists on Capitol Hill did not yet constitute a majority, but the Egyptian leader added to their ranks by announcing at just this time that Egypt would adopt a neutralist course in the cold war. Indeed he went further. Through a spokesman he asserted that although his government sought balanced relations with East and West, he felt obliged, since the status quo favored the West, to move toward the East. Accordingly Egypt would pursue closer ties with the Soviet Union, recognize China, strengthen its diplomatic representation in East Germany, and strive for improved trading arrangements with countries of Eastern Europe. In addition Egypt's delegate would feel free to support Moscow's initiatives at the United Nations.[53]

Just as Nehru's public opposition to American arms for Pakistan—at this very same moment—nearly compelled the administration to go ahead with that deal, Nasser's shift to the left forced the Eisenhower administration to shelve its plans for assistance to Egypt. Dulles explained to Caffery:

> The U.S. could not appear to be granting aid in direct response to this type of Egyptian pressure, not only because of adverse domestic (especially Congressional) reaction, but also because of the very adverse effect in other Middle Eastern countries, where such action would undercut moderate elements and embolden extremists to demand that their governments exert similar pressures.[54]

Caffery thought Dulles was overreacting and he feared that the miscalculation would play into the hands of radical elements in Egypt. "Neutralism is a menace here," the ambassador admitted. But he predicted that withholding aid would make the neutralists stronger. Despite the recent announcement Caffery did not believe Nasser and his group had thrown their lot irrevocably in with the neutralists. On the contrary, he declared that the R.C.C. was "definitely not neutralist minded." For the United States to treat Nasser as unfriendly would be premature and perhaps self-fulfilling.[55]

For the time being Caffery lost the argument. Dulles recognized that aid to Egypt might yet play an important role in American diplomacy toward the Middle East, but the cost—in terms of relations with Britain, with Congress, and with moderate potential allies in the Middle East— was too high. Nor did events of he first half of 1954 dispose the secretary to change his mind. With the crisis in Indochina coming to a head, Dulles and Eisenhower hoped to create an Anglo-American united front against the communists on the ground in Indochina and later in negotiations at Geneva. Aid to Cairo would only make the task more difficult.

X

BY THE end of July, however, the West had salvaged what it could of Indochina, London had agreed to a Suez withdrawal timetable Cairo could accept, and half a year had passed since Nasser's declaration of left-neutralism. Knowing that Israel's supporters and hard-core antineutralists would still object, Eisenhower and Dulles nonetheless decided to give aid to Egypt a chance. On July 30 the secretary notified Caffery that the administration planned to include $40 million for assistance to Egypt in its budget for fiscal 1955. Half would go for military aid, half for economic.[56]

After the long delay Caffery found the numbers disappointingly small, and he told Dulles the Egyptians would feel the same way. Cairo's hopes regarding American aid had escalated during the two years since the new regime had first approached the embassy. American intimations that a settlement with Britain would unlock the doors of the American treasury had done nothing to deflate these hopes. With the recent Suez agreement, Caffery said, the Egyptians' expectations had "soared." Forty million dollars would hardly seem to justify Cairo's patience.[57]

In the event, Egyptian leaders accepted the American offer with little overt complaint, as the first installment of a larger program. To Washington's surprise they requested a change in the program's mix, preferring to take all $40 million in economic aid. American arms came with more strings than did American dollars, and so soon after ejecting one Western overlord they did not want to appear to be accepting another. Anyway, as Foreign Minister Mahmoud Fawzi commented, American economic aid would free Egypt's reserves for weapons purchases.

Caffery suggested that this shift in Cairo's priorities could work to the advantage of the United States. It would relieve America of the burden of arming Egypt; it would ease potential problems with Israel; and it would prevent the inspection and supervision problems that plagued military aid to Yugoslavia. On the whole the ambassador thought Washington still enjoyed "an excellent opportunity to improve the U.S. position while strengthening a forward-looking regime."[58]

XI

CAFFERY PLACED more faith in the good will of the Egyptians than did some others in the administration, but Washington in the latter half of 1954 generally agreed that it might yet work with Nasser. What neutralism meant for Egypt remained to be seen; one could not help taking the anti-Western rhetoric of the prime minister (Naguib had been ousted in February) with a grain of salt, as part of a negotiating strategy against Britain. Now that the British were on their way out accommodation might be achieved. Egypt needed foreign aid; the United States could supply it. Undoubtedly Nasser had his own agenda—what self-respecting nationalist did not?—but there seemed enough overlap between his and America's to allow for collaboration. At least the United States ought to test the possibility. When Eisenhower's NSC revised its policy statement for the Middle East, cooperation with Egypt remained on the list of goals worth pursuing. Although the administration had shifted its regional focus to the northern tier, the NSC advocated making clear to Nasser that this shift in no way derogated from the importance the United States placed on Egypt.[59]

So far was the administration willing to go toward accommodating Nasser, in fact, that Eisenhower's top-level Operations Coordinating Board authorized a special program of covert military aid to Cairo. In the two years since the overthrow of Farouk the CIA had strengthened its relations with Nasser, not least because the prime minister and the agency's Near East expert, Kermit Roosevelt, hit it off far better than did Nasser and Caffery. Nasser also preferred doing business with Roosevelt because the CIA operated under fewer political constraints than did the American embassy, and its money, some $3 million of which the agency had delivered to Cairo, came with relatively few conditions. Unwilling to accept the strictures Congress placed upon arms transfers and financing, Nasser inquired of Roosevelt whether some special arrangement might be possible. At a September meeting the OCB, which consisted of representatives from the State and Defense departments, the CIA, and the Foreign Operations Administration, advocated an end run around Congress.

We should advise Prime Minister Nasir that we cannot undertake a full scale military aid program unless and until he is able to conclude a normal military assistance agreement. However, in view of our special friendship and our desire to assist his regime to maintain and consolidate itself, we are willing to make available a modest additional amount of economic aid in such a way that it will release dollars for the purchase by Egypt of American military equipment. This would be kept strictly secret.

The figure the OCB set for this program was not large—up to $10 million—but it would get things started and demonstrate the administration's good faith. In passing this recommendation along to Dulles, John Jernegan, the deputy secretary of state for Near Eastern affairs, said of Nasser: "He can be very useful to us in the Near Eastern picture if properly supported and cultivated. Therefore, I think a special gesture of this kind is worth trying."[60]

Dulles approved and the project proceeded. Unfortunately for its success, the two American officers dispatched to Cairo to make the offer soon learned that what Washington proposed would not begin to cover what the Egyptians had in mind. Nasser's chief of staff handed Colonel H. Alan Gerhardt and Captain Wilbur Eveland a list of Egypt's requirements, including bombers, tanks, and heavy artillery, totaling well over $100 million. Nasser made the sum academic, however, by declaring that he could not accept American military aid at this time, secret or otherwise. His political enemies would discover it and attack him for selling out to the United States. When the American officers inquired how long it might be before he would feel free to receive American weapons, he responded that "when the last British soldier left Egypt"— in 1956—he would think about an agreement with Washington.

Aside from military aid, Nasser and the Americans discussed the general state of the Middle East. Gerhardt and Eveland were impressed by the Egyptian leader's personal presence and grasp of regional issues. In his report to the Defense Department Gerhardt wrote:

Nasir displays a keen understanding of the strategic importance of the area and the critical role which Egypt plays in it. He also is keenly aware of the vacuum that exists between the northern tier of defense and the Egyptian base. In a brief strategic estimate he considered that the Soviets would strike first at the oilfields and as a second priority the Egyptian base crossroads. . . . He said that there were neutralist elements in Egypt who felt that with a strong national army the frontiers could be defended and the Soviets would bypass Egypt. He did not accept this view since he did not see within Egypt the capability of developing a sufficiently strong force to deter a Soviet attack on Egypt. Hence the vacuum between the northern tier and Egypt must be filled.

What Nasser suggested filling the vacuum with was not MEDO, of course, but an alliance strictly of the countries of the region.

In Gerhardt's view Nasser's comments indicated that the United States ought to drop its plans for military aid to Egypt for the near future. Gerhardt conceded that if Nasser consolidated his political strength and if he were "continuously worked upon" by American agents he might reconsider. But this was a long shot. Gerhardt recommended that the administration take this opportunity to get itself off a potentially uncomfortable hook.

> Unless after further reflection on the discussion he indicates a changed position, it would seem that the proper course of action would be to drop any further negotiations for an MDAP [Mutual Defense Assistance Program] agreement and on the face accept his timing of approximately 18 months. This has been his decision based on his estimate of what he can get away with and would relieve the U.S. of its commitment at least insofar as a grant aid program is concerned.[61]

As matters turned out, Nasser did reconsider his rejection of American military aid. Shortly before the end of 1954 he told the administration changing circumstances had led him to conclude that American arms would provide a necessary boost to army morale. Indeed he declared Egypt's need for military aid "desperate." Although Nasser still deemed it politically impossible to sign a formal MDAP agreement, he asked whether a personal letter from himself to Eisenhower covering all points required by legislation would suffice.

But the back door for weapons had closed. After the State and Defense departments and the CIA discussed Nasser's latest proposal, Dulles sent a reply declaring that unfortunately the funds previously earmarked for Egypt had, upon Nasser's expression of lack of interest, been reallocated. Congress would have to appropriate new monies; in any event Egypt must accept standard MDAP terms.[62]

XII

ONE REASON for the change of heart in Washington—even Allen Dulles, whose CIA had instigated the covert-aid effort, signed off on the rejection—was a belief that if conditions in Egypt were as desperate as Nasser contended there was no point giving away weapons without compensation. In particular the administration might use the lure of military aid to induce Nasser to come to terms with Israel. John Jernegan explained the thinking of those at the State-Defense-CIA meeting who drafted the reply to Nasser, in a cover letter to Foster Dulles.

> As you know, our plans for making progress toward a solution of the Arab-Israel problem count heavily on Egypt as the potential leader in a settlement with Israel. To induce Nasir to accept this role, we must (1) help to strengthen his position at home and (2) show him that such a policy will pay dividends. By the proposed message we would hold out to him the carrot of possible military assistance (which he wants more than anything else) while at the same time making it clear that he must earn this by an improved attitude toward Israel.[63]

Another factor inclining the administration away from military aid to Egypt also had to do with Israel. Even those in Washington most enamored of the CIA and America's covert-operations capability—in the post-Mossadeq, post-Arbenz, pre–U-2, pre–Bay of Pigs days there were many—had to concede, on sober second thought, that American military aid to Egypt would not long remain secret from the Israelis, who would have every reason to leak the news to their friends in America. The repercussions for the administration of being caught circumventing Congress could be imagined. (Something similar would happen three decades later to another Republican president, to his enormous embarrassment.)

In 1954 the Israelis opposed military aid to Egypt as vigorously as they had two years earlier when the Democrats first floated the idea. Before the ink was dry on the Anglo-Egyptian pact Dulles found Israeli Ambassador Abba Eban at his door, ready to describe in detail the danger American weapons in Egyptian hands would pose to Israel's security. Of course Israel did not presume to tell the government of the United States how to manage its affairs, but the ambassador considered it reasonable to ask compensation for his country. The particulars had changed only slightly from 1952: similar aid to Israel, firm guarantees against Arab aggression, and American help in forcing Cairo to lift its blockade against Israeli traffic through the Suez Canal.[64]

A week later Israeli Prime Minister Moshe Sharett amplified the point to the American chargé in Tel Aviv. Sharett expressed his concern that

253

the United States would become so involved with Egypt that Washington would lose its ability to push Cairo toward peace. The prime minister therefore urged the Eisenhower administration to declare that Egypt would receive no aid until Nasser redressed Israel's legitimate grievances. Shortly afterward the embassy in Tel Aviv learned that Sharett's government was planning a four-pronged diplomatic offensive, including all-out opposition to American weapons for Arab countries, insistence on arms for Israel, demands that Washington hold up economic aid to Egypt until Cairo met its international obligations, and efforts to obtain a commitment of military forces to guarantee Israel's borders.[65]

As part of this offensive, Rabbi Abba Hillel Silver paid visits to the White House and the State Department. At the latter he told Walter Bedell Smith that the prospect of weapons for Egypt was causing "the deepest concern" in Israel. Many in that country, he said, believed the Eisenhower administration had "turned its back" on them. Silver hastened to add that he did not agree with these people, but he remarked a "conspicuous lack of friendly statements toward Israel" and a number of "unfortunate" speeches by administration officials. Israel did not ask much—at least Silver did not ask much in Israel's name. If the administration could make some public gesture to encourage the Israelis to feel they could "look on the United States as a big brother," the situation would be greatly relieved.[66]

XIII

THE ADMINISTRATION, as noted above, chose the path of least resistance, scrapping plans for covert military aid to Cairo and insisting on congressionally mandated conditions, which it knew Nasser would reject, on any above-board arms assistance. But the administration refused to surrender all levers for encouraging Egyptian cooperation, and Dulles and others pursued the possibility of increasing economic aid.

As early as 1952 the Egyptian government had indicated interest in American help financing a new dam at Aswan on the Nile. During the following year the World Bank began feasibility studies. In January 1954 the bank sent a representative, Dorsey Stevens, to Cairo to commence financial discussions. Stevens took care to remind the Egyptians that his employer was not an agency of the United States; but aside from the fact that the American government underwrote most of the bank's projects,

Stevens' disclaimer rang hollow as he repeatedly stressed that the bank's contribution of $125 million toward the dam's projected $500 million cost would depend on Washington's donating a significant sum as well.[67]

Through 1954, as the funding package took shape, Eisenhower and Dulles anticipated objections from those who feared anything that strengthened an enemy of Israel; but the approaching storm did not appear to be of major proportions. In important respects the dam was to American policy toward Egypt what food aid was to policy toward India and Yugoslavia. Supporters could don the mantle of humanitarianism—in the Aswan case, uplifting the downtrodden fellahin—and opponents tended to look like ogres. Consequently aid for the dam offered the Eisenhower administration an ideal vehicle for demonstrating American support for Egypt and encouraging a friendly attitude on Nasser's part.

As 1955 began, however, the Middle East's always unpredictable political weather forced some changes in administration forecasts. The first indication of new turbulence came in February, when Israeli troops attacked an Egyptian base at Gaza, killing more than thirty Egyptian soldiers. Nasser was surprised—"caught with my pants down," he told a reporter—and determined not to let it happen again. In one respect the Gaza raid put Israel's supporters on the defensive and promised to make a pro-Egyptian policy easier for the administration to sell. On the other hand, coming just a week after David Ben-Gurion's return to government, the attack indicated a hardening of the Israeli line toward Egypt, with repercussions in American politics that could be guessed.[68]

A second new twist was Nasser's increasing identification with the neutralist movement, highlighted by his appearance at the Bandung Conference in April. Nasser and Nehru first met two months earlier. "They had a deep and instantaneous effect on one another," according to Nasser intimate Mohamed Heikal. "It was rather like a man looking across a crowded room and falling in love with a woman he has never seen before." (Anthony Nutting, who also knew both leaders, took a different view of the relationship: "Nasser never really warmed to Nehru's lofty intellectualism, which made him feel inferior." Perhaps Nasser lacked ability Yugoslavia's Tito's to laugh off Nehru's deep background analyses. When the Indian prime minister would begin explaining the roots of present conflicts Tito would turn to friends and explain that "with Nehru everything starts B.C.") During the next half-year Nasser and Nehru exchanged eight visits. Nasser also met Tito during this period, tying Egypt still more closely to the neutralist cause. Even among American conservatives neutralism was not quite a hanging offense, but by associating with Nehru and Tito, Nasser lost a few more votes in Congress and raised the political costs to the administration of doing business with him.[69]

The third and most seriously troublesome development occurred in September when Nasser announced an arms agreement with Czechoslovakia. Since Washington had rejected his arms request at the end of 1954 Nasser had been looking to the East for weapons, but the Russians had to be convinced of his bona fides. "Our attitude was cautious," Khrushchev recalled.

> For a certain period after the coup and Colonel Nasser's emergence as chief of state we couldn't be sure what direction this new government of army officers would take, either in foreign or in domestic policies. The new Egyptian leadership came mostly from the upper ranks of the Egyptian army, in other words from the bourgeoisie and not from the working class. . . .
>
> We were inclined to think that Nasser's coup was just another one of those military take-overs which we had become so accustomed to in South America. We didn't expect much new to come of it.

Eventually, however, Moscow decided Nasser deserved help. When the Egyptian prime minister told Zhou Enlai at Bandung he needed arms, Zhou passed the request along and the Kremlin responded favorably.[70]

Nasser made no secret of the arrangement. Early in 1955 Caffery retired and was replaced by Henry Byroade. The former assistant secretary was much more Nasser's type. A precocious soldier, he had become the youngest general in the history of the U.S. Army before turning to diplomacy. At the time of his posting to Cairo *Look* magazine, in a column about "Men Who Fascinate Women," described the forty-one-year-old ambassador (Nasser was the same age) as an "authentic Horatio Alger character" and the "prototype of the grown-up American boy." Unlike many diplomats, Byroade was on friendly terms with the CIA—which also helped with Nasser—to the point that when he finally retired after holding a near-record six ambassadorships the intelligence agency held a special going-away party at headquarters in Langley, Virginia. In any event Nasser and Byroade got along famously and in May the prime minister told the ambassador that he had a firm commitment from Moscow for weapons.[71]

Washington reacted slowly at first. Dulles thought Nasser might be bluffing, hoping to pressure Washington into releasing American arms. Some in the State Department doubted that Moscow had the guns to spare. During the course of the summer, however, the administration became convinced of the reality of the Soviet offer. In mid-September the CIA reported that an announcement was imminent.[72]

At the last minute Dulles sought to dissuade Nasser, sending two special envoys to Cairo: first Kermit Roosevelt, then George Allen, formerly ambassador to Belgrade, now in Byroade's old job. Neither succeeded in changing Nasser's mind.[73]

On its merits the arms agreement between Egypt and Czechoslovakia did not augur a major shift in the balance of power in the Middle East. As an NSC paper phrased the issue, the Czech deal produced a change "of degree rather than of kind" in the situation facing the United States. In public Dulles treated the matter almost casually, telling reporters that what Nasser did was entirely his own business. To the extent the secretary spoke of the arms pact as a problem, it principally involved Soviet-American relations. Dulles declared that weapons shipments to the Middle East "would not contribute to relaxation of tensions" between the United States and the Soviet Union.[74]

Part of Washington's relative calm followed from the fact that Nasser himself still expressed a desire for good relations with the United States. Byroade reported from Cairo early in November that the Egyptian prime minister had said he was aware of an increasing internal communist challenge in his country; as a consequence he was planning a crackdown. Nasser assured Byroade that Egypt was not supplying weapons to other countries in the area. Most indicative of Cairo's reasons for cultivating Washington—and the principal grounds for the administration's belief that cooperation might yet be achieved—was Nasser's comment that he hoped to move ahead with planning for the Aswan Dam.[75]

Equally important in conditioning Washington's reaction to Nasser's eastward shift was the opinion that turning to Moscow was precisely what should be expected of one in Nasser's position. Jefferson Caffery earlier had identified Egyptian neutralism as "a primeval impulse," arising out of Egypt's millennia as a pawn in great-power rivalries. Others in the administration saw the matter in more rational terms. In a September 1955 study entitled "The Mainsprings of Egyptian Foreign Policy," the State Department's Office of Intelligence Research described Nasser's neutralism as a thoroughly comprehensible response to Egypt's international circumstances and a policy likely to persist.

> The role of a weak neutral, maintaining the fiction of international importance and applying its statecraft to best advantage in playing off, one against the other, the primary antagonists in the global conflict, appears to be marked out for Egypt for at least several years to come.

While this situation would not make life easy for the West, neither did it represent a sellout to the Soviets. The OIR analysts explained that while Nasser's policies would be inhibited by the "narrow and restricted outlook" he had developed during the years of British occupation, as well as by continuing American support for Israel, the prime minister was no more likely to allow Russian exploitation of Egypt than he was willing to countenance Western control.[76]

Even as confirmed a cold warrior as Allen Dulles considered Nasser's attempt to balance East against West a perfectly understandable policy. Some while later the CIA director sent an associate to brief former president Truman on the Middle East. Dulles' agent carried a paper describing Nasser as a shrewd manipulator of his diplomatic environment. The memo pointed out that although Nasser valued the "prestige" and the "position of leadership in the Arab world" that the Soviet arms pact had brought, he recognized the dangers of dealing with the communists. "If he can maintain his independence and prestige through an arrangement with the West, he would prefer that to a close tie-up with the Soviets." But should the West fail to cooperate, Nasser would not hesitate to look to Moscow. "If he feels that the West has definitely turned its back on him, he will accept further Soviet aid, if proffered, and endeavor, probably with a good chance of success, to bring Syria and Saudi Arabia along with him." All the same, Egypt seemed unlikely to fall under communist control while Nasser remained at the helm. "He is today no more anxious to come under Soviet domination than to join a Western alliance."[77]

XIV

FROM THE administration's perspective the Czech deal created two worrisome problems. The first and lesser was domestic. By moving toward Moscow Nasser guaranteed a new round of criticism in the United States, making him politically more expensive to deal with. Although Congress had adjourned, the periodical press indicated what the administration could expect when the legislators came back. Until now most mainstream publications had been willing to accept Nasser as a progressive, antimonarchist reformer; but the arms agreement changed many editorial minds. *Newsweek* characterized Nasser's activities as "nonsense on the Nile." The *New Republic,* asserting that Cairo's "single preoccupation" was "empire," likened Nasser to Hitler by asking, "Can Egypt be appeased?" The *Nation* described the execution of two Jews charged with espionage as "sadistic," attributing the sentence to "the shakiness of the regime and the ruthless measures Nasser and company are prepared to employ to remain in power." *Time* offered the most telling criticism, declaring that Egypt's decision to accept Soviet aid afforded Moscow "a firm and influential hold on an area hitherto dominated by the West."[78]

The greater problem was strategic, arising from the possibility that arms for Egypt would lead to a weapons race in the Middle East, perhaps provoking the Israelis to a preemptive attack. An assault by Israel was Washington's nightmare. It would force the administration to choose between a pair of excruciating alternatives: to oppose the Israelis, with all such opposition entailed in terms of domestic political troubles, or to overlook the offense. Despite the problems inherent in the former course the latter appeared even worse. In October Eisenhower's NSC weighed the available responses to a renewal of fighting in the Middle East. A report prepared for the council put the matter in stark terms.

If the U.S. adopted a "hands-off" policy in the event of an Israeli attack on its neighbors, it may be confidently predicted that Egypt and Syria would appeal to the U.S.S.R. for political and material support which the U.S.S.R. has indicated it would provide. Jordan and Lebanon would presumably first look to the other Western powers but if dissatisfied with their response might well turn to the U.S.S.R. Saudi Arabia and Iraq would be unlikely targets of Israeli invasion, but the former's bitterly anti-Israel regime would react strongly against the Western powers. Iraq might well succumb to anti-Western emotions and Arab pressures and withdraw from the Baghdad Pact.

In the chaotic aftermath of an Israeli success, political conditions in the Arab states would be ripe for Communist exploitation. A likely result would be to solidify the Arab world under Soviet political guidance and with further Soviet support.[79]

XV

IN AN effort to poll this dilemma Eisenhower authorized a top-level, top-secret diplomatic initiative. In January 1956 the president brought Robert Anderson, former secretary of the navy and more recently deputy secretary of defense, to the White House to discuss a mission he and Dulles had in mind. Anderson had already been to the Middle East once. In December he had met separately with Nasser and Ben-Gurion to sound out the possibility of a settlement between the two principal antagonists in the Arab-Israeli dispute. His talks had not been especially encouraging, but aside from the fact that Nasser had refused to allow him to fly directly from Egypt to Israel, insisting on an intermediate stop in a third country, neither had Anderson discovered grounds for particular pessimism.[80]

In the January session at the White House, Dulles laid out a plan for a comprehensive Arab-Israeli agreement. The secretary of state prefaced his proposal by admitting the difficulty of the situation in the Middle East, especially between Egypt and Israel, but he asserted that problems insoluble in isolation often yielded to solutions drawing from a "larger context." In this case the larger context involved the "future leadership of the Arab world." Nasser sought preeminence but found his claim challenged by Iraq's Nuri al-Said. The Iraqis had cast their lot with Britain, Turkey, Iran, and Pakistan, and in doing so were attempting to shift the Arab center of gravity away from Cairo toward Baghdad. Nasser naturally opposed the idea. So far he had managed to line up Syria and Saudi Arabia against Nuri's scheme. The United States had maintained "a position of flexibility" by holding apart from both the Baghdad pact and Egypt's countermeasures. This flexibility, Dulles said, placed America in a position to throw its weight to Nasser's side if the Egyptian leader indicated a desire to cooperate.

I believe that Nasser would be willing to pay a considerable price to get the support of the United States in limiting the Baghdad Pact to its present Arab membership with concentration upon the peril from the North, with Egypt maintaining its hegemony of the Arab countries.

The price Dulles hoped to exact was a peace treaty with Israel.

But the administration was prepared to enhance the attractiveness of the deal considerably beyond American help in reading Iraq out of the Arab world. (Dulles pointed out that this aspect of the proposal was "particularly delicate" in view of the fact that the British would not look with favor on American efforts to undermine what had become their principal remaining link with the Middle East.) A first sweetener was a solid commitment of American funding for the Aswan Dam. A second was an offer to renovate the Suez Canal. A third was a plan to dig a new canal across the isthmus, wider and deeper than the original and under Egypt's undisputed control. Fourth and finally, Dulles directed Anderson to pledge American assistance in finding a home for the Palestinian refugees. The secretary acknowledged the political complexities involved in relocating the Palestinians but did not regard these as overwhelming. "Money," Dulles said, would "deal basically with the problem of the refugees."[81]

Shortly after this meeting Anderson again set off for the Middle East. During much of the next two months he traveled back and forth between Cairo and Jerusalem, stopping at Athens or Rome in between. He offered a wide range of enticements in addition to those described at the White House meeting with Dulles and Eisenhower. He suggested a bridge spanning the Gulf of Aqaba to remedy Israel's geographic sundering of the Arab world, or, to achieve the same end, transit rights across the Negev, with an overpass-underpass arrangement to allow Arabs and Israelis to move without blocking each other. To the latter scheme Nasser objected: "If an Arab on the upper level had to relieve himself and accidentally hit an Israeli, it would mean war!" Despite Anderson's best efforts, the envoy failed to break through Nasser's skepticism and resistance to concessions. (Ben-Gurion was only marginally more cooperative.) At one point Anderson thought he had secured the prime minister's agreement to begin talks with the Israelis, and he left the meeting eager to cable the good news to Washington. As matters turned out, Nasser had found Anderson's Texas accent and idiom incomprehensible.

In nodding what Anderson took for assent the prime minister was merely being polite. Upon Anderson's exit Nasser asked Kermit Roosevelt, also present, what in the world Anderson had been talking about. Roosevelt replied, "I think he believes he was getting your firm pledge to meet with Ben-Gurion and resolve all your differences." Nasser was floored. "I could never do that. I'd be assassinated! Go stop him. Don't let him send that cable!"[82]

VII

To Beirut and Back: 1956–1960

ROBERT ANDERSON returned to Washington empty-handed, and the demise of his mission left the Eisenhower administration few cards to play in the Middle East. At a moment when the administration was learning to appreciate the value of a neutral India as a "bulwark of democracy" in Asia, and even as it convinced itself that Tito would not sell out to Stalin's successors, Eisenhower and Dulles were coming to view Nasser as an impediment to American interests in the Middle East. It remains unclear how much hope the president and the secretary of state put in Anderson's mission; certainly, as Dulles' remark that the Palestinian problem would yield to American money indicates, they grossly underestimated the intractability of the divisions of the region. In any event the administration, Eisenhower especially, laid the blame for Anderson's failure at Nasser's feet. Shortly after the envoy came home the president reflected in his diary:

> Nasser proved to be a complete stumbling block. He is apparently seeking to be acknowledged as the political leader of the Arab world.
>
> In reaching for this, Nasser has a number of fears. First of all, he fears the military junta that placed him in power, which is extremist in its position to Israel. Next he fears creating any antagonism toward himself on the part of the Egyptian people; he constantly cites the fate of King Farouk. Because he wants to be the most popular man in all the Arab

world, he also has to consider public opinion in each of the other countries. The result is that he finally concludes he should take no action whatsoever—rather he should just make speeches, all of which must breathe defiance of Israel.[1]

Eisenhower overestimated the fear factor as it contributed to Nasser's actions, but the president hit the mark directly when he asserted that Nasser aimed to become the leader of the Arab world. For the first few years after 1952 Nasser had been too busy consolidating his power in Cairo and effecting the evacuation of the British to see much beyond the frontiers of Egypt. During that period his foreign policy, such as it was, lacked focus. His indecisiveness regarding American military aid attested to this fact. By 1955, however, Nasser's diplomatic objectives were becoming clearer—in his own mind as well as to outside observers. Foremost among these objectives was leadership among the Arabs.

Nasser later said, "The stirrings of an Arab consciousness crept into my thinking when I was a secondary school student." He may or may not have been so precocious. Certainly the Palestine war of 1948 played a role in turning him toward Arab nationalism. Events of 1955 did more. In January of that year Iraq joined Britain in the Baghdad pact. Not only did this arrangement strike Nasser as a device by London to hedge the Anglo-Egyptian accord on Suez (it was), but it appeared a challenge to what Nasser considered Egypt's historic and rightful place at the head of the Arab peoples by Baghdad's Nuri el-Said (it was this too). Nuri's move touched off a bitter personal feud that would last until 1958, when revolution in Iraq claimed Nuri's life, and it continued an international rivalry ages old. Refusing to concede Arab leadership to Nuri, Nasser sought means to strike back. The Israeli raid on Gaza in February 1955 provided one weapon. The attack allowed—indeed required—Nasser to play the part of defender of the Arab nation against the Zionist aggressors. "I promise all the Arabs that I will always be the faithful soldier to Arabism, who works for its strength and unity," Nasser said.[2]

The Bandung Conference of April 1955 provided another, more promising, avenue to Nasser's goal of Arab unity under Egyptian—and Nasserite—primacy. Bandung brought Nasser forward on the world stage; at the same time it opened his eyes to the uses of neutralism as a tool of Egyptian foreign policy. By playing off the Soviets against the West, Nasser calculated, at a time when Iraq remained tied to the British, he would score a great coup in the Arab world. This reasoning lay behind his decision in favor of Soviet-bloc weapons, and his logic proved impeccable. As one close student of Nasser's career writes: "The announcement in September 1955 of the Soviet arms deal had an immediate and electrifying propaganda effect on the rest of the Arabs. It catapulted Nasser to a position of prominence among the Arab heads of state." The intensity of the enthusiasm surprised even Nasser, who told an associate, "I did not expect all this commotion over a purchase of arms."[3]

Nasser was not about to spoil the effect of his brilliant victory by buying into the package Anderson tried to sell him at the beginning of 1956. At some point he might move back toward the West. But not yet, for the balance of power in the Middle East still favored the West, and until the balance drew more nearly level he would tilt toward Moscow.

Thus Eisenhower spoke with full accuracy when he characterized Nasser as a "stumbling block" to American interests in the region; and the president was justified, from the American point of view, in taking measures to limit Nasser's influence. On March 28 Eisenhower summoned most of his foreign-policy team to the White House to reconsider America's position vis-à-vis Egypt. Dulles was there, of course; so were Hoover, George Allen, Deputy Assistant Secretary of State William Rountree, Defense Secretary Charles Wilson, Deputy Defense Secretary Reuben Robertson, and Joint Chiefs Chairman Arthur Radford. Conversation focused on a memorandum Dulles brought entitled "Near Eastern Policies," outlining a new approach to the region. Speaking from this paper Dulles noted the inability of the administration to persuade Nasser to compromise on the Israel issue, and he recommended a shift from persuasion to coercion. Referring to the Czech arms deal, Dulles recommended that the administration "let Colonel Nasser realize that he cannot cooperate as he is doing with the Soviet Union and at the same time enjoy most-favored–nation treatment from the United States." Pressure on Nasser must be applied subtly: the administration ought to avoid "an open break which would throw Nasser irrevocably into a Soviet satellite status" and should leave "a bridge back to good relations with the West." But since Nasser had not responded to American enticements something else was in order. Among the penalties Dulles suggested were a tightened trade policy, a slowdown in American economic aid, footdragging in negotiations on the Aswan project, diplomatic and other support for the Baghdad Pact, and assistance to Lebanon and Saudi Arabia in an effort to lure those countries away from Cairo. Dulles also recommended certain covert actions against Egypt, but what these comprised is impossible to ascertain since this part of the memorandum did not survive the declassification process.[4]

Eisenhower liked Dulles' ideas and authorized the secretary of state to begin implementation at once. Commenting on the discussion and on the trouble facing the United States in the Middle East, the president wrote:

> A fundamental factor in the problem is the growing ambition of Nasser, the sense of power he has gained out of his associations with the Soviets, his belief that he can emerge as a true leader of the entire Arab world—and because of these beliefs, his rejection of every proposition advanced as a measure of conciliation between the Arabs and Israel.
>
> Because of this, I suggested to the State Department that we begin to build up some other individual as a prospective leader of the Arab world —in the thought that mutually antagonistic personal ambitions might disrupt the aggressive plans that Nasser is evidently developing. My own choice of such a rival is King Saud.

Eisenhower aimed to use Nasser's desire for Arab unification against him, believing the idea of losing the support of other Arabs would incline Nasser toward conciliation. "I am certain of one thing," the president wrote. "If Egypt finds herself thus isolated from the rest of the Arab world, and with no ally in sight except Soviet Russia, she would very quickly get sick of that prospect and would join us in the search for a just and decent peace in that region."[5]

Eisenhower's preference for King Saud—an odd selection if one were looking for a charismatic nationalist to counter Nasser's appeal—arose partly from an appreciation of the monarch's importance as guardian of Islam's holy places, but in greater measure from an understanding of Saud's significance as keeper of Christendom's oil. The administration's concern regarding access to oil was well known. In February 1956, even as Anderson was mystifying Nasser with his Texan, Arthur Radford told the Senate Foreign Relations Committee that Middle Eastern oil was "essential to the free world." Eighty-five percent of Western Europe's petroleum came from the region.

> Any stoppage of oil from the Middle East—if the Arabs wanted to shut it off—would thoroughly disrupt the NATO plans that we have, and we

would not be able to supply from other sources in the free world enough oil to make up that difference without a great deal of difficulty.

Eisenhower shared the JCS chairman's view completely. "The oil of the Arab world has grown increasingly important to all of Europe," the president wrote. "The economy of European countries would collapse if those oil supplies were cut off. If the economy of Europe would collapse, the United States would be in a situation of which the difficulty could scarcely be exaggerated." With Iran and Iraq tied to the West through the Baghdad pact, Saudi Arabia remained the question mark among the large oil-producing state. By building up Saud the administration could secure two objectives at once: access to oil and neutralization of Nasser.[6]

By the spring of 1956 American policy was moving in a decidedly anti-Nasser direction. Significantly this shift did not reflect a belief that Nasser was abandoning nonalignment. American analysts continued to recognize the genuineness of Egyptian neutralism. They never thought Nasser was a Russian puppet; they knew he was not. Even after Egypt began receiving Soviet-bloc weapons and economic aid, and after Egypt recognized China in May 1956, the administration understood that Nasser was stringing the Soviets along fully as much or little as they were manipulating him. Commenting on the present coincidence of interests between Moscow and Cairo, the State Department's Office of Intelligence Research wrote in July:

> Despite increasingly close ties, the Egyptian Government has maintained its freedom of action and is in no sense a Soviet satellite. No privilege has been granted any Bloc state that is not also enjoyed by the West, although there is a tendency to eliminate Western privileges that are not also enjoyed by the Bloc. Egyptians remember their recent hampering dependence on the British Commonwealth for cotton purchases and arms and they are reluctant to substitute the U.S.S.R. for Britain in the equation.

Several months later, after Nasser's seizure of the Suez Canal, Eisenhower told King Saud, of all people, that Nasser's inclinations toward the Soviet Union were "greatly exaggerated."[7]

But this recognition that Nasser was his own man was precisely what turned the administration against him. In an area as vital to Western security as the Middle East, Washington did not want independent-minded neutralists; it wanted clients. Heretofore the Middle East had been a relatively secure Western sphere of influence. Nasser intended to change that, in part by summoning the East to right the balance against the West; his independence therefore worked against American interests. An NSC progress report summarized the administration's attitude in a sentence: "Arab neutralism actually works in favor of the Soviet bloc since it is directed against established Western positions."[8]

II

THE ADMINISTRATION'S principal device for registering disapproval of Nasser was the curtailment of American aid. More precisely, since the United States at this time was providing relatively little assistance to Cairo, disapproval involved withdrawing the American offer to underwrite the Aswan Dam.

Yet backing out of the Aswan project was no easy matter. While Robert Anderson had been trying to get Nasser to meet Ben-Gurion, administration officials had been working to secure congressional support for the dam, at the time a prerequisite to Nasser's cooperation. In January Hoover spent a long session on Capitol Hill explaining the necessity of moving ahead quickly to a firm commitment on Aswan aid. Hoover's exposition was significant for policy toward Egypt; it also provided one of the clearest views into administration thinking on the Soviet challenge in the third world.

Shortly after the announcement of the Czech arms deal Moscow had offered to fund the dam, reportedly with a $400 million loan repayable over fifty years at two percent. Dulles countered in December 1955 with a proposal for a $1.3 billion package of loans and grants from the United States, Britain, and the World Bank, including an initial American gift of $56 million. Hoover assured the Senate Foreign Relations Committee that the administration's plan was not simply a response to Soviet initiatives in the Middle East. The dam was "a very old project," one which the World Bank had been investigating for years. It bore "no relationship" to the Czech weapons pact, nor had it been "dreamed up simply to meet a Russian threat." Nonetheless the flurry of Soviet interest demonstrated that Egypt now had an alternative to Western funding. "This dam is going to be built, whether we build it or whether the Russians build it."

Hoover described several factors making Moscow "extremely keen" on gaining a foothold in Egypt.

First, Egypt lies athwart the lifeline of communications of Europe with the Middle East and the Far East. The Suez Canal has been the gateway through which commerce has traditionally always gone, or in modern time, between Europe and those areas.

It certainly lies completely across the lifeline of Europe in terms of oil. The whole of NATO is dependent upon oil from the Middle East, which flows through the Suez Canal. . . .

It is also the gateway to Africa, and we know that the Soviets are doing their utmost to penetrate into Africa, and as Egypt went, so would probably a large part of Africa go, too.

Egypt has become, in many ways, one of the leaders in the Arab States, and its movement on one side or the other would have a very profound effect on the whole character of the Middle East.[9]

Hoover's questioners wanted to know what promises the United States had made to Egypt. The undersecretary said the administration had given a "firm commitment" to underwrite the first phase of the project, costing some $55 million. Beyond that the American government had no obligations.

William Fulbright was skeptical. "Do you think it is really true that we are not committed to complete this whole project? . . . As a practical matter, in your heart you know we are committed, don't you?" When Hoover responded that the administration had pledged to nothing beyond the first phase, Fulbright continued, "Well, you wouldn't want to run off and let the Russians take you $150 million." Hoover corrected: "$50 million." Undeterred, Fulbright asserted, "The Russians would be delighted to have you make the initial stages, and they would get the full credit for finishing it."[10]

Democrat Theodore Green of Rhode Island said he feared America would find itself in a bidding war with the Soviet Union; Hoover responded that the administration would not allow any such thing to happen. William Langer expressed a related concern: that the United States would feel obliged to counter similar Soviet offers in the future. "Suppose Russia comes along and says, 'We are going to build an aluminum plant.' Does this mean we are going to advance money for an aluminum plant, too, to keep Russia out of Egypt?"

Hoover replied that the administration would treat each request on its merits. He added that Nasser and his associates would have their hands full for a decade simply trying to complete the Aswan Dam. "They know that this will require all of their resources and all of their efforts for the next ten years, and they are thoroughly reconciled to that fact." Beyond precluding further requests, the dam would keep Nasser out of mischief. Hoover estimated that Aswan, relative to the size of the Egyptian economy, was comparable to all the public-works projects the United States had built in the twentieth century. As a result of this massive burden, the Egyptian government would have to choose between making trouble and building the dam.[11]

Fulbright asked the perennial question: Did the American offer include political conditions? The Arkansas senator inquired specifically about a possible agreement by Cairo to forgo future arms deals with the Soviet bloc. When Hoover said the administration had demanded no such assurance, Fulbright expressed surprise. "You don't ask them to restrict any further commitments of arms?"

Hoover replied that the administration had not. "If we did so, I don't think they would agree. I think they take it as a matter of their own sovereignty."[12]

Representatives of American cotton growers had objected to the Aswan project on grounds that it would increase the world supply of cotton and lower the price. Hoover contended that this would not be a problem. The Egyptians, he said, had "a pretty good record on cotton," by which he meant that they were attempting to curtail production.[13]

Returning to the broader question of the Soviet challenge in the third world, Hoover underlined the importance of countering Russian offers to countries like Egypt, countries for which the goal of economic advancement often mattered more than the means by which that goal was pursued. The communist model was seductive. "Under communism the Soviet Union has developed from an almost wholly agricultural 'Kulak' state into a state which ranks as one of the most important industrial powers." The model held special appeal for Asian and African states. "This is the first time in history that a non-Western Power has equipped itself to meet the industrial challenge which began in the West with the industrial revolution." The cost, of course, had been tremendous. Development had come only through "cruel and evil treatment of people," through "total disregard of human rights," and by "use of slave or compulsory labor." Hoover continued:

> Nevertheless, it has been done, and that fact has had a profound influence upon the nations of Asia which covet for themselves industrial power.

They feel they have not wholly achieved their independence unless, in addition to political independence, they gain a corresponding measure of industrial capacity which will free them from dependence upon their former colonial rulers.

The ultimate significance of Aswan lay in the opportunity it afforded the United States to demonstrate that development and democracy could coexist, indeed reinforced each other. As such, Hoover said, the project was "vitally necessary to the security of the United States."[14]

III

THAT WAS in January. Even then critics had attacked the administration for considering a major commitment to a regime that apparently preferred Moscow's company to America's. Democratic Congressman Eugene Keogh of New York spoke for several of his colleagues when he argued that American money would be better spent on arms for Israel to counter the Soviet buildup in Egypt. The Kremlin, Keogh said, had a "timetable" for conquest of the Middle East; the Czech deal to Cairo represented the opening move of the operation. In the Senate Estes Kefauver, a Tennessee Democrat and once and future presidential contender, labeled the arms pact a "turning point" in Middle Eastern history, in that it brought the cold war directly into regional politics. McCarthyite Republican William Jenner asserted that the administration's passivity if not complicity in the face of undeniable provocation was playing right into Soviet hands, allowing the Kremlin to establish a "fifth column" in Egypt.[15]

During the next several months the drums only beat louder. After Cairo recognized Beijing, Senator Mike Monroney declared it incomprehensible that the administration could still consider financing the Aswan Dam. "We have gone far enough toward appeasing Mr. Nasser," the Oklahoma Democrat said. Oregon's two senators, Democrats Wayne Morse and Richard Neuberger, wondered where the administration found the gall and funds to underwrite a dam for Egypt while denying money to expand the Bonneville Power Administration. Neuberger asked, "What are we using to help pay for the Egyptian dam—Confederate dollars, counterfeit coins, or wampum?" In the House, Democrats Gracie Pfost of Idaho and Victor Wickersham of Oklahoma took a similar approach, the former demanding preference for projects on the Snake

River, the latter saying flood-control and irrigation facilities in Oklahoma deserved priority.[16]

When the Egyptian government celebrated the evacuation of the last British troops in June by inviting Soviet Foreign Minister Dmitri Shepilov to Cairo, Democrat James Roosevelt asserted that this changing of the guard symbolized "a new defeat in the Mediterranean." Reminding his audience of administration predictions that the removal of the British irritant would open the way to friendlier U.S.–Egyptian relations, the California congressman announced that Dulles and Eisenhower had been duped. Unless they mended their ways they would be duped again. "Democracy will not be able to organize the defense of freedom in the Near East if it continues to capitulate to the pressures and intrigue of rulers who have no interest in democracy and who are concerned primarily with the search for power." Illinois Republican Paul Douglas located the source of the problem in Ambassador Byroade, whose "misguided urging" of support for Nasser had allowed the Egyptian leader to play the United States against the Soviets. Democrat Frank Thompson of New Jersey agreed, suggesting that if Byroade possessed decency or honor he would resign.[17]

These complaints were not the cause of the administration's decision to abandon the Aswan project—Nasser's rejection of the Anderson plan accounted for that—but they certainly militated against a reversal of the earlier choice. As the administration's luck would have it, they also eased what otherwise would have been an embarrassing volte-face. Having made such an issue of Aswan's being "vitally necessary" to American security, as Hoover had phrased the matter, Dulles and Eisenhower might have found their pullout hard to justify had Nasser not provoked such criticism. Dulles cited congressional problems, as well as concerns about Cairo's ability to hold up its end of the financing, when he told the Egyptian ambassador on July 19 that the United States no longer intended to contribute to the construction of the Aswan Dam.[18]

IV

WHILE DULLES was preparing to break the news of the Aswan withdrawal, Nasser was in Brioni with Tito and Nehru. This session was the first bringing the three neutralists together, although by now each knew the other two well. They had not yet achieved the sense of solidarity that would inspire Mohamed Heikal to write, perhaps a bit too enthusiastically: "Defeat for one was defeat for them all, victory for one was victory for them all. They rejoiced in one another's successes and commiserated with one another in failure." But already they were seen as the big three of the neutralist world, and the American decision against Aswan, coming while they met and only three weeks after Dulles' declaration that neutrality in the cold war was "immoral," appeared a blow against the idea they embodied. The Egyptians certainly interpreted the American announcement as such. Heikal wrote that from Dulles' point of view

> this rebuff could not have been better timed. Dulles always believed any form of neutralism to be immoral, and the Brioni meeting, attended by the three high priests of nonalignment, was just the sort of occasion he most disapproved of. What a devastating curtain he had been able to drop on their deliberations!

The Brioni summit was ending when Dulles delivered the decision on Aswan; Nehru and Nasser heard it on a plane from Brioni to Cairo. "Those people, how arrogant they are," Nehru responded. Nasser declared, "This is not a withdrawal; it is an attack on the regime." [19]

A week later Nasser launched his counterattack. "We will not allow the domination of force and the dollar," he declared in a speech on July 24.

> When Washington sheds every decent principle on which foreign relations are based and broadcasts the lie, smear, and delusion that Egypt's economy is unsound, then I look them in the face and say: Drop dead of your fury for you will never be able to dictate to Egypt.

Two days after this he announced the nationalization of the Suez Canal Company, with tolls to go toward the Aswan project. [20]

Nasser's move took Washington by surprise—Allen Dulles detected a "note of desperation" in the decision—but it was not especial cause for alarm. The Egyptian president had acted "within his rights," as Eisenhower admitted; the United States had no financial interest in the canal company; and there was no particular reason to believe Egypt would interfere with the operation of the canal. Compensation and other related matters could be worked out by the diplomats. [21]

What *was* alarming was the violent reaction of Britain and France, especially the former, to the nationalization. Eisenhower and Dulles recognized the distrust Anthony Eden felt toward Nasser. Several months earlier, when Washington still hoped to strike a bargain with Egypt, Dulles had told the British prime minister that the United States intended to make use of Nasser in much the same way it was using Tito. Eden warned against overoptimism in this regard. He also asserted that it would be a mistake to assume Nasser represented the will of the Egyptian masses—hinting at the possibility of finding someone more pliable to replace the Egyptian leader. But this knowledge had not prepared Eisenhower and Dulles for the prime minister's July 27 cable: "My colleagues and I are convinced that we must be ready, in the last resort, to use force to bring Nasser to his senses. For our part, we are prepared to do so. I have this morning instructed our Chiefs of Staff to prepare a military plan accordingly." [22]

Some in the administration thought Eden had the right idea. Two days after Nasser's seizure of the canal, Air Force Chief of Staff Nathan Twining described Egyptian management of the vital waterway as "militarily unacceptable" and asserted that the United States should take action "to assure that the canal is under the control of friendly and responsible authority." Two days later the joint chiefs of staff, while admitting an initial role for diplomacy, advocated contingency planning for a military response. "Timeliness in effecting this action," the chiefs declared, "is essential." [23]

Eisenhower and Dulles did not entirely rule out the military option, but neither, at this stage, did they rule it in. The use of force entailed grave consequences, not least with respect to American credibility in Asia and Africa. As Eisenhower put it, to join with the British in an attack on Nasser would probably "array the world from Dakar to the Philippines against us." At a meeting early in August the president and the secretary of state agreed that the administration should give no hint to Eden of support for a military venture until negotiations had failed, and even then it should move only with the concurrence of Congress. [24]

V

WITHIN SIX months the administration would go to Congress for authorization to use military force in the Middle East; it would do so then with the well-founded belief that the legislature would support the idea. Egypt's seizure of the canal unleashed a new wave of criticism of

274

Nasser—and not a little of the administration for failing to take stern action against him. Among the more reliable critics Emanuel Celler charged Eisenhower and Dulles with pursuing "a consistent policy of appeasement, subordinating national self-respect to the fog of fear." By trying to win Nasser's favor with foreign aid, Celler said, the administration had merely fed his "arrogance." Another Democrat, Representative William Dorn of South Carolina, characterized the nationalization of the canal company as a fresh example of the bankrupt nature of the administration's "ridiculous policy of buying friends with money." If any country should have been grateful for American help, Dorn said, Egypt should. "Now, because we did not advance the money to build the Aswan Dam on her terms, Dictator Nasser is ready to join up with Russia and possibly start another world war." Without naming names —but with obvious implications for Nehru and Tito—Dorn predicted similar treatment from other countries America had assisted. "One by one they will kick us in the teeth when they find the money is running out."[25]

James Roosevelt detected a grand conspiracy between Nasser and the Soviets. The Suez seizure, he said, was "part of a calculated plan to undermine the influence of the West and to expropriate its assets in the region." Unless Nasser were effectively challenged, Roosevelt continued, others would soon follow his example. "Oil wells, mines, refineries, pipelines, air bases, landing fields—none of these will be immune from the grasp of political adventurers seeking to expand domination and wealth." Let the United States have no more illusions about Nasser, Roosevelt warned. "Let us understand fully that this man, in the name of neutralism . . . is attempting to undermine and destroy the position of the West in the Mediterranean, in the Middle East, and throughout Africa."

Although the Democrats fired the heaviest barrages against the administration at this time, Republicans expressed concern as well. Alexander Wiley, the ranking GOP member of the Senate Foreign Relations Committee, spoke for many when he declared that the great danger to American interests in the Middle East came not from the Suez seizure itself, bad as that was, but from the precedent it set. If Nasser succeeded in snatching the canal, what would stop the leaders of the oil states from nationalizing the operations of the oil fields?[26]

VI

EISENHOWER AND Dulles did not intend to let Nasser get off free, but for the moment they were more worried about the British. After receiving Eden's bellicose cable the president dispatched Robert Murphy to London with orders to "hold the fort." When Murphy discovered the seriousness and extent of Britain's military preparations he called for reinforcements. Dulles flew to London, and together the two managed to talk Eden and the French into putting off military action until after an international conference scheduled for the middle of August.[27]

On his return to Washington the secretary of state joined Eisenhower for a briefing of key members of Congress. Dulles began with an analysis of Nasser's intentions. Above all, the secretary said, the Egyptian president sought to become the leading figure of a united Arab world—if possible of the Moslem world as well, though this seemed more problematic. As a means to his goal Nasser attacked the West with weapons of propaganda and, as recent events had proved, property. Nor did it appear likely, to Dulles anyway, that Nasser would stop at Suez. If he could manage the feat the Egyptian leader would not hesitate to use Middle Eastern oil against the West. The secretary declared that fulfillment of Nasser's ambitions would result "in reducing Western Europe literally to a state of dependency." Pointing out that two-thirds of the Atlantic allies' petroleum passed through the Suez Canal, Dulles said, "It is almost intolerable to Western Europe to feel that it cannot rely on access to the oil of the Middle East." The British and French considered the matter nothing less than "a life and death issue."

Eisenhower agreed with Dulles' analysis and went even further, likening Nasser to Hitler. The Egyptian leader's statements, Eisenhower said, reminded him of *Mein Kampf*, which "no one believed" either. Dulles picked up on this theme, comparing Nasser's *Philosophy of the Revolution* to the Nazi manifesto and asserting that its author possessed a "Hitlerite" personality. When one lawmaker asked whether efforts to undermine Nasser might open the way to someone still less desirable, the secretary replied that the Egyptian president was "the worst we have had so far." The administration had tried to get along with him but to no avail. "We finally became convinced that he is an extremely dangerous fanatic."

Although neither Eisenhower nor Dulles would specify what the administration had in mind in the event Britain and France intervened militarily, they clearly indicated sympathy for the allies' fears. "We can't accept an inconclusive outcome leaving Nasser in control," the president declared. "We do not intend to stand by helplessly and let this one man get away with what he is trying to do."[28]

VII

THE HARD part was figuring out just what Nasser was trying to do. The general trend of his policy was evident: he continued to pursue the objective of Arab unification, under Cairo's leadership, and neutralism was his means to that end. In certain respects, the American and British withdrawal from the Aswan project, by providing a pretext for seizing the Suez Canal and affording a platform for denouncing the West, played directly into Nasser's hands. But he certainly realized the British and French were considering military action, which he might easily not survive. How far he would press his luck, American officials could only guess.

At the end of August some insight—although not much—arrived through a diplomatic side channel. Dulles received a letter from Charles Jones, president of Richfield Oil Company, describing a conversation with Ali Sabri, one of Nasser's co-conspirators in the days before the 1952 coup, still a close aide, and later to be prime minister. "My Chief is at a loss," Sabri said, "to understand why the Western Powers do not want to cooperate with him and appear content to see Egypt drawn closer and closer into the Soviet sphere of influence." Referring to the Czech arms pact, Sabri explained that his country had tried "endlessly" to acquire weapons from the West, out of fear of an Israeli attack. "But all our requests were turned down." Soviet military aid, however, implied no commitment to the communists. "After we were satisfied with our secure position vis-à-vis the Israelis, we decided to have no further dealings with the Soviets, lest they absorb us."

Sabri said his government had then hoped to turn its attention to economic development, central to which was the Aswan project. The promise of American aid had encouraged Nasser and his associates greatly. "The truth is that we felt very much happier in dealing with the West than with Russia." Yet all at once the pledged assistance disappeared. "The blow was staggering." Nasser had planned a major address on the fourth anniversary of the revolution. "The main topic of the speech was to have been the announcement of the approaching commencement of work on the High Dam. Then suddenly these hopes were shattered." Sabri denied that Egypt had any intention of using the canal for blackmail, and he declared that his government would rescind the expropriation upon receiving guarantees of an acceptable level of Egyptian participation in operating the canal. He also rejected the notion that Egypt would encourage the Arab oil producers to seize the assets of Western companies, agreeing with Jones that such an action would lead to economic chaos. "This is quite unthinkable. Creating chaos in the Middle East could only ruin it and open the door to foreign invasion." But he did feel compelled to add that Egypt would not be cowed. "Neither intimidation nor physical force will succeed in making us back down."[29]

Eisenhower and Dulles could not know how accurately Sabri's statement as a whole reflected his chief's attitude; certainly the suggestion that Nasser might be persuaded to rescind the nationalization strained credulity. They had no difficulty, however, believing his final remark. In Nasser the administration realized it was dealing with a dedicated and determined individual who indeed would not be intimidated. Two years earlier Eisenhower had ordered the CIA to engineer the ouster of the government of Guatemala. The agency's success there had resulted largely from a failure of nerve on the part of Arbenz, who was essentially terrorized into exile. Nasser, Eisenhower realized, was not an Arbenz. The year before the Guatemala operation Kermit Roosevelt had helped restore the shah in Iran. In that case the plan had depended on widespread dissatisfaction with Mossadeq; Roosevelt's rioters gave the final push to a tottering regime. The situation in Egypt had not reached any comparable stage; on the contrary, Nasser was more popular than ever and the center of world attention.[30]

For this reason Eisenhower rejected covert operations to overthrow the Egyptian president. In the middle of October Hoover described a visit by an unnamed (in the record of the conversation) "group"—probably British—to "one of our agencies"—the CIA, no doubt—regarding "how to topple Nasser." Hoover, filling in for the hospitalized Dulles, allowed that events might necessitate such action at some point but questioned "whether this was the time to attempt this." Eisenhower agreed that the United States could not make a move "when there is as much active hostility as at present." Eisenhower hardly opposed subversion on principle; regarding Nasser he simply thought he could not get away with it. "For a thing like this to be done without inflaming the Arab world," he said, "a time free from heated stress holding the world's attention as at present would have to be chosen."[31]

Eisenhower also thought Nasser might be overreaching himself in regional terms. Other Arab leaders, he commented, were becoming "uneasy at Egyptian developments." The United States would do well to allow Nasser a little more rope. The Egyptian president's handling of the Suez affair afforded America "a great chance to split the Arab world."[32]

(Some evidence exists that others in the administration were willing to try covert measures to bring Nasser down. On February 12, 1976, the *Washington Post* carried a report citing an unnamed CIA official who described a confused plan to assassinate the Egyptian president. According to this source, Allen Dulles misinterpreted a comment by his brother to the effect that something must be done to "eliminate the problem" of Nasser, and in response the CIA chief fielded agents to kill him. After they failed, Allen Dulles discovered that assassination was not what Foster Dulles had intended, to the intelligence director's great embarrassment.)

VIII

IT WAS Eisenhower's hope of isolating Nasser, as much as anything else, that led to his outrage three weeks later when the British and French colluded with Israel to attack Egypt. Eden apparently thought the United States would acquiesce in a military strike; he later wrote that when Dulles had said in London that some way must be found to make Nasser "disgorge" what the Egyptian leader was trying to swallow, he had been "encouraged" by the secretary of state's remarks. "These were forthright words. They rang in my ears for months." On October 25 Eden told his cabinet that Washington would go along with action designed to "prevent interference with the free flow of traffic through the Canal." American leaders, he asserted, had supported the principle in question "on many occasions in the last hundred years." Other cabinet ministers objected, doubting Eden's prediction, fearing "lasting damage" to Anglo-American relations, and suggesting that he ought at least to notify Eisenhower in advance.[33]

Eden's failure to give notice rankled Eisenhower—"Nothing justifies double-crossing us," the president told Hoover—but what really upset him was the fact that a frontal assault on Nasser would certainly prove completely counterproductive. At a moment when Moscow was revealing its true nature in Hungary, by what Eisenhower called "colonialism by the bayonet," the British and French were ravaging the credibility of the West and making Nasser a neutralist hero in the process.[34]

Administration officials took just this line in a briefing of the leaders of Congress. Allen Dulles explained how the attack on Nasser had disrupted a favorable trend in Egypt and throughout the region. Growing distrust of Nasser's ambitions, the CIA chief asserted, had been "drowned out by a wave of revival of age-old hatred of Western imperialism and colonialism." The primary consequence of the Suez invasion was a "unanimous revulsion" against the West. In Egypt Nasser's critics were lying low. "Politically, there is no organized opposition." Eisenhower interjected that he had warned Eden against rash action and had recommended that "time be allowed to run against Nasser, probably ending in his isolation." The president said he had predicted that any obvious effort to remove Nasser would alienate world opinion. Events had proved him right.[35]

Under such circumstances the administration had no choice but to oppose the British-French-Israeli action. Already the colonialists had gravely destabilized the Middle East. The CIA reported the strong possibility of a radical coup in Syria and declared that the repercussions might spread to Iran and Iraq. Foster Dulles judged the odds "high" that the British would be evicted from the latter country. Allen Dulles agreed, telling Eisenhower, "Nuri may not be able to survive very long."[36]

More disturbing still was the likelihood of an increased Soviet presence in the Middle East. The administration took quite seriously Moscow's intimations of support for Egypt against Western aggression. Arthur Radford described the "concern" of the joint chiefs that the Soviets might be contemplating "major hostilities." Allen Dulles said the CIA had learned that Nasser had "assurances from the Soviet Ambassador in Cairo that Russia was prepared to support Egypt all the way, even risking World War III." Eisenhower initially shared these fears but after the worst of the crisis passed he concurred with Allen Dulles' revised view that Moscow would content itself with "keeping the pot boiling." Still, as the CIA director pointed out, the United States could not ignore "the possibility of chain reactions which might ultimately lead to general war without being so intended."[37]

Radford pointed out that even if the United States managed to prevent broader hostilities its problems in the region had only begun. According to the joint chiefs chairman the Kremlin was "absolutely determined to delay or prevent any solution of the crisis in the Middle East," in the belief—which Radford considered well founded—that the United States eventually would have to repair relations with the Europeans. "This will turn the Arabs against us."[38]

Foster Dulles agreed that the Russians would continue to make trouble. In a conversation with Eisenhower at Walter Reed Hospital the secretary expressed worry that the Soviets "might really take advantage of the situation by coming to the aid of the Arabs." The president responded that if they did the United States would have to move into opposition, with the likely result that America would end up "getting into the Arab doghouse." Yet Eisenhower did not consider such an outcome inevitable. He hoped some of the Arab leaders would shun close ties with the Russians, preferring cooperation with the West.[39]

The Soviet challenge, however serious, remained distant; the principal problem at the moment was Nasser. Put differently, the Egyptian president and the Russians represented two facets of the same danger: the loss of control of the Middle East. Nasser was the narrow front of a wedge that could open a seam between the West and its oil supplies; the Kremlin was the broader back that would rip the region apart. Eisenhower and Dulles knew Nasser did not intend to exchange Western imperialism for Moscow's variety, but they worried he might not be able to control events. In any case Egypt and the Soviet Union both stood to gain from cracking the Middle Eastern status quo. The Suez invasion had been designed to restore the position of the West in the region; instead the invaders dealt it a mortal blow. Eden had hoped to force Eisenhower's hand in support; he succeeded only in guaranteeing opposition—by diplomatic means at the UN and by economic methods on the world currency and oil markets. The invasion ended with the disgrace of the status quo's erstwhile defenders; Washington was left trying to figure out how to shore up that crumbling structure.

IX

CONCEIVED IN the shambles of Suez, the Eisenhower Doctrine first saw the light of day at the beginning of 1957. The president and the secretary of state pulled more than a score of leading legislators from their hearths and football games on January 1 for a preview of administration plans for the Middle East. Eisenhower began with a reminder of what he called "traditional Russian ambitions" in the area. He did not go into detail; his listeners knew what he was talking about. (In his memoirs the president spoke more explicitly: "The Soviet objective was, in plain fact, power politics: to seize the oil, to cut the Canal and pipelines of the Middle East, and thus seriously to weaken Western civilization.") Describing "the present impossibility of France and Britain acting as a counterweight" in the region, Eisenhower went on to say, "The existing vacuum must be filled by the United States before it is filled by Russia."[40]

The president then outlined a message he intended to convey to Congress in a few days, requesting authorization for a special Middle East economic aid fund and for the use of American troops in the region at his discretion. Asserting that the crisis demanded immediate action, Eisenhower urged the legislators to make passage of his Middle East resolution their first order of business in the session about to begin. "The United States must put the entire world on notice that we are ready to move instantly if necessary." The president affirmed his respect for the legislature's war-declaring prerogative, but he commented that modern war might be "a matter of hours only." If Congress would grant him the authority he requested—to dispatch American forces to the Middle East in response to a communist challenge—that authority might well serve to deter aggression and never have to be used.

The legislators at this session demonstrated no open hostility to Eisenhower's proposal; neither were they about to be stampeded. Democrat Richard Russell of Georgia stated that while all could see that something must be done in the Middle East, he personally required "much more information" before he could support any specific action. Russell went on to ask whether it might not be preferable to work through normal treaty procedures to strengthen American allies in the region. Dulles and Eisenhower responded that this would prove impractical, given the deep animosities in the area, especially toward Israel. Eisenhower admitted that a set of several bilateral security pacts might do the job if they could be negotiated simultaneously, but this was unlikely.

Democrat John McCormack wondered if Eisenhower really needed the authority he was requesting. Did not such power already reside in the president as commander-in-chief? Eisenhower responded that the point of the exercise was deterrence, not constitutionality. An American statement of resolve regarding the Middle East would gain great weight from demonstrating the combined convictions of the executive and legislative branches of the government. What America's friends in the Middle East desired, Eisenhower said, was "reassurance now that the United States would stand ready to help."[41]

As this meeting broke up, the president told the lawmakers Dulles would explain the administration's plan in greater detail before its public unveiling; the next day the secretary addressed the Senate Foreign Relations Committee. Although the administration would couch its Middle East resolution in ideological language and would defend it publicly in ideological terms, at this closed hearing Dulles' exposition was basic geopolitics. "There is a highly dangerous situation in the Middle East," the secretary declared.

> There is today there a vacuum of power as a result of the recent British-French action, so that if we do not find some way in which to put our support back of the free nations of the area to reassure them and give them strength . . . that critical area will almost certainly be taken over by Soviet communism with disastrous effects upon our own security position in the world.

For more than a century, Dulles said, Britain had been the "bulwark" against czarist and Soviet ambitions in the Middle East. "That bulwark has been swept away, due to what I consider to be the very improvident and unwise action of the British in the attack upon Egypt." Britain was "finished"; America must move in. "Only the United States can, I think, save that area and, indeed, save itself from very great peril."[42]

Dulles read to the committee the text of the resolution the administration would submit to Congress. The operative passage empowered the president to deploy the armed forces of the United States "to secure and protect the territorial independence and political integrity" of cooperating countries "in the general area of the Middle East" against "overt armed aggression from any nation controlled by international communism."

When the questioning began Republican Homer Capehart of Indiana wanted to know precisely what the administration meant by "overt armed aggression." "Would that mean one of the Middle East countries fighting another, or a couple of them fighting one, or do you mean directly an attack by Russia?" Dulles replied that the answer was contained in the language declaring that the attack had to originate in a country controlled by international communism. Capehart asked, "Is there a single Arab country which would come under that category at the present moment?" Dulles responded that there was not.

Democrat Hubert Humphrey stated that it sounded to him as though Eisenhower and Dulles were proposing de facto membership in the Baghdad system. "Why would it not be better, Mr. Secretary, just to bring the Baghdad Pact up here and consider its provisions and see whether or not we should join?" Dulles replied that the arguments against participating in that organization were "overwhelming." For one thing the administration did not want to appear as Britain's cat's paw at a moment when Britain was so widely anathematized in the region. For another, Saudi Arabia, which the United States had been trying to encourage as a rival of Egypt, was "violently opposed" to the pact. Finally, any association with such an avowedly anti-Israel country as Iraq would create substantial political difficulties.

Humphrey remained unconvinced. The Minnesota senator resisted the idea of the advance authorization Eisenhower was requesting, saying it amounted to "a predated declaration of war." Dulles objected to the use of such language but did not deny its essential accuracy. The secretary emphasized that what the president hoped to achieve was the prevention of war: by announcing its willingness to use force to defend American interests in the Middle East, the administration would render unnecessary the actual use of that force.

Other senators joined the attack. Chairman Richard Russell thought the language of the resolution too vague. He worried that the administration would involve the United States in local affairs having little to do with vital American interests. Russell said he feared America was "going to get chewed up over there over a period of time with a lot of little wars." Democrat Mike Mansfield, the majority whip, questioned the unilateral nature of the administration's proposal. During the Suez crisis the president had placed much emphasis on the role of the United Nations. Now, Mansfield said, the administration seemed intent on going it alone. American resources were stretched thin already. "There are other vacuums in the world, and we cannot be expected to cover the world with our Armed Forces."

Alexander Wiley wanted to know what the resolution meant for relations between Egypt and Israel. Noting the influx of Soviet arms to Egypt, Wiley worried about the possibility of an "all-out scrap" between Egyptians and Israelis. "If this resolution is passed, where do we stand?" Dulles said the administration did not intend to invoke the resolution in any strictly Arab-Israeli clash. This response was designed to reassure those like Russell who thought the administration was pushing the United States into an endless round of regional fighting. The secretary, however, went on to appeal to pro-Israel sentiment by pointing out that communist penetration of the Middle East posed a great danger to Israel's existence and by characterizing the administration's measure as essential to Israel's safety. "If the United States does not make itself strongly felt in that area, I think it is curtains for Israel."[43]

X

DULLES COULD not have come away from this session encouraged about the prospects for the administration's resolution, but he and the president chose to push ahead. As a result of Eisenhower's decision to force the Suez invaders to pull back, American stock in the Middle East and throughout the third world had risen—but so had Nasser's. In facing down the imperialists Nasser achieved a prestige that made his combination of neutralism and nationalism more attractive and potent than ever. Consequently his threat to the privileged position of the West had increased, and the Eisenhower administration sought means to meet it.

To take Nasser on directly, however, would be to repeat the mistake of Britain and France. It would squander the credit the United States had recently gained and would increase Nasser's stature the more. So the administration sought to contain Egypt indirectly, by calling up the reliable bogey of Soviet-backed communism. For Washington to denounce communism was entirely expected and would not alienate anyone not already alienated. Moreover, although Nasser counted considerably more enemies than friends in America, Congress was not about to sign away its war-declaring power in an anti-Nasserist crusade. But it might do so in a battle against communism. If McCarthy was in decline, the spirit that made a generation of lawmakers tremble at his charges still stalked the halls of the Capitol.

This is not to say the Eisenhower Doctrine was solely a device to thwart Nasser. Far from it. In the thinking of the administration, the Soviet menace in the Middle East was indeed real. Yet it lacked the immediacy of Nasser's challenge to the status quo, and it depended on the destabilizing activities of people like Nasser who, for reasons of their own, found the status quo intolerable. As long as Nasser and other radical nationalists agitated the region, the Soviets would make headway. Shortly after Nasser seized the Suez Canal, Alexander Wiley asked Eisenhower about the Russian role in the matter. The president responded that the Soviets had had little to do with it directly, but he added that they would certainly take the opportunity to "fish in troubled water." This comment exactly summarized the administration's assessment of the relationship between Nasserism and communism. Since the Egyptian leader appeared intent on keeping the waters troubled, calming them required containing him.[44]

So Eisenhower's Middle East resolution took the form of an anticommunist measure, and the administration promoted it in those terms. Two days after the president formally offered the bill, which included $200 million in economic aid, the secretary of state returned to Capitol Hill, this time to brief the House Committee on Foreign Affairs. Dulles painted a grim picture of what the future would hold for the Middle East and the world if the administration's proposal failed. "Atheistic, materialistic communism" was on the march and was heading straight for the Middle East. A communist victory there would be a political, economic, and religious disaster for the peoples of the region, and its shock waves would spread far. "A Communist breakthrough in the Middle East would encourage the Soviet rulers to resort everywhere, at home and abroad, to more aggressive policies."[45]

The committee members had heard this sort of thing before and were not particularly impressed. The discussion quickly moved to a consideration of the specific language of the administration's resolution. Chairman Thomas Gordon, an Illinois Democrat, wondered what "the general area of the Middle East" meant. Dulles—no doubt recalling Dean Acheson's faux pas in declaring Korea in January 1950 beyond the American security perimeter—preferred not to answer in public. "There is always danger in drawing a line on the map because the inference is if you step across the line you are in trouble, but as long as you do not step across the line you are not in trouble."

Gordon then asked whether the administration's measure might back-fire, polarizing the Middle East into explicitly pro-American and pro-Soviet camps and increasing the risk of regional conflict. Quite the contrary, Dulles replied. The administration's approach would minimize local tensions by making the countries of the area stronger and more stable. Gordon persisted in his doubts, suggesting that the resolution would dissipate the political capital America had gained during the Suez affair. Dulles rejected this notion as well. What the administration proposed was simply an extension of the principle that had guided American policy during the crisis: that the states of the Middle East should be safe from aggression.[46]

Despite the skepticism surrounding Dulles' appearance before this committee of the House, the lower chamber as a whole proved willing to accept the administration's arguments. The Foreign Affairs Committee recalled Dulles twice during the next week and continued hearings on the issue through most of January, but at the end of the month the House approved the Middle East resolution by a vote of 355 to 61.

In the Senate the measure ran into considerably more difficulty. The Democratic leadership took its time scheduling hearings and debate; during the delay the resolution became enmeshed in problems involving Israel's refusal to pull out of Gaza. Eisenhower and Dulles pressed for withdrawal as ordered by the United Nations, believing American credibility among the Arabs was on the line. Should the administration acquiesce in Israeli occupation, Dulles said, "virtually all of the Middle East countries would feel that United States policy toward the area was in the last analysis controlled by the Jewish influence in the United States and that accordingly the only hope of the Arab states was in association with the Soviet Union."[47]

Predictably the administration's pressure on Israel did not suit that country's backers in the Senate. Styles Bridges railed at the "double standard of international morality" that would force Israel to bow to UN pressure while taking no strong stand against Soviet aggression in Hungary. Jacob Javits of New York criticized the "muddled thinking" of the administration in charming the Arabs while squeezing the Israelis. Hubert Humphrey demanded to know whether the president would "restrain and reprimand" only the friends of the United States, or whether the administration was prepared "to apply with equal justice the same rule on those who have not been so kind to us." Humphrey added, "I think we have a right to ask whether the Eisenhower doctrine means the sending of tanks and planes to Saudi Arabia and the imposition of sanctions upon Israel, or whether it means justice to both parties."[48]

Lyndon Johnson particularly opposed anything that smacked of trading Israel's security for Arab favor. In mid-February the majority leader wrote Dulles denouncing American support for sanctions against Israel as "most unwise" and implying that the administration should expect no action on its Middle East resolution if it voted for sanctions in the UN. Johnson, like other members of the Democratic leadership, took many of his cues on foreign policy from Dean Acheson. The former secretary of state, who had little good to say about Eisenhower-Dulles diplomacy generally, was especially scornful of the Republicans' Middle East policy. The day before Johnson and his colleagues were scheduled to return to the White House for another arm-twisting session, the Texas senator called Acheson for advice. Acheson urged Johnson not to commit the party to anything in haste, decrying the administration's approach to Middle Eastern affairs as "very short-sighted," as "idiocy." Acheson thought Eisenhower and Dulles were engaged in a transparent effort to appease Egypt and the Arabs. By trying to force the Israelis to withdraw, the administration had "played into Nasser's hands."[49]

Johnson carried these opinions to the White House the next day, but Eisenhower and Dulles refused to reconsider. Israel must pull back, they declared. Addressing the double-standard charge, the president said the United States had voted against the Soviets on numerous occasions in the past; for good measure he added that the administration had applied pressure on Egypt as well. Dulles argued that if the Israelis remained obstinate guerrilla war would break out, oil would stop flowing to Europe, and Russian influence would grow. "In short, there would be all those disasters that the United States has been trying to avoid since the creation of the state of Israel." UN Ambassador Henry Cabot Lodge, brought in from New York for the occasion, asserted that the administration had no alternative to accepting an Arab resolution calling for sanctions against Tel Aviv. Citing the enthusiasm that had greeted American actions during the Suez crisis, Lodge declared, "The Arabs will feel we have abandoned our position if we do not support some effective measures to accomplish Israeli withdrawal."

Eisenhower and Dulles had convened this gathering in hope of gaining Democratic cooperation in a policy leading to Israel's withdrawal, but Johnson and his colleagues rejected the idea. When Republican John Taber proposed a press release—drafted in the State Department, no doubt—calling for an Israeli pullback, the Democrats would not touch it. Some, like Johnson, opposed the idea on principle. Others simply preferred to let the administration take the heat. Richard Russell suggested that since the group had not achieved a consensus the president would have to act on his own authority. The Georgia Democrat recommended a televised address to "crystallize public opinion." House Speaker Sam Rayburn added, "America has either one voice or none; and the one voice is the voice of the president, even though not everyone agrees with him."[50]

Eisenhower, recognizing that his burden-sharing plan had failed, followed Russell's and Rayburn's advice and carried his case to the American people. At the same time, he privately turned the screws on Israel. While Lodge delayed a vote in the UN the president wrote Ben-Gurion a strong letter warning the Israelis to get out of Gaza before they found themselves with fewer friends than they had already.[51]

The Israeli prime minister chose to be persuaded. On March 1 Ben-Gurion's foreign minister, Golda Meir, announced Israel's intention to withdraw.[52]

With this roadblock removed the Senate proceeded to act on the administration's Middle East resolution. On March 2 the upper house rejected a watered-down substitute. Three days later it approved the original by a vote of 72 to 19.

XI

THROUGH 1957 the anti-Nasserist implications of the Eisenhower Doctrine went largely unrealized, although the spring and summer brought two close calls. In April a revolt against Jordan's King Hussein, led by a pro-Nasser army faction, resulted in the redeployment of the Sixth Fleet and the dispatch of $10 million in emergency aid to Amman. In August Syria's already left-leaning government announced a substantial increase in Soviet economic and military assistance, prompting some of Syria's neighbors to suggest to Washington that Damascus was falling into Moscow's orbit. Again the Sixth Fleet steamed east; arms deliveries to Iraq, Lebanon, and Jordan were stepped up; the administration repositioned fighter planes to Turkey; Turkish troops massed on Syria's borders. But the president never explicitly invoked the Eisenhower Doctrine, since Syria seemed incapable of seriously threatening the countries nearby.[53]

As the pressure leaked out of the latter crisis the administration considered trying to determine "what Nasser might have learned from the Syrian experience," as Dulles put it. Eisenhower went so far as to suggest a detente with Cairo. "Do you think there would be any percentage in initiating a drive to attempt to bring back Nasser to our side?" the president asked Dulles. Eisenhower cautioned that he had nothing "spectacular" in mind and that any initiative would have to remain closely guarded.

> My thought would be that either through the Ambassador or anybody else you can trust, you would start inquiring from him whether he saw any basis for rapprochement and what he would be prepared to do in the way of easing tensions in the Mid East if we on our part would resume efforts to help him over some of his difficulties.

The president acknowledged that any such effort would be exceedingly delicate. "If we do this it will, of course, have to be skillfully done— certainly we don't want to be in the position of 'bootlicking a dictator.'"[54]

Dulles effectively nixed Eisenhower's plan two days later at a meeting of the cabinet. The State Department, Dulles said, was giving the matter of reconciliation with Cairo its "closest consideration," but the problem involved great complexity. At present, the secretary asserted, the United States enjoyed good relations with all the Arab countries except Egypt and Syria. In seeking to win Nasser's favor the administration would run the risk of antagonizing Nasser's rivals. Moreover, evidence indicated that the Egyptian president would be satisfied "with nothing less than our willingness to treat him as the leader of the Arab world." That was the position Nasser "coveted." To grant him his ambition would infuriate King Saud and severely damage relations with Jordan, Lebanon, and Iraq. The rulers of those countries looked primarily to Saud and were "somewhat fearful of Nasser." Eisenhower admitted it would be a mistake to be "disloyal to King Saud or to attempt to push Nasser into leadership ahead of Saud," and he let the matter drop.[55]

Within six weeks events appeared to confirm Dulles' estimate regarding Nasser's expansionist designs. At the beginning of 1958 Egypt and Syria merged to form the United Arab Republic, an unequal and ill-fated union that joined Nasser's leadership skills and unmatched prestige in the Arab world to the revolutionary socialism of the Syrian Ba'ath party. Nasser affected reluctance, telling American Ambassador Raymond Hare that it would probably prove "a great headache." He had reason for fearing headaches, since Syria's Shukri al-Quwatli himself warned Nasser:

> Ah, Mr. President! You don't know what you have taken on. You have taken on people of whom every one believes he is a politician. Fifty percent consider themselves national leaders; twenty-five percent of them think they are prophets; and at least ten percent believe they are gods. You have taken on people of which there are those who worship God, and there are those who adore fire; and there are those who idolize the devil.

Nasser had to accept Quwatli's word on the subject, since he had never been to Syria. But the riotous reception he received in Damascus following publication of the banns stilled some of his concerns.[56]

They hardly silenced American worries. Not inaccurately, officials in the Eisenhower administration interpreted the merger—by which Nasser became president of the U.A.R. and Cairo the capital—as the first solid step toward the realization of Nasser's pan-Arab aims. Dulles voiced the prevailing opinion in Washington when he asked the CIA's Wilbur Eveland: "What do you make of Nasser's plan to take over Syria?"[57]

Analyzing these developments, the staff of the National Security Council considered two aspects of the situation in the Middle East. Militarily, matters were essentially under control. According to NSC 5801, the Baghdad system was "a going concern," its resilience demonstrated by the fact that it had survived the Suez crisis. Arguments for American membership were not inconsequential but were outweighed by the trouble such membership would cause with Israel and Saudi Arabia; therefore the United States should continue to provide support and advice short of formal adherence. Politically, things were more complex. The underlying struggle between the United States and the Soviet Union for control of the area was primarily "a battle for men's minds." To date America could not claim to be winning, as the predominant mood among the Arabs was neutralist rather than pro-Western. Two factors accounted for this mood: "the feeling that the Arabs can only gain in an East-West competition for their favor, and a fear of the consequences which a third world war might bring." American lapses contributed to the problem. "We have not defined, on an area basis, with any precision the degree of Soviet presence and influence in a country which we would be prepared to tolerate." Nor had the administration enunciated "a definition of 'neutralism' which would be acceptable to us."[58]

A slightly revised version of this paper described in greater detail the sources of Arab neutralism. Nationalists in the region were convinced that "the Arab place in the sun" could not be achieved in the present setting of more than a dozen political entities, some still under Western tutelage. What the nationalists, of whom the most prominent was Nasser, desired was "an Arab empire reaching from Casablanca to the Persian Gulf." Although this vision was illusory—the Arab world historically tended toward fragmentation—"the mystique of Arab unity has become a basic element of Arab political thought." The status quo stood between the nationalists and their pan-Arab dream; therefore they opposed the status quo. Since the United States supported the status quo the nationalists attacked the United States. As long as American policy favored conservative Arab regimes, the nationalists would continue to believe that "the United States desires to keep the Arab world disunited and is committed to work with 'reactionary' elements to that end."

Meanwhile the Soviet Union was getting a free ride in the region. Russia, the NSC report said, was "not inhibited in proclaiming all-out support for Arab unity and for the most extreme Arab nationalist aspirations, because it has no stake in the economic or political status quo in the area." Nationalists like Nasser encouraged Soviet penetration, in the belief "that their own interests are best served by a competition between the Free World and the Soviet bloc for Arab favor." The nationalists realized, to some degree at least, the risks involved in balancing East against West, but these risks did not deter them. "They are confident of their ability to play such a game." Besides, communism to them was not the principal danger. "The Arabs sincerely believe that Israel poses a greater threat to their interests than does international Communism."

Under the circumstances the United States could do little to improve its standing in nationalist and Nasserist circles; consequently the report, which upon Eisenhower's approval on January 24 became the authoritative statement of American policy, specified a continued tilt toward conservatism in the region. In public the United States should "proclaim support for the ideal of Arab unity." Behind the scenes American officials should "discreetly encourage" Nasser's rivals, especially the leaders of Saudi Arabia, Jordan, and Iraq.[59]

XII

IN DESCRIPTIVE terms NSC 5801 could hardly be faulted; its identification of the basic incompatibility of Arab nationalism–neutralism and the desire of the United States to preserve the status quo defined the crux of America's problems in the Middle East. The Eisenhower administration had a clear view of the interplay of Egyptian, Soviet, and American objectives. Prescriptively, however, the paper left something to be desired. Betraying its bureaucratic roots, it was cautious to the point of silence on the likelihood of American success in "discreet" encouragement of conservative regimes. Whether defending the status quo was a wise policy or a foolish one depended on the viability of that structure.

In the spring of 1958 the status quo in the Middle East most needed defending in Lebanon. The Lebanese president, Camille Chamoun, had enthusiastically embraced the Eisenhower Doctrine and in doing so had incurred the wrath of Arab nationalists. He compounded his troubles by indicating that he would seek an amendment to Lebanon's constitution allowing him another term in office. From Cairo Nasser fueled Lebanese discontent with propaganda, money, and weapons. In May tension flared into civil war, prompting Chamoun to ask Washington to consider military intervention.

Eisenhower responded that he would send troops but only if another Arab state concurred in the request and only with the understanding that the troops' purpose was to keep peace, not to maintain Chamoun in office. For several weeks the question hung fire, as the situation stabilized temporarily. In July, however, a bloody coup in Baghdad toppled Iraq's monarchy (and Nasser's archrival Nuri) and sent tremors throughout the region. In Beirut Chamoun summoned the American ambassador and demanded American soldiers.[60]

Administration officials detected no sign of "overt armed aggression" against Lebanon from a nation "controlled by international communism"—the language of the Middle East resolution—but they had little difficulty spotting Nasser's influence. Foster Dulles said, "The mastermind is very apparent." Allen Dulles told a group of legislative leaders that the CIA saw "the hand of Nasser" very clearly in recent events. Henry Cabot Lodge agreed that the coup in Iraq and the turmoil in Lebanon betrayed "a plot by Nasser to take over the whole thing." Joint Chiefs of Staff Chairman Nathan Twining concurred in the opinion that if the United States failed to move swiftly "Nasser would take over the whole area."[61]

Eisenhower considered the crisis part of Nasser's campaign to eject the West from the Middle East. The United States had come to the "cross roads," he told Vice President Nixon.

> Since 1945 we have been trying to maintain the opportunity to reach vitally needed petroleum supplies peaceably, without hindrance on the part of anyone. The present incident comes about by the struggle of Nasser to get control of these supplies—to get the income and the power to destroy the Western world. Somewhere along the line we have got to face up to the issue.[62]

Eisenhower overspoke when he said Nasser was aiming to destroy the Western world. Nasser was ambitious, but not even he set his sights quite that high. Yet American officials were correct in believing the Egyptian leader hoped to turn Lebanon's troubles to his benefit. He would be more than happy to see the pro-American Chamoun regime brought down, and he would gladly assist in its replacement by leadership amenable to Egypt's friendly persuasion. If this undermined other Western-oriented governments in the region, all the better.

While Eisenhower did not intend to save Chamoun, he did hope to prevent a wave of Nasserist sentiment from sweeping across the Middle East. To accomplish this goal he dispatched nearly 15,000 troops to Beirut. The president and Dulles understood the hazards of military intervention. Dulles told a gathering of legislators at the White House:

> If we go in, our action is likely to accentuate the anti-Western feeling of the Arab masses, even though the governments of many of the neighboring states would probably like for us to intervene—however, their leaders do not dare to say so. Our intervention would not therefore be likely to be a quick and easy solution.

But failure to intervene would cost more. "The first consequence of not going in," Dulles continued, "would certainly be that the non-Nasser governments in the Middle East and adjoining areas would be quickly overthrown." American vacillation would demoralize America's allies around the world. "They will therefore lose confidence and tend toward neutralism."[63]

As a morale-building exercise, the landing in Beirut was aimed as much at other countries as at Lebanon. In certain respects Lebanon was the least of the administration's worries. Allen Dulles said recent events had frightened pro-Western governments in the region "very badly." Foster Dulles put the matter more emphatically: "There is panic throughout the entire area." Reports from the field substantiated the Dulleses' assessment. King Hussein uncovered a Nasserist plot in the Jordanian army; even after the monarch arrested the ringleaders his position, in the CIA's opinion, hung "in the balance." From Riyadh, King Saud declared that unless the United States took immediate and decisive action his country would be forced to "go along" with the U.A.R. The shah of Iran described Nasser as "the heart of the octopus which is strangling the Middle East."[64]

The strongest response came from Israel. Ben-Gurion wrote to Eisenhower describing his country's alarm at "the present grave crisis," his advisers' conviction that Nasser's expansionist designs lay behind the region's troubles and Moscow behind Nasser, and his government's plans for a secret alliance with Iran, Turkey, Sudan, and Ethiopia to build "a strong dam against the Nasserist-Soviet torrent." Regarding the last point he asked American support.

> With your assistance, Mr. President, it will thus be possible to salvage freedom in this crucial part of the Middle East, and even amongst some of the Arabic-speaking countries of North Africa. With the flanks of the region assured, it will be easier to develop resistance to Nasserist and Soviet penetration in the remaining areas of the Arab world.[65]

American officials shared Ben-Gurion's suspicions of Nasser's expansionist ambitions. "These ambitions," Dulles told Eisenhower, "include at least a truncation of Israel and the overthrow of present governments in Lebanon, Jordan, Morocco, Tunis, Libya, the Sudan, Saudi Arabia, etc., and their replacement by his stooges." Washington also agreed that the Kremlin would benefit from Nasser's destabilizing activities. "The

Soviet Union . . ." Dulles continued, "can and does help Nasser to achieve these extravagant goals, believing it will be the ultimate heir."[66]

But neither Dulles nor Eisenhower was inclined to accept Ben-Gurion's invitation to support an anti-Nasser pact. Both aimed to keep Israel at arm's length. Responding to a comment that the Soviets consistently scored points against America by siding with Arab nationalists, Eisenhower said, "We always come back to Israel as the basic problem." Obviously the president took a more diplomatic approach in telling Ben-Gurion that the United States wanted nothing to do with his proposal, but his coolness was evident. Regarding Israel's security concerns, Eisenhower limited himself to a restatement of American policy. He declared that "the independence and integrity of the nations of the Middle East are vital to world peace and the national interest." The president did add however, that "since the Middle East comprehends Israel, you can be confident of United States interest in the integrity and independence of Israel," and he instructed Dulles to tell the Israeli ambassador in private that Israel should take the intervention in Lebanon as an example of what the administration would do in response to a threat to Israel's existence.[67]

XIII

REINFORCING EISENHOWER'S reluctance to join Israel in an anti-Nasserist venture was the president's growing belief that the policy of opposition was failing. "Arab sympathies toward Nasser . . ." Eisenhower conceded, "are probably greater than we thought." At a White House strategy session in the third week of July, the president cautioned against any appearance of directly challenging Egypt. "We do not wish to be jockeyed into the position of having to attack Nasser publicly." The coup in Baghdad demonstrated that the status quo was crumbling faster than Washington had realized. Whatever the outcome of the Lebanon venture, the nationalists would continue to gain ground. "We must win them to us," the president said, "or adjust to them."[68]

As a first step toward accommodating the nationalists, if not Nasser himself, the State Department advocated an approach to Baghdad. "Iraq is the big thing," Dulles remarked. George Allen contended that the overthrow of Nuri, who was widely distrusted among the Arabs, provided an unforeseen opportunity. "We should try to live with the new government in Iraq," Allen said, arguing that General Kassim and his associates would not settle for a place in Nasser's shadow and that Iraq, now under a credibly nationalist government, could become a counterweight to Egypt. Economically—since Iraq had oil and Egypt did not—and historically—since Baghdad and Cairo had contested for ascendancy for centuries—there existed a "natural cleavage" between Kassim and Nasser. The United States should play on this division.[69]

Agreeing, Eisenhower approved recognition of the Kassim regime and ordered Robert Murphy, then in Lebanon persuading Chamoun to leave office peacefully, to proceed to Iraq. There Murphy confirmed Allen's prediction that Kassim did not intend to subordinate Iraq's interest to the cause of Nasserism. Recalling their conversation later, Murphy wrote that the general spoke with "quiet ferocity" when he declared his determination to put a stop to the activities of Nasser's agents in Iraq. Kassim admitted agreement with some aspects of Egypt's foreign policy but on the whole he impressed Murphy as being "grimly determined" to maintain Iraq's independence.[70]

XIV

THE AMERICAN approach to Iraq proved a dead end—when the expected rivalry between Nasser and Kassim developed, Washington found itself on the side of the former—but the idea that the United States must accommodate Arab nationalism took hold. Whatever the symbolic value of the show of military force in Lebanon, the actual outcome of the affair was distinctly anticlimactic, involving a solution Nasser himself had suggested in June: Fuad Chehab as president and Rashid Karami as prime minister. Since Karami was a leader of the rebels, Chamoun and many of his supporters interpreted this denouement as a vindication of armed revolt and a triumph for Nasser.[71]

Although certainly not in public, the administration granted as much. On November 4 Eisenhower approved a new NSC policy statement which was remarkable both for its candor and for the divergence of its prescriptions from those of its predecessors. NSC 5820/1 described the situation in the Middle East as having gone from bad to worse despite the intervention in Lebanon. The "two basic trends" in the region— "the emergence of the radical pan-Arab nationalist movement and the intrusion of the Soviet Union into the area"—continued unabated. If anything the radicals' momentum was increasing and the nationalists and the West were more at odds than ever. The threat to the United States increased commensurately. "The virtual collapse during 1958 of conservative resistance, leaving the radical nationalist regimes almost without opposition in the area, has brought a grave challenge to Western interests." Until now the United States had sought to block Russian penetration by opposing the nationalists. But this opposition had rested on the conservative base which had largely vanished; as a result the United States was left without a policy.

Given this fact, the NSC paper continued, the United States must change tactics. The objectives of American policy remained as before: first, to deny the Middle East to the Soviet Union and preserve Western access to oil; second, to secure basing and transit rights, facilitate an Arab-Israeli settlement, and encourage the evolution of stable, noncommunist, and pro-American governments. But where the United States heretofore had pursued these objectives by opposing the radical nationalists, especially Nasser, now the administration ought to explore the possibility of cooperating with the nationalists, who for better or worse controlled the only game left in town.

> It has become increasingly apparent that the prevention of further Soviet penetration of the Near East and progress in solving Near Eastern problems depend on the degree to which the United States is able to work more closely with Arab nationalism and associate itself more closely with such aims and aspirations of the Arab people as are not contrary to the basic interests of the United States.

Washington's attitude toward Nasser would serve as the touchstone of American credibility in the region. "In the eyes of the great mass of Arabs, considerable significance will be attached to the position which the United States adopts toward the foremost current spokesman of radical pan-Arab nationalism, Gamal Abdel Nasser." As hazardous and distasteful as collaboration with Nasser might be, the Egyptian president's stature in the Arab world and the absence of any believable conservative alternative made other courses even less desirable. "To be cast in the role of Nasser's opponent would be to leave the Soviets as his champion."

It was a narrow path the United States must walk, since Nasser's agenda included items "strongly inimical" to American interests. Nasser remained as antipathetic as ever to what he considered undue Western influence in the Middle East. He opposed Israel. He challenged the surviving conservative regimes, with which the United States had close ties. He aspired to a larger role in regional politics. Consequently, even while the United States should seek to forge a more cooperative relationship with the Egyptian leader, American officials must take pains to ensure that this was accomplished "without destroying our freedom of action in dealings with other Arab leaders." Further, the American government ought to maintain its policy of "discreetly encouraging" rivals to Nasser, and under no circumstances should it indicate that it accepted Nasser's claims to primacy in the Arab world.

One goal of this new policy was the prevention of deeper Soviet penetration of the Middle East; another was the encouragement of moderation on the part of the nationalists. Boring from within had definite limits, to be sure, for the nationalists would be on their guard against American pressure. Nonetheless, in endeavoring to establish "an effective working relationship with Arab nationalism," American leaders might hope "constructively to influence and stabilize the movement and contain its outward thrust."

There were no guarantees that the new policy would work, and some of the paper's recommendations sounded suspiciously like counsels of despair; but the report did offer concrete suggestions for limiting the damage the West had incurred in the Middle East. In particular the authors urged that the administration "accept the neutralist policies of the states of the area when necessary," even though the neutralists maintained friendly relations with the Soviet Union. More specifically still, the United States should "normalize" relations with Egypt at the same time it endeavored to circumscribe Cairo's contacts with Moscow and to "take discreet advantage of trends in the area which might render less likely further expansion of Nasser's position."[72]

XV

FORTUNATELY FOR Washington, this reversal of policy coincided with a pro-Western trend on Nasser's part. During 1959 the new regime in Baghdad proved as independent of Cairo as Kassim promised Murphy it would be, and in an effort to wrest Arab leadership from Nasser Kassim turned to the Iraqi Communist party and the Soviet Union. The quarrel between the two leaders centered on Syria; in January, following fighting in that eastern wing of the U.A.R. between Nasserists and communists, the Egyptian president jailed hundreds of the latter. When Khrushchev complained about this persecution of his co-ideologists Nasser told the Kremlin to mind its own business. At the beginning of March Egypt initialized an agreement with Britain resolving disputes arising from the Suez war. By year's end Cairo and London had resumed normal diplomatic relations.[73]

As part of this campaign to reopen channels to the West Nasser addressed the American people. In a feature article in the July issue of *Life* magazine he explained his philosophy of "nonalignment and positive neutrality." He held that "Western imperialism" had not entirely disappeared; but the rest of his argument made plain that he worried more about imperialism from the East. Communism, Nasser said, had declared its hostility to his country and to the movement he represented. His struggle with the communists was to the death. "We know they can never relent in their opposition to Arab nationalism and the U.A.R. . . . Their ultimate objective is that of Communist parties everywhere: to take power." Nasser described the stern measures he had adopted to stem the communist threat, pointing out that the Communist party was illegal in Egypt. (He could not resist adding that such was not the case in Israel.) Although Egypt sought "coexistence between countries of differing social and political systems," the communists recognized no such principle. As a result they did not deserve political consideration. "While the Communists have been attacking me, I have been attacking them."[74]

The Eisenhower administration interpreted Nasser's statements and actions as evincing a desire for rapprochement. Dulles told congressional leaders it seemed apparent that Nasser would welcome "a measure of association with the West." Accordingly, as an indication of a reciprocal wish, the administration announced in July the first new economic aid package in three years.[75]

When Eisenhower's Operations Coordinating Board in February 1960 reviewed Middle Eastern developments, it described recent trends as "broadly favorable" to the United States. The increase in Russian influence in Iraq was worrisome but was more than offset by the emergence of "a deep and widening gulf between the two principal political forces of the area—communism and Arab nationalism." This encouraging news portended a fundamental shift in the ideological balance in the region.

To be sure, Arab nationalists were not exactly leaping into the Western embrace; suspicion of Western motives remained. Nevertheless Nasser and others had concluded that communism was no longer friend but foe. This conclusion gained all the more significance from the fact the nationalists had demonstrated that "against communism they can muster ideological weapons far more powerful than anything the U.S. or its allies could bring to bear."

Regarding developments between Washington and Cairo specifically, the OCB report detected a "marked improvement" in the diplomatic atmosphere. "Nasser himself now views relations between the two countries as 'normal.' " The Egyptian president had turned his propaganda guns away from the West and toward the communists; the American government was providing ammunition in the form of anticommunist radio scripts written by the United States Information Service and grants earmarked for newsprint. Cultural and political exchanges were increasing, including an effort by the AFL-CIO to forge an alliance with its Egyptian counterpart.[76]

XVI

FOR ALL the warming, Nasser remained controversial in the United States. During the summer of 1960, as the Egyptian president made arrangements to travel to New York for the fall session of the UN, the administration carefully considered how to handle the visit. Although Eisenhower had no hesitation at this point about being seen with Nehru and Tito, Nasser presented greater difficulties. As Undersecretary of State C. Douglas Dillon pointed out, a personal interview with Nasser would set off alarms in Israel and stir ill feelings in Congress. On balance, Dillon argued, a meeting between Eisenhower and Nasser would do more harm than good. He advised the president to stay away.[77]

Eisenhower rejected the advice, believing, as Dillon himself admitted, that Nasser had become a moderating force in the cold war. With his final months in office slipping past, Eisenhower sought every opportunity to encourage further moderation.[78]

As was true of the president's talks with Nehru and Tito, the substance of the Eisenhower-Nasser interview had less significance than its general tone. Although some basic issues—Israel in particular—still separated Washington and Cairo, the two presidents expressed a genuine interest in minimizing differences and concentrating on areas of cooperation. Nasser, who told the American ambassador in Cairo he had admired Eisenhower ever since studying World War II in staff college, thanked his host for America's "great help" during the Suez crisis. Speaking against a backdrop of UN operations in the Congo, Nasser recounted how the UN had acted to deter aggression four years earlier. He hoped it would continue to do so. Eisenhower agreed that the UN was a great influence for peace. It had served well during the Suez affair; it must continue to serve. World leaders should give it every support.[79]

The discussion was not entirely harmonious. Eisenhower had a hard time treating Nasser on the terms of equality that marked his conversations with Nehru and Tito. The age difference doubtless contributed; so too, it seems, did a lingering resentment at Nasser for refusing a settlement with Israel and opening the Middle East to Soviet influence. When Nasser averred that he had always sought good relations with the United States but that Israel had been and remained an intransigent obstacle, Eisenhower retorted that the United States was getting "very tired" of the situation in the Middle East and that Americans were weary of "putting up 23 million dollars each year to keep a million Arab refugees alive with no progress towards settlement." Israel, Eisenhower asserted, was a "fact" which the countries of the region must learn to accept. Eisenhower added that his administration had been "very suspicious" of Russian aid to Egypt, since Americans always worried "when the Soviets touch a country." In a somewhat inquisitorial voice Eisenhower asked Nasser to tell what he knew of the situation in Jordan, where Hussein's prime minister had recently been assassinated.

Nasser stood his ground. Regarding the Zionists he stated that "to accept Israel as a fact would be to permit a thief to keep what he has stolen." As to Russian aid, he denied that he had allowed Moscow excessive influence over his actions. Egypt, he said, "would accept no price for its liberty or independence." Describing the Egyptians as "a very sensitive people," Nasser commented that the withdrawal of the American offer of funding for the Aswan Dam had come as a "great shock," leaving his government no choice but to turn to the Soviets. On dissent in Jordan against Hussein he declared that he had no "agents" there, although he admitted that many Jordanians supported the cause he represented. "I do not know who they are, but they believe in me, and they believe in Arab unity." He added that he would not accept the adherence of other Middle Eastern countries to his movement for Arab nationalism if this were accomplished "through a coup or through subversion." He welcomed cooperation but only if it represented a "voluntary decision" by the people involved.

As the conversation ended, Eisenhower stressed the importance of avoiding a military buildup in the Middle East. If the U.A.R. wished to accept weapons from the Soviets, "without coming under Soviet domination," the United States would not object. "We respect the U.A.R.'s position as a neutral." But he could not help believing an arms race would be counterproductive. Peace was what the people of the region needed. Eisenhower concluded by remarking that he appreciated Nasser's recent straightforward profession that Egypt did not intend to destroy Israel.

Without accepting Israel's legitimacy, Nasser commented that it would be "foolish" to try to liquidate the Zionist state. "Nowadays anyone can begin a war, but it will not stay limited and no one can win." [80]

CONCLUSION

The Triumph of Geopolitics

A FEW days before John Foster Dulles delivered his opinion on the "immorality" of neutralism Dwight Eisenhower addressed the same issue. At a news conference the president provided advance publicity for his secretary of state, directing reporters' attention to what Dulles would say, especially on the subject of nonalignment. Eisenhower took pains to stamp his imprimatur on Dulles' remarks. He said the secretary would be speaking "not only with my approval but really with my great support."

Because the journalists had not previewed Dulles' speech they could not know that what the president said next essentially contradicted the secretary's argument. After his enthusiastic buildup of a statement that would come across as a typically Dullesian and predictably moralistic broadside, Eisenhower proceeded to characterize neutralism in the most moderate of terms. Reminding his listeners that the United States had followed a neutral course for a century and a half, he suggested that nonalignment reflected less an ethical choice than a political and military one, and he said he could understand how, under certain circumstances, the national self-interest of a country might dictate a middle course between the superpower blocs.[1]

On this day the president's observations seemed unobjectionable enough, and the reporters moved on to other matters; but after Dulles

Conclusion

commented on the same subject in decidedly harsher tones they took the first opportunity to investigate the discrepancy. It appeared, they said, that the White House and the State Department viewed neutralism in different lights. Was this the case? Of course not, Dulles replied. What was the administration's position, then? Dulles responded that as always the president's remarks represented American policy. If there appeared any divergence between those remarks and his own, such divergence was entirely a matter of semantics. When a correspondent asked Dulles to expand on the circumstances that might justify, in the administration's opinion, a neutralist position for a country, the secretary declined to elaborate.[2]

The journalists were left to puzzle out precisely what the administration thought of neutralism, as were foreign observers, some of whom had an immediate and direct interest in the issue. The government of India, for example, found the matter incomprehensible. A spokeswoman for Nehru wondered to a friend of Dulles how the secretary managed to get away with espousing a view so at variance with Eisenhower's. "Mr. Dulles," she said, "made a statement on neutralism which we consider is directly opposite of the president's statement." She added that in India, as in most countries with parliamentary governments, such a contradiction would provoke either a retraction or a resignation.[3]

In America, of course, inspired confusion of this sort does no such thing. Rather it forms the stuff of bureaucratic politics and allows an administration to cast its leading characters in their most useful roles. This certainly was the case with Eisenhower and Dulles, who played the good-cop, bad-cop routine to substantial effect through the six years the president and the secretary worked together. Dean Acheson noted this ability in a commiserating and slightly envious letter to Lyndon Johnson in 1957. Acheson's message related to disarmament and in the instance he described, two understudies shared the spotlight, but the basic strategy was the same.

> The methods of this Administration would, I should suppose, drive the leader of an opposition trying to do his duty responsibly into schizophrenia. The idea of Messrs. Eisenhower and Dulles seems to be to occupy both extremes at the same time. They back belligerency and appeasement in the persons of Admiral Radford and Harold Stassen, stage a combat which they can throw either way, and outflank any opposition.[4]

306

The Eisenhower-Dulles crossfire on neutralism fell into this category. The secretary's sermonizing was designed to please conservatives, Republicans for the most part, who distrusted neutralists and continually threatened to block administration initiatives toward countries of the third world. In this context a point repeatedly in evidence in the previous chapters but often overlooked bears underscoring: that on the subject of nonalignment the Eisenhower administration faced more serious criticism from the right than from the left. Dulles lives in memory as an unbending moralist, but to his conservative contemporaries he more commonly seemed a trimmer. To be sure, Dulles' pulpit-thumping elicited groans from liberals, but Eisenhower's administration had less to fear from Stevensonites than from McCarthy, Knowland, and their ilk. In any event, with Dulles disarming the right Eisenhower could and did climb the high ground of moderation and statesmanship.

But after allowances are made for political posturing, more remains to the neutralist question. A close reader of Eisenhower's and Dulles' comments on the subject could discern that the administration considered neutralism an issue of two distinct parts. At the moral level neither the president nor the secretary of state accepted a place for neutralism. Morality, in their view, demanded commitment, and to the degree diplomacy reflected morality there was no middle ground between West and East, between democracy and dictatorship. This was the thrust of Eisenhower's remark to Tito in 1960: "There can be no neutrals when the question is one of moral values or right and wrong."[5]

But Eisenhower and Dulles had lived long enough to know that morality alone did not carry diplomacy very far and that the arena of military strategy and great-power politics was essentially amoral. The United States had joined forces with Stalin against Hitler during World War II and been happy for the help. The cold war was a struggle of a different sort but its stakes were no less. "How many divisions has the pope?" asked Stalin in dismissing morality as a guide to foreign policy. "How many divisions has Tito?" asked American leaders in doing essentially the same thing.

Writing to his brother Edgar, Eisenhower explained the difference between what might be termed ideological-ethical neutralism and political-military neutralism. This letter bears repeating at some length, because it affords the clearest view of Eisenhower's beliefs on nonalignment.

Conclusion

You and I, of course, know that there is no neutral position as between honesty and falsehood, or, indeed, as between any moral value and its opposite. However, the concept of neutrality for a nation does not necessarily mean that that nation is trying to occupy a position midway between right and wrong. In the ordinary sense, neutrality applies to military combinations.

Now it is very true that we want every nation we can reach to stand with us in support of the basic principles of free government. But for a long time, I have held that it is a very grave error to ask some of these nations to announce themselves as being on our side in the event of a possible conflict. Such a statement on the part of a weak nation like Burma, or even India, would at once make them our all-out ally and we would have the impossible task of helping them arm for defense.

Moreover, if a country would declare itself our military ally, then any attack made upon it by Communist groups would be viewed in most areas of the world as a more or less logical consequence. Since so much of the world thinks of the existing *ideological* struggle as a *power* struggle, the reaction to the kind of conflict I talk about would be, "Well, they asked for it."

On the other hand, if the Soviets attacked an avowed neutral, world opinion would be outraged.[6]

Eisenhower's comments in this 1956 letter represented the matured opinion of his administration regarding neutralism, and they reflected most of a decade of American experience dealing with nonaligned states. By the mid-1950s international tensions had abated somewhat and the president could take a more equanimous view of neutralism than was possible earlier. Even so, almost from the beginning of the cold war American policy, as distinct from the rhetoric in which that policy was sometimes shrouded, demonstrated a pragmatic ability to deal with neutralism on its merits. If the neutralist actions of a particular country worked to the advantage of the United States, that country deserved, and usually received, American support. If a neutralist challenged American interests, opposition was the rule. Ideology counted little in the business.

II

YUGOSLAVIA WAS the principal test case. Tito never wavered in his adherence to the tenets of communism, but from the moment American leaders learned of his break with Stalin they had few qualms about providing assistance, and the doubts they did have related chiefly to the efficacy, not the ethics, of such aid. As George Kennan wrote only days after the schism became evident, Yugoslavia's internal affairs were "its own business"; what mattered to the Truman administration was the redirecting of Yugoslavia's armed forces. Omar Bradley explained the situation most plainly in his testimony before the House Foreign Affairs Committee in 1950. Should Tito simply remain neutral in a conflict with the Russians, Bradley said, his neutrality would significantly assist the United States and the West. Should he choose a more overt form of cooperation, all the better.[7]

Easing the military strain on the Central European front constituted the first order of diplomacy toward Yugoslavia; a close second involved promoting Titoism among the Soviet Union's allies. Whether American officials spoke in the language of the joint chiefs of staff, who described Tito as "an ideological threat to Kremlin control of the world communist movement," or of Dulles, who characterized Yugoslavia as a symbol of "the possibility of breaking up the Soviet empire without war," the point was the same; and it is in this context that the latitudinarianism of American policymakers shows most clearly. Recognizing that the Titoist model would possess attractive power for Eastern Europe and China only to the degree independence of Moscow did not imply subordination to Washington, and only to the extent rejection of Stalinism in the international realm did not demand abandonment of communism as a domestic organizing principle, American officials actually preferred that Tito remain a demonstrably orthodox Marxist-Leninist. To be sure, they encouraged moderation at the margins, but their concern had considerably less to do with the civil liberties of Yugoslavia's people than with the political sensibilities of Congress. In those McCarthyite days supporting aid for a communist of any variety could shorten a legislator's career. When one's constituency embraced large numbers of Catholics who objected to Yugoslavia's treatment of Archbishop Stepinac, a vote for Tito entailed double jeopardy. Besides, politics apart, wasn't the cold war supposed to be about opposing communism? What made Tito's brand so much better than Stalin's? These were fair questions, and they caused officials in the Truman and Eisenhower administrations no little difficulty in testimony before congressional committees.[8]

Nonetheless, as their actions if not always their public statements made apparent, what the two administrations opposed was not communism but the Soviet Union. If a communist like Tito could sow discontent within the Russian alliance system, the United States would collaborate with him. If his effectiveness required that he remain a good communist at home, American decision makers had no great difficulty with that. George Allen put the issue succinctly in 1950 when he declared that although America's "ultimate aim" in Yugoslavia, as everywhere else, should be democracy, "for the moment a Marxist state independent of Moscow suits our purposes." George Perkins reiterated the argument when he asserted that Yugoslavia's existence as "an anti-Soviet but still Communist state" would create "the maximum dissension within and magnetism upon the other satellites." This opinion continued to inform American policy toward Tito's regime eight years later when the authors of NSC 5805 described the primary American objective as the mainte-nance of "an independent Yugoslavia" with the potential for "weaken-ing the monolithic front and internal cohesiveness of the Soviet Bloc." A definitely subordinate goal, one to be pursued only without risk to the first—which meant, in effect, hardly at all—was domestic liberaliza-tion.[9]

If the advantages of a neutralist Yugoslavia were obvious from the beginning, a nonaligned India was an acquired taste. After the commu-nist victory in China and the outbreak of Korean War, during the manic phase of American alliance-building, officials in the Truman administra-tion would have welcomed India into the ranks of the enlightened aligned. But their disappointment at Nehru's aloofness was tempered by their belief that India would join forces with the West in the event of the war many of them expected. The prime minister himself said as much when he told Loy Henderson that although India might try to avoid involve-ment in a general conflict, eventually it would be drawn in, and on the Western side.[10]

As the perceived danger of war diminished, as the tenacity of Nehru's neutralism sank into the American official mind, and after an adminis-tration headed by a president with a broader grasp of the significance of military alliances took office, the virtues of Indian nonalignment became more evident. American leaders never looked kindly on Nehru's efforts to spread the neutralist gospel, and they greeted his apparent failures, as at Bandung, with private satisfaction. But they understood that India was solidly in the democratic, if not the Western, camp, and they appre-ciated that Nehru intended to keep the Indian Communist party firmly under control. They recognized that for all the annoyance the prime minister's diplomacy caused, India served as an anchor for Asia. By its sheer mass it prevented the continent from drifting further East. Besides, as American officials realized and Eisenhower specifically pointed out, the West could not reasonably defend India militarily. To accept India as an ally would imply a commitment the United States was not prepared to fulfill. Better to leave the country on its own, providing assistance as necessary to keep Nehru in control and the country progressing toward economic development. Chester Bowles was ahead of his time on other matters, but he summarized top-level American opinion in 1952 when he described Nehru as "much the strongest pillar of strength against Communism in Asia." This view motivated the increasingly explicit commitment to Indian development during the middle and last part of the decade, and it provided the basis for an NSC policy statement just days before Eisenhower left office: "While India's policy of non-alignment will on occasion bring India into opposition to U.S. programs and activities, and a strong and increasingly successful India will add weight to this opposition, over the longer run, the risks to U.S. security from a weak and vulnerable India would be far greater than the risks of a strong, stable, even though neutral, India."[11]

Nasser's neutralist brew proved considerably harder to swallow than Nehru's, and only when the Eisenhower administration discovered that the alternative tasted worse did the United States accept the idea of cooperation with Cairo. The essential trouble with Nasser, and the reason he provoked American enmity, was that he proposed neutralism for a country at once vitally important to the West and hitherto under effective Western control. Compounding the problem was the fact that American leaders had a more difficult time fathoming Nasser than understanding either Nehru or Tito. Allen Dulles put the matter generously, by Washington's standards, when he commented in 1957: "It is not always easy to work with Nasser. One wonders at times whether he is really seeking the welfare of his people or his own personal aggrandizement." Foster Dulles, in one of his less histrionic moods, found Nasser "rather undependable," adding, "It is not that he is intentionally dishonest, but he has an urge that pushes him from one thing to another. He is not the kind of person who settles down." Despite this uncertainty regarding Nasser personally, officials in the Eisenhower administration recognized the trend of his policy, and they realized that it did not augur well for the privileged position of the West. Eisenhower got carried away when he asserted that Nasser was seeking to bring down Western civilization by seizing control of Middle Eastern oil. (Dulles, publicly thought the administration's spokesman for the apocalypse, predicted that no matter what Nasser managed among the Arabs, Iran would elude him.) But the fact remained that Nasser's destabilizing activities were opening the region to Soviet influence. The 1958 crisis sent shudders through Washington; at the moment of ordering American troops into Lebanon Eisenhower exclaimed that Nasser was "a puppet even though he probably doesn't think so." In calmer moments the administration possessed greater appreciation for Nasser's ability to steer an independent and genuinely neutralist course, but this hardly inspired confidence. As an NSC progress report put the matter—quite correctly—in the spring of 1956, "Arab neutralism actually works in favor of the Soviet bloc since it is directed against established Western positions." The same authors drew the logical conclusion some months later: "The United States cannot successfully deal with President Nasser." [12]

But the situation changed after the revolution in Iraq, as the Eisenhower administration was astute and flexible enough to see. With Kassim in Baghdad challenging Nasser from the left and threatening, in the process, to give the Russians entrée to the Persian Gulf, Nasser's neutralism began to appear, if not quite a rock of stability, at least an improvement over Iraq's pro-Soviet tilt. Consequently the administration decided to make its peace with the man it had so recently opposed. It never got especially excited about the idea, understanding that collaboration with Nasser, like most forms of international cooperation, was a matter of mutual and probably passing convenience. Nonetheless, by the summer of 1960 American officials had come to the conclusion that Nasser's neutralism, in the words of an NSC paper, "need not be an insurmountable obstacle" to the achievement of American goals in the Middle East.[13]

III

THE STANDARD criticism of American relations with the third world charges that American leaders, beguiled by the experience of the 1930s and preoccupied if not obsessed with containing communism, have adopted an overly ideological approach toward nonaligned and

developing nations. In doing so and in forcing events to fit their precon-
ceptions, they have misinterpreted the revolutionary changes shaping
that international middle ground and have pursued rigid policies often
productive of the very results they aimed to prevent.

If the experience of the Truman and Eisenhower administrations, and
the policies they formulated toward India, Yugoslavia, and Egypt, are
any guide—and there is little reason to believe they are not—this criticism is unfounded. Perhaps the most distinctive characteristic of the
approach of the two administrations to the three leading neutralists was
the remarkable absence of ideology at the policy-making level. In the
realm of abstract morality, to be sure, American leaders believed without
question in the superiority of the "free world" over its communist
challengers. In the arena of political oratory, they denounced neutralism
as "immoral." But in the domain where policy took shape, where progress called for compromise and making use of the instruments at hand,
ideology carried little weight. Geopolitics—the pragmatic pursuit of
strategic, military, and other solid material, including economic, interests—was what mattered. For all Nehru's "double standard," for all his
efforts on behalf of China, for all his attempts to prevent the organization of Asia and the Middle East into collective security pacts, both the
Truman and Eisenhower administrations supported him as the best
guarantor of a stable India, independent of the Soviet bloc. Despite
Tito's unswerving devotion to communism, despite his belligerently anti-
Western rhetoric, despite his later return to Moscow's good graces, both
administrations backed him as a distracter of Russian attention and an
example of one satellite that had spun out of the Kremlin's control.
When Eisenhower and Dulles moved into opposition against Nasser,
their shift had nothing to do with a belief that the Egyptian leader was
soft on communism, for they had solid evidence to the contrary; it
followed instead from a well-founded fear that he would disrupt the
pro-Western status quo in the Middle East. After most of that status quo
collapsed, they swung back toward cooperation, in an effort to shore up
what remained against a more serious threat.

This said, it *is* true that officials in the Truman and Eisenhower
administrations viewed events in the third world through the lens of the
cold war, that they always saw Bandung in the context of Yalta. But
again interests, not ideology, commanded their attention. As policy toward
Yugoslavia demonstrated, their cold war was chiefly a struggle against

the Soviet Union. Only coincidentally—to the degree communism served as a vehicle for the expansion of Soviet influence—was it a battle against communism. Admittedly they sometimes failed to distinguish clearly between the two in the hubbub of debate, but this failure owed more to the political necessities of the time than to any conceptual confusion on their part. In the best of worlds they would have wished communism away. Its atheism offended their moral scruples, its totalitarianism their political preferences, its socialism their economic sensibilities. But they understood that the cold war did not turn on taste; it was a contest for power. Where communism contributed to Soviet power, they opposed it. Where it undermined Soviet power, as in Yugoslavia, they were quite willing to exploit it.

If Yalta took priority in the attention of American leaders, and if in the process Bandung got slighted, that was unfortunate—but understandable. After all, only Moscow could directly threaten the physical security of the United States. At a time when they could not know the Kremlin's intentions, for them not to have been preoccupied with the Soviet Union would have amounted nearly to a derelection of duty.

But there is more to the criticism of American policy as insufficiently attentive to Bandung's concerns, for it commonly implies, if it does not state explicitly, that American interests would have been better served had American leaders concentrated less on the struggle with the Soviets and more on the priorities of the developing countries. This argument possesses a certain plausibility, especially as it relates to India and Egypt. Greater support for India, and less concern with bringing Pakistan into the American system, might have promoted warmer relations with New Delhi. Greater sympathy toward Egypt early on, and less deference to Britain, might have elicited increased cooperation in return.

But the argument soon runs aground. In the first place it assumes American officials had significant ability to shape the policies of India and Egypt, that those policies were essentially responses to what Washington did. This is an extremely tenuous assumption. Indeed, a fundamental objective of the diplomacy of India and Egypt, and Yugoslavia as well—the very raison d'être of Bandung—was to avoid being placed in the position of having simply to react to the moves of the major powers. To some degree American leaders might have improved the tone of relations with New Delhi, Cairo, and Belgrade. On issues of substance they had far less influence. India, Egypt, and Yugoslavia ordered their own priorities and charted their own courses. Events demonstrated the accuracy of C. D. Jackson's prediction that American pressure on Yugoslavia to settle the Trieste issue would not drive Tito into Moscow's arms. Jackson's point, mutatis mutandis, applied equally to India and Egypt. The converse—that enticements would not bring Nehru, Tito, and Nasser into the American embrace—was no less true.[14]

The second difficulty with the argument for greater attention to the third world is that it largely ignores the context in which decisions were made. American diplomacy involves balancing conflicting interests. The United States might have placated Nehru by avoiding an alliance with Pakistan. It might have backed Tito sooner and more forcefully at the risk of a confrontation with the Soviets. It might have given Nasser the weapons he wanted but alienated the British in doing so. In each case, improving relations with Bandung would have exacted a cost from Yalta. The third world's basic problem in American diplomacy is reflected in its name (which is why some members and friends object to the appellation). Although the nonaligned nations as a group—to the admittedly problematic extent it makes sense to speak of such a diverse agglomeration as a group—count for a great deal to the United States, rarely can relations with a single member outweigh contending claims of pledged allies or competing challenges from sworn rivals.

Tradeoffs on the domestic side were equally important. Never throughout the period under examination could the White House and the State Department plan an initiative toward India, Yugoslavia, or Egypt without evaluating the impact of such a move in Congress. Rarely did critics in the legislature totally block an effort on behalf of one of these countries, but the dissenters' influence went far beyond their success in roll calls. Although Congress approved the 1951 wheat loan to India, the debate the bill provoked deterred Acheson from backing Bowles' aid program, despite the secretary's agreement that it made diplomatic good sense. Congressional hostility elicited the same reaction from Dulles to Jackson's assistance scheme. In large part because of resentment on Capitol Hill toward Nehru's neutralism, American support for Indian development came several years later than it would have otherwise.

Similar remarks apply to policy toward Yugoslavia and Egypt. Tito's congressional opponents kept aid requests below what the administration would have liked; they commonly slashed even those cautious requests during the authorization and appropriation process. Once, in 1956, they forced a cutoff of new weapons. In 1957 they vetoed Eisenhower's plan to try personal diplomacy with Tito. In the case of Egypt, both the Truman and Eisenhower administrations constantly looked over their shoulders toward the pro-Israel posse; when Nasser's neutralism emerged, the ranks of the opposition swelled. Congressional complaints did not kill American funding of the Aswan Dam, but they greatly influenced the timing of its demise. Dulles commented to brother Allen on the afternoon of his announcement of withdrawal of funding: "If I don't do it Congress will chop it off tomorrow." Domestic politics also shaped the Middle East resolution, causing Eisenhower to cast his anti-Nasserist doctrine in anticommunist terms.[15]

IV

THE WISDOM of a foreign policy can be judged in various ways, but for the present purpose a four-part test will suffice. First, is the policy based on a realistic view of the world? That is, do the policymakers understand the forces—both foreign and domestic—at work in the situation at hand? Second, are the ends of the policy worth pursuing, and do they lie in the realm of the possible? In other words, does the policy point in the right direction and have a reasonable chance of reaching its goal? Third, are the means for pursuing these ends appropriate? Here the question is one of cost versus benefit: a prudent policy pays no more than necessary to accomplish its objectives. Finally, do the means achieve the desired ends? A policy need not be successful to be sound—sometimes success is not in the cards—but it helps.

Applied to India, Yugoslavia, and Egypt, the test yields broadly if not uniformly positive results. In each instance American policymakers perceived fairly clearly the forces at work. They understood Nehru's neutralism for what it was: a device to protect India's independence and expand India's freedom of maneuver by keeping the cold war out of South Asia. They early realized New Delhi would not join an anticommunist alliance. Although they underestimated the degree of strain the arming of Pakistan would engender in U.S.–Indian relations, they predicted accurately that the weapons deal would not throw Nehru into the Soviet camp. And eventually they came to the correct conclusion that a nonaligned India could serve the stability of Asia as well as or better than an India tied to the West.

Regarding Yugoslavia, American policymakers might sooner have detected the fissure in the Cominform; but once they discerned the reality of Tito's break they had little difficulty seeing its significance. They labored under no illusions that Tito's need for help made him intrinsically any friendlier toward the United States. They understood that collaboration between the two countries was entirely an alliance of convenience. Tito used the Americans for his purposes; the Americans used him for theirs.

The Egyptian case yields mixed results. Washington experienced difficulty determining that Nasser was the power behind Naguib for several months after the 1952 coup. The Eisenhower administration should have known before May 1953 that rumors of MEDO's death were not exaggerated. American officials might have guessed prior to Anderson's mission in 1956 that Nasser would not—in the context of Egyptian and Arab politics, perhaps could not—agree to a settlement the Israelis would buy. But Washington got the central issues of nationalism and neutralism right. For all the exasperation Nasser provoked, the Eisenhower administration understood that Egyptian neutralism was an expression of Arab nationalism and not of crypto-communism. Yet Nasser threatened the status quo in the Middle East, and by cracking the quo he certainly opened the door to Soviet involvement. Had Nasser succeeded in his pan-Arab aims, he would have used oil as a weapon against the West—as even conservative regimes have used it. Washington initially failed to appreciate the strength of the radical nationalist movement; on the other hand, the fact that the monarchies in Jordan and Saudi Arabia have survived for another three decades indicates that confidence in conservatism was not entirely misplaced. In any event, American policymakers revised their forecasts after the revolution in Iraq.

In terms of other forces impinging on policy, both the Truman and Eisenhower administrations understood the constraints relations with allies, especially the British, and the sensitivities of Congress placed upon their dealings with the third world. Did the administrations defer too much to London? Perhaps. But in any rational calculation of security interests, Britain, America's bridgehead in Europe, had to take precedence over India, Egypt, and all other countries. Did they cower before

Congress? Probably. For the Eisenhower administration particularly, an unwillingness to educate the country was a consistent failing. In numerous White House briefings and committee hearings, administration officials made their case for supporting the neutralists; but these exclusive sessions lacked the mobilizing power of some straightforward bully pulpiteering. Dulles was too afraid of becoming another Acheson, and by placating the right with his bombast he compounded his and the administration's problems. Eisenhower did not sufficiently appreciate that a president who leaves office more popular than he entered has probably failed to make full use of his political capital—as in the pursuit of development capital for India.

On the second issue, whether the ends of policy were possible and worth pursuing, the answers are complex. The fundamental complications arise from the fact that policy toward each country was part of larger regional and global policies. Assessing the objectives of policy toward India requires a judgment on the wisdom of an alliance-based containment of the Soviet Union. (One questioning the alliance with Pakistan might ask whether NATO was necessary.) Evaluating aid to Yugoslavia demands gauging the significance of Central Europe to American security. (Was Berlin worth a war?) As to Egypt: how badly did the Europeans require Middle Eastern oil? (And how much did the United States need Europe?) The answers here lie in the realm of the unknowable, since what American policies guarded against did not occur. Might the Russians have moved to the Gulf if the Baghdad system had not materialized? Absent American aid, would Tito have gone the way of Nagy? To whom would an oil-starved Europe have turned for help?

Also involved here is the more fundamental issue of cui bono: whose interests is American foreign policy supposed to serve? What do American policymakers owe themselves, their constituents, the world at large? Ought they be expected to make decisions that will lead to their own rejection? Should Acheson have braved the "massacre" he predicted for another India-aid request? Is majoritarianism a rational principle in foreign policy? Was Eisenhower right to drop Tito from his guest list when Congress objected? What weight does one assign to the interests of other countries and their inhabitants in evaluating American policy? Assuming the alliance with Pakistan did help hold the Middle East for the West, does this offset its undeniable effect in raising tensions in the subcontinent, contributing to an arms race and eventually war? Letting Tito be Tito no doubt increased his attractiveness to other national communists, but it did little good for the Yugoslav people. Should Washington have been more respectful of Arab nationalism as an honest expression of the self-determining aspirations of millions of people? Put bluntly, must American interests, however defined, come first simply because the United States has the capacity to enforce those interests?

These are cosmic questions, requiring deep reflection; on narrower grounds, fortunately, conclusions flow more readily. Regarding India, the basic goal was to keep that country out of the Soviet sphere. This goal was worth pursuing and, as events proved, entirely possible. Active cooperation on New Delhi's part would have been nice but was not essential. For Yugoslavia, similar remarks apply. Tito's thirty divisions counted for much merely by leaving the ranks of the East bloc. Preserving this defection was desirable and possible. Militarily, overt collaboration would have helped even more, but politically it would have diminished Tito's drawing power with potential emulators. As to Egypt, the initial aim was active cooperation in regional defense. This was desirable and not unreasonable, but it turned out to be impossible. The same can be said of subsequent efforts to achieve an Israeli-Egyptian settlement. Regarding the underlying objective—an Egypt closely tied to the West—this proved impossible. Considering Nasser's character and ambitions it may even have been unreasonable. But until Nasser demonstrated its unreasonableness, one could never know. Anyway, when its impossibility became apparent, American leaders reduced their aims and contented themselves with trying to get along with a neutral and independent Egypt.

Were the means appropriate to achieve these goals; did the benefits outweigh the costs? In the case of India, the direct costs were principally the sums spent on economic aid. As policymakers recognized from the first and Congress later came to realize, funds devoted to Indian development were monies well spent. The chief indirect cost was the fallout from the Pakistan alliance. Between the United States and India, this part of the bill entailed mostly hard feelings, which matter, but in themselves not much. Doubtless the pact with Karachi helped the Kremlin gain a foothold in India. This would have come in any event, since Nehru would not have accepted American aid without balancing Soviet help. The American alliance with Pakistan certainly strained relations between Pakistan and India; by impelling New Delhi to spend more on weapons American leaders undid some of their own work in promoting Indian development. In addition they made life difficult for lots of people in the subcontinent, including those who died when the tensions flared into war. The costs of these deaths to America cannot be calculated; the exercise is repugnant.

The means of supporting Tito's independence—diplomatic, economic, and military aid—were appropriate to the goal. Whether Belgrade would have fallen back into Stalin's snares without American aid is unclear; but the insurance the aid bought was not exorbitantly priced. Hungarian general Béla Király suggests that the vigorous American response to the North Korean invasion of South Korea was as important in deterring Stalin from attacking Yugoslavia as American actions toward Yugoslavia per se. If this is true, the insurance was unnecessary. But most insurance is, and a bit extra rarely hurts. Backing Tito took a toll in American credibility, as critics of aid to Yugoslavia continually reminded. Should the last, best hope for humanity underwrite a repressive regime? Was it not important to bring clean hands to the bar of world opinion? Fortunately for Tito's supporters, the appeal to ideals also cut the other way. The United States opposes aggression and defends the right of small countries to national independence. However checkered Tito's record domestically, Yugoslavia as a country deserved to stand free from Soviet hegemony and the threat of Soviet invasion.[16]

Depending on who is accounting, the costs of opposing Nasser included or did not include the Suez affair. Beyond the deaths and destruction of the invasion, the 1956 fiasco helped set the one-war-per-decade pattern that has marked the Arab-Israeli struggle since 1948. An additional cost to the United States was the near rupture of relations with America's two most important allies. Finally, Suez led to the Eisenhower Doctrine, which produced the invasion of Lebanon in 1958, which proved worse than useless. The operation failed to achieve its goal of salvaging the status quo (although the concomitant British intervention in Jordan helped Hussein keep his crown) and it cast Americans in the same unfavorable—albeit less intense—light that illuminated Britain and France at Suez. That Chamoun invited the American marines convinced many only that he had been bought.

On the final test—whether the policies achieved their goals—the results are also mixed. India remained beyond the Kremlin's orbit, although the United States could hardly claim credit. Nehru never became as helpful internationally as Washington desired, but this resulted less from anything American leaders did or left undone than from the fact that India's objectives were not America's. Tito kept his distance from Moscow, even after Stalin died. Again non-American factors weighed more than Washington's actions, although the latter were not insignificant, if only because they put the Kremlin on notice that the United States would object, to a degree kept tactically obscure, to forcible efforts at reamalgamation. While Titoism proved a bust for Eastern Europe, as Eisenhower left office the long-awaited spread of the Tito "virus" to China was just becoming apparent—although the Sino-Soviet split had almost nothing to do with Tito or the United States.

In Egypt, the policy of maintaining a pro-Western status quo failed utterly. As remarked above, failure alone does not demonstrate the unsoundness of a policy; sometimes wisdom lies in making the best of a bad situation. Eisenhower and Dulles did not make the best of this bad situation, as the Lebanon affair demonstrated. But neither did they make the worst: they might have joined the Suez invaders. To their credit, when they recognized their failure they changed course.

On balance and considering the complications involved, American policy toward India, Yugoslavia, and Egypt turned out about as well as could have been expected. Relations with the three countries, Egypt especially, might have been smoother; yet smoothness is not an end in itself. While American leaders committed mistakes, these generally resulted less from clouded perceptions, and less still from a rigid application of anticommunist ideology, than from the problems created by an honest clash of interests. Where fault existed, it usually lay not in the protagonists but in their stars.

EPILOGUE
From Bandung to Stanleyville

THE THIRD world of the 1980s differs significantly from the third world of the 1950s. While political nonalignment, or aspiration thereto, tended to distinguish the original "tiers monde," economic underdevelopment has increasingly become the common denominator of the group. The emphasis changed most noticeably during the early 1960s, as dozens of impoverished African states joined the movement; indeed, the shift was beginning by the time Eisenhower left office.

During the late summer of 1960, while Eisenhower conferred with Nehru, Tito, and Nasser at the UN, international attention focused on troubling events in the Congo. At the beginning of the previous year the government of the Belgian colony had announced a timetable for devolution, leading ultimately to independence after several years. But the winds of change buffeting the continent had fanned nationalist and tribal violence in the Congo, and the timetable collapsed. Belgians in the colony decamped for the metropolis while contenders for the succession jostled for position. Frightened and disillusioned at the incipient chaos in what they had considered their model colony, Belgian leaders cut and ran, tossing independence over their shoulder in June 1960.

Self-rule merely heightened the confusion. Even had it been willing, the new regime proved unable to guarantee the personal safety and property of the tens of thousands of Belgian nationals still in the Congo;

consequently Brussels dispatched a force of paratroopers in July, invading the country it had set free only weeks before. Needless to say, the reoccupation inflamed matters further. When Belgian copper interests backed a secessionist movement in Katanga province against the government of Prime Minister Patrice Lumumba and President Joseph Kasavubu, Lumumba appealed first to the United Nations and then to Moscow for aid. The UN was slower to respond than the Soviets, who dispatched equipment and advisers at once. By the time a UN contingent arrived Lumumba denounced it as a tool of the imperialists.

The prospect of a Russian presence in the mineral-rich heart of Africa, until recently under the secure control of the West, had much the same effect on the Eisenhower administration as Egypt's earlier efforts toward nonalignment. At an August meeting of the National Security Council Eisenhower declared it "simply inconceivable" that Lumumba and his Soviet allies should be able to block the UN troops. "We are talking of one man forcing us out of the Congo," the president said, "of Lumumba supported by the Soviets." As Eisenhower had sought to frustrate Nasser's designs, so he authorized efforts to undermine Lumumba. This time he turned directly to the CIA. During the next three months agency operatives, on orders from Washington, plotted various means of assassinating Lumumba. Even after Kasavubu sacked Lumumba and the former prime minister handed himself over to the UN for protection against his erstwhile colleagues, the administration feared a comeback. Lumumba's persuasive skills were well known. "He had this tremendous ability to stir up a crowd or a group," Undersecretary of State Dillon commented afterward. "And if he could have gotten out and started to talk to a battalion of the Congolese Army, he probably would have had them in the palm of his hand in five minutes." Lumumba's supporters in the area of Stanleyville had proclaimed an independent, pro-Soviet republic; should the former premier make it to Stanleyville he would pose a greater threat than ever.

Until the end of November the CIA did its best to murder Lumumba, but he remained out of sight, surrounded by both Congolese enemies and UN protectors. On the night of November 27 Lumumba slipped through the double ring of troops. In the middle of a raging thunderstorm he climbed into a darkened car and sped off toward Stanleyville.

He never arrived. Arrested at some point along the way by government soldiers, he was imprisoned and killed early in 1961. The CIA apparently had little to do with the final deed, but it certainly applauded the result. "Thanks for Patrice," an agency officer wrote after Lumumba's arrest. "If we had known he was coming we would have baked a snake." [1]

Washington's reaction to events in the Congo was hardly unique, although responses to instability did not always include assassination attempts. American Congo policy was of a piece with opposition to Nasser from 1956 to 1958, and with other efforts in various parts of the world to guarantee a favorable status quo against attack. In Iran in 1953 Washington conspired to bring down the government of Mohamed Mosadeq; in Guatemala in 1954 the target was Jacobo Arbenz Guzman; in 1958 the CIA backed an abortive revolt against Indonesian President Sukarno. Castro's rise in Cuba provoked political and economic pressure and covert operations ranging from Mafia contracts on Castro's life to a paramilitary invasion. As the 1960s wore on, American troops by the thousands occupied the Dominican Republic; by the hundreds of thousands they fought in South Vietnam. Later efforts to preserve a favored position for the United States included the sabotage of the Chilean economy under Salvadore Allende Gossens, the invasion of Grenada, and pressure on the Sandinista government of Nicaragua by nearly all means short of direct military intervention.

The thread uniting these campaigns of opposition is an American desire to keep as much of the world as possible under friendly control. Most of the individuals and groups contesting for control were leftists or had ties to the left; this was inevitable where the left offered the only alternative to regimes dominated by a pro-American right. But Mosadeq in Iran, Arbenz in Guatemala, Sukarno in Indonesia—to name three— were no more communists than were Nehru and Nasser, and far less than Tito, as Washington knew full well. Their crime was not adherence to Marxism-Leninism but a refusal to remain within a Western sphere of influence, which seemed to American officials the only proof against Soviet encroachment.

As the foregoing chapters demonstrate, Washington's ability to get along with Nehru and Tito, and its troubles with Nasser, had almost nothing to do with ideology and everything to do with geopolitics. The same holds true for relations with other countries. Had India and Yugoslavia, and Egypt after 1959, continued to typify the third world, American leaders would have experienced a much easier time during the 1960s and later. But as independence swept across Africa, poverty, often accompanied by the turmoil that wracked the Congo, became the characteristic feature of countries beyond the great blocs, and a North-South split superimposed itself on the East-West divide. Metaphorically, Stanleyville supplanted Bandung as defining the third world. In these new circumstances defending the status quo became a never-ending task.

India and Yugoslavia, and Egypt by Eisenhower's last years in office, shared at least some stake in the status quo. With such countries Washington could work out a modus vivendi. But the third world of the 1960s and after was a world predominantly of have-not nations. Impatient at their peoples' poverty and at the unwillingness of the West to cut them a larger piece of the pie, leaders like Lumumba naturally turned to the Soviet Union for help.

For the United States calmly to accommodate the demands of the newcomers was nearly impossible. It is not in the nature of empires, whether democratic and informal or otherwise, to cede territory and relinquish power gracefully; a step in any direction from the top of the mountain is a step down. The fact that the United States is a democratic republic simply made it more difficult to accept change than it would have been for a nation with a less representative political system. As the preceding pages make clear, the greatest resistance to accommodation of the third world came from Congress, which on this matter probably reflected the views of the American people. Far more than the Truman and Eisenhower administrations, conservatives in the legislature insisted on treating neutralists as fellow-travelers and worse. Administration officials were not innocent of calling up the communist bogey when it suited their purposes, or of branding neutralism as immoral. But their overall sophistication and flexibility were not matched on Capitol Hill, where opposition to any regime even slightly left of center remained the rule among powerful groups. By the time Congress finally got used to the likes of Nehru, the third world he represented was giving way to one more radical.

The crux of America's problem with the third world—an essential difficulty facing American leaders since 1947—is that the postwar status quo suited the United States better than it did any other country. For all its deficiencies, Yalta attempted to lock in the status quo. The third world, whether defined in terms of Bandung or of Stanleyville, represented a rejection of Yalta and of that status quo. The Truman and Eisenhower administrations succeeded, not without missteps, in dealing with the issues Bandung raised. To their successors they left the challenge of Stanleyville.

NOTES

In the following citations, only short labels and titles are given for manuscript collections and published works. Locations of collections, full titles, publishers, and the like are included in the section on sources cited.

For the sake of readability, understood words and punctuation omitted from telegraphic communications have been reinserted. Likewise, nontransparent abbreviations have been expanded.

Many of the cables and memoranda referred to can be found in more than one location, for example at the Truman Library and the National Archives. In addition, as time passes and more volumes of the *Foreign Relations* series appear, increasing numbers of documents are coming into print. No effort has been made below to indicate the multiplicity of locations in which particular items can be found.

Introduction

1. Finer, *Dulles over Suez*, 42; Hoopes, *Devil and Dulles*, 316; Neff, *Warriors at Suez*, 77. A rare, more sophisticated analysis, but one based primarily on textual criticism rather than on an examination of the (then generally unavailable) archival record, is Guhin, *Dulles*, 252–264.

2. *New Republic*, Aug. 6, 1956; Banerjee, *Nonaligned Movement*, 10–11; Jackson, *Nonaligned, the UN, and the Superpowers*, 14; Sengupta, *Non-Alignment*, dedication.

3. Gurtov, *United States Against the Third World*, 203–204; Barnet, *Intervention and Revolution*, 9–10; Kolko, *Confronting the Third World*, 62. Read-

ers looking for other general treatments of American policy toward the third world during this period should consult especially Packenham, *Liberal America and the Third World;* Girling, *America and the Third World;* Gurtov and Maghroori, *Roots of Failure;* and Shafer, *Deadly Paradigms.*

4. Wolpert, *Roots of Confrontation in South Asia,* 140–142; Stookey, *America and the Arab States,* 148–149, 157; Paterson, *Meeting the Communist Threat,* 190.

5. Noer, *Cold War and Black Liberation,* 35–36; LaFeber, *Inevitable Revolutions,* 143; Immerman, *CIA in Guatemala,* 16–19. McMahon, "Eisenhower and Third World Nationalism," surveys recent literature covering the 1950s.

6. Rao, *Non-Alignment in International Law and Politics,* 18–23; Brecher, "Neutralism," 225; Lyon, *Neutralism,* 15–16; Sayegh, "Anatomy of Neutralism," 1–2.

1. Laissez Faire, 1947–1950

1. Background on American perceptions of India can be found in Rosinger, *India and the United States;* Vyas, *Dawning on the Capitol;* Brown, *United States and India, Pakistan, Bangladesh;* Isaacs, *Scratches on Our Minds;* Hess, *America Encounters India;* and Palmer, *United States and India.* Hess's book includes a valuable, if now slightly dated, bibliography of published works dealing with pre-World War II relations between the two countries. More up-to-date and more concerned with the postwar period is the same author's "Global Expansion and Regional Balances."

2. The best source on the American reaction to the Quit India movement is Venkataramani and Shrivastava, *Quit India.* See also the same authors' *Roosevelt, Gandhi, Churchill.*

3. Venkataramani and Shrivastava, *Quit India,* 78.

4. Hess, *America Encounters India,* 95.

5. Department of State *Bulletin,* March 9, 1947, 450; State Department to London, April 4, 1947, State Department decimal file 845.00/3–2747, record group (RG) 59.

6. *Bulletin,* June 22, 1947, 1249–1250. For a more thorough treatment of the American role in Indian independence, see, in addition to the works by Venkataramani and Shrivastava, Hope, *America and Swaraj.*

7. New Delhi to State Department, Oct. 5, 1947, 845.00/10–547, RG 59; State Department to London, Nov. 14, 1947, 845.00/11–1047, RG 59.

8. Henderson to Lovett, Oct. 8, 1947, 845.00/10–847, RG 59; State Department to New Delhi, Oct. 9, 1947, 845.00/10–947, RG 59; New Delhi to State Department, Nov. 10, 1947, 845.00/11–1047, RG 59.

9. Statement by Lord Ismay at Joint Defense Council meeting, Aug. 6, 1947, DEFE 11/31, British Defense Ministry records. This file also contains various memoranda outlining Britain's options in the event of Indian withdrawal from the Commonwealth.

10. London to State Department, Oct. 10, 1947, 845.00/10–1047, RG 59.

11. New Delhi to State Department, Oct. 25, 1947, 845.00/10–2547, RG 59; memorandum of conversation, Dec. 26, 1947, 845.00/12–2647, RG 59.

12. New Delhi to State Department, June 27, 1947, 845.00/6–2747, RG 59; New Delhi to State Department, Sept. 2, 1947, 102.78/9–247, RG 59; New Delhi to State Department, Sept. 3, 1947, 845.01/9–347, RG 59.

13. New Delhi to State Department, Sept. 3, 1947, 845.01/9–347, RG 59; State Department to New Delhi, Oct. 3, 1947, 102.78/10–347, RG 59.

14. Memorandum of conversation, Dec. 26, 1947, 845.00/12–2647, RG 59.

15. Grady to Bechtel, Oct. 16, 1947, Grady papers.

16. Memorandum of conversation, Dec. 26, 1947, 845.00/12–2647, RG 59.

17. Nehru quoted in Burke, *Mainsprings,* 93; Pillai, *India's Foreign Policy,* 28.

18. Heimsath and Mansingh, *Diplomatic History of Modern India,* 55–81, 350–351.

19. The 25,000 was a CIA estimate: Hillenkoetter to Forrestal, Jan. 14, 1949, CD 6–2–7, Office of the Secretary of Defense (OSD) records, RG 330.

20. On the U.S. role in the Kashmir dispute, see Talbot and Poplai, *India and America,* 71–86; and Lamb, *Kashmir Problem,* passim.

21. "India's Future in Relations with the Commonwealth," March 14, 1949, C.P. (49) 58, British Cabinet records.

22. Memorandum of conversation, Jan. 10, 1947, 501.BC/1–1048, RG 59.

23. State Department to New Delhi, March 4, 1948, 745.45F/3–448, RG 59.

24. Memorandum of conversation, Jan. 10, 1948, 501.BC/1–1048, RG 59.

25. Henderson to Lovett, Jan. 9, 1948, 501.BC/1–948, RG 59.

26. CIA report ORE 2 49: "Review of the World Situation," Feb. 16, 1949, President's secretary's file, Truman papers.

27. SANACC (State-Army-Navy-Air Force Coordinating Committee) 360/14, March 30, 1949, SWNCC (State-War-Navy Coordinating Committee) files, RG 353. On the nature of Britain's continued connections with the Indian military, see file DEFE 7/106 and subsequent files in British Defense Ministry records, and file DO 133/14 in British Dominions Office records.

28. Memorandum from joint chiefs of staff, March 24, 1949, RG 353.

29. CIA report ORE 93–49: "The Possibility of Britain's Abandonment of Overseas Military Commitments," Dec. 23, 1949, President's secretary's file, Truman papers.

30. *New Republic,* Oct. 10, 1949; *Newsweek,* Oct. 17, 1949; *Time,* Oct. 17, 1949; *Nation,* Oct. 22, 1949.

31. *New York Times,* Oct. 11 and 13, 1949; *Washington Post,* Oct. 11, 1949; *New York Post,* Oct. 14, 1949.

32. *Congressional Record* 95 (1949), A5445–A5446, A6581, A6409, A6463.

33. McGhee, *Envoy,* 52; *Congressional Record* 95 (1949), A2374, 14230.

34. On the administration's embarrassment at the Nehru-induced hoopla, see British embassy in Washington to Foreign Office, Oct. 1, 1949, FO371/F13432, British Foreign Office records. Grady to Henderson, Aug. 9, 1947, 845.00/8–947, RG 59.

35. Henderson to Acheson, quoted without date in background memorandum on Nehru visit, Oct. 3, 1949, President's secretary's file, Truman papers.

36. State Department OIR report 5052, Oct. 4, 1949, 845.002/10–549, RG 59.

37. Henderson quoted in British high commissioner in India to Foreign Office, Dec. 9, 1949, FO371/F18771, Foreign Office records; McGhee, *Envoy*, 47.

38. Acheson, *Present at the Creation*, 334–336.

39. Moraes, *Nehru*, 471; attachment to CIA memorandum by Hillenkoetter, Dec. 20, 1949, President's secretary's file, Truman papers.

40. Memorandum of conversation, Oct. 12, 1949, Acheson papers (Truman Library).

41. Memorandum of conversation, Oct. 19, 1949, 845.002/10–1949, RG 59.

42. NSC 48/1, Dec. 23, 1949, NSC records, RG 273.

43. NSC 48/2 with cover letter by Souers, Dec. 30, 1949, RG 273.

44. McGhee to Acheson, Jan. 6, 1950, 690D.91/1–650, RG 59; Acheson to Bevin in State Department to London, ibid.; Acheson to Bevin in State Department to London, Feb. 13, 1950, 357.AB/2–1350, RG 59.

45. British high commissioner in Pakistan to Dominions Office, Jan. 10, 1950, DO 134/10; memorandum of conversation, March 28, 1950, 357.AB/3–2850, RG 59.

46. Mansingh, "India and the United States," 162; Pandit, *Scope of Happiness,* 258. On Indian policy during the Korean war, see also Gopal, *Nehru,* vol. 2, ch. 5; Kaushik, *Crucial Years;* Heimsath and Mansingh, *Diplomatic History of Modern India,* 66–74.

47. New Delhi to State Department, June 27 and 28, 1950, *FRUS* 50:7, 204–206, 218–220.

48. New Delhi to State Department, June 29, 1950, 795.00/6–2950, RG 59.

49. Moscow to State Department, June 29, 1950, 795.00/6–2950, RG 59; Menon quoted in Reid, *Envoy to Nehru,* 193.

50. State Department to Moscow, July 3, 1950, *FRUS* 50:7, 294; New Delhi to State Department, July 28, 1950, 691.00/7–2850, RG 59.

51. *New York Times,* July 4, 1950; New Delhi to State Department, July 5, 1950, 791.00/7–550, RG 59.

52. Gopal, *Nehru,* 2:102; Nehru to Acheson in Pandit to Acheson, July 17, 1950, 330/7–1750, RG 59.

53. Memorandum of conversation, July 28, 1950, *FRUS* 50:7, 490, n. 1.

54. Acheson to Nehru in State Department to New Delhi, July 25, 1950, 795.00/7–2550, RG 59; Nehru to Acheson, July 30, 1950, 795.00/7–3050, RG 59.

55. State Department to New Delhi, July 22, 1950, 795.00/7–2250, RG 59.

56. State Department to New Delhi, Sept. 16, 1950, 330/9–450, RG 59; New Delhi to State Department, Sept. 18, 1950, 795.00/9–1850, RG 59.

57. New Delhi to State Department, July 28, 1950, 795B.00/7–2850, RG 59; memorandum of conversation, Sept. 27, 1950, 795.00/9–2750, RG 59.

58. Panikkar, *In Two Chinas,* 109–111; New Delhi to State Department, Sept. 28, 1950, *FRUS* 50:7, 808–810.

59. Truman, *Memoirs,* 2:362; State Department to New Delhi, Oct. 4, 1950, *FRUS* 50:7, 875–876.

60. New Delhi to State Department, Oct. 6, 1950, *FRUS* 50:7, 886; New Delhi to State Department, Oct. 6, 1950, ibid., 889; New Delhi to State Department, Oct. 7, 1950, ibid., 901.

61. New Delhi to State Department, Oct. 10, 1950, *FRUS* 50:7, 921; UN mission to State Department, Dec. 4, 1950, ibid., 1379–1380.

62. Donovan, *Tumultuous Years,* 308; Nehru, *Speeches,* 418.

63. Memorandum of telephone conversation, Dec. 3, 1950, 795.00/12–350, RG 59; State Department to New Delhi, Dec. 4, 1950, *FRUS* 50:7, 1358–1359.

64. On the Indian role in achieving a truce, see for example Heimsath and Mansingh, *Diplomatic History of Modern India,* 70–74.

65. CIA report 6–49: "Review of the World Situation," June 15, 1949, President's secretary's file, Truman papers; memorandum of conversation, Sept. 18, 1950, 780.00/9–1850, RG 59.

2. Write-Off: 1951–1954

1. National Intelligence Estimate NIE-3: "Soviet Intentions and Capabilities," Nov. 15, 1950, President's secretary's file, Truman papers.

2. NSC 98, Jan. 5, 1951, RG 273.

3. Joint chiefs of staff to secretary of defense, Jan. 16, 1951, President's secretary's file, Truman papers; minutes of 80th NSC meeting, Jan. 18, 1951, ibid.; NSC 98/1, Jan. 22, 1951, RG 273.

4. Noel-Baker in Commonwealth Relations Office to New Delhi, Dec. 27, 1951, DO 133/72, Dominions Office records.

5. Report of South Asian conference, Feb. 26–March 3, 1951, McGhee papers, 7–10.

6. Ibid., 17–19; notes for Ceylon conference, undated (Feb. 1951), Henderson papers.

7. Report of South Asian conference, Feb. 26–March 3, 1951, McGhee papers, 1–3.

8. Memorandum of conversation, March 8, 1951, McGhee papers.

9. Memorandum of conversation, Dec. 16, 1950, Acheson papers (Truman Library). McMahon discusses the 1951 India aid bill in "Food as a Diplomatic Weapon."

10. Memorandum by Fluker: "The Indian Food Crisis," Jan. 15, 1951, *FRUS* 51:6, 2085.

11. Memorandum by McGhee: "Indian Request for Food Grains: Political Considerations," Jan. 24, 1951, *FRUS* 51:6, 2103.

12. Senate, *Executive Sessions,* vol. 3, pt. 1, 27–29.

13. Ibid., 31–32.

14. Ibid., 32, 39.

15. Ibid., 33–34.

16. Ibid., 34.

17. Ibid., 37–39.

18. Ibid., 43.

19. Ibid., 35, 39, 43.

20. Ibid., 45–46.

21. Memorandum of conversation, Feb. 1, 1951, *FRUS* 51:6, 2106–2107; message to Congress, Feb. 12, 1951, *Public Papers,* 149–152; Hoover quoted in McMahon, "Food as a Diplomatic Weapon," 364.

22. New Delhi to State Department, Feb. 21, 1951, *FRUS* 51:6, 2118.

23. House of Representatives, *Hearings on the India Emergency Assistance Act of 1951;* Senate, *Executive Sessions,* 3:368.

24. Senate, *Executive Sessions,* 3:369.

25. Ibid., 370–377.

26. Ibid., 373.

27. Ibid., 493–494, 383, 497–498.

28. *New York Times,* May 2, 1951; Senate, *Executive Sessions,* 3:460.

29. Nehru in Brecher, *Nehru,* 566; Dutt, *With Nehru,* 240. Further assessment of the negative fallout of the aid bill can be found in McMahon, "Food as a Diplomatic Weapon."

30. Government of India note to United States, Aug. 23, 1951, *Bulletin,* 25 (1951), 385.

31. *New York Times,* Aug. 28, 1951.

32. New Delhi to State Department, June 23, 1950, 791.00/6–2350, RG 59; New Delhi to State Department, Sept. 6, 1951, 611.91/9–651, RG 59.

33. New Delhi to State Department, Sept. 6, 1951, 611.91/9–651, RG 59.

34. Gopal, *Nehru,* 2:137–138; Heimsath and Mansingh, *Diplomatic History of Modern India,* 354, 491.

35. Heimsath and Mansingh, *Diplomatic History of Modern India,* 60–65; Burke, *Mainsprings,* 144–153.

36. "Means to Combat India's Policy of Neutralism," Aug. 30, 1951, *FRUS* 51:6, 2172–2174.

37. NIE 23, Sept. 4, 1951, President's secretary's file, Truman papers.

38. On the back-channel suggestion, see British high commissioner in India to Commonwealth Relations Office, Feb. 16, 1951, FO371/FL10345, Foreign Office records. Sulzberger, *Long Row of Candles,* 791; Bombay *Current,* Sept. 5, 1951, clipping in Henderson papers.

39. Senate, *Executive Sessions,* 3:416–419.

40. Ibid., 417–419.

41. Ibid., 420, 439–441, 493, 409–410; *Congressional Record* 95 (1951), 12848–12851.

42. British embassy in Washington to Commonwealth Relations Office, Dec. 15, 1953, FO371/FL10345, Foreign Office records; Pandit, *Scope of Happiness,* 261.

43. Acheson to Bowles, Dec. 31, 1959, Acheson papers (Yale); New Delhi to State Department, Dec. 6, 1951, *FRUS* 51:6, 2191–2201; Bowles to Austin, Dec. 29, 1951, Bowles papers.

44. State Department to New Delhi, Jan. 14, 1952, *FRUS* 51:6, 2202, n. 5.

45. Senate, *Executive Sessions,* 4:62.

46. Ibid., 64–68.

47. Ibid., 76, 85.

48. Ibid., 85–89.

49. Berry to Matthews, Feb. 8, 1952, *FRUS* 52–54:11, 1634–1635.

50. Bowles to Bajpai, June 22, 1952, Bowles papers; memorandum of conversation, June 9, 1952, Acheson papers (Truman Library).

51. Dulles to Eisenhower, Nov. 14, 1952, John Foster Dulles papers (Princeton).

52. Bowles to Dulles, March 10, 1952, ibid.; New Delhi to State Department, Feb. 5, 1953, International series, Eisenhower papers.

53. Minutes of special NSC meeting, March 31, 1953, NSC series, Eisenhower papers.

54. Wiley to Dulles, April 14, 1953, 611.91/4–1453, RG 59.

55. Nanda, éd., *Indian Foreign Policy,* 4; Heimsath and Mansingh, *Diplomatic History of Modern India,* 328–329; Menon, *Many Worlds,* 292. Reston in Hoopes, *Devil and Dulles,* 311.

56. Dulles to Eisenhower in Karachi to State Department, May 22, 1953, Dulles-Herter series, Eisenhower papers.

57. See ch. 7 below.

58. Dulles to Eisenhower in Karachi to State Department, May 22, 1953, Dulles-Herter series, Eisenhower papers. For a brief account of this conversation from the Indian side, see Gopal, *Nehru,* 2:184.

59. New Delhi to State Department, May 29, 1953, 611.91/5–2953, RG 59; British high commissioner to Commonwealth Relations Office, May 29, 1953, FO371/FL10345, Foreign Office records.

60. Brecher, *Nehru,* 582; Gopal, *Nehru,* 2:186–190.

61. Minutes of 147th NSC meeting, June 1, 1953, NSC series, Eisenhower papers; Menon, *Flying Troika,* 38.

62. NIE–79, June 30, 1953, *FRUS* 52–54:11, 1072–1088.

63. NSC 155/1, July 14, 1953, RG 273. On the development of American strategy toward Pakistan, see Brands, "India and Pakistan in American Strategic Planning"; and McMahon, "United States Cold War Strategy in South Asia."

64. New Delhi to State Department, July 28, 1953, *FRUS* 52–54:11, 1700.

65. Ibid., 1700–1702; State Department to New Delhi, Aug. 3, 1953, ibid., 1706–1708.

66. State Department to New Delhi, Sept. 3, 1953, *FRUS* 52–54:11, 1717–1718.

67. Stassen to Dulles, July 2, 1954, with attachments, *FRUS* 52–54:11, 1762–1764.

68. Karachi to State Department, July 24, 1953, 611.90D/7–2453, RG 59;

2. Write-Off: 1951–1954

British embassy in Washington to Foreign Office, Oct. 9, 1953, FO371/FY1192, Foreign Office records; Bowles, *Promises,* 478; Venkataramani, *American Role in Pakistan,* 222–224; Barnds, *India, Pakistan, and the Great Powers,* 95; Harrison, *Widening Gulf,* 266.

69. Memorandum of conversation, Oct. 7, 1953, 611.91/10–753, RG 59.

70. Nixon, *RN,* 131–132.

71. Minutes of 176th NSC meeting, Dec. 16, 1953, NSC series, Eisenhower papers.

72. Bowles, *Promises,* 477–481; Dudley to Dulles, Dec. 24, 1953, 611.91/12–2453, RG 59; New Delhi to State Department, Jan. 12, 1954, *FRUS* 52–54, 1731; memorandum of conversation, Jan. 27, 1954, 611.91/1–2754, RG 59; British Commonwealth Relations Office to embassy in Washington, Nov. 9, 1953, FO371/FY1192, Foreign Office records; Commonwealth Relations Office to high commissioners in India and Pakistan, Nov. 12, 1953, FO371/FY1192, Foreign Office records; Nehru to Eisenhower, Dec. 10, 1953, White House memoranda series, Dulles papers (Eisenhower Library).

73. State Department to Karachi, Jan. 8, 1954, 611.90D/1–854; Dulles to Eisenhower, undated (January 1954), White House memoranda series, Dulles papers (Eisenhower Library).

74. Dulles to Eisenhower, undated (January 1954), White House memoranda series, Dulles papers (Eisenhower Library).

75. Memorandum of conversation, Jan. 5, 1954, White House memoranda series, Dulles papers (Eisenhower Library).

76. Eisenhower to Nehru in State Department to New Delhi, Feb. 18, 1954, International series, Eisenhower papers.

77. New Delhi to State Department, Feb. 24, 1954, 611.91/2–2454, RG 59; State Department to Rangoon, Feb. 25, 1954, 611.91/2–2554, RG 59.

3. A Virtue of Necessity: 1954–1960

1. *New York Times,* Feb. 19, 1954.

2. "U.S. Position on Participation in the Indochina Phase of the Geneva Conference," March 24, 1954, *FRUS* 52–54:16, 481.

3. Menon, *Flying Troika,* 74; Nehru quoted in Sardesai, "India and Southeast Asia," 87; *New York Times,* April 24, 1954.

4. New Delhi to State Department, April 25, 1954, *FRUS* 52–54:13, 1406–1408.

5. As reported, on the basis of an official transcript provided by the Ceylonese government, in Colombo to State Department, April 29, 1954, *FRUS* 52–54:16, 610–611.

6. Stelle to Bowie, April 30, 1954, *FRUS* 52–54:16, 635–638.

7. Geneva to State Department, May 22, 1954, 396.1GE/5–2254, RG 59.

8. State Department to Geneva, May 22, 1954, *FRUS* 52–54:16, 889–890.

9. Moraes, *Nehru,* 453; Harrison, ed., *India and the United States,* 36; Reid, *Envoy to Nehru,* 181–182; Dutt, *With Nehru,* 241; Jha, *Bandung to Tashkent,* 74; Menon, *Many Worlds,* 221.

10. Dulles to Eisenhower, March 14, 1955, Dulles-Herter series, Eisenhower papers; memorandum of conversation, June 20, 1955, White House memoranda series, Dulles papers (Eisenhower Library).

11. Diary entry, July 14, 1955, Diary series, Eisenhower papers.

12. Quoted in Brecher, *India and World Politics,* 190.

13. Dulles backgrounder in Geneva to State Department, April 25, 1954, 396.1GE/4–2554, RG 59; Dulles to Eisenhower, March 14, 1955, Dulles-Herter series, Eisenhower papers.

14. Geneva to State Department, May 25, 1954, 396.1GE/5–2554, RG 59.

15. U.S. delegation in Geneva to State Department, May 26, 1954, *FRUS* 52–54:16, 931–933.

16. U.S. delegation to State Department, June 5, 1954, *FRUS* 52–54:16, 1045.

17. Gopal, *Nehru,* 2:195; Heimsath and Mansingh, *Diplomatic History,* 191–192; Sardesai, "India and Southeast Asia," 87–88.

18. Johnson, *Right Hand,* 222; Geneva to State Department, July 13, 1954, 396.1GE/7–1354, RG 59.

19. NSC 5409, Feb. 19, 1954, RG 273.

20. The evolution of the Eisenhower administration's attitude on foreign aid is a main theme of Kaufman's *Trade and Aid.* See also Rostow, *Eisenhower, Kennedy, and Foreign Aid.* On India particularly, the best work is Merrill, "Bread and the Ballot."

21. Millikan to Jackson, Nov. 12, 1954, Jackson papers; Kaufman, *Trade and Aid,* 49–51; Rostow, *Eisenhower, Kennedy, and Foreign Aid,* ch. 6; Cook, *Declassified Eisenhower,* 298ff.; Jackson to Rockefeller, Nov. 10, 1955, Jackson papers; Jackson to Dulles, Aug. 3, 1954, General correspondence series, Dulles papers (Eisenhower Library). On Soviet aid to the third world, see Becker, "The Soviet Union and the Third World."

22. Dulles to Jackson, Aug. 24, 1954, Jackson papers.

23. Ibid.

24. Eisenhower to Dulles, Dec. 5, 1955, White House memoranda series, Dulles papers (Eisenhower Library).

25. *Public Papers,* 404–414.

26. Kaufman, *Trade and Aid,* 55; *Congressional Record* 101 (1955), 11264–11265.

27. Gopal, *Nehru,* 2:166.

28. *New York Times,* Feb. 26, 1955.

29. Dulles to Eisenhower in Rangoon to State Department, Feb. 26, 1955, Dulles-Herter series, Eisenhower papers.

30. Dulles to Adams, March 31, 1955, White House memoranda series, Dulles papers (Eisenhower Library).

31. *Congressional Record* 101 (1955), 4144.

32. Memorandum of telephone conversation, April 1, 1955, Telephone calls series, Dulles papers (Eisenhower Library); *Bulletin*, May 2, 1955, 728.

33. Jha, *Bandung to Tashkent*, 64–65.

34. Kahin, *Asian-African Conference*, 15–29.

35. Menon in Brecher, *India and World Politics*, 57; Jha, *Bandung to Tashkent*, 70; Dutt, *With Nehru*, 98; Kahin, *Asian-African Conference*, 36; Zhou in Burke, *Mainsprings*, 91; Gopal, *Nehru*, 2:239.

36. *Bulletin*, May 9, 1955, 754.

37. James C. Hagerty diary, April 27, 1955, Hagerty papers; cabinet minutes, April 29, 1955, Cabinet series, Eisenhower papers.

38. Menon in Brecher, *India and World Politics*, 53; progress report on South Asia, Aug. 24, 1955, NSC series, papers of the Office of the Special Assistant for National Security Affairs (OSANSA). The nature of the "advice" offered to various American friends is described in intelligence reports 6830.1 (Feb. 21, 1955), 6830.2 (March 4, 1955), 6830.3 (March 18, 1955), and 6830.4 (April 1, 1955), OIR records, RG 59. Jackson to Jessup, Oct. 5, 1955, Jackson papers.

39. Cabinet minutes, April 29, 1955, Cabinet series, Eisenhower papers.

40. Jansen, *Afro-Asia and Non-Alignment*, 187; memorandum of conversation, May 11, 1955, Whitman diary series, Eisenhower papers.

41. Goodpaster to Adams, Nov. 8, 1955, Dulles-Herter series, Eisenhower papers; memoranda of conversations, Oct. 27 and Nov. 16, 1955, Subject series, Dulles papers (Eisenhower Library).

42. Memorandum of telephone conversation, Nov. 21, 1955, Telephone calls series, Dulles papers (Eisenhower Library); Dulles to Hoover, Nov. 23, 1955, White House memoranda series, Dulles papers (Eisenhower Library).

43. Macmillan to Dulles, Dec. 21, 1955, Subject series, Dulles papers (Eisenhower Library); Dulles to Macmillan, Jan. 6, 1956, ibid.; Macmillan to Dulles, Jan. 30, 1956, ibid.

44. Memorandum of conversation, April 6, 1956, General correspondence series, Dulles papers (Eisenhower Library); Cohen, *Rusk*, 82–83.

45. *U.S. News and World Report*, Feb. 25, 1955.

46. Nehru in Wolpert, *Roots of Confrontation*, 142.

47. Menon, *Flying Troika*, 110; *Newsweek*, July 4, 1955.

48. Nehru in Gopal, *Nehru*, 2:253; *U.S. News and World Report*, Dec. 2, 1955; *New York Times*, Dec. 15, 1955. Additional information on the exchange of visits, and on Soviet–Indian relations generally during this period, can be found in Stein, *India and the Soviet Union;* and Donaldson, *Soviet Policy toward India.*

49. On the Indian reaction to the Goa statement, see Bandyopadhyaya, *Making of India's Foreign Policy*, 250–253. Johnson, *Right Hand*, 243–257; Nehru to Eisenhower in New Delhi to State Department, July 29, 1955, International series, Eisenhower papers.

50. Memorandum of conversation, July 29, 1955, White House memoranda series, Dulles papers (Eisenhower Library).

51. Memorandum of conversation, July 28, 1955, General correspondence series, Dulles papers (Eisenhower Library). See also Dutt, *With Nehru,*231.

52. Cooper to Eisenhower, July 30, 1955, Dulles-Herter series, Eisenhower papers.

53. Eisenhower to Nehru, Aug. 1, 1955, Dulles-Herter series, Eisenhower papers.

54. Nehru to Eisenhower, Aug. 15, 1955, Dulles-Herter series, Eisenhower papers.

55. Lodge to Eisenhower, Sept. 26, 1955, Administration series, Eisenhower papers. Emphasis Lodge's.

56. Menon, *Flying Troika,* 128–129.

57. Lodge to Eisenhower, Nov. 16, 1954, Lodge papers; Lodge to Eisenhower, March 28, 1956, ibid.; Lodge to Eisenhower, May 25, 1956, ibid.

58. Dulles to Eisenhower, Feb. 2, 1956, White House memoranda series, Dulles papers (Eisenhower Library).

59. Choudhury, *India, Pakistan, Bangladesh, and the Major Powers,* 23; Heimsath and Mansingh, *Diplomatic History,* 444. See also the works by Stein and Donaldson.

60. Dulles to Eisenhower in Colombo to State Department, March 12, 1956, Dulles-Herter series, Eisenhower papers; Gopal, *Nehru,* 2:274–275; Dulles memo, March 10, 1956, *FRUS* 55–57:8, 306–308. On Dulles' earlier opinion of Indian anti-Americanism, see State Department to New Delhi, Jan. 6, 1954, 611.91/1–654, RG 59.

61. Dulles to Eisenhower in Colombo to State Department, March 12, 1956, Dulles-Herter series, Eisenhower papers; Dulles memo, March 10, 1956, *FRUS* 55–57:8, 306–308; Gopal, *Nehru,* 2:274–275.

62. Hoopes, *Devil and Dulles,* 353–354; Brecher, *India and World Politics,* 64; Dulles to Eisenhower in London to State Department, Aug. 22, 1956, Dulles-Herter series, Eisenhower papers; Dulles to Eisenhower in London to State Department, Aug. 20, 1956, ibid.

63. Memorandum of conference, Nov. 2, 1956, White House memoranda series, Dulles papers (Eisenhower Library).

64. Gopal, *Nehru,* 2:291–299.

65. *New Republic,* Nov. 26, 1956.

66. Hoover to Eisenhower, Dec. 13, 1956, Subject series, Eisenhower staff secretary records; Greene to Goodpaster with attachments, Dec. 14, 1956, ibid; Hoffman to Dulles, April 28, 1953, Hoffman papers; Wallace to Eisenhower, Nov. 26, 1956, White House memoranda series, Dulles papers (Eisenhower Library); Cousins to Eisenhower in Whitman to Dulles, Aug. 30, 1956, ibid.

67. Hagerty diary, March 15, 1955, Hagerty papers; Eisenhower to Dulles, March 23, 1955, Dulles-Herter series, Eisenhower papers.

68. Eisenhower, *Waging Peace,* 113–114.

69. Eisenhower memorandum of conversations, Dec. 17–18, 1956, International series, Eisenhower papers; memorandum of conversation, Dec. 19, 1956, *FRUS* 55–57:8, 331–340.

70. Memorandum by Layton for joint chiefs, June 8, 1956, *Declassified Documents,* 460a.

71. NSC 5617, Dec. 7, 1956, RG 273. (Approved Jan. 10, 1957, as NSC 5701.)

72. New Delhi to State Department, Nov. 6, 1956, Confidential series, Eisenhower White House central file.

73. Cooper memorandum, Dec. 13, 1956, International series, Eisenhower papers.

74. Eisenhower to Nehru in State Department to New Delhi, Jan. 7, 1957, International series, Eisenhower papers; Gopal, *Nehru,* 3:42; Eisenhower telephone conversation with Dulles, Jan. 12, 1957, Eisenhower diary series, Eisenhower papers.

75. Rostow, *Eisenhower, Kennedy, and Foreign Aid,* 38–40; Merrill, "Bread and the Ballot," 252–253.

76. Merrill, "Bread and the Ballot," 255; Mason and Asher, *World Bank,* 514. For additional arguments in favor of aid, see Bartlett to Rountree, Sept. 30, 1957, *FRUS* 55–57:8, 377–382; Dulles to Eisenhower, Nov. 4, 1957, *FRUS* 55–57:8, 393–395; Goodpaster memo, Nov. 12, 1957, *FRUS* 55–57:8, 404–406.

77. Merrill, "Bread and the Ballot," 255–256. See also Rostow, *Eisenhower, Kennedy, and Foreign Aid,* 152–169.

78. Memorandum of conversation, Jan. 17, 1958, Confidential series, Eisenhower White House central file.

79. Memorandum of telephone conversation, Jan. 27, 1957, Eisenhower diary series, Eisenhower papers.

80. Dulles to Eisenhower, with Eisenhower reply in margin, April 17, 1958, Dulles-Herter series, Eisenhower papers.

81. Memorandum of conversation, May 2, 1958, White House memoranda series, Dulles papers (Eisenhower Library); Gopal, *Nehru,* 3:85.

82. Nehru to Eisenhower in New Delhi to State Department, July 19, 1958, International series, Eisenhower papers; Eisenhower to Nehru in State Department to New Delhi, July 25, 1958, ibid.; NSC 5909/1, Aug. 21, 1959, RG 273; report 7727, June 3, 1958, OIR records, RG 59.

83. Eisenhower, *Waging Peace,* 499–500.

84. Ibid., 501–504; Gopal, *Nehru,* 3:103–105.

85. New Delhi to State Department, Dec. 22, 1959, International series, Eisenhower papers; Hoffman to Eisenhower, March 14, 1960, Eisenhower diary series, Eisenhower papers; Eisenhower to Champion, March 25, 1960, ibid.

86. Memorandum by John Eisenhower, Sept. 26, 1960, International series, Eisenhower papers; State Department memorandum of conversation, Sept. 26, 1960, ibid.

4. Bolt from the Blue Danube: 1948–1950

1. The most complete account of American relations with Yugoslavia is Campbell, *Tito's Separate Road.* See also Larson, *United States Foreign Policy*

4. Bolt from the Blue Danube: 1948–1950

toward Yugoslavia; Garrett, "On Dealing with National Communism"; Kousalas, "Truman Doctrine and the Stalin-Tito Rift"; Lees, "American Decision to Assist Tito"; Stefan, "Emergence of Soviet-Yugoslav Break"; Hathaway, "Truman, Tito, and the Politics of Hunger"; Blum, "Surprised by Tito"; Heuser, "Western Containment Policies in the Cold War"; and Brands, "Redefining the Cold War."

2. Kidrić in Dedijer, *Battle Stalin Lost,* 74; Ulam, *Expansion and Coexistence,* 461–462.

3. Belgrade to State Department, Jan. 4, 1948, *FRUS* 48:4, 1056–1058. Dedijer, *Battle Stalin Lost,* ch. 3, describes Yugoslavia's economic difficulties with the Soviets.

4. Belgrade to State Department, June 8, 1948, 860H.00/6–848, RG 59.

5. Belgrade to State Department, June 18, 1948, *FRUS* 48:4, 1073–1075. For the Yugoslav view of the split with Stalin, see Djilas, *Conversations with Stalin,* and *Rise and Fall.* Other treatments of the rift include Armstrong, *Tito and Goliath;* Ulam, *Titoism and the Cominform;* Vucinich, *At the Brink;* and Dragnich, "Soviet-Yugoslav Conflict." On the failure of American intelligence to foresee the split, see Blum, "Surprised by Tito."

6. Belgrade to State Department, June 29, 1948, 860H.00/6–2948, RG 59; Belgrade to State, July 2, 1948, 860H.00/7–248, RG 59; Belgrade to State Department, June 29, 1948, 860H.00/6–2948, RG 59; military and naval attachés in Belgrade to State Department, June 29, 1948, 860H.00/6–2948, RG 59.

7. PPS 35: "The Attitude of This Government Toward Events in Yugoslavia," June 30, 1948, President's secretary's file, Truman papers.

8. Hillenkoetter to Truman, June 29, 1948, President's secretary's file, Truman papers; Hillenkoetter to Truman, June 30, 1948, ibid.

9. In a cabinet meeting early in July, Ernest Bevin asserted that with respect to Greece, Tito and Stalin could be expected to display only "differences of method, not of ultimate aim." (Minutes of cabinet meeting, July 1, 1948, C.M. 46 (48), Cabinet records.) London to State Department, July 1, 1948, 860H.00/7–148, RG 59; Paris to State Department, ibid.

10. Moscow to State Department, July 2, 1948, 860H.00/7–248, RG 59; Zagreb to Belgrade, July 1 and 22, 1948, 800/Yugoslavia, RG 84.

11. Keyes to Royall in Draper to Royall, July 6, 1948, *FRUS* 48:4, 1085–1087.

12. State Department to London, July 10, 1948, 860H.00/7–1048, RG 59. See also James V. Forrestal diary entry for July 9, 1948, Forrestal papers.

13. Paris to State Department, July 7, 1948, *FRUS* 48:4, 1088.

14. Moscow to State Department, July 23, 1948, 860H.00/7–2348, RG 59.

15. See *Bulletin,* Aug. 1, 1948, 137–140; Wisner to Harriman, July 22, 1948, *FRUS* 48:4, 1095–1096.

16. Belgrade to State Department, July 26, 1948, *FRUS* 48:4, 1907–1098.

17. Forrestal diary, July 19, 1948, Forrestal papers; State Department to Belgrade, July 28, 1948, 860H.00/7–2848, RG 59.

18. Belgrade to State Department, July 29, 1948, 860H.00/7–2948, RG 59; Lees, "American Decision to Assist Tito."

19. Belgrade to State Department, Aug. 12, 1948, 860H.00/8–1248, RG 59; Belgrade to State Department, Aug. 14, 1948, 860H.00/8–1448, RG 59.

20. Belgrade to State Department, Aug. 31, 1948, *FRUS* 48:4, 1102–1105.

21. State Department to Belgrade, Sept. 3, 1948, *FRUS* 48:4, 1105–1106.

22. CIA report ORE 22–48: "The Possibility of Direct Soviet Military Action During 1948–1949," Sept. 16, 1948, President's secretary's file, Truman papers.

23. Moscow to State Department, Sept. 26, 1948, 860H.00/9–2648, RG 59; Belgrade to State Department, Sept. 27, 1948, 860H.00/9–2748, RG 59.

24. State Department to Belgrade, Oct. 1, 1948, 860H.00/10–148, RG 59.

25. Belgrade to State Department, Oct. 4, 1948, 860H.00/10–448, RG 59.

26. Belgrade to State Department, Oct. 5, 1948, 860H.00/10–548, RG 59; memorandum for president re 34th NSC meeting, Feb. 18, 1949, President's secretary's file, Truman papers; Reams to Cannon, Oct. 29, 1948, 710/Yugoslavia 800B, RG 84; CIA report ORE 49–48: "The Trend of Soviet-Yugoslav Relations," Nov. 18, 1948, President's secretary's file, Truman papers.

27. Hickerson to Kennan, Nov. 26, 1948, 860H.00/11–2648, RG 59.

28. Report 4850, Dec. 31, 1948, OIR records, RG 59; CIA report ORE 16–49: "The Yugoslav Dilemma," Feb. 10, 1949, President's secretary's file, Truman papers.

29. Belgrade to State Department, Jan. 10, 1949, *FRUS* 49:5, 854–856.

30. CIA report ORE 16–49, Feb. 10, 1949, President's secretary's file, Truman papers; CIA report: "Review of the World Situation," Jan. 19, 1949, ibid.

31. See Thompson to Acheson, Feb. 12, 1949, 860H.00/2–1249, RG 59.

32. UM D-3: "Economic Relations Between the United States and Yugoslavia," Feb. 14, 1949, *FRUS* 49:5, 866–868.

33. NSC 18/1, Feb. 15, 1949, RG 273.

34. See editorial note, *FRUS* 49:5, 868–869.

35. See Thorp to Acheson, July 8, 1949, *FRUS* 49:5, 905–907.

36. Ibid.; memorandum of conversation, July 21, 1949, 660H.119/7–2149, RG 59. This meeting is discussed further in Lees, "American Decision to Assist Tito."

37. Attachment to Allen to Acheson, July 28, 1949, *FRUS* 49:5, 911 n.

38. Ibid.; Acheson to Johnson, Aug. 4, 1949, ibid., 915–920. The State Department staff study is described in ibid., 918 n. On the destabilizing effect of a reversal, see also memorandum of telephone conversation, July 12, 1949, 660H.119/7–1249, RG 59.

39. Acheson to Webb, Aug. 8, 1949, 660H.119/8–849, RG 59.

40. Belgrade to State Department, March 3, 1949, 860H.00/3–349, RG 59; CIA report 8–49, Aug. 17, 1949, President's secretary's file, Truman papers; Hillenkoetter memorandum, Aug. 22, 1949, ibid.

41. PPS 60, Sept. 12, 1949, *FRUS* 49:5, 947–954. Király, "Aborted Soviet Military Plans against Tito's Yugoslavia," assesses Stalin's designs against Tito, including invasion preparations.

42. NSC 18/3, Nov. 10, 1949, RG 273.

43. Bradley to Marshall, Nov. 16, 1949, *FRUS* 50:4, 1339–1341.

44. NSC 18/4, Nov. 17, 1949, RG 273.

45. CIA report: "Review of the World Situation," Nov. 16, 1949, President's secretary's file, Truman papers; report 5058, Feb. 6, 1950, OIR records, RG 59; Belgrade to State Department, Dec. 8, 1949, *FRUS* 49:5, 981–983.

46. State Department to Belgrade, March 11, 1950, 768.00/3–1150, RG 59; *New York Times*, Dec. 23, 1949; Allen to Zalene, Jan. 3, 1950, Allen papers; *Public Papers*, 585.

47. Rusinow, *Yugoslav Experiment*, 52–53; Wilson, *Tito's Yugoslavia*, 63–65.

48. Memorandum of conversation, Jan. 14, 1950, *FRUS* 50:4, 1354–1355.

49. Belgrade to State Department, Feb. 19, 1950, 668.00/2–1950, RG 59; memorandum of conversation, June 19, 1950, Acheson papers (Truman Library).

50. Memorandum by Hillenkoetter, Jan. 18, 1950, President's secretary's file, Truman papers.

51. Belgrade to State Department, Feb. 2, 1950, 768.00/2–250, RG 59; Belgrade to State Department, April 20, 1950, *FRUS* 50:4, 1404–1407.

52. Allen to parents, March 6/7, 1950, Allen papers.

53. State Department to Paris, Feb. 22, 1950, 868.10/2–2250, RG 59.

54. Wilson, *Tito's Yugoslavia*, 66; Perkins to Acheson, Feb. 8, 1950, *FRUS* 50:4, 1366–1369.

55. Memorandum of conversation, Feb. 2, 1950, Acheson papers (Truman Library); memorandum by Battle, Feb. 17, 1950, ibid.; Acheson to Gaston, Feb. 21, 1950, 868.10/2–2150, RG 59; State Department to Belgrade, March 1, 1950, 868.10/3–150, RG 59.

56. Belgrade to State Department, March 2, 1950, *FRUS* 50:4, 1378 n.; CIA report ORE 8–50, May 11, 1950, President's secretary's file, Truman papers; Belgrade to State Department, May 18, 1950, 768.00/5–1850, RG 59; Belgrade to State Department, Aug. 18, 1950, 668.00/8–1850, RG 59.

57. Belgrade to State Department, June 30, 1950, 768.00 (W)/6–3050, RG 59; Campbell, *Tito's Separate Road*, 26; Wilson, *Tito's Yugoslavia*, 123.

58. CIA Special Evaluation 40, July 29, 1950, President's secretary's file, Truman papers; United Nations to State Department, July 20, 1950, 768.00/7–2050, RG 59.

59. State Department to Belgrade, June 28, 1950, 768.5/6–2850, RG 59.

60. State Department-Defense Department study, undated, *FRUS* 50:4, 1432 n.

61. Bradley to Johnson, Aug. 23, 1950, *FRUS* 50:4, 1441–1444.

62. NSC 73/4, Aug. 25, 1950, RG 273.

63. Memorandum of conversation, Oct. 19, 1950, Acheson papers (Truman Library).

64. Acheson to Thorp, Oct. 20, 1950, Acheson papers (Truman Library); Acheson memorandum, Oct. 27, 1950, ibid.; Campbell, *Tito's Separate Road*,

23; Hathaway, "Truman, Tito, and the Politics of Hunger," 138–139; State Department to Belgrade, Nov. 25, 1950, 868.00/11–2550, RG 59.

65. Acheson to Connally et al., Oct. 31, 1950, 868.00/10–3150, RG 59.

66. Message to Congress, *Public Papers*, 721–722.

67. House Foreign Affairs Committee, *Hearings on H.R. 9853*, 2–3. On Tito's treatment of the Greek insurgents, see Pappas, "Soviet-Yugoslav Conflict and the Greek Civil War."

68. House Foreign Affairs Committee, *Hearings on H.R. 9853*, 5–6.

69. Ibid., 8, 15.

70. Ibid., 16.

71. Ibid., 16–18.

72. Ibid., 20, 26.

73. Ibid., 36–39. On Yugoslavia and American policy in Greece, see Wittner, *American Intervention in Greece*, chs. 8–9.

74. House Foreign Affairs Committee, *Hearings on H.R. 9853*, 40–42.

75. *Congressional Record* 96 (1950), 16335–16336.

76. Ibid., 16347.

77. Ibid., 16354.

78. Ibid., 16461, 16387, 16523.

79. Ibid., 16343.

5. The Devil's Due: 1951–1960

1. Belgrade to State Department, Dec. 29, 1950, *FRUS* 50:4, 1514–1515.

2. Belgrade to State Department, Feb. 19, 1951, 668.00/2–1951, RG 59.

3. Matthews to Lovett, Jan. 17, 1951, *FRUS* 51:4, 1684–1686.

4. Belgrade to State Department, Jan. 24, 1951, *FRUS* 51:4, 1697–1698.

5. Belgrade to State Department, Jan. 26, 1951, *FRUS* 51:4, 1701–1702.

6. Joyce to Webb, Jan. 31, 1951, 768.5/1–3151, RG 59.

7. Bradley to Marshall, Feb. 2, 1951, *FRUS* 51:4, 1719–1721; Joint Logistics Plans Committee report, April 10, 1951, JLPC 461/6, JCS reports, RG 218; State Department memorandum, March 2, 1951, 768.5/3–251, RG 59.

8. *FRUS* 51:4, 1815 n.; memorandum of conversation, June 18, 1951, Acheson papers (Truman Library).

9. Memorandum of conversation, June 18, 1951, Acheson papers (Truman Library).

10. Popović to Acheson, June 28, 1951, Acheson papers (Truman Library).

11. Memorandum by Bevin for cabinet meeting, Oct. 21, 1949, C.P. (49) 212, British Cabinet reports; "Economic Aid for Yugoslavia," June 18, 1951, C.P. (51) 160, Cabinet records; ministry of defense to mission in Washington, Feb. 28, 1951, DEFE7/215/81/051, British Defense Ministry reports; minute by Gore-Booth, March 10, 1949, FO371/R2800, British Foreign Office reports; British embassy in Belgrade to Foreign Office, Jan. 27, 1950, FO371/RY1071, Foreign Office records.

12. State Department to London, Paris, and Rome, July 14, 1951, *FRUS* 51:4, 1827–1829; State Department to NATO, July 20, 1951, ibid., 1831–1833; memorandum of conversation, Aug. 3, 1951, Acheson papers (Truman Library); editorial note, *FRUS* 51:4, 1838.

13. Walters, *Silent Missions*, 266–267.

14. Harriman to Truman in London to State, Aug. 27, 1951, *FRUS* 51:4, 1842–1843.

15. Memorandum of conversation, Aug. 28, 1951, Acheson papers (Truman Library); Belgrade to State Department, July 24, 1951, 768.00/7–2451, RG 59.

16. Belgrade to State Department, Nov. 29, 1951, *FRUS* 51:4, 1866–1867.

17. CIA intelligence report, Dec. 7, 1950, President's secretary's file, Truman papers; memorandum of conversation, Aug. 28, 1951, 768.00/8–2851, RG 59; Bern to State Department, Nov. 7, 1951, 768.00/11–751, RG 59; Belgrade to State Department, Sept. 27, 1951, 768.00/9–2751, RG 59.

18. Belgrade to State Department, Oct. 11, 1951, *FRUS* 51:4, 1854–1855.

19. *Congressional Record* 97 (1951), 10938.

20. House of Representatives, *Selected Executive Session Hearings*, 15:111–112.

21. Ibid., 113, 108, 110.

22. *Bulletin*, Nov. 26, 1951, 863–864; report 5863, March 31, 1952, OIR records, RG 59; Truman to Acheson, Sept. 22, 1952, 768.00/9–2252, RG 59; memorandum of conversation, March 6, 1952, Acheson papers (Truman Library); memorandum of conversation, July 18, 1952, ibid.; minutes of cabinet meeting, Jan. 9, 1953, Connelly papers.

23. Campbell, *Tito's Separate Road*, 26–27.

24. On Dulles' role at the 1952 Republican convention, see Hoopes, *Devil and Dulles*, 129–130. Memorandum of conversation, June 24, 1953, Dulles-Herter series, Eisenhower papers.

25. Dedijer, *Battle Stalin Lost*, 322.

26. Ibid., 324; Ulam, *Expansion and Coexistence*, 539–547.

27. Wilson, *Tito's Yugoslavia*, 87–88; Ulam, *Expansion and Coexistence*, 543–546; Campbell, *Tito's Separate Road*, 30–31.

28. Summary of NIE 93: "Probable Developments in Yugoslavia," in Armstrong to Dulles, June 30, 1953, 768.00/6–3053, RG 59; Allen Dulles to Roman, Nov. 3, 1965, Allen Dulles papers.

29. Wilson, *Tito's Yugoslavia*, 87.

30. Jackson to Eisenhower, Sept. 29, 1953, Dulles-Herter series, Eisenhower papers.

31. British Defense Ministry to mission in Washington, Nov. 9, 1951, FO371/RT1203, British Foreign Office records; British Defense Ministry to mission in Washington, Nov. 19, 1951, FO371/RT1203, Foreign Office records; Zagreb to State Department, Oct. 10, 1953, 768.00/10–953, RG 59; minutes of 167th NSC meeting, Oct. 22, 1953, NSC series, Eisenhower papers; Eisenhower, *Mandate for Change*, 414

32. Cook, *Declassified Eisenhower*, 193.

33. State Department to Belgrade, Oct. 14, 1953, 768.00/10–1453, RG 59; Eisenhower, *Mandate for Change*, 409–419.

34. Murphy, *Diplomat among Warriors*, 42.

35. Eisenhower to Tito, Sept. 10, 1954, Diary series, Eisenhower papers.

36. Murphy, *Diplomat among Warriors*, 424.

37. Belgrade to State Department, July 13, 1954, 668.00/7–1354, RG 59.

38. State of the Union address, Jan. 6, 1955, *Public Papers*, 8; special messages to Congress, April 20, 1955, ibid., 405.

39. State Department press release, May 24, 1955, *Bulletin*, June 6, 1955; Dulles statement, May 25, 1955, ibid.

40. *U.S. News*, Oct. 30, 1953; *New York Times*, Jan. 23, 1955.

41. *U.S. News*, June 15, 1956; ibid., Oct. 30, 1953; ibid., Jan. 15, 1955; ibid., July 20, 1956; *Time*, Aug. 8, 1955; *Newsweek*, Aug. 8, 1955; *New Republic*, Jan. 10, 1955; ibid., July 9, 1956.

42. *New York Times*, July 28, 1955; *Congressional Record* 101 (1955), 9405–9406.

43. *Congressional Record* 101 (1955), 9477.

44. Ibid., 9502.

45. Ibid., 9504–9505, 9655.

46. Legislative leadership meeting, June 14, 1955, Legislative meeting series, Eisenhower papers.

47. Ibid., June 28, 1955.

48. Kaufman, *Trade and Aid*, 54–56; Eisenhower to Tito, Sept. 19, 1955, Dulles-Herter series, Eisenhower papers; memorandum of telephone conversation, Aug. 8, 1955, Eisenhower diary series, Eisenhower papers.

49. Murphy, *Diplomat among Warriors*, 426–427.

50. Memorandum of conversation, Oct. 11, 1955, White House memoranda series, Dulles papers (Eisenhower Library).

51. Memorandum of conversation, July 13, 1954, *FRUS* 52–54:16, 1352; Hoopes, *Devil and Dulles*, 222; Ambrose, *Eisenhower*, 2:260.

52. Dulles to Eisenhower, Nov. 7, 1955, Dulles-Herter series, Eisenhower papers.

53. Ibid.; memorandum of conversation, Nov. 6, 1955, General series, Dulles papers (Eisenhower Library); Goodpaster to Adams, Nov. 8, 1955, Dulles-Herter series, Eisenhower papers.

54. *New York Times*, Jan. 6, 1956. On Tito and Nasser (and Tito and Nehru), see Rubinstein, *Yugoslavia and the Non-aligned World*, passim. Accounts of Tito's Moscow visit are in Mićunović, *Moscow Diary*, ch. 4; and Khrushchev, *Khrushchev Remembers*, ch. 12.

55. *Congressional Record* 102 (1956), 10788, 10948, 11103–11107, 14172–14173.

56. Dulles news conference, *Bulletin*, July 9, 1956.

57. Kaufman, *Trade and Aid*, 68–69.

58. For an early defense of the policy of aiding Tito—in this case by an easing

of trade restrictions—see Blaisdell to Bricker, May 11, 1949, 93126/64, Commerce Departments records, RG 40. Minutes of 298th NSC meeting, Sept. 27, 1956, NSC series, Eisenhower papers.

59. Radford to Wilson, Oct. 11, 1956, JCS 1901/42, RG 218.

60. Memorandum of conversation, Oct. 11, 1956, White House memoranda series, Dulles papers (Eisenhower Library).

61. Eisenhower news conference, Oct. 11, 1956, *Public Papers,* 888; Eisenhower to Nixon and Rayburn, Oct. 15, 1956, ibid., 928–930.

62. Kennan to Bowles, Oct. 15, 1956, Kennan papers; Murphy speech, Oct. 24, 1956, *Bulletin,* Nov. 5, 1956.

63. Mićunović, *Moscow Diary,* 144; Wilson, *Tito's Yugoslavia,* 104–106; Clissold, *Yugoslavia and the Soviet Union,* 66–69.

64. *New York Times,* Nov. 6 and 9, 1956.

65. Memorandum of conversation, Jan. 17, 1957, White House memoranda series, Dulles papers (Eisenhower Library); *Congressional Record* 103 (1957), 2052, A874, 1024, 2012.

66. Press release, May 14, 1957, *Bulletin,* June 10, 1957.

67. Memorandum of conversation, May 21, 1957, Eisenhower diary series, Eisenhower papers.

68. NSC 5805, Feb. 28, 1958, RG 273.

69. Minutes of 315th NSC meeting, March 7, 1957, NSC series, Eisenhower papers.

70. On the renewal of trouble between Belgrade and Moscow, see Benes et al., *Second Soviet–Yugoslav Dispute;* and Clissold, *Yugoslavia and the Soviet Union,* 70–75.

71. *Congressional Record* 104 (1958), 8724.

72. Memorandum of conversation, May 19, 1959, Rankin papers.

73. Memorandum of conversation by John Eisenhower, Sept. 22, 1960, International series, Eisenhower papers; memorandum of conversation by Goodpaster, Oct. 5, 1960, ibid.

6. The Riddle of the Sphinx: 1952–1956

1. Campbell, *Defense of the Middle East,* 85–87; Polk, *United States and the Arab World,* 363–372.

2. Joint Strategic Survey Committee to secretary of defense, Dec. 28, 1951, JCS 1887/33, RG 218; Nitze for PPS to Cabell et al., May 26, 1952, ibid. See also Hahn, "Containment and Egyptian Nationalism."

3. Churchill to Cherwell, Nov. 10, 1951, PREM11/208, British Prime Minister's records; *Congressional Record* 98 (1952), 276–279.

4. *New York Times,* Jan. 1 and 10, 1952; *Congressional Record* 98 (1952), 288, 317.

5. National Intelligence Special Estimate, SE-23, "Prospects for an Inclusive Middle East Defense Organization," March 17, 1952, President's secretary's file, Truman papers.

6. Hoskins for Board of Policy Planning to Byroade, April 7, 1952, *FRUS* 52–54:9, 204–213.

7. Acheson in cabinet meeting, March 28, 1952, Connelly papers; National Intelligence Special Estimate, SE-23, "Prospects for an Inclusive Middle East Defense Organization," March 17, 1952, President's secretary's file, Truman papers.

8. Minutes of State-JCS meeting, June 18, 1952, *FRUS* 52–54:9, 237–247.

9. Hoskins to Byroade, July 25, 1952, *FRUS* 52–54:9, 256–262.

10. Rubin, "America and the Egyptian Revolution," 75–76; Vatikiotis, *Nasser and His Generation*, 107–109. See also Nutting, *Nasser*, 12–37; Baker, *Egypt's Uncertain Revolution*, 23–31; Sadat, *Revolt on the Nile*, 138–159. The question of how much American agents and officials knew of preparations for the coup has occasioned debate. Copeland (*Game of Nations*, 62–64) claims that the CIA was aware of what Nasser and his associates were about, to the point of encouraging the plotters. Ranelagh (*Agency*, 297–298) agrees. Eveland (*Ropes of Sand*, 97–98) states emphatically that the revolt took the CIA by surprise.

11. Cairo to State Department, July 21, 1952, 774.00/7–2152, RG 59; Cairo to State Department, July 23, 1952, 350/Egypt, RG 84; London to Cairo, July 23, 1952, 350/Egypt, RG 84; Cairo to State Department, July 23, 1952, 774.00/7–2352, RG 59.

12. Cairo to State Department, July 25, 1952, 774.00/7–2552, RG 59; Evans to Caffery, July 28, 1952, 350/Egypt, RG 84; Cairo to State Department, July 24, 1952, 774.00/7–2452, RG 59. See also Evans to Caffery, July 30, 1952, 350/Egypt, RG 84.

13. Cairo to State Department, July 25, 1952, 774.00/7–2552, RG 59.

14. Fowler in weekly summary of events, July 28, 1952, 774.00/7–2852, RG 59; Nasser in Baker, *Egypt's Uncertain Revolution*, 29.

15. Weekly summary of events, July 28, 1952, 774.00/7–2852, RG 59.

16. Cairo to State Department, July 24, 1952, 350/Egypt, RG 84; Cairo to State Department, Aug. 20, 1952, 774.00/8–2052, RG 59. See also Cairo to State Department, July 28, 1952, 350/Egypt, RG 84.

17. Cairo to State Department, Aug. 19, 1952, 350/Egypt, RG 84; *Bulletin*, Sept. 15, 1952.

18. Minute by Parsons, June 6, 1952, FO371/10345, British Foreign Office records.

19. Minute by Mackworth, Sept. 27, 1952, FO371/JE1024, and minute by Morris, Sept. 8, 1952, FO371/JE10345, British Foreign Office records; Eden in State Department to Cairo, Sept. 8, 1952, *FRUS* 52–54:9, 1857–1858.

20. Cairo to State Department, Sept. 8, 1952, 774.00/9–852, RG 59; State Department to Cairo, ibid.; Cairo to State Department, July 28, 1952, 774.00/7–2852, RG 59; Cairo to State Department, Sept. 9, 1952, 774.00/9–952, RG 59; Cairo to State Department, Sept. 10, 1952, 774.00/9–1052, RG 59.

21. Cairo to State Department, Sept. 10, 1952 (two cables), *FRUS* 52–54:9, 1858–1859.

22. Cairo to State Department, Sept. 18, 1952, President's secretary's file, Truman papers.

23. Memorandum of conversation, Sept. 8, 1952, Acheson papers (Truman Library); Acheson to Truman, Sept. 30, 1952, President's secretary's file, Truman papers; State Department to Cairo, Sept. 30, 1952, 774.00/9–3052, RG 59.

24. Cairo to State Department, Nov. 10, 1952, *FRUS* 52–54:9, 1877–1878.

25. Memorandum of conversation, Nov. 15, 1952, Acheson papers (Truman Library).

26. Ibid.

27. Cairo to State Department, Nov. 25, 1952, 780.5/11–2552, RG 59.

28. Cairo to State Department, Nov. 26, 1952, 774.00/11–2652, RG 59.

29. Cairo to State Department, Nov. 18, 1952, 774.00/11–1852, RG 59; Nasser to Love in Aronson, *From Sideshow to Center Stage*, 98.

30. Cairo to State Department, Dec. 3, 1952, *FRUS* 52–54:9, 1903–1904.

31. Memorandum of cabinet meeting, Nov. 17, 1953, CC 67 (53), British Cabinet records; record of meetings, Dec. 31, 1952–Jan. 7, 1953, DEFE7/797, British Defense Ministry records; London to State Department, Nov. 25, 1952, *FRUS* 52–54:9, 1895–1896; memorandum of conversation, Dec. 31, 1952, Acheson papers (Truman Library); Acheson to Wilson, Dec. 11, 1952, CD 091.3/Egypt, RG 330; Bradley to Wilson, Dec. 16, 1952, ibid.

32. Joint Strategic Plans Committee to JCS: "Force Bases for the Middle East Area," June 13, 1953, JCS 2099/296, RG 218.

33. Jernegan to Acheson, Dec. 30, 1952, 774.5MSP/12–3052, RG 59.

34. Memorandum of conversation, Dec. 31, 1952, Acheson papers (Truman Library).

35. Memorandum of conversation, Jan. 5, 1953, Acheson papers (Truman Library); memorandum of conversation, Jan. 7, 1953, 774.5MSP/1–753, RG 59.

36. Memorandum of conversation, Jan. 7, 1953, Acheson papers (Truman Library); Jernegan to Acheson, Jan. 6, 1953, 774.5MSP/1–653, RG 59.

37. Eisenhower to Dulles, Nov. 15, 1982, Dulles-Herter series, Eisenhower papers.

38. Cairo to State Department, May 18, 1953, 774.00/5–1853, RG 59.

39. Memorandum of conversation, May 12, 1953, *FRUS* 52–54:9, 19–25; Heikal, *Cutting the Lion's Tail*, 39; Heikal, *Nasser*, 51.

40. Dulles to Eisenhower, May 12, 1953, Dulles-Herter series, Eisenhower papers.

41. Dulles to Smith in Cairo to State Department, May 13, 1953, *FRUS* 52–54:9, 25–26; Nasser quoted in Monroe, *Britain's Moment in the Middle East*, 173.

42. Dulles to Eisenhower in Baghdad to State Department (two parts), May 18, 1953, Dulles-Herter series, Eisenhower papers.

43. Heikal, *Cutting the Lion's Tail*, 40–41.

44. Minutes of 147th NSC meeting, June 1, 1953, NSC series, Eisenhower papers.

45. NSC 155/1, July 14, 1953, RG 273.

46. Joint Strategic Plans Committee to JCS: "Force Bases for the Middle East Area," June 13, 1953, JCS 2099/296, RG 218.

47. Memorandum of conversation, June 5, 1953, 774.00/6–553, RG 59; Cairo to State Department, June 29, 1953, 774.56/6–2953, RG 59.

48. State Department to Cairo, June 23, 1954, 774.00/6–2354, RG 59; Cairo to State Department, June 24, 1953, 774.00/6–2454, RG 59. On Nasser's struggle with Naguib, see Vatikiotis, *Nasser and His Generation,* 126–151.

49. Cairo to State Department, June 29, 1953, *FRUS* 52–54:9, 2104–2106.

50. British embassy in Washington to Foreign Office, Nov. 14, 1953, FO371/JE11345, British Foreign Office records.

51. Byroade to Dulles, Nov. 12, 1953, 874.00TA/11–1253, RG 59.

52. *Congressional Record* 100 (1954), 1674–1675, 410–411.

53. *New York Times,* Dec. 28, 1953.

54. State Department to Cairo, Dec. 31, 1953, 874.00TA/12–3153, RG 59.

55. Cairo to State Department, Jan. 6, 1954, 874.00TA/1–651, RG 59.

56. State Department to Cairo, July 30, 1954, *FRUS* 52–54:9, 2290 n. For the terms of the Anglo-Egyptian agreement, see Sachar, *Europe Leaves the Middle East,* 600–608.

57. Cairo to State Department, July 31, 1954, *FRUS* 52–54:9, 2290–2291.

58. Cairo to State Department, Aug. 29, 1954, *FRUS* 52–54:9, 2297–2298.

59. NSC 5428, July 23, 1954, RG 273.

60. Heikal, *Nasser,* 54–55; Jernegan to Smith, Sept. 28, 1954, *FRUS* 52–54:9, 2305–2306.

61. Gerhardt to Davis, Nov. 29, 1954, *FRUS* 52–54:9, 2319–2322; Eveland, *Ropes of Sand,* 90–102; Copeland, *Game of Nations,* 145–148.

62. Jernegan to Dulles, Dec. 31, 1954, *FRUS* 52–54:9, 2322–2323.

63. Ibid.

64. State Department to Tel Aviv, Aug. 4, 1954, *FRUS* 52–54:9, 1600–1602. For more on opposition by Israel and Israel's American supporters to arms for Egypt, see Safran, *Israel,* 348–350; Spiegel, *Other Arab-Israeli Conflict,* 64; and Kenen, *Israel's Defense Line,* 95–96.

65. Tel Aviv to State Department, Aug. 10, 1954, *FRUS* 52–54:9, 1608–1610; Tel Aviv to State Department, Aug. 22, 1954, ibid., 1621.

66. Memorandum of conversation, Aug. 16, 1954, *FRUS* 52–54:9, 1613–1614.

67. Cairo to State Department, Dec. 11, 1952, 874.00TA/12–1152, RG 59; Cairo to State Department, *FRUS* 52–54:9, 2192–2197; Stookey, *America and the Arab States,* 139–140; Mason and Asher, *World Bank,* 631.

68. Kimche, *Second Arab Awakening,* 104.

69. Heikal, *Nasser,* 229, 251–252; Nutting, *Nasser,* 100.

70. Khrushchev, *Khrushchev Remembers,* 431–432; Nutting, *Nasser,* 101. See also Glassman, *Arms for the Arabs,* 7–12.

71. Bonner, *Waltzing with a Dictator,* 3–4; Heikal, *Nasser,* 53; Copeland, *Game of Nations,* 152–155.

72. Heikal, *Nasser,* 50–52; Copeland, *Game of Nations,* 157; Eveland, *Ropes of Sand,* 135; Jabber, *Not by War Alone,* 164.

73. Hoopes, *Devil and Dulles,* 326–327.

74. Draft report: "Deterrence of Major Armed Conflict between Israel and Egypt or Other Arab States," Oct. 17, 1955, NSC series, OSANSA records; *Bulletin,* Oct. 17, 1955.

75. Goodpaster intelligence summary for Egypt, Nov. 3, 1955, Dulles-Herter series, Eisenhower papers.

76. Cairo to State Department, Jan. 9, 1954, 674.0021/1–954, RG 59; report 7042, Sept. 12, 1955, OIR Records, RG 59.

77. Attachment to Allen Dulles to Eisenhower, Aug. 1, 1958, White House memoranda series, John Foster Dulles papers (Eisenhower Library).

78. *Newsweek,* June 6, 1955; *New Republic,* April 16, 1956; *Nation,* Feb. 19, 1955; *Time,* Oct. 10, 1955.

79. Draft report: "Deterrence of Major Armed Conflict between Israel and Egypt or Other Arab States," Oct. 17, 1955, NSC series, OSANSA records.

80. Heikal, *Cutting the Lion's Tail,* 91–92.

81. Memorandum of conversation, Jan. 11, 1956, NSC series, OSANSA records. It is perhaps worth noting that this memorandum, which was declassified in "sanitized" form in 1985, records a conversation that Neff, whose book on the Suez crisis is the first to make substantial use of materials from the Eisenhower Library, believes went unrecorded. (*Warriors at Suez,* 131.)

82. Ewald, *Eisenhower,* 194–195; Neff, *Warriors at Suez,* 133–136; Burns, *Economic Aid and American Policy toward Egypt,* 58–63, 70–73; Heikal, *Cutting the Lion's Tail,* 92–94, 232–236.

7. To Beirut and Back: 1956–1960

1. Diary entry for March 13, 1956, Ferrell, *Eisenhower Diaries,* 319.

2. Vatikiotis, *Nasser and His Generation,* 227; Hasou, *Struggle for the Arab World,* 56–57.

3. Vatikiotis, *Nasser and His Generation,* 231.

4. Dulles to Eisenhower, March 28, 1956, Dulles-Herter series, Eisenhower papers.

5. Diary entry for March 28, 1956, Ferrell, *Eisenhower Diaries,* 323; Eisenhower memorandum, March 8, 1956, Eisenhower diary series, Eisenhower papers.

6. Radford in Senate, *Executive Sessions,* 8:111; diary entry for March 13, 1956, Ferrell, *Eisenhower Diaries,* 319.

7. Report 7292, July 9, 1956, OIR records, RG 59; memorandum of conversation (Eisenhower and Saud), Jan. 30, 1957, Dulles-Herter series, Eisenhower papers.

8. Progress report on NSC 5428, May 17, 1956, NSC series, OSANSA records.

9. Senate, *Executive Sessions,* 8:44–50.

10. Ibid., 49, 59–60.

11. Ibid., 60, 50–51, 56.

12. Ibid., 55–56.

13. Ibid., 53–54, 63.

14. Ibid., 61–62, 57.

15. *Congressional Record* 102 (1956), 7223, 1817, 910.

16. Ibid., 1443, 1545, 9709, 9819.

17. Ibid., 10622, 10956, 9739.

18. Heikal, *Cutting the Lion's Tail,* 115.

19. Heikal, *Nasser,* 73–74, 228–229; Heikal, *Cutting the Lion's Tail,* 117; Gopal, *Nehru,* 2:277; *Bulletin,* June 18, 1956, 999–1000. See also Burns, *Economic Aid and American Policy toward Egypt,* 105–106.

20. Neff, *Warriors at Suez,* 267–272.

21. Memorandum of conversation, July 27, 1956, International series, Eisenhower papers; Ambrose, *Eisenhower,* 2:332.

22. British embassy in Paris to Foreign Office, Oct. 26, 1955, FO371/JE1072, British Foreign Office records; Eden, *Full Circle,* 476–477.

23. Twining to JCS, July 29, 1956, *Declassified Documents* 78:369b; Wentworth to JCS, July 31, 1956, JCS 2105/38, RG 218.

24. Ambrose, *Eisenhower,* 2:331–332; memorandum of conference, Aug. 8, 1956, Eisenhower diary series, Eisenhower papers.

25. *Congressional Record* 102 (1956), 15376, 15415.

26. Ibid., 15653, 15455–15456.

27. Murphy, *Diplomat among Warriors,* 379; Macmillan, *Riding the Storm,* 105.

28. Minutes of bipartisan leadership meeting, Aug. 12, 1956, Legislative meetings series, Eisenhower papers.

29. Lind to Jones, passed to Dulles, Aug. 25, 1956, White House memoranda series, Dulles papers (Eisenhower Library).

30. On the American role in the overthrow of Arbenz, see Immerman, *CIA in Guatemala;* Schlesinger and Kinzer, *Bitter Fruit;* and Cook, *Declassified Eisenhower.* On the toppling of Mossadeq: Rubin, *Paved with Good Intentions;* and Roosevelt, *Countercoup.*

31. Memorandum of conference, Oct. 8, 1956, Eisenhower diary series, Eisenhower papers.

32. Memorandum of conversation, Oct. 29, 1956, Eisenhower diary series, Eisenhower papers.

33. Notes of cabinet meeting, Oct. 25, 1956, C.M. 74 (56), British Cabinet records; Eden, *Full Circle,* 487.

34. Memoranda of conversation, Oct. 29 and Nov. 5, 1956, Eisenhower diary series, Eisenhower papers.

35. Memorandum of meeting with legislative leaders, Nov. 9, 1956, Legislative meetings series, Staff secretary records.

36. Minutes of 303rd NSC meeting, Nov. 9, 1956, NSC series, Eisenhower papers; memoranda of conversations, Oct. 30 and Nov. 21, 1956, Eisenhower diary series, Eisenhower papers.

37. Memorandum of conference with legislative leaders, Nov. 9, 1956, Legislative meetings series, Staff secretary records; memorandum of conversation, Oct. 30, 1956, Eisenhower diary series, Eisenhower papers; minutes of 303rd NSC meeting, NSC series, Eisenhower papers.

38. Minutes of 303rd NSC meeting, NSC series, Eisenhower papers.

39. Memorandum of conversation, Nov. 7, 1956, White House memoranda series, Dulles papers (Eisenhower Library).

40. Minutes of bipartisan legislative leadership meeting, Jan. 1, 1957, Legislative meetings series, Eisenhower papers; Eisenhower, *Waging Peace,* 178.

41. Minutes of bipartisan legislative leadership meeting, Jan. 1, 1957, Legislative meetings series, Eisenhower papers.

42. Senate, *Executive Series,* 9:3, 21.

43. Ibid., 5–10, 19–28.

44. Bipartisan leadership meeting, Aug. 12, 1956, Legislative meetings series, Eisenhower papers.

45. *Hearings on H.J. Res. 117,* 3–4.

46. Ibid., 7–13.

47. Ambrose, *Eisenhower,* 2:386.

48. *Congressional Record* 103 (1957), 1835–1841.

49. Johnson to Dulles, Feb. 11, 1957, George Reedy file, Johnson Senate papers; Johnson telephone conversation with Acheson, Feb. 19, 1957, ibid.

50. Minutes of bipartisan legislative meeting, Feb. 20, 1957, Legislative meetings series, Eisenhower papers.

51. Ambrose, *Eisenhower,* 2:388.

52. Brecher, *Decisions in Israel's Foreign Policy,* 299–303.

53. Meyer, *Egypt and the United States,* 187–192; Spiegel, *Other Arab-Israeli Conflict,* 86.

54. Memorandum of conversation, Oct. 28, 1957, White House memoranda series, Dulles papers (Eisenhower Library); Eisenhower to Dulles, Nov. 13, 1957, ibid.

55. Memorandum for the record, Nov. 15, 1957, White House memoranda series, Dulles papers (Eisenhower Library).

56. Kerr, *Arab Cold War,* 1–16; Nutting, *Nasser,* 218; Hasou, *Struggle for the Arab World,* 113.

57. Eveland, *Ropes of Sand,* 270.

58. NSC 5801, Jan. 16, 1958, RG 273.

59. NSC 5801/1, Jan. 24, 1958, RG 273.

60. Stookey, *America and the Arab States,* 153–154.

61. John Foster Dulles telephone conversation with Knowland, July 16, 1958, Telephone calls series, Dulles papers (Eisenhower Library); minutes of meeting with legislative leaders, July 14, 1958, International series, Staff Secretary rec-

ords; John Foster Dulles telephone conversation with Lodge, July 14, 1958, Telephone calls series, Dulles papers (Eisenhower Library); memorandum for the record, July 14, 1958, *Declassified Documents*, R:628h.

62. Staff notes, July 15, 1958, International series, Eisenhower papers.

63. Memorandum of conference, July 14, 1958, Subject series, Staff Secretary records.

64. Memorandum of conference, July 21, 1958, Subject series, Staff secretary records; John Foster Dulles telephone conversation with Lodge, July 14, 1958, Telephone calls series, Dulles papers (Eisenhower Library); memorandum of conference, July 14, 1958, International series, Eisenhower papers; Ambrose, *Eisenhower*, 2:469; Tehran to State Department, July 19, 1958, Subject series, Staff secretary records.

65. Ben-Gurion to Eisenhower, July 24, 1958, White House memoranda series, Dulles papers (Eisenhower Library).

66. Dulles to Eisenhower, July 28, 1958, Chronological series, Dulles papers (Eisenhower Library).

67. Memorandum of conversation, July 20, 1958, Subject series, Staff secretary records; Eisenhower to Ben-Gurion in State Department to Tel Aviv, July 25, 1958, International series, Eisenhower papers; Eban, *Autobiography*, 262–264.

68. Ambrose, *Eisenhower*, 2:331; memorandum of conference, July 20, 1958, Subject series, Staff secretary records; memorandum of conference, July 21, 1958, ibid.

69. Memorandum of conference, July 21, 1958, Subject series, Staff secretary records; memorandum of telephone conversation, July 15, 1958, Telephone calls series, Dulles papers (Eisenhower Library).

70. Murphy, *Diplomat among Warriors*, 412–414.

71. Stookey, *America and the Arab States*, 155–156.

72. NSC 5820/1, Nov. 4, 1958, RG 273.

73. On the Nasser-Kassim dispute, see Kerr, *Arab Cold War*, 16–21.

74. *Life*, July 20, 1959.

75. Memorandum of conversation, Jan. 5, 1959, John Foster Dulles papers (Princeton).

76. OCB report on the Near East (NSC 5820/1), Feb. 3, 1960, OCB series, OSANSA records.

77. Dillon to Eisenhower, Aug. 25, 1960, International series, Eisenhower papers.

78. Dillon to Eisenhower, Sept. 25, 1960, International series, Eisenhower papers.

79. Memorandum of conversation by Jones, Sept. 26, 1960, International series, Eisenhower papers; memorandum by Goodpaster, Sept. 28, 1960 (of Sept. 26 conversation), ibid.; excerpt from Cairo to State Department, Nov. 15, 1960, ibid.

80. Memorandum of conversation by Jones, Sept. 26, International series,

354

Eisenhower papers; memorandum by Goodpaster, Sept. 28, 1960 (of Sept. 26 conversation), ibid.

Conclusion: The Triumph of Geopolitics

1. *Public Papers 1956,* 554–556.
2. *Bulletin,* June 25, 1956, 1064–1065.
3. Hotchkis to Dulles, June 27, 1956, John Foster Dulles papers (Princeton).
4. Acheson to Johnson, June 19, 1957, Acheson papers (Yale).
5. Memorandum of conversation by John Eisenhower, Sept. 22, 1960, International series, Eisenhower papers; memorandum of conversation by Goodpaster, Oct. 5, 1960, ibid.
6. Eisenhower to Edgar Eisenhower, Feb. 27, 1956, Eisenhower diary series, Eisenhower papers. Emphasis Eisenhower's.
7. PPS 35, June 30, 1948, President's secretary's file, Truman papers; *Hearings on H.R. 9853, 36–39.*
8. JCS Joint Intelligence Committee 501/6, March 21, 1951, RG 218; memorandum of conversation, June 24, 1953, Dulles-Herter series, Eisenhower papers.
9. Belgrade to State Department, Feb. 2, 1950, 768.00/2–250, RG 59; Perkins to Acheson, Feb. 8, 1950, *FRUS* 50:4, 1366–1369; NSC 5805, Feb. 28, 1958, RG 273.
10. Memorandum of conversation, undated (Feb. 1950), Henderson papers.
11. Bowles to Truman, Jan. 31, 1952, 320/India, RG 84; NSC 6105, Jan. 19, 1961, RG 273.
12. Allen Dulles to John Foster Dulles, March 26, 1957, Allen Dulles papers; notes of John Foster Dulles background interview, April 3, 1958, John Foster Dulles papers (Princeton); staff notes, July 15, 1958, International series, Eisenhower papers; progress reports on NSC 5428, May 17 and Dec. 22, 1956, RG 273.
13. NSC 6011, July 19, 1960, RG 273.
14. Jackson to Eisenhower, Sept. 29, 1953, Dulles-Herter series, Eisenhower papers.
15. Neff, *Warriors at Suez,* 261.
16. Kiraly, "Aborted Soviet Military Plans against Tito's Yugoslavia." See also Dragnich, "Soviet-Yugoslav Conflict."

Epilogue: From Bandung to Stanleyville

1. Brands, *Cold Warriors,* 63–66. For a more thorough treatment of the Congo affair, see Kalb, *Congo Cables;* Weissman, *American Foreign Policy in the Congo;* and Mahoney, *Ordeal in Africa.*

SOURCES CITED

I. Archival Collections

National Archives, Washington:
    Department of Commerce records, record group (RG) 40.
    Department of State central files, RG 59.
    Joint Chiefs of Staff records, RG 218.
    National Security Council records, RG 273.
    Office of the Secretary of Defense records, RG 330.
    State-War-Navy Coordinating Committee records, RG 353.
Washington National Records Center, Suitland, Maryland:
    Department of State consular and diplomatic post files, RG 84.
Harry S. Truman Library, Independence, Missouri:
    Dean G. Acheson papers.
    George V. Allen papers.
    Matthew J. Connelly papers.
    Paul G. Hoffman papers.
    Henry F. Grady papers.
    George McGhee papers.
    Harry S. Truman papers.
Dwight D. Eisenhower Library, Abilene, Kansas:
    John Foster Dulles papers.
    Dwight D. Eisenhower papers (Ann Whitman file).
    James C. Hagerty papers.
    C. D. Jackson papers.

Sources Cited

Office of the Special Assistant for National Security Affairs (OSANSA) records.
Staff Secretary records.
White House central file.
Princeton University Library, Princeton, New Jersey:
  Allen W. Dulles papers.
  John Foster Dulles papers.
  James V. Forrestal papers.
  George F. Kennan papers.
  Karl Lott Rankin papers.
Yale University Library, New Haven, Connecticut:
  Dean G. Acheson papers.
  Chester W. Bowles papers.
Library of Congress, Washington:
  Loy W. Henderson papers.
Massachusetts Historical Society, Boston:
  Henry Cabot Lodge papers.
Lyndon B. Johnson Library, Austin:
  Lyndon B. Johnson papers.
British Public Record Office, Kew, England:
  Cabinet records.
  Defense Ministry records.
  Dominions Office records.
  Foreign Office records.
  Prime Minister's records.

II. United States Government Publications

Congress. *Congressional Record.*
Congress, House of Representatives, Committee on Foreign Affairs. *Hearings on H.R. 9853.* 1950.
Congress, House of Representatives, Committee on Foreign Affairs. *Hearings on the India Emergency Assistance Act.* 1951.
Congress, House of Representatives, Committee on Foreign Affairs. *Hearings on H.J. Res. 117.* 1957.
Congress, House of Representatives, Committee on Foreign Affairs. *Selected Executive Session Hearings* (Historical series).
Congress, Senate, Committee on Foreign Relations. *Executive Sessions of the Senate Foreign Relations Committee* (Historical series).
Department of State. *Bulletin.*
Department of State. *Foreign Relations of the United States.* (Abbreviated in the notes as *FRUS,* with appropriate year and volume, e.g.: *FRUS* 50:7.)
Office of the Federal Register. *Public Papers of the Presidents of the United States.*

III. Microfiche Collection

Declassified Documents Reference System. Washington: Carrollton Press.

IV. Secondary Sources

Acheson, Dean. *Present at the Creation: My Years at the State Department.* New York: Norton, 1969.

Adelman, Jonathan R., ed. *Superpowers and Revolution.* New York: Praeger, 1986.

Ambrose, Stephen E. *Eisenhower.* New York: Simon and Schuster, 1983–1984.

Armstrong, Hamilton Fish. *Tito and Goliath.* New York: Macmillan, 1951.

Aronson, Geoffrey. *From Sideshow to Center Stage: U.S. Policy toward Egypt, 1946–1956.* Boulder, Colo.: Rienner, 1986.

Baker, Raymond William. *Egypt's Uncertain Revolution under Nasser and Sadat.* Cambridge, Mass.: Harvard University Press, 1978.

Bandyopadhyaya, J. *The Making of India's Foreign Policy: Determinants, Institutions, Processes and Personalities.* Bombay: Allied, 1970.

Banerjee, Malabika. *The Nonaligned Movement.* Calcutta: Firma, 1982.

Barnds, William J. *India, Pakistan, and the Great Powers.* New York: Praeger, 1972.

Barnet, Richard J. *Intervention and Revolution: The United States in the Third World.* New York: World, 1968.

Becker, Abraham S. "The Soviet Union and the Third World: The Economic Dimension." In Korbonski and Fukuyama, eds., *Soviet Union and Third World,* 67–93.

Benes, Vaclav L. et al., eds. *The Second Soviet-Yugoslav Dispute.* Bloomington: Indiana University Publications, 1959.

Blum, Robert M. "Surprised by Tito: The Anatomy of an Intelligence Failure." *Diplomatic History* 12 (1988), 39–58.

Bonner, Raymond. *Waltzing with a Dictator: The Marcoses and the Making of American Foreign Policy.* New York: Times Books, 1987.

Bowles, Chester. *Promises to Keep: My Years in Public Life, 1941–1969.* New York: Harper and Row, 1971.

Brands, H. W., Jr. *Cold Warriors: Eisenhower's Generation and American Foreign Policy.* New York: Columbia University Press, 1988.

Brands, H. W., Jr. "India and Pakistan in American Strategic Planning, 1947–1954: Commonwealth as Collaborator." *Journal of Imperial and Commonwealth History* 15 (1986), 41–54.

Brands, H. W., Jr. "Redefining the Cold War: American Policy toward Yugoslavia, 1948–1960." *Diplomatic History* 11 (1987), 41–54.

Brecher, Michael. *Decisions in Israel's Foreign Policy.* New Haven: Yale University Press, 1975.

Brecher, Michael. *India and World Politics: Krishna Menon's View of the World.* New York: Praeger, 1968.

Sources Cited

Brecher, Michael. *Nehru: A Political Biography*. London: Oxford University Press, 1959.

Brecher, Michael. "Neutralism: An Analysis," *International Journal* 17 (1962), 224–236.

Brown, W. Norman. *The United States and India, Pakistan, Bangladesh*. Cambridge: Harvard University Press, 1972.

Burke, S. M. *Mainsprings of Indian and Pakistani Foreign Policies*. Minneapolis: University of Minnesota Press, 1974.

Burns, William J. *Economic Aid and American Policy toward Egypt, 1955–1981*. Albany: State University of New York Press, 1985.

Campbell, John C. *Defense of the Middle East: Problems of American Policy*. New York: Praeger, 1960.

Campbell, John C. *Tito's Separate Road: America and Yugoslavia in World Politics*. New York: Harper and Row, 1967.

Choudhury, G. W. *India, Pakistan, Bangladesh, and the Major Powers*. New York: Free Press, 1975.

Clissold, Stephen, ed. *Yugoslavia and the Soviet Union, 1939–1973: A Documentary Survey*. London: Oxford University Press, 1975.

Cohen, Warren I. *Dean Rusk*. Totowa, N.J.: Cooper Square, 1982.

Cook, Blanche Weisen. *The Declassified Eisenhower: A Divided Legacy*. Garden City, N.Y.: Doubleday, 1981.

Copeland, Miles. *The Game of Nations: The Amorality of Power Politics*. New York: Simon and Schuster, 1969.

Dedijer, Vladimir. *The Battle Stalin Lost: Memoirs of Yugoslavia, 1948–1953*. New York: Viking, 1971.

Dedijer, Vladimir. *Tito Speaks: His Self Portrait and Struggle with Stalin*. London: Weidenfeld and Nicolson, 1953.

Divine, Robert A. *Eisenhower and the Cold War*. New York: Oxford University Press, 1981.

Djilas, Milovan. *Conversations with Stalin*. New York: Harcourt, Brace and World, 1962.

Djilas, Milovan. *Rise and Fall*. San Diego: Harcourt Brace Jovanovich, 1985.

Donaldson, Robert H. *Soviet Policy toward India: Ideology and Strategy*. Cambridge: Harvard University Press, 1974.

Donovan, Robert J. *Tumultuous Years: The Presidency of Harry S. Truman, 1949–1953*. New York: Norton, 1982.

Dragnich, Alex N. "The Soviet-Yugoslav Conflict." In Adelman, ed., *Superpowers and Revolution*, 169–180.

Dutt, Subimal. *With Nehru in the Foreign Office*. Calcutta: Minerva, 1977.

Eban, Abba. *An Autobiography*. New York: Random House, 1977.

Eden, Anthony. *Full Circle*. Boston: Houghton Mifflin, 1960.

Eisenhower, Dwight D. *The White House Years: Mandate for Change, 1953–1956*. Garden City, N.Y.: Doubleday, 1963.

Eisenhower, Dwight D. *The White House Years: Waging Peace, 1956–1961*. Garden City, N.Y.: Doubleday, 1965.

Eveland, Wilbur Crane. *Ropes of Sand: America's Failure in the Middle East.* London: Norton, 1980.

Ewald, William Bragg, Jr. *Eisenhower the President: Crucial Days, 1951–1960.* Englewood Cliffs, N.J.: Prentice-Hall, 1981.

Ferrell, Robert H., ed. *The Eisenhower Diaries.* New York: Norton, 1981.

Finer, Herman. *Dulles over Suez: The Theory and Practice of His Diplomacy.* Chicago: Quadrangle, 1964.

Garrett, Stephen A. "On Dealing with National Communism: The Lessons of Yugoslavia." *Western Political Quarterly* 26 (1973), 529–549.

Girling, John L. S. *America and the Third World: Revolution and Intervention.* London: Routledge and Kegan Paul, 1980.

Glassman, Jon D. *Arms for the Arabs: The Soviet Union and War in the Middle East.* Baltimore: Johns Hopkins University Press, 1975.

Gopal, Sarvepalli. *Jawaharlal Nehru: A Biography.* Cambridge: Harvard University Press, 1976–1984.

Guhin, Michael A. *John Foster Dulles: A Statesman and His Times.* New York: Columbia University Press, 1972.

Gurtov, Melvin. *The United States Against the World: Anti-Nationalism and Intervention.* New York: Praeger, 1974.

Gurtov, Melvin, and Ray Maghroori. *The Roots of Failure: United States Policy in the Third World.* Westport, Conn.: Greenwood, 1984.

Hahn, Peter L. "Containment and Egyptian Nationalism: The Unsuccessful Effort to Establish the Middle East Command, 1950–53." *Diplomatic History* 11 (1987), 23–40.

Harrison, Selig S., ed. *India and the United States.* New York: Macmillan, 1961.

Harrison, Selig S. *The Widening Gulf: Asian Nationalism and American Policy.* New York: Free Press, 1978.

Hasou, Tawfig Y. *The Struggle for the Arab World: Egypt's Nasser and the Arab League.* London: KPI, 1985.

Hathaway, Robert M. "Truman, Tito, and the Politics of Hunger." In Levantrosser, ed., *Truman,* 129–150.

Heikal, Mohamed H. *Cutting the Lion's Tail: Suez through Egyptian Eyes.* New York: Arbor House, 1987.

Heikal, Muhammad. *Nasser: The Cairo Documents.* London: New English Library, 1972.

Heimsath, Charles H., and Surjit Mansingh. *A Diplomatic History of Modern India.* Bombay: Allied, 1971.

Hess, Gary R. *America Encounters India.* Baltimore: Johns Hopkins University Press, 1971.

Hess, Gary R. "Global Expansion and Regional Balances: The Emerging Scholarship on United States Relations with India and Pakistan." *Pacific Historical Review* 61 (1987), 263–297.

Heuser, Beatrice. "Western Containment Policies in the Cold War—The Yugoslav Case, 1948–1953." Dissertation, Oxford University, 1987.

Sources Cited

Hoopes, Townsend. *The Devil and John Foster Dulles.* Boston: Little, Brown, 1973.

Hope, A. Guy. *America and Swaraj: The U.S. Role in Indian Independence.* Washington: Public Affairs Press, 1968.

Immerman, Richard H. *The CIA in Guatemala: The Foreign Policy of Intervention.* Austin: University of Texas Press, 1982.

Isaacs, Harold R. *Scratches on Our Minds: American Images of China and India.* New York: John Day, 1958.

Jabber, Paul. *Not by War Alone: Security and Arms Control in the Middle East.* Berkeley: University of California Press, 1981.

Jackson, Richard L. *The Non-Aligned, the UN and the Superpowers.* New York: Praeger, 1983.

Jansen, G. H. *Afro-Asia and Non-Alignment.* London: Faber and Faber, 1966.

Jha, C. S. *From Bandung to Tashkent: Glimpses of India's Foreign Policy.* Madras: Sangam, 1983.

Johnson, U. Alexis, with Jef Olivarius McAllister. *The Right Hand of Power.* Englewood Cliffs, N.J.: Prentice-Hall, 1984.

Kahin, George McTurnan. *The Asian-African Conference: Bandung, Indonesia, April 1955.* Ithaca, N.Y.: Cornell University Press, 1956.

Kalb, Madeleine G. *The Congo Cables: The Cold War in Africa, from Eisenhower to Kennedy.* New York: Macmillan, 1982.

Kaufman, Burton I. *Trade and Aid: Eisenhower's Foreign Economic Policy.* Baltimore: Johns Hopkins University Press, 1981.

Kaushik, R. P. *The Crucial Years of Non-alignment: U.S.A.—Korean War—India.* New Delhi: Kumar, 1972.

Kenen, I. L. *Israel's Defense Line: Her Friends and Foes in Washington.* Buffalo: Prometheus, 1981.

Kerr, Malcolm H. *The Arab Cold War: Gamal Abd al-Nasir and His Rivals, 1958–1970.* London: Oxford University Press, 1971.

Khrushchev, Nikita S. *Khrushchev Remembers.* Boston: Little, Brown, 1970.

Kimche, Jon. *The Second Arab Awakening.* London: Thames and Hudson, 1970.

Király, Béla. "The Aborted Soviet Military Plans against Tito's Yugoslavia." In Vucinich, ed., *At the Brink,* 273–288.

Kolko, Gabriel. *Confronting the Third World: United States Foreign Policy, 1945–1980.* New York: Pantheon, 1988.

Korbonski, Andrzej, and Francis Fukuyama. *The Soviet Union and the Third World: The Last Three Decades.* Ithaca, N.Y.: Cornell University Press, 1987.

Kousalas, D. George. "The Truman Doctrine and the Stalin-Tito Rift: A Reappraisal." *South Atlantic Quarterly* 72 (1973), 427–439.

Kwitny, Jonathan. *Endless Enemies: The Making of an Unfriendly World.* New York: Congdon and Weed/St. Martin's Press, 1984.

LaFeber, Walter. *Inevitable Revolutions: The United States in Central America.* New York: Norton, 1984.

Lamb, Alastair. *The Kashmir Problem: A Historical Survey.* New York: Praeger, 1966.

Larson, David L. *United States Foreign Policy toward Yugoslavia, 1943–1963.* Washington: University Presses of America, 1979.

Lees, Lorraine M. "The American Decision to Assist Tito, 1948–1949." *Diplomatic History* 2 (1978), 407–422.

Levantrosser, William F., ed. *Harry S. Truman: The Man from Independence.* New York: Greenwood, 1986.

Lyon, Peter. *Neutralism.* Leicester: Leicester University Press, 1963.

Macmillan, Harold. *Riding the Storm, 1956–1959.* New York: Harper and Row, 1971.

Mahoney, Richard D. *JFK: Ordeal in Africa.* New York: Oxford University Press, 1983.

Mallik, Deva Narayan. *The Development of Non-Alignment in India's Foreign Policy.* Allahabad: Chaitanya, 1967.

Mansingh, Surjit. "India and the United States." In Nanda, ed., *Indian Foreign Policy,* 150–169.

Mason, Edward S., and Robert E. Asher. *The World Bank since Bretton Woods.* Washington: Brookings Institution, 1973.

McGhee, George. *Envoy to the Middle World: Adventures in Diplomacy.* New York: Harper and Row, 1983.

McMahon, Robert J. "Eisenhower and Third World Nationalism: A Critique of the Revisionists." *Political Science Quarterly* 101 (1986), 453–473.

McMahon, Robert J. "Food as a Diplomatic Weapon: The India Wheat Loan of 1951." *Pacific Historical Review* 56 (1987), 349–377.

McMahon, Robert J. "United States Cold War Strategy in South Asia: Making a Military Commitment to Pakistan, 1947–1954." *Journal of American History* 75 (1988), 812–840.

Menon, K. P. S. *The Flying Troika.* London: Oxford University Press, 1963.

Menon, K. P. S. *Many Worlds.* London: Oxford University Press, 1965.

Merrill, Dennis J. "Bread and the Ballot: The United States and India's Economic Development, 1947–1961." University of Connecticut dissertation, 1986.

Meyer, Gail E. *Egypt and the United States: The Formative Years.* Rutherford, N.J.: Fairleigh Dickinson University Press, 1980.

Mićunović, Veljko. *Moscow Diary.* Garden City, N.Y.: Doubleday, 1980.

Monroe, Elizabeth. *Britain's Moment in the Middle East, 1914–1971.* Baltimore: Johns Hopkins University Press, 1981.

Moraes, Frank. *Jawaharlal Nehru: A Biography.* New York: Macmillan, 1956.

Murphy, Robert. *Diplomat among Warriors.* Garden City, N.Y.: Doubleday, 1964.

Nanda, B. R., ed. *Indian Foreign Policy.* Delhi: Vikas, 1976.

Neff, Donald. *Warriors at Suez: Eisenhower Takes America into the Middle East.* New York: Linden/Simon and Schuster, 1981.

Nehru, Jawaharlal. *Jawaharlal Nehru's Speeches, 1949–1953.* Delhi: Publications Division, Ministry of Information and Broadcasting, 1961.

Sources Cited

Nixon, Richard M. *RN: The Memoirs of Richard Nixon.* New York: Grosset and Dunlap, 1978.

Noer, Thomas J. *Cold War and Black Liberation: The United States and White Rule in Africa, 1948–1968.* Columbia: University of Missouri Press, 1985.

Nutting, Anthony. *Nasser.* New York: Dutton, 1972.

Packenham, Robert A. *Liberal America and the Third World: Political Development Ideas in Foreign Aid and Social Science.* Princeton, N.J.: Princeton University Press, 1973.

Palmer, Norman D. *The United States and India: The Dimensions of Influence.* New York: Praeger, 1984.

Pandit, Vijaya Lakshmi. *The Scope of Happiness: A Personal Memoir.* New York: Crown, 1979.

Panikkar, K. M. *An Autobiography.* Madras: Oxford University Press, 1977.

Panikkar, K. M. *In Two Chinas: Memoirs of a Diplomat.* London: Allen and Unwin, 1955.

Pappas, Nicholas. "Soviet-Yugoslav Conflict and the Greek Civil War." In Vucinich, ed., *At the Brink,* 219–238.

Paterson, Thomas G. *Meeting the Communist Threat: Truman to Reagan.* New York: Oxford University Press, 1988.

Pillai, K. Raman. *India's Foreign Policy: Basic Issues and Attitudes.* Meerut: Meenakshi Prakashan, 1969.

Polk, William R. *The United States and the Arab World.* Cambridge, Mass.: Harvard University Press, 1975.

Ranelagh, John. *The Agency: The Rise and Decline of the CIA.* New York: Simon and Schuster, 1986.

Rao, T. V. Subra. *Non-Alignment in International Law and Politics.* New Delhi: Deep and Deep, 1981.

Reid, Escott. *Envoy to Nehru.* Delhi: Oxford University Press, 1981.

Roosevelt, Kermit. *Countercoup: The Struggle for the Control of Iran.* New York: McGraw-Hill, 1979.

Rosinger, Lawrence K. *India and the United States: Political and Economic Relations.* New York: Macmillan, 1950.

Rostow, W. W. *Eisenhower, Kennedy, and Foreign Aid.* Austin: University of Texas Press, 1985.

Rubin, Barry. "America and the Egyptian Revolution, 1950–1957." *Political Science Quarterly* 97 (1982), 73–90.

Rubin, Barry. *Paved with Good Intentions: The American Experience and Iran.* New York: Oxford University Press, 1980.

Rubinstein, Alvin Z. *Yugoslavia and the Non-aligned World.* Princeton, N.J.: Princeton University Press, 1970.

Rusinow, Dennison. *The Yugoslav Experiment, 1948–1974.* Berkeley: University of California Press, 1977.

Sachar, Howard M. *Europe Leaves the Middle East, 1936–1954.* New York: Knopf, 1972.

Sadat, Anwar El. *Revolt on the Nile.* New York: John Day, 1957.

Sources Cited

Safran, Nadav. *Israel: The Embattled Ally*. Cambridge, Mass.: Harvard University Press, 1978.

Sardesai, D. R. "India and Southeast Asia." In Nanda, ed., *Indian Foreign Policy*, 78–101.

Sayegh, Fayez A. "Anatomy of Neutralism: A Typological Analysis." In Sayegh, ed., *Dynamics of Neutralism*, 1–102.

Sayegh, Fayez A., ed. *The Dynamics of Neutralism in the Arab World: A Symposium*. San Francisco: Chandler, 1964.

Schlesinger, Stephen, and Stephen Kinzer. *Bitter Fruit: The Untold Story of the American Coup in Guatemala*. Garden City, N.Y.: Doubleday, 1982.

Sengupta, Jyoti. *Non-Alignment: Search for a Destination*. Calcutta: Naya Prokash, 1979.

Shafer, D. Michael. *Deadly Paradigms: The Failure of U.S. Counterinsurgency Policy*. Princeton, N.J.: Princeton University Press, 1988.

Spiegel, Steven L. *The Other Arab-Israeli Conflict: Making America's Middle East Policy, from Truman to Reagan*. Chicago: University of Chicago Press, 1985.

Stefan, Charles G. "The Emergence of the Soviet-Yugoslav Break: A Personal View from the Belgrade Embassy." *Diplomatic History* 6 (1982), 387–404.

Stein, Arthur. *India and the Soviet Union: The Nehru Era*. Chicago: University of Chicago Press, 1969.

Stookey, Robert W. *America and the Arab States: An Uneasy Encounter*. New York: Wiley, 1975.

Sulzberger, C. L. *A Long Row of Candles: Memoirs and Diaries, 1934–1954*. New York: Macmillan, 1969.

Talbot, Phillips, and S. L. Poplai. *India and America: A Study of Their Relations*. New York: Harper, 1958.

Truman, Harry W. *Memoirs: Years of Trial and Hope*. Garden City, N.Y.: Doubleday, 1956.

Ulam, Adam B. *Expansion and Coexistence: The History of Soviet Foreign Policy, 1917–67*. New York: Praeger, 1968.

Ulam, Adam B. *Titoism and the Cominform*. Cambridge, Mass.: Harvard University Press, 1952.

Vatikiotis, P. J. *Nasser and His Generation*. New York: St. Martin's, 1978.

Venkataramani, M. S. *The American Role in Pakistan, 1947–1958*. New Delhi: Radiant, 1982.

Venkataramani, M. S., and B. K. Shrivastava. *Quit India: The American Response to the 1942 Struggle*. New Delhi: Vikas, 1979.

Venkataramani, M. S., and B. K. Shrivastava. *Roosevelt, Gandhi, Churchill: America and the Last Phase of India's Freedom Struggle*. New Delhi: Radiant, 1983.

Vucinich, Wayne S., ed. *At the Brink of War and Peace: The Tito-Stalin Split in Historical Perspective*. New York: Brooklyn College/Columbia University Press, 1982.

Sources Cited

Vyas, Pramod. *Dawning on the Capitol: U.S. Congress and India.* Calcutta: Mascott, 1967.

Walters, Vernon A. *Silent Missions.* Garden City, N.Y.: Doubleday, 1978.

Weissman, Stephen. *American Foreign Policy in the Congo, 1960–1964.* Ithaca, N.Y.: Cornell University Press, 1974.

Wilson, Duncan. *Tito's Yugoslavia.* Cambridge: Cambridge, Mass.: Harvard University Press, 1979.

Wittner, Lawrence S. *American Intervention in Greece, 1943–1949.* New York: Columbia University Press, 1982.

Wolpert, Stanley. *Roots of Confrontation in South Asia: Afghanistan, Pakistan, India, and the Superpowers.* New York: Oxford University Press, 1982.

INDEX

Index

Index

Index

Truman, Harry S., 9, 48, 66; and Egypt, 240; and India, 14, 39–40; and Nehru, 34, 37; and Yugoslavia, 162–163, 171–172, 180
Truman Doctrine, 2, 5, 227
Turkey, 2, 19, 91, 290
Twining, Nathan, 274, 294

U.S. News and World Report, 118–119, 196–197
Ulam, Adam, 191–192
United Nations, 10

Vietminh, *see* Indochina; Geneva Conference
Vietnam, 103
Vorys, John, 180

Wallace, Henry, 127–128
Washington Post, 29
Webb, James, 46
Wickersham, Victor, 271
Wiley, Alexander, 63–64, 69, 275, 285–286

Wilkins, Fraser, 85
Willkie, Wendell, 17
Wilson, Charles, 92, 216, 265
Wilson, Woodrow, 16
Wolpert, Stanley, 8

Yalta: as metaphor, 2–10, 15, 51, 73, 182, 313–314, 327
Yalta Conference, 1
Yugoslavia, 3, 6, 9; and American aid, 146, 154–155, 161–162, 166–167, 169–180, 182–190, 201–202, 208–211, 213–216; and China, 157, 218; and Greece, 153; and Hungary, 211–212; and Korean War, 167–170, 176; and Marshall Plan, 149; and NATO, 177, 185–186, 193; and neutralism, 141, 206–207, 217–218, 308–310; and Soviet Union, 142–152, 161–162, 182, 184–185, 189–190, 192–193, 195–196, 214–216; and Trieste, 153; and United States, 141–219

Zhou Enlai, 38, 46–47, 102, 113–115, 118, 256